TRANCEWORK

*An Introduction
to the Practice of
Clinical Hypnosis*

Second Edition

Other Books by Michael D. Yapko

WHEN LIVING HURTS
Directives for Treating Depression

BRIEF THERAPY APPROACHES TO
TREATING ANXIETY AND DEPRESSION *(Ed.)*

HYPNOTIC AND STRATEGIC INTERVENTIONS
Principles and Practice (Ed.)

TRANCEWORK

*An Introduction
to the Practice of
Clinical Hypnosis*

Second Edition

MICHAEL D. YAPKO, Ph.D.

BRUNNER/MAZEL, A member of the Taylor & Francis Group

Library of Congress Cataloging-in-Publication Data

Yapko, Michael D.

    Trancework : an introduction to the practice of clinical hypnosis
    / by Michael D. Yapko.—2nd ed.
    p. cm.
    Includes bibliographical references.
    ISBN 0–87630–568–0
    1. Hypnotism—Therapeutic use. I. Title.
    [DNLM: 1. Hypnosis—methods. WM 415 y25t]
RC495.Y373 1989
615.8′512—dc20
DNLM/DLC
for Library of Congress   89–22173
                                             CIP

For information and ordering, contact:
Taylor & Francis
7625 Empire Drive
Florence, KY 41042
1-800-634-7064

Manufactured in the United States of America

10 9

This book is dedicated with love to my wife Diane,
who has kept me in the happiest of trance states.

Foreword to the Second Edition

Although I am not a practitioner of the Ericksonian approach, nor a strategic therapist, and hold different opinions on aspects of hypnotism than Michael Yapko, I believe I can correctly state that *Trancework* is an excellent exposition of current teachings on Ericksonian therapy or, as the author prefers to say, of the naturalistic approach originated by Milton H. Erickson.

The naturalistic approach to therapy and to hypnotism can be summed up in a few words: It is the "utilization," that is, the use by the therapist of whatever capacities and kinds of responses the patient has and is capable of giving at any particular moment; even his or her symptoms can be used.

Trancework is also an excellent introduction to strategic therapy, which is an outgrowth of this naturalistic approach. Strategic therapy was originally defined quite broadly by Jay Haley (as a result of his study of Erickson's therapeutic work) as any therapy in which the therapist takes the responsibility of directly influencing the patient according to a plan of treatment determined by the presenting problem. But to be a true reflection of Erickson's approach, as it was intended to be, this definition should have added that the plan is also determined by what can be utilized out of what is offered by the patient at any given moment, a plan that is both fluid and unique for each patient. It is in this sense that I see *Trancework* as an exposition of strategic therapy.

However, *Trancework* is not just an exposition of Ericksonian methods or of strategic therapy. It is more, being a reflection of Michael Yapko's personal understandings, skills, and experience as a psychotherapist and psychologist. One way of summing up Erickson's approach to psychotherapy is to say that it is an integration of hypnotic and nonhypnotic phenomena brought about naturalistically for therapeutic purposes. It is to Yapko's credit that he not only has been able to capture the essence of this approach, but he has also been able to make it available in a practical way.

While the author's subject matter is primarily clinical hypnotism as viewed from within a naturalistic framework, he does not ignore matters pertaining to traditional hypnotism and introduces the reader to its principal concepts and methods. With fairness, he points out the strengths and weaknesses of the two approaches as he sees them, although clearly giving his overall preference to the naturalistic approach.

There is considerable didactic material in *Trancework,* but the book remains above all a practical work aiming not only to teach the reader the art of doing hypnotherapy but, more importantly, the art of doing effective psychotherapy. For, as already intimated, it is in the nature of the Ericksonian approach not to separate the use of hypnotic patterns of communication from therapeutic communications in general. For both Erickson and Yapko, effective communication is the key to both the skilled use of hypnotic phenomena and to effective psychotherapy. One may not necessarily agree with the author that all influencing communications constitute hypnosis—which seems to be his position—but there is no question that readers who practice the communication techniques he details will be well on their way to becoming skilled clinical hypnotists and therapists.

A valuable pedagogical feature of the work that should not be overlooked are the lists of topics for discussion and the assignments with which each chapter terminates. Readers would be well advised to give them their attention.

Trancework will be a good starting point for beginners, and a good review for more advanced workers that brings together a great deal of material, and should be particularly instructive for practitioners who have thus far limited themselves strictly to the traditional approach.

ANDRÉ M. WEITZENHOFFER, PH.D.
Nathrop, Colorado

Foreword to the First Edition

Milton Erickson was known for his flexible and effective therapeutic communication which was predicated to a great extent on his ability to read nonverbal behavior. Early in my training with Erickson, I asked for instruction to be able to better understand nonverbal behavior. In an amused fashion, he asked if I knew the definition of "zyzzyx." I replied that I did not and asked what it meant. He instructed me to look it up in the dictionary, stating that you first learn the alphabet, then the words, then the grammar. There is no substitute for direct experience and, before one goes on to complex tasks, it is important to really know the basics.

In this volume, Michael Yapko presents the alphabet of hypnotic influence communication based in part on Erickson's strategic and symptom-based therapy, a methodology that uses hypnosis both formally and naturalistically to promote change. Whereas traditional therapy made understanding and insight primary, Ericksonian methods center on promoting effective living independent of the therapeutic situation. To accomplish goals and to maximize patient-based change, Erickson pioneered indirect techniques, noting that communication occurs on multiple levels, including the verbal content, the implications, and such extraverbal factors as tone, duration, intensity, and body language. In fact, some experts maintain that only a small fraction of our response to communication is due to the verbal content.

Traditional therapists interpret the patient's multiple level communication, i.e., describe back to the patient what he "really means." Modern Ericksonian methods, however, are predicated on the idea that if the patient is intelligent enough to communicate on more than one level, the therapist should be equally intelligent. Therapeutic communication does not need to be interpretive, concrete, direct, or linear to be effective. In fact, therapeutic communication is best when the therapist is flexible, uses indirect techniques, and focuses as many output channels of communication as possible (Zeig, 1980c).

Yapko gently eases us into the world of hypnotic communication. He provides a balance between direct and indirect techniques, integrating clear examples of each approach into the text. Examples also are given of content and process techniques (roughly, those that are specific and those that are more general). Direct and indirect techniques along with process and content suggestions have their place in therapy. Yapko does not tell us which to use or when to use them; rather, he examines possibilities, presenting the advantages and disadvantages of each, reminding us that the amount of indirection to be used is directly proportional to the perceived resistance.

Yapko's approach to hypnosis is a radical departure from other authorities. He defines hypnosis as influence communication—a position sure to be considered controversial because some might think that definition too general, thereby unnecessarily diluting the territory. However, Yapko presents his arguments cogently and has a position that deserves recognition in the literature and can be supported by citations and references.

Trancework was written to promote clinical hypnosis and make it more available to psychotherapists. It will motivate many to enter the field and broaden their interests so that there will be active use of and research into hypnotic communication.

I find this book particularly interesting when it describes the induction process, the utilization of trance phenomena, and the wording of different types of suggestions. Professionals will appreciate the attention given to the ethical use of hypnosis. In good Ericksonian fashion, we are admonished to attend to individual differences and meet the patient at his frame of reference; the emphasis is on communication skills, not on rigid formulas.

Trancework provides the building blocks necessary to learn the vocabulary and grammar of hypnotherapy and effective forms of influence communication. We look forward to other expositions from this talented writer.

JEFFREY K. ZEIG, PH.D.,
Director, The Milton H. Erickson Foundation
Phoenix, Arizona

Contents

Frames of Reference

Relevant comments from leading figures in the fields of hypnosis and psychotherapy.

Tables

Introduction to the Second Edition

When *Trancework* first came out in 1984, it was riding on a wave of enthusiasm for the creative approaches to hypnosis and hypnotically-based psychotherapy of the late Milton H. Erickson, M.D. The focus on Erickson and his innovative methods has spawned a whole new generation of clinicians interested in hypnosis and the applications it may have in various clinical contexts. *Trancework* is not a book about Erickson, though. It is a book about practical methods for developing the kinds of relationship and communication skills that will increase the effectiveness of your clinical methods, regardless of the context in which they are applied. I am a practical-minded fellow who is interested in therapeutic patterns that *work*. Erickson's emphasis was also a practical one, which I can appreciate. His influence on the material contained here is significant.

This second edition represents an effort to make the acquisition of skills to apply hypnosis more easily accomplished by the reader. The exercises and discussions can be the most powerful teachers of hypnotic skill, but this revised edition presents new features that will enhance the learning process. First, two new chapters have been added. Chapter 19 contains transcripts of portions of actual hypnosis sessions conducted with bona fide clients. Chapter 20 presents a verbatim clinical session in its entirety, including commentary intended to amplify points of interest in the learning of hypnotic communication. Both new chapters are intended to provide greater insight into the clinical applications of hypnosis and are considered a valuable addition to the text.

Another new feature are the *Frames of Reference* sections, which include worthwhile quotes on a variety of stimulating topics from leading figures in the field. These *Frames of Reference* provide an enjoyable glimpse into the thinking and the history of notable authorities. The reader will note that the *Frames of Reference* are listed separately, immediately following the table of contents.

Also new to this edition are 20 tables that clearly and succinctly provide key information. These tables can be easily memorized, allowing more rapid integration of the material.

What makes hypnosis so potentially useful a tool? Is it the emphasis on acknowledging and respecting the subjective reality of each individual client? Is it the emphasis on the cooperative nature of the therapeutic relationship? Is it the enhanced appreciation and use of the recognition that words can heal? Certainly, all these are factors contributing to the effectiveness of hypnotic patterns, but the strength of doing trancework comes from undefinable sources within each human being. Whether these are termed the "unconscious," "inner wisdom," "the God within," or some other equally ambiguous name, there is a remarkable potential in each person that surfaces during those states of absorption called "trance" that one can readily appreciate. If there is a more dynamic and potent means of empowering individuals than by working hypnotically, I am not yet aware of it.

It is unfortunate, but nonetheless true, that the field of hypnosis remains an internally conflicted one. The focus on the clinical approaches of Erickson has been substantial in the last decade, and it is a basic truth that every movement creates a countermovement. While many were (noncritically) touting the wonders of "Ericksonian hypnosis," others were openly criticizing the apparent lack of objectivity in such strong claims. Just as there are divisions in the field of psychotherapy, there are those who align themselves with one model of hypnosis and openly express disapproval for any other model. It is my hope that *Trancework* will permit you to sidestep issues of alignment and instead focus on issues associated with discovering how *you as an individual practitioner can best apply these approaches in a manner congruent with your training and personality*. While I generally favor the flexibility of less direct and imposing techniques, I am quite aware that what works well for me may not work as well for someone else.

Knowing what I know about trance states and ways to induce and utilize them, I am inclined to integrate the seemingly irreconcilable views about hypnosis. I generally promote the perspective that while the experimental production of specific trance phenomena is not an apparent capability of all people, the "real life" utilization of specific trance phenomena to create reality (including wellness and illness) is evident in all. The question of what is and what is not "trance" is interesting fodder for debates which cannot be won, but is irrelevant when a client is in distress and needs a skilled, flexible, creative therapist to interrupt self-limiting patterns while building self-enhancing ones.

Technique is inevitably bound to context. What succeeds in one context can be faithfully duplicated but still yield unfortunate results in another context. What *Trancework* is ultimately about is synthesizing what is known about social influence, communication, psychotherapy, and clinical hypnosis in order to sensitize you to the healing power of words, the healing power of beliefs, and the healing power of relationships.

In that regard, I have chosen not to focus on facts and issues unrelated to the development of actual skills in using hypnosis. Detailing the ancient history of hypnosis or reporting unusual experiments with hypnosis that lead to nonclinical questions such as whether or not hypnosis can be used to get someone to rob a bank is simply not consistent with my aim in writing *Trancework*. I am all too aware that most professionals do *not* get their hypnosis training in academic institutions—they get it in privately sponsored workshops. If you are taking a university-sponsored course in hypnosis, consider yourself fortunate to have *some* progressive aspects in your curriculum. Most hypnosis training takes place in small groups of interested and experienced clinicians. As one who routinely offers such training, I am aware of the participants' desire to focus on skill-building above all else. For this reason, I have included things to discuss and things to do in every chapter. The conceptual framework of the first part of the book is simply a foundation for more easily assimilating the techniques of the second part of the book. The true skills, however, come only with practice, as you would naturally expect.

I would like to make one final point about usage in this edition. Rather than refer to people exclusively as male, as tradition suggests, or exclusively as female, as I did in the first edition, I have consistently made use of both male and female pronouns in an inconsistent way, thoughout the book. Male and female therapists; male and female clients. Just like in the real world.

I hope you find *Trancework* a valued ally in your efforts to learn clinical hypnosis. More importantly, I hope you find resources in yourself you can appreciate as you learn.

MICHAEL D. YAPKO, PH.D.
San Diego, California

Introduction to the First Edition

If the word "hypnosis" conjures up images of a powerful, magician-like figure dangling a gold watch in the face of a stuporous subject while giving the command to "sleep deeply," then you are in a for a pleasant surprise. Not only is that *not* what clinical hypnosis is all about, but that old stereotype of hypnosis has little relevance to the current perspective of hypnosis as a rich system of communication.

Hypnotic patterns are evident wherever influential communication occurs. The artistry of meaningful applications of hypnosis can be appreciated when one considers the dynamics of how one person can use communication to alter the experience of another.

It is my hope and anticipation that hypnosis will become a significant part of your range of interactional skills, even if after reading this book you never formally induce a trance in anyone for the remainder of your life. Although that may seem a grandiose goal for a hypnosis book, many years of teaching hypnosis to practicing professionals and graduate students have convinced me that the skills in communication described in this book can make a positive difference in the work you do and in the relationships you form with virtually everyone.

So much has happened in recent years in the fields of clinical hypnosis, clinical psychology, communications, linguistics, neurology, and others relevant to understanding human behavior that the impact has yet to be fully appreciated. Certainly a revolution has taken place in perspectives on hypnosis, described throughout this book. In the past there have been numerous theories explaining the various phenomena associated with the trance state, yet the practice of hypnosis was generally limited to one of two forms: 1) the "traditional" application of hypnosis emphasizing the power of the hypnotist in relationship to an obedient subject (this approach is best represented by the stage hypnotist), and 2) a "standardized" approach emphasizing the responsibility of the client to adapt herself to a scripted, and therefore non-individualized, program of the hypnotist (best represented by prepackaged tapes and "cookbook" treatments). Both approaches have been quite limited in their ability to obtain positive results reliably (see Appendix A).

Fortunately, the field of hypnosis has evolved past these two limited approaches in recent years, This development is due in large part to the innovative and untiring work of the late psychiatrist and hypnosis pioneer Milton H. Erickson, M.D. Erickson evolved his own unique techniques which could recognize and use the creativity and individuality of each person. Recently, numerous texts and articles have flooded the hypnosis literature promoting Erickson's methods, collectively called the "utilization" approach, though also referred to as "Ericksonian hypnosis." In this model, emphasis is placed upon the utilization of as many dimensions of the client's inner world as possible, particularly the unconscious mind's unique resources.

The progression of hypnosis as a field beyond demanding blind obedience and offering scripted routines has radically changed its conceptual and practical frameworks. Hypnosis is no longer the "occultish" mystery it once was, although undeniably there are still things about hypnosis remaining to be explained. With the progression in understandings about hypnosis has also come acceptance. Although most people encountering hypnosis for the first time still do so in a stage show context, increasing numbers of people are also being made aware of its clinical and other appropriate professional uses. Typically, they have been made aware through the media, which frequently runs programs and articles on hypnosis, or through friends who have obtained help through hypnosis.

The sole purpose of this book is to introduce professionals to the rich and complex world of clinical hypnosis. I hope it will allow you to acquire a comprehensive understanding of the concepts and issues related to its practice, and to acquire the basic skills that only years of regular practice and continued pursuit of excellence can build upon. Reread, if you don't mind, the last sentence. It is one written with great sincerity. To become truly skilled in the use of hypnosis (or any other worthwhile endeavor for that matter) takes a great deal of time and commitment. This book can provide a broad and solid framework of understanding and experience that more advanced, specialized studies of hypnosis can build upon.

There are plenty of books, cassette and videotape packages, and training programs that promise to make you a hypnotist "overnight." They are not lying, either, for you can be a hypnotist overnight. Guiding a person into trance is not particularly difficult, nor is reading a prepared script to the hypnotized subject. Such approaches may even get some positive results occasionally. However, obtaining consistent results across a wider range of client concerns requires a sensitivity and deeper knowledge that is not available in such approaches. Developing sensitivity to the individual needs of the client and learning how to best develop her unique inner resources is not taught in the "overnight hypnotist" programs. Only rigid formulas are. The oversimplifications of the traditional and standardized approaches make them, in many instances, undesirable for use.

Unfortunately, a powerful tool like hypnosis can be placed in the hands of people who are not in a position to appreciate the full implications of its use. This is another reason why anyone can be a hypnotist: It is legal for anyone who wants to to hang out the "hypnotist" shingle on her door with no formal credentials, not even a high school diploma. Hypnotists who are untrained in the health professions are routinely providing physical and psychological health care, under ambiguous names of course, but health care nonetheless. Some are really quite good at what they do, but the potential dangers should be apparent.

After you have read this book you will be faced with decisions about how much more, if any, training and proficiency you want to obtain. Beyond what you will be aware of learning, you can learn a great deal more without even realizing you are learning, and perhaps you can decide to learn just enough to take pride in your knowledge and skills.

This is a book for training in hypnosis. There are exercises to do, concepts and terms to master, and points to discuss. I encourage you to experience and practice all the techniques you can. Ultimately, you can read about hypnosis, then read more about it, and talk about it, and then read still more about it, but there is no substitute for hours and hours of working with it. A lot of commitment, but the payoff is most rewarding.

MICHAEL D. YAPKO PH.D.
San Diego, California

Acknowledgments

I have no idea whether psychotherapist Neil Simon had any foresight as to what kind of impact he would have when he offered me the opportunity to learn the concepts and techniques of clinical hypnosis. I gratefully acknowledge Neil's investment in me—his thoroughness, sensitivity and patience provided a solid foundation on which to build.

The ideas expressed in this book have developed as a result of the influences of many special people. I would like to gratefully acknowledge the following friends and colleagues for their valued contributions on both personal and professional levels:

Stephen G. Gilligan	Bill Kroger
Linda M. Griebel	Ernest L. Rossi
Jay Haley	Martin E.P. Seligman
Sam Janus	André M. Weitzenhoffer
John Koriath	Jeffrey K. Zeig

I would like to express my deep appreciation to my wife, Diane, for her love and support. Without the support and encouragement of my family and friends, I doubt this project could have been realized. Finally, I would like to thank the editorial staff at Brunner/Mazel, particularly Natalie Gilman and Laura Greeney, for their efforts on my behalf. Many thanks.

SECTION I

*Conceptual
Framework*

1

Perspectives

A few years ago, a local high school student called me and asked whether I would be willing to speak to his psychology class about clinical applications of hypnosis. I said I would, but knowing from previous experience the red tape generally involved in such undertakings, I advised him to first obtain permission from his teacher and school administration. That was the last I heard from him. Several days later I received a very "official looking" letter from the school district superintendent's office stating that it was district policy to "prohibit use of school facilities for demonstrations of hypnosis or any other use of hypnosis involving students as observers or as subjects." No demonstration of hypnosis was going to be done by me in this setting anyway, but the school board apparently thought any discussion of clinical hypnosis must also involve a show of some sort.

Now, I do not consider myself particularly dangerous as an individual and, although somewhat ornery on occasion, I am hardly a threat to humanity. However, it seems that merely being a practitioner of hypnosis has apparently made me capable of committing such serious atrocities that students should not even be observers of hypnosis lest they become victims of an unspeakable fate, according to a local school board.

In reality, I know the school board wasn't concerned about me as an individual. Rather, the school board was concerned about the dangers associated with hypnosis, and did not have enough knowledge about clinical hypnosis to establish guidelines that would distinguish an appropriate professional presentation from a stage show.

Fortunately, not everyone is as unenlightened. More and more frequently I encounter people who have had positive exposure to the applications of clinical hypnosis. There is still a long way to go in making hypnotic principles and techniques a part of most helping professionals' repertoire of skills, but my experience in teaching hypnosis to professionals of diverse backgrounds and interests suggests that when hypnosis is made a more

3

practical and understandable tool, its positive use grows and the appreciation spreads.

Hypnosis has been very up and very down on the roller coaster of acceptability to both layperson and professional alike. To gain acceptance, some practitioners have made wild claims, sensationalized treatment results, and, in general, built hypnosis into a magical, mystical process that has everything going for it but a formal endorsement from Above. Unfortunately, the more grandiose a claim for any product or service, the more skeptical the consumer and the more extreme a position its advocates are subsequently forced into. The result is inevitably more turn-offs than turn-ons.

This book is not intended to sensationalize hypnosis, nor is it intended to make a statement about how hypnosis is *the* answer to all of life's challenges. Rather, hypnosis is conceptualized and treated as a system of skilled communication able to enhance those interactions requiring a wide range of communication skills. Hypnosis offers a way to conceptualize how individual human beings construct their individual realities, and it offers insights about ways to interact more effectively with others. Acquiring hypnotic skills is one way to enhance your clinical abilities, and can allow you to obtain lasting results in the therapy work you do. Perhaps best of all, use of hypnosis can be a way to promote self-sufficiency and independence in those clients you work with, helping them to be happier and more self-assured.

Clinical hypnosis is a skill of using words and gestures in particular ways to achieve specific outcomes. The emphasis throughout this text will be on the use of hypnotic processes as agents of effective communication and change. This orientation minimizes the use of rituals in its use and maximizes rapid assessment of and responsiveness to individual client needs according to specific guidelines provided throughout.

With the emphasis always on "practical" and "understandable," it is my intention to present the concepts and techniques of hypnosis in a way that will allow you to let go of old, useless misunderstandings in favor of new, useful understandings. In doing so, I would like to avoid, whenever possible, the unanswerable questions that knowledgeable people have debated endlessly about (such as whether there is such a thing as "reality") and instead focus on specific skills that can be obtained through the study of hypnotic communication.

Almost everyone has an established attitude about hypnosis. Most people have seen it or heard of it, and whatever they saw, heard, or felt at the time left an impression as the basis for their attitude. Hypnosis has been demonstrated in movies, kiddie cartoons, television programs, stage shows, state fairs, and classrooms everywhere. Uncle Melvin dabbles in the art at parties (usually just before his lampshade-on-the-head routine). It helped your third cousin twice removed quit smoking. It took the Smith boy you vaguely knew away from his family when he joined that cult in California. With this kind of exposure, it is little wonder that many feel certain that whatever hypnosis is, it is beyond understanding . . . and probably dangerous.

For stage artists, keeping the mystery in hypnosis means more bread and butter. Unfortunately, these are the people least able to use hypnosis effectively to its greatest potential as a tool for helping people to improve their lives. Instead, hypnosis is misrepresented to the public, both layperson and professional, as a mind-controlling instrument with frightening implications. As sophisticated and enlightened as many people are becoming in many areas, change comes hard in the field of hypnosis. The school board I mentioned at the outset is just one of many testimonials to this fact.

Few fields have had the ups and downs hypnosis has had. Hypnosis has been around, in various forms, for thousands of years. Acceptability has varied from moderate to none. People who practiced hypnosis had their rituals ("techniques") and superstitions ("this induction worked pretty well on the last client I had with freckles . . . ") but very little cognitive understanding of what they were doing. With acceptability and applicability of hypnotic processes growing in scope, the need for a sensible, understandable approach is necessary for maximizing positive exposure to hypnosis for all concerned. That is my intention.

When people discover I practice hypnosis, typically they are both fascinated and skeptical. Almost everyone has had some direct or indirect experience with hypnosis, and it is incorrectly assumed that whatever I do with it is the same as whatever anyone and everyone else who uses hypnosis does with it. Few people have had enough exposure to hypnosis to be able to differentiate the different types and applications of hypnosis from one another. This is a drawback to being an overt practitioner of therapeutic hypnosis; the general public assumes that "hypnosis is hypnosis is hypnosis," and all they have to do as consumers is shop around to find the most inexpensive deal with the most promises attached.

Used skillfully, however, this problem can become an asset. By exploring with the consumer seeking information about my work the various approaches and possibilities, I can help the person become knowledgeable enough to make meaningful decisions. Making certain that consumers have the information necessary to make an informed decision about treatment should, in my opinion, be basic to any professional practice. Just because someone doesn't ask questions does not mean she has none. It usually means she just doesn't know what to ask.

By involving people in a brief discussion about their needs and the nature of clinical hypnosis as a tool, one can provide information that helps consumers more realistically assess their needs, and the best means for meeting them. Often, formal hypnosis aimed at symptom removal alone is not a desirable or realistic treatment alternative, but was turned to initially by the person for some "magic" and a chance to avoid the maze of pursuing other, more personally threatening, approaches to treatment.

The fact that hypnosis is used as a stage act in the media (live shows especially, but also cinema and television) contributes to popular stereo-types of hypnosis as a magical means for instant problem resolution through powerful suggestions. I wish I had a nickel for every person who has asked for a "quick suggestion" to stop some unwanted behavior. Rational explanations of why the work to be done might be a little more involved than they think are often met with puzzled looks and some variation of the question, "Then how does the stage hypnotist just snap his fingers to get his subject to do whatever he wants him to?" Unrealistic concepts can lead to disappointment and disillusionment in the client.

Clarifying the purposes and capacities of hypnosis as a therapeutic tool is almost always beneficial for the client. If the situation arises where it may be of benefit to the client to not be directly active in treatment, one might choose not to hold an informative discussion, occasionally an excellent alternative. Clarification, however, leads the person to face the fact that there will be no miracle cures other than the ones she provides for herself. It means accepting personal responsibility for the problem, and it means being active in its resolution.

Almost as dangerous as the stage hypnotist in promoting misconception, perhaps even more so, is the hypnotist who through ignorance or greed uses hypnosis in a practice that caters to public misconception. Such persons usually have little or no formal education in hypnosis and the healing sciences, but know just enough to mislead people with claims of sensational power.

These are just a few of the problems faced by hypnosis as a field. Others are discussed in later sections of the book. The point is made throughout that if hypnosis is to be considered a serious treatment alternative, it must be promoted with a sensitivity to the issues of concern both to consumers and other health-care providers. It starts with you, the reader.

For Discussion

1. Why do you want to learn hypnosis? What about hypnosis do you find appealing?

2. What things have you heard are possible to do with hypnosis? What is your reaction to these claims?

3. What exposure have you had to hypnosis? What were the circumstances, and what were the outcomes?

4. Should the use of hypnosis be restricted in some way? Why or why not? If you think it should, how would you recommend it be done?

5. What things, if any, are you apprehensive about in learning hypnosis? What is the basis for your apprehensions?

Things to Do

1. Watch the media for stories on hypnosis. How is it represented? Keep a scrapbook of articles that appear over the next few months as you study hypnosis.

2. Interview a variety of health professionals (such as physicians, dentists, etc.) about their attitudes toward hypnosis. What do you discover?

3. Go through the Yellow Page listings under "Hypnotism." How do you react to the claims made there of what hypnosis can do?

2

Broadening
Perspectives

Sometimes when one tries to describe or define an experience, attaching a specific label to the experience limits the way the experience will be perceived. For example, if a new co-worker is introduced to you as a psychiatric patient recently released from the hospital, how will your perception of the person be influenced by the label "psychiatric patient?" Would someone react to the person in the same way if no such introduction were given? When one is considering a simple, concrete object, such as a chair, the tendency for labels to get in the way of experience is not so troublesome. The word "chair" represents something tangible that most people can experience similarly. In considering something as abstract, complex, and subjective as "hypnosis," however, the difficulties arise almost immediately. The word represents different experiences to different people, preventing the attainment of a precise shared meaning.

Traditionally, hypnosis has been considered a subjective state of experience ("in hypnosis") in which the individual has capabilities or experiences generally regarded as atypical of the "normal waking" state. Hypnosis has also been considered to be a process ("doing hypnosis") in which a hypnotist offers suggestions to a subject. Both of these concepts are correct, yet are limited in their both using the word "hypnosis" to describe an individual subjective state and a process of offering suggestions to another person.

Hypnosis as a word has been overused to the point of robbing it of any real meaning. When one word comes to describe as many different experiences as "hypnosis" has, there is ample opportunity for misunderstanding, mislabeling, misconception, and ultimately, confusion. It is precisely because hypnosis is one word for many different experiences that the layperson is led to believe that "hypnosis is hypnosis," regardless of context. Furthermore, because hypnosis is only one word for many different experiences, even helping professionals untrained in hypnosis are skeptical about its use in clinical contexts, uncertain whether it differs appreciably from that which is demonstrated in stage shows.

Proponents of hypnosis have long recognized this, generally feeling more misunderstood as a group than others, yet the term remains virtually unchanged in common usage. For practitioners, it seems imperative to be clear in describing the context in which hypnosis is used so others may be continually reminded of the variety of applications.

Arranging the concepts and techniques of hypnosis into a useful definition is a difficult task. Moving in that direction, some perspectives from the past may be useful for the purpose of illustrating some of the earlier views of hypnosis. If one were to review past definitions of hypnosis, one would typically find offerings such as:

1. Hypnosis is guided daydreaming. The hypnotist, either another person (heterohypnosis) or one's self (autohypnosis, self-hypnosis) acts as a guide for an experience regarded as fantasy.
2. Hypnosis is a natural, altered state of consciousness. The person enters a trance state, a state distinctly different from the person's "normal" state, through a natural process not involving ingestion of any substances or other physical treatments.
3. Hypnosis is a relaxed, hypersuggestible state. The person enters a very relaxed state of mind and body, and subsequently is more responsive to suggestion.
4. Hypnosis is a twilight state. The hypnotic state is considered a sort of halfway point between sleep and the waking state, a state in which the unconscious mind is more receptive to change.

Each of the above definitions of hypnosis contains an element of truth, but is limited in its usefulness. All describe hypnosis from the standpoint of the person in the trance state, with no mention of the role of the hypnotist or the quality of the relationship between the two. All imply a passive responsiveness to suggestion on the part of the hypnotic subject, a tendency to accept offered suggestions due to the presence of a state ambiguously called "trance." Other definitions will be described along with the theories of hypnosis in the later chapter "Conceptualizing Hypnosis."

When people think of hypnosis, they typically think of the hypnotized person behaving in unpredictable and unexplainable ways in response to a

hypnotist's suggestions. Traditional perspectives on hypnosis consider theoretical constructs of the mind and human personality to explain hypnotic
phenomena. Such explanations have been quite unclear and are usually
bound to one theoretical view. Perhaps the most obvious example is the
psychoanalytic view of hypnosis as a transference response and regression
in which the hypnotist is responded to as a parent figure.

It is possible to transcend theoretical considerations of the structure of
the mind or personality when considering how such structures become
known. In other words, if there are detectable structures of the mind and
personality that may be recognized and developed into theories or models,
the level of consideration it seems most worthwhile to study is the means by
which such structures become evidenced in the person. Very simply, the
person evidences them by somehow *communicating* them.

Every person who works with people in a professional capacity makes
continuous assessments of clients' needs, motivations, skills, limitations,
and further assesses the likelihood of success in reaching the goals of their
relationship. These assessments are made in accordance with how the
person intervening in the problem chooses to conceptualize the problem
from the way it is communicated—the framework she uses to organize
perceptions while experiencing the client. One's framework is one's way of
viewing people and their problems. It varies from clinician to clinician
according to formal training, personal experience, and the resulting belief
system from the interaction of the two. Someone who believes in one
particular theory will conceptualize a problem's dynamics very differently
from someone else who believes in and practices from a different theory.
For example, someone with a weight problem will be given different
alternatives and instructed in different concepts while undergoing behavioral treatment than will someone undergoing treatment for the same
problem while undergoing psychoanalysis. Likewise, a psychological approach
to the problem will be different from a medical approach.

Arguments about theoretical perspective are hard to avoid, but they can
be sidestepped to some degree if one can appreciate that such arguments
can not be won. No one theory to date adequately explains why people
do what they do or how to intervene in a uniformly successful way. The
evidence for this point is in the limitation clinicians face in their capacity
to heal the people in distress they work with. No therapist succeeds with
all clients, perhaps not even with most. I am not saying psychotherapy is
failing to help people, but I am saying that it is not 100% effective, nor

is it ever likely to be, given the varied and unpredictable nature of human beings. The idealistic goal is to learn its limitations and to strive to surpass them.

This, then, is my point. It seems that taking a client's communications about his problems and altering them from their original form in order to fit with some preferred theoretical belief is a step that is both arbitrary and unnecessary. Responding to a client's communications in their original form as a reflection of what the person is experiencing can lead one to communicate in a way that will enhance the quality of the interaction. The approach to hypnosis promoted in this book is essentially a way of organizing one's therapeutic communications to best fit an individual's needs, using words and gestures selectively in order to arrive at some worthwhile outcome. Which therapeutic framework one chooses to work from is not an issue here. *All* the therapeutic approaches work, which is why each has devotees. The skill lies in knowing which approach to use at any given moment.

The client who senses being understood by the clinician is the client more likely to benefit from the relationship. Of course, this is not an original idea, for every clinician is trained to appreciate the importance of the quality of the relationship with the client. Literature in hypnosis and psychotherapy generally employs the word "rapport" to describe the ideal positive interrelationship between hypnotist/clinician and client. How one attained rapport was left up to the individual clinician, as it must be, but such noticeable lack of consideration has resulted in a de-emphasis of the interpersonal components of effective clinical hypnosis. Consequently, rigid approaches have flourished.

The process of clinical intervention can be described as a series of communications between clinician and client. No matter what one's orientation, one is using the communications of the client to make assessments, and one is using communications as the vehicle for the therapy. A therapeutic communication is one that somehow influences the person in distress to feel or behave differently in a way that is considered more adaptive or beneficial.

The essence of what I am discussing here is communication and interpersonal influence, and that is precisely where hypnosis comes in. If one rejects the passive view of hypnosis as simply an individual's subjective state, and instead considers the dynamics of interpersonal communication that a clinician employs in order to influence a client to have a suggested therapeutic experience, then a rich and complex new world opens up. Somewhere in the communications of both the hypnotist and psychotherapist are some components that enable a client's subjective experience to be altered and therapeutic influence to take place.

To use words and gestures skillfully in the creation of therapeutic experiences for an individual in distress (or any other person one would want a specific outcome with) is the nuts and bolts of what hypnosis is all about. Approaching hypnosis from this standpoint places emphasis on being an effective communicator, one who is able to recognize and competently relate to the communications of others. This allows the clinician to adapt her communications in ways that maximize their opportunity for being understood at one or more levels, and then integrated in a way that proves beneficial.

When one shifts the focus to dimensions of communications that increase the potential for influence of another person's experience, the emphasis is much less on ritual and attaining particular levels of trance, and much more on the use of words and gestures in specific ways. Thus, elements of *any* piece of communication can have hypnotic qualities without formally being "hypnosis." This point especially allows the study of hypnosis to be of great potential value for those who work with people. Even if one chooses not to pursue expertise in doing formal trancework, one can benefit greatly from learning about the power of effective communication. An insensitively used word can hinder or prevent a positive treatment result. Likewise, a sensitively used phrase can engender a positive belief that dramatically improves the chances for a successful treatment outcome.

It is important to recognize the everpresent nature of interpersonal influence. In one course I teach, Social Psychology, I usually make the statement at the start of class that, "You will do things when you are by yourself that you will not do as soon as one other person is around."* Recognizing hypnotic elements in everyday situations is a skill that can allow you to use hypnosis more flexibly and with greater success.

---

*The point is that the mere presence of another person alters your behavior. It is not a question of *whether* you will influence your client—you undoubtedly will—but rather a question of *how* you will influence him. Learning to use patterns of influence responsibly while respecting the integrity of those we work with is a demanding challenge. Patterns of influence do not just exist in the contexts of therapy or hypnosis, though. If you are observant, you will see them literally everywhere that you see social interaction.

An inevitable by-product of using communication in hypnotic ways is the de-emphasis on performing structured hypnotic rituals in order to obtain trance, or what I call "formal hypnosis." The recent popularity of indirect techniques of hypnosis is the direct result of the recognition that a person's experience can be guided and trance responses are possible without any formal induction taking place at all. Since trance is an everyday experience, all a good hypnotist does is create trance phenomena deliberately instead of waiting for them to occur randomly. No hypnotist is creating experiences outside the realm of what occurs routinely in other contexts. When we describe the trance phenomena later, this point will become clearer.

An original aim of this chapter was to provide some definition of hypnosis for the reader. The limitations of some earlier definitions were discussed, and the case for hypnosis as a process of influential communication was presented. Defining hypnosis as a process of influential communication is a very general definition, and as so often happens when one is trying to define abstract concepts, a more specific definition can be provided only when the variables of a specific context can be considered. Included in a context-determined definition, as I am recommending, would be the client's subjective experience, noticeably absent from the discussion thus far and discussed at length later.

For Discussion

1. What do you think makes one an effective communicator?

2. What is your belief system about why people do the things they do? How do your beliefs both help and hurt your ability to interact with others?

3. How do you sense what a person is capable of doing? For example, how do you decide that someone is trustworthy?

4. What is your definition of "rapport"? How do you know when you have rapport with someone?

5. Why do definitions of abstract terms, such as "love," differ so much from person to person? What are the implications for effective communications?

Things to Do

1. Give your discussion partner instructions *not* to communicate for three minutes while you observe her. Does she communicate anything to you in spite of your instructions? What? Why is it not possible to prevent communication?

2. List and define the basic constructs of personality from your perspective. How do you become aware of these in the people you interact with?

3. List those people closest to you whom you influence. How do you do so? Do you influence them in ways you would like to?

3

The Origins of Myth

The process of hypnosis can be viewed as a complex interaction in which the quality of the communications is the inescapable bottom line in describing the quality of interaction. In other words, the relationship between clinician and client is characterized by the quality of the communications exchanged, specifically whether the communication "fits" well enough to be incorporated.

By describing the hypnotic interaction in terms of communication and influence, much of the mystery of "hypnotic power" can be eliminated. The recency of the understanding of hypnotic techniques as rooted in communications is a primary reason for the limited exposure of most persons to the positive aspects of clinical hypnosis. Clinical hypnosis with an emphasis on effective communication is a relatively new perspective with a great deal to offer professional communicators. In order to be acknowledged as such, however, it will take a great deal of competent ethical exposure on the part of its proponents.

Laypeople and professionals alike generally have pre-existing attitudes about hypnosis. Since hypnosis from a communications perspective is burdened with the same name as any other hypnosis, the tendency of others is to assume that what they already know about hypnosis from prior exposure is accurate. People do not know they are misinformed until their existing information and beliefs come into direct conflict with some new information. It is especially important to spend time with clients discussing directly or indirectly their views and expectations about the therapeutic relationship. Only through such discussion can a clinician discover the client's expectations and needs in order to assess their realistic or unrealistic nature.

In the practice of clinical hypnosis, the opportunity for dealing with misinformation is constant. Most misconceptions are predictable, which can make their identification and rebuttal easier. Most people hold the stereotypical view of hypnosis as a powerful form of mind control, and the most common misconceptions are based on that notion.

It is difficult to change people's thinking when they are convinced they are knowledgeable in their opinions. In fact, the more knowledgeable a person views himself, the more difficult it is to introduce a piece of conflicting information. In general, people ignore contradictions or twist them around until everything they believe fits together comfortably, even if incorrectly. The classic defense mechanisms (such as rationalization) are examples of this point. I had what seemed to be the 10,000th experience of this recently when I was unable to convince an obstetrician that hypnosis would not be harmful to his pregnant patient wanting hypnosis. I pointed out ways that hypnosis would, in fact, be helpful to her, and though he could agree at the intellectual level, he could not bring himself to give her permission to experience hypnosis, so strong were his fears and doubts. This is the same doctor who said, "Lamaze is bunk; the only way to go is with a saddle block." With many people, unfortunately, the predominant attitude is "Don't bother me with facts, my mind is made up!"

The misconceptions that run rampant in this field are kept alive by those who profit from them. Stage hypnotists, script writers for the entertainment industry, and fast-buck seekers who like "the power" are contributors to the ever-present body of misinformation that has kept hypnosis on the periphery of acceptable therapeutic procedure.

Involving the client in a discussion about her beliefs and expectations for the hypnotic and psychotherapeutic experience is necessary to make certain she is knowledgeable enough to make worthwhile decisions about her treatment. Since the client's understanding of the process is likely to be inaccurate, incomplete, or both, the ethical and competent professional can provide the person with as much information as she may require in order to be fully involved in the process in a cooperative and positive way. You may note that I say that as much information should be provided as the person "requires," implying that on some occasions the amount of information dispensed may be marginal, while in other instances it is substantial. Individual needs differ, and only by communicating clearly with your client will you discover her needs. Generally, though, a well-informed client is in a better position to make the therapy a more meaningful collaboration.

Many clinicians are helpful in reaction to the questions and concerns the client raises, but this may be only a portion of what is required in order for the client to be positively involved in the treatment. The client is sometimes too self-conscious to ask questions of the clinician, and the risk of seeming ignorant in addition to already having presented one's self as experiencing problems that are out of control and in need of professional help is a risk too great for some to take. The result is a silent hope that the clinician is skilled enough to read minds and take the necessary steps to effect a cure with as little involvement as possible on the part of the client. Another facet of the concern for providing information to the client whether or not one is asked for it is the observation that many people simply don't know what to ask. If a client already feels comfortably knowledgeable about hypnosis, she is unlikely to seek new information. If a client is experiencing hypnosis as something totally new, she may not know what to ask the clinician. Only a gentle inquiry will help you decide what seems important for this person to know.

The hazard of not giving the client enough information is matched by the hazard of giving *too much* information to a client who is not ready for it or wanting it. A favorite story of mine illustrates the point: A boy about six years old came home from one of his first days at school and with a manner of intensity asked his mother, "Mommy, where did I come from?" The mother got a pained look on her face, took a deep sigh and said "Well, I had desperately hoped we wouldn't have to have this talk for a few more years yet, but since you've asked I may as well tell you. The psychologist on the talk show said that if you're old enough to ask, you're old enough to know." The mother proceeded to explain the "facts of life" in vivid detail, describing anatomical differences between males and females, the process of intercourse, the fertilization process, pregnancy, and finally the birth process. The little boy sat unmoving and wide-eyed while listening to his mother throughout the entire explanation. Finally, the mother completed her explanation and asked her son "Does that answer your question?" The boy replied, "No, mommy, it doesn't. My friend Mitchell says he comes from Detroit. Where did I come from?"

Only by engaging the person seeking help in discussion can one discover how much he knows and simultaneously take advantage of the opportunity to confirm or deny the beliefs as they are presented. Three basic questions that have been useful for me to ask are: Have you ever had experience with hypnosis before? Was it personal experience or was it something you saw, read, or heard about? What impression did you form?

If the client has had personal experience with hypnosis, good questions to ask might include: What was the situation in which you experienced hypnosis? Who was the hypnotist and what were his or her qualifications? What was the explanation given to you about hypnosis at the time? What was the technique used with you? Was it successful? Why or why not? How did you feel about the experience? What is the basis for your seeking further experience with hypnosis? The information you gather will be vital in determining your approach. Asking a lot of questions can be threatening and tiresome to the client, and so must be done gently; interrogations under a bright light are not recommended.

If the person has not had personal experience with hypnosis, good questions to ask might include: Have you seen hypnosis demonstrated? Have you heard about hypnosis before? In what context? How have you heard hypnosis may be used? Do you know anyone personally who has experienced hypnosis? What did he tell you about it? What is your understanding of how hypnosis works and what it can do? What is the basis for your requesting hypnosis? In asking some or all of these questions, one elicits the client's experiences and attitudes concerning hypnosis. Misconceptions can be dealt with, unrealistic fears alleviated, and a positive belief system engendered.

Asking about specific hypnotic techniques the client may have previously experienced is very important. If she experienced a process that was ineffective or unpleasant, then using the same or a similar technique is one way of assuring a similar failure. Unless one specifically asks about prior experience, one runs the risk of duplicating past negative experiences.

If the client has not had personal experience with hypnosis before, but is only indirectly familiar with it through entertainment media or the experiences of an acquaintance, it becomes even more important to discover her beliefs and attitudes. Second- and third-hand stories from "knowledgeable" friends have a tendency to get distorted and can sometimes be as misleading as the entertainer's version of hypnosis. Many clients are fearful of the "mind-control" potential, but seek the associated "magic wand" for quick results.

The major issue that arises for most people, experienced with trance or not, is that of "control." The client's fear of losing control of herself is the single greatest obstacle you are likely to encounter. In one form or another, almost every common misconception is grounded in this fear. Unless it is acknowledged and dealt with in a sensitive and positive way, it will undoubtedly hinder or even prevent the attainment of therapeutic results. The belief that hypnosis has the power to take self-control away has been fostered in ways mentioned previously, and until one has had the experience of therapeutic hypnosis in a positive atmosphere of caring and professionalism, the fear is a real one.

Stage hypnosis seems to be the biggest culprit for making control an issue of such huge proportions. The typical viewer of a hypnosis stage act has no idea how the hypnotist can "make" those seemingly normal volunteers do all those crazy things on stage before an audience. The erroneous conclusion is that the hypnotist has some mysterious power that can make people do things they would not ordinarily do.

THE SECRETS OF STAGE HYPNOSIS

How stage hypnotists get their subjects to perform is not difficult to understand if one has an appreciation both of hypnotic principles and of certain aspects of human behavior perhaps best described in the literature of social psychology.

Most stage shows begin with a call for volunteers. The volunteers are asked to *come up on the stage only if they truly want to be hypnotized.* Some stage hypnotists are so well known that volunteers eagerly make themselves available as soon as the opportunity arises. When a stage hypnotist gets volunteers, he knows several things about these people with a large measure of certainty:

1) They are aware of what they are volunteering for, and thus are willing to perform. There is an exception to this discussed shortly.

2) A general personality trait common to volunteer performers is a degree of exhibitionism; the greater the degree, the more useful the subject. Someone shy and introverted is unlikely to go on stage before a crowd. If someone shy were to go on stage, one of two things would probably occur: Either the person would "let loose" and consider hypnosis responsible for her behavior, or the subject would fail the hypnotist's tests for determining subject acceptability and be returned to the audience. For the most part, however, the people who go on stage to become a part of the act are aware of what their role will be. They are actively seeking the role, and they are agreeable to carry out its demands. You may notice my use of the word "role." The faces and names of hypnotic subjects change from show to show, but not the routines. Undeniably and invariably, the volunteer subject knows what is expected and tacitly agrees to provide it.

3) The experienced stage hypnotist also knows that some individuals are volunteering to participate with the intention of proving to the hypnotist that he is not omnipotent. Others are intent on proving to themselves that their personal will is strong, and that this fact may be evidenced by the inability of the hypnotist to "control" them. Insecure people may be boosted by an inability to be hypnotized when they interpret it as "having too strong a will."

In order to discover which subjects are the performers and which are the ones intent on proving themselves through noncooperative behavior, the hypnotist next administers traditional hypnotic suggestibility tests. These are discussed in greater detail in a later chapter, but are defined here simply as brief hypnotic interactions that can reveal the degree to which the subject will respond to suggestion. The stage hypnotist offers suggestions of specific feelings and behaviors; the most responsive subjects are kept on stage to be used in the show, and the others are told to return to their seats in the audience. Typically, the hypnotist offers an indirect suggestion to those remaining on stage about how good and responsive they are as subjects by stating directly to those dismissed from the stage how unfortunate it is that they were not (open, secure, smart . . .) enough to succeed as hypnotic subjects. I have observed one stage hypnotist in particular who bluntly says to those he dismisses as stage subjects that they "are very probably failures in life in addition to being failures as hypnotic subjects" because of their "resistant" nature. This, of course, involves the self-image of those remaining on stage, who do not want to be called failures in front of a large group and so comply even more readily with the hypnotist's whims. What does that kind of insult do to the rejected person's self-esteem? One can't be certain, but nothing positive seems possible from such an interaction.

It is at this point, where the subjects have been chosen, that the pressure to perform becomes very intense. The subjects have been chosen for whatever qualities (primarily obedience) they possess that will be conducive to putting on a good show. There is a great deal of pressure to meet the expectations of the hypnotist, of the crowd, and, not least, of themselves. The pressure is to be successful, and success in this context is directly proportional to the level of obedience displayed. Now that the subjects have been chosen and motivated to obey, the show can begin. From the perspective of the audience, the show is ready to begin. From the hypnotist's perspective, the work for the night is over! Subjects have been properly conditioned to comply, and now the show becomes a matter of simply running them through "tricks."

The hypnotist has cultivated almost unquestioned cooperation in the subject by running the person through tests and then "passing" her, in essence telling the subject, "You are the person I want here because I know you will do as I suggest." The literature of social psychology calls attention to how much more valuable a position of membership or a relationship is viewed if it is difficult to attain. Being accepted as a subject is a position earned, not one given charitably.

The audience expects the hypnotic subject to behave in particular ways, just as the subjects themselves know they will be "made" to act in certain entertaining ways. When a group of people have an expectation of how one is supposed to act, a temporary social norm is established. Deviation from a norm in any situation is generally undesirable, and the strong sense of independence it takes not to conform to the norm (the expected behavior) in the stage show context is virtually absent in the chosen subjects. Research on the need for peer approval and its relationship to the phenomenon of conformity describes this concept clearly. Thus, conforming behavior in order to get hypnotist and audience approval is a major ingredient in the stage show formula.

While the reader may not be familiar with or appreciate the lengths to which the perceived desirability of conforming will drive one, a review of literature on conformity will reveal that the need to conform to others' expectations has led research subjects to express obviously incorrect judgments, adopt others' perceptions of ambiguous events, and even to comply with mistrusted authorities. Compromising one's self even in potentially damaging situations is possible if the rewards for doing so are viewed as worthwhile enough. Witness the number of people injured doing stunts while looking for just a brief moment's exposure on national television. In a situation like a hypnosis stage show, where the subject is confident she will not be injured, being the center of attention and the source of a large group's amusement may be reward enough to comply with the hypnotist's suggestions. Any negative side-effects (e.g., embarrassment) from the performance can be readily attributed to the hypnosis, and not to the subject herself.

Research shows that people are far more willing to take risks, exercise questionable judgment, and even hurt others when they are not held accountable for their actions. If someone else assumes responsibility, or the person can act anonymously, or some other factor (such as alcohol or hypnosis) is a viable alibi, then inhibitions may disappear. Hypnosis is made the culprit for silly behavior, and the subject is free to act "as if" out of personal control. It is to the hypnotist's advantage to maintain this illusion, for if the subject appears to not be maintaining personal control, then it must be the hypnotist who is in control of the subject. This conclusion on the part of the audience is the very belief of power the hypnotist strives to foster. It's all a part of the act, and it is very convincing for most people.

Last, but not least, the expectations the subject has toward herself are involved in this process. The smart hypnotist uses the person's desire for a positive self-image and can make the subject's positive self-image contingent on carrying out the suggestions. Essentially, the hypnotist is saying, "Smart (secure, strong, successful . . .) people respond in this way to this suggestion. Now how are you going to respond?" Unless one wants to be viewed by one's self and others negatively, one will respond in the manner suggested. Furthermore, the person wants to succeed, not fail; in this instance, success is defined as following the given suggestions to the letter.

All the forces described above are working on the subject in the hypnotist's favor. The competent hypnotist, before giving any suggestions at all, knows all these things and knows that if all the pressures to perform are developed carefully and used properly, the subject will be most cooperative. If the pressures to perform have not been developed and used correctly, or if a suggestion is perceived by the subject as too threatening to carry out, the subject is unlikely to respond well to the hypnotist.

At all times, the subject is able to refuse to accept suggestions should she choose to. Given the great amount of pressure to accept them, however, this capacity is rarely used. It is actually easier just to go ahead and comply than it is to refuse; it takes more energy and inner strength to actively reject a suggestion than it does to passively comply and blame hypnosis as responsible. The key point is that the subject *is* able to reject the hypnotist's suggestions, but for the reasons given typically chooses not to.

The structure of the suggestions given to stage show subjects is another factor in the apparent ease with which the hypnotist seems to control his subjects. The typical layperson does not understand how saying, "You would not forget your name, would you?" can induce someone to forget her name. This is an example of "indirect negative suggestion," which carries the hypnotist's requests in a more subtle form but is recognizable all the same. This and other types of suggestions are described in a later chapter. Suggestions for amnesia are typically given in the same covert way, furthering the illusion that the hypnotist has control of the subject's mind.

Stage hypnotists are, as a group, skilled in their use of hypnosis. All the principles and techniques of stage hypnosis are identical to those of clinical hypnosis. Only the application is different. I can respect their skills and knowledge in hypnosis, but I must admit I have strong negative feelings about their chosen application. Using something potentially beneficial to people in a misleading and even degrading way is unethical and should be discouraged. Many people will not seek out hypnosis as a therapeutic alternative because they cannot even begin to comprehend how what they have seen in a night club show can be used clinically to help someone in distress. Colleagues of mine have pointed out that many people seek out hypnosis in therapy because of the stage hypnotist, but such people tend to believe that hypnotists have mysterious powers and so they approach treatment unrealistically. Stage hypnosis and its negative connotations rob people in need of help of what could be a valuable choice as a treatment alternative by promoting misconception and mystery.

Having a good understanding of how stage hypnosis works will be invaluable to you in terms of understanding dynamics of influence and assisting you in dealing with the general public's fears and doubts about hypnosis. Addressing misconceptions is the subject of the next chapter.

For Discussion

1. What is peer group pressure? How does it cause one to conform?

2. What qualities might allow one to resist peer group pressure? In general, are these positive or negative qualities?

3. How do one's expectations influence one's experiences? How is a "self-fulfilling prophecy" likely to be part of a stage hypnosis show?

4. How does a fear of losing control of one's self surface in everyday behavior? Cite examples.

5. What fears did you or do you have about experiencing trance? What apprehensions do you have about hypnotizing others?

4

Responding to Misconceptions

If someone were to come to you, take you by the hand and say "Come with me," would you go with the person and allow yourself to be led? Or would you first demand to know where you are being taken? Try this simple exercise on a number of people you know in varying degrees of intimacy. It should highlight to you the recognition that different people respond differently to direction and uncertainty, an important observation relevant to doing trancework. The issue of "control" surfaces immediately.

Taking the time to identify and correct misconceptions can help sidestep the issue of control, particularly if you emphasize the naturalistic nature of trance through the use of examples of trance taken directly from the client's routine experience. Furthermore, you can reinforce for the client the virtually total self-control the hypnotized person maintains during the trance experience. Clinicians must be sensitive to the issue of control and respond to it in some way, either directly or indirectly. Avoiding the issue of control can be anxiety-producing for the already uncertain client, and may create a force ("resistance") that works against the aims of treatment. If a client senses an imminent loss of control, the typical result is a power struggle with the clinician. Would *you* want to be hypnotized if you thought you would lose control of yourself? The goal is to do all one can to avoid a power struggle and define the relationship as a cooperative one. After all, there is really no way to win a power struggle with the client—to win, all she has to do is *nothing!*

Using the power struggle, and any other interpersonal factors that arise for that matter, as a hypnotic device to enhance the therapy is possible when it is based on the recognition that there is a paradox present in hypnosis and psychotherapy. Jay Haley (1963) described this paradox in terms of the hypnotist's seemingly contradictory messages: "I can only hypnotize you by you hypnotizing yourself; I can only help you by you helping yourself." Essentially, the message emphasizes the responsibility and control on the part of the client, but which is shared with the clinician. If I say to you, "Here. I'm giving you control of me," then who is really in control? If I have the control to give you control, then all I am really doing is suspending my decision to exercise my choices and instead use yours. I remain free, though, to begin exercising my choices again at any time I either have to or want to.

If you have ever been involved in a group decision-making process, you may think of the dynamics in that situation as analogous to what takes place in the hypnotic interaction. If it seems unnecessary to express your opinion because others are already acting in a way that is consistent with your beliefs, then you are less likely to make any further contributions to a system that is already working in a desirable way. If the group acts in ways contrary to your belief system, however, you can either go along with them peacefully but not really internalizing their beliefs, or you can resist and contradict them overtly, or you can resist covertly in a passive-aggressive manner. If you choose to just go along, you have control of yourself, but that control is not overtly expressed *by choice* in order to avoid contradictory encounters. The client, likewise, is free to overtly or covertly reject suggestions that don't fit for whatever reason. So even though the client seems to be saying, "Control me," the clinician can appreciate that control of the client is not his responsibility. Rather, the responsibility of the clinician is to structure suggestions responsibly and competently to maximize the likelihood that they will be accepted and translated into a therapeutic change. There is never a guarantee that even the most well-formed suggestion will be accepted and acted upon. Sensitivity to the client's unique needs only increases the *probability*.

The role of choice in the hypnotic encounter cannot be overemphasized. Hypnosis has been accused of making good people do bad things, but such accusations do not consider the choices the individual made (or *didn't* make, which is also a choice). At any given time, a person in trance is in a position to lighten, deepen, maintain, or end the trance state. One cannot be forced to concentrate and respond, the basic components of trance. One may choose to suspend judgment or decision-making, but that is a choice and not a surrendering of will. It takes control to yield control. I learned that particular lesson with people generally regarded as out of control, the residents of a locked, intensive-care psychiatric unit. Having spent several years working with these patients, I often noticed that frequently the outbursts and apparent loss of control were actually not a loss of control at all. Sometimes they were a call for help, sometimes a statement of anger, sometimes a request for more medication, sometimes a manipulation for attention . . . The "crazy outbursts" were often quite well calculated, for patients were occasionally overheard discussing which staff member was all right to "act out" on, or which was a "soft touch" for more medication. Loss of control was not necessarily a loss of control at all, even in locked-up psychiatric patients.

Identification and correction of misconceptions alleviates fear and uncertainty, and modifies expectations to be more consistent with the natural course of therapy. Unrealistic expectations at either extreme of wanting hypnosis to be a "magic wand" that can effect instantaneous cures for complex problems or, conversely, feeling the problem is hopeless altogether are expectations that are likely to reduce the effectiveness of intervention. Such obstacles are unnecessary and you can avoid them by promoting correct information and involving the person in forming newer, more useful concepts. This is the essence of an informed consent to treatment.

Control has been identified as an issue for persons seeking hypnosis, but an observation of mine derived from teaching hypnosis over the years is that students of hypnosis inevitably confront the issue of control from an opposite perspective. If the typical client is fearful of being controlled, it is easy to appreciate how the misinformed practitioner can be fearful of being the "controller" and having an awesome responsibility.

Typically, persons entering their first course in clinical hypnosis are intrigued and excited by the potential applications of trance phenomena. There is also a sense of concern, even fear, that they will be developing powers that they might "lose control" of at some point to someone's detriment. Developing skills in hypnosis presupposes a directive style (taking responsibility for initiating and guiding the course of therapy), and there arises for some students the issue of how they will deal with the "power" they think they will obtain from studying hypnosis. For some, the ability to direct another person's experience is used egotistically, evidenced in demonstrations of power by requiring the "subject" to respond to such degrading things as finger-snaps. Usually, I become aware of the concerns in a more positive way, however, when students express their thoughts and feelings about developing hypnotic skills.

As one becomes more experienced with hypnosis, the issues of power from the clinician's standpoint become less prominent. Experience with hypnosis demonstrates quickly and repeatedly that suggestions can be, and often are, rejected. One's sense of omnipotence is rapidly lost, a fortunate outcome of failure. The fear of losing control of the hypnosis and of the hypnotized client comes to be recognized as an unnecessary concern, since control is ultimately maintained by the client. Adopting this view affords one the comfort of knowing that even if a client reacts in unexpected ways, the person is choosing (at some level) to do so and the clinician's role is to be as supportive and helpful as possible.

Listed in the remainder of this chapter are the most frequently encountered misconceptions about clinical hypnosis. Following each is a discussion containing ideas that may be used to clarify the issues related to the misconception. As you become more familiar with hypnosis, responding to these and other misconceptions will become quite automatic. You may be surprised how many people, including "hypnotists," believe some of these erroneous ideas.

MISCONCEPTION: HYPNOSIS IS CAUSED BY THE POWER OF THE HYPNOTIST

Most stage hypnotists are skilled at creating the illusion that they possess a magical and mysterious power over other people. The communication and contextual variables of stage hypnosis were detailed in the previous chapter, and it is through the systematic and deliberate manipulation of these variables that the hypnotist attains and maintains the illusion of power. In the clinical context, the hypnotist is able to use her skills in communication to make acceptance of suggestions more likely, but there is no control over the client other than the control the client gives to the hypnotist. If you allow someone to guide you through an experience, who is in control? The hypnotist directs the client's experience, but only to the degree that the client permits it. It is a relationship of mutual responsiveness.

Hypnosis involves concentration on some stimulus (such as the clinician's words or the client's own associations). When used formally, hypnosis usually involves a relaxation process as well. One cannot force someone to concentrate or relax; thus, technically, entering trance is a personal choice. Even in the use of covert or indirect techniques one is capable of resisting having one's attention directed. Everyone has had the experience of turning someone "off," consciously or unconsciously, in order to not have to respond to the person.

Without the client's cooperation on *some* level, the likelihood of thera-peutic gain is greatly reduced or eliminated. Allowing the client to feel accepted, understood, and likely to be helped is important for that reason.

Realistically, the clinician is given power by the average client because of her title, education, reputation, etc. That power can be given suspiciously or openly as a reflection of the level of trust involved. The success of the hypnotic interaction depends on the quality of interpersonal communica-tion relative to the structure and goals of the relationship. If the clinician does not emphasize personal power on the part of the client, the issue of who is in control may arise, hindering treatment. Furthermore, if the clinician were truly in absolute control, then treatment results would be uniformly successful. It is because the client is in control that treatment results vary so much from individual to individual. The clinician is a guide for the experience, but the client permits that role and thus is the ultimate check in the process.

MISCONCEPTION: ONLY CERTAIN KINDS OF PEOPLE CAN BE HYPNOTIZED

This is a tricky issue, and pertains primarily to the induction of formal trance. In theory, anyone can be hypnotized, whether directly or indirectly. Even the people whom many practitioners claim are unhypnotizable (such as retarded, psychotic, or senile individuals) can, in fact, be hypnotized, but will require the use of specialized techniques.

In practice, there are definitely some people in whom it is more difficult to induce a formal trance than others. Such persons are not less capable than others, but are less responsive for any of a wide range of reasons: fear of losing control, inability to distinguish ambiguous (for them) internal states such as tension or relaxation, fear of impending change, negative situational factors, etc. When the point(s) of resistance is identified and resolved, the "difficult" person can usually be transformed from a poor trance subject into a good one.

In traditional literature addressing this misconception, there are often statistical averages provided describing what percentage of the population can reach each given level of trance, as well as what percentage of the population cannot be hypnotized at all. For example, one such source states that of "normal adults," 5% cannot go into trance at all, 95% can attain light trance, 55% can attain medium trance, and only 20% are capable of attaining deep trance (these figures, for example, appeared in the American Society of Clinical Hypnosis' *Syllabus on Hypnosis and Handbook of Therapeutic Suggestions,* 1973. There are many other, differing estimates).

When I first moved to San Diego some years ago, I made a number of inquiries into the status of the profession locally in order to get acquainted with other professionals also involved in clinical hypnosis. I spoke with one gentleman who told me about his practice and his beliefs about hypnosis. He told me very matter-of-factly that when a client seeks hypnosis, he views that person as "trying out for the choir. Maybe they'll make it, maybe they won't." In his practice, he tests persons seeking help for their hypnotizability, and if they pass his tests he accepts them as clients. Asked what percentage pass, he answered, "About 50% don't make it." This particular clinician claimed that one out of every two people he attempted to work with hypnotically could not be hypnotized! Is that a statement of fact or an indication of his limited skills as a hypnotist? How does being in the half that "don't make the choir" affect someone he rejects? Whatever he tells them at their dismissal, one can be fairly certain the experience is a negative one for the rejected person. Unfortunately, the typical layperson will actually believe the professional who says she cannot be hypnotized and the degree to which the episode will affect her self-image negatively is unknown. Misinformed clinicians representing the field of hypnosis can be doing damage unintentionally.

When the clinician states that *any* percentage of the population cannot be hypnotized, the responsibility to obtain the greatest results possible is taken from the clinician. The clinician mentioned above has plenty of room to fail comfortably with people without taking personal responsibility. After all, 50% of the people who approach him for help are expected to fail! Even if only 5% are expected to be unhypnotizable, when someone has difficulty experiencing trance, she may be written off irresponsibly as "one of those impossible types." That takes the clinician off the hook to be more responsible for making greater effort to reach that person and other "difficult" clients as well.

The figures claiming degree of hypnotizability are *not* to be believed or relied on as a cushion against failure. I think it is imperative to assume that 100% of the population can be hypnotized, and that if trance is not accomplished the clinician must take the initiative and attempt other techniques in other styles until trance is accomplished (assuming the client is equally intent on attaining successful results). Believing that the client can be hypnotized seems a much more positive framework for an interaction than anticipating a possible failure, which is likely to become a self-fulfilling prophecy. Clients are already limiting themselves, which is why they are seeking help in the first place. Why should the clinician place her own limitations on the client as well? Furthermore, consider the role of expectancy in the hypnotic interaction. What effect does the clinician's assumption that the client can meaningfully experience trance have on the person's responses?

Statistical averages for hypnotizability are essentially useless to a clinician, in my opinion. They say nothing about a given individual's capacity for attaining trance and, furthermore, they are derived under circumstances that have little bearing on the therapeutic interaction. How these figures are obtained is important in understanding why they are invalid. The figures are based on getting a sample of research subjects, running each of them through a standardized procedure as required by research, and determining how many of them were able to demonstrate behavior thought to be associated with specific levels of trance. The flaws in such studies are numerous:

1) The most serious fault of such hypnotizability studies is that standardized induction procedures do not recognize individual differences in subjects. Assessing individual differences and then specifically forming suggestions on the basis of those differences is the most fundamental prerequisite for successful clinical hypnosis. Using the same technique with each person without variation is one way of assuring failure with a significant number of people.

Realistically, standardization of procedure is essential for objective studies of hypnosis, but to use standardization to measure hypnotizability as a general trait is unnecessarily misleading. Experimental subjects who can respond to impersonal procedures are demonstrating considerable flexibility. Subjects who don't respond well to such standardized procedures are certainly hypnotizable, but will require greater individual consideration. In one-on-one psychotherapy with a competent clinician, such individuals would, one hopes, get that kind of individual consideration and would thus be much more likely to respond favorably.

2) In studies of hypnotizability, the person's trance depth is measured by demonstration of particular behaviors associated with certain levels of trance. For example, in order for a subject to demonstrate a trance phenomenon such as age regression, the subject is assumed to be in at least a medium level trance. Traditional concepts of hypnosis assume that if one can demonstrate phenomenon "X," then one must be at trance level "Y."

This is an invalid assumption, for people demonstrate hypnotic phenomena continually in their everyday "waking" state. For example, almost everyone has had the experience of being engrossed in a task, and only upon its completion noticing they have injured (e.g., cut, bruised) themselves slightly: "I'm bleeding! Now how did that happen?" According to the traditional literature, such a demonstration of hypnotic anesthesia is possible only in medium to deep levels of trance! In the skilled use of indirect techniques of hypnosis, formal trance has not even been induced and yet subjects can demonstrate hypnotic phenomena quite nicely.

3) Formal studies of hypnotizability also make the assumption that one must employ formal trance inductions in order for hypnosis to occur, which is not necessarily the case. People enter spontaneous, informal trances continuously, and these transient episodes of absorption are every bit as useful to a clinician who knows how to recognize and utilize them as are the formal trance states.

This last point, especially, is a source of contradiction for the misconception under consideration. Since people enter spontaneous trances continuously (in absorbing conversations, while watching television, while reading, while making love . . .), all conscious, information processing people can be induced either formally or informally. Some may take longer or require more complex approaches than others, but I make the assumption that each client I encounter can be induced either directly or indirectly, *if* I am competent enough to discover the best approach for that particular individual. The issue of hypnotizability will be addressed in greater detail in a later chapter.

FRAME OF REFERENCE*: ANDRÉ M. WEITZENHOFFER

One of the most knowledgeable researchers and clinicians to ever study and practice hypnosis is André M. Weitzenhoffer, Ph.D. With a strong "hard science" background in Physics, Engineering, and Physiology, and an insatiable appetite for understanding hypnosis,

---

*Sections entitled "Frames of Reference" appear throughout this book. Each "Frame of Reference" presents relevant comments from a leading authority on hypnosis, providing a more personal glimpse of his or her perspectives.

Weitzenhoffer gathered and integrated a broad array of hypnosis literature that eventually became his first book, a classic called *Hypnotism: An Objective Study in Suggestibility*. After its completion, Weitzenhoffer was contacted by Ernest (Jack) Hilgard, who initiated a collaborative attempt to establish a hypnosis research laboratory at Stanford University, which the two successfully did. Major effort was put forth to develop a scale to measure hypnotic responsiveness, and the result was the Stanford Profile Scales of Hypnotic Susceptibility, Forms I and II. These scales continue to be a backbone of the research wing of the field of hypnosis.

The Stanford lab closed over a decade ago, and Hilgard and Weitzenhoffer have gone their separate ways. Weitzenhoffer enjoys his "retirement" by working almost as hard as ever. He is continually traveling and teaching; when he is not working someplace else, he enjoys his mountain home in Colorado.

On the Beginning of His Interest in Hypnosis: "I think, initially, it was a demonstration at a summer camp, done by a camp counselor, that kind of intrigued me. He did postural sway tests. He was a mesmerist, so he used passes. He would put people into a sort of hypnotic sleep, which was kind of weird.

Later on, I went to a stage show and saw a magician that I don't think hypnotized anyone, but everyone was convinced he was hypnotizing people.

So, I began to look it up in the encyclopedia to find out more about it. I had an inquisitive mind for most of my childhood, and it sometimes got me into trouble, too. But anyway, that's how my interest arose."

On the Start of the Stanford Hypnosis Research Laboratory: "Jack Hilgard came down just as I was doing the last six months of my dissertation. He told me at the time that he had read my book and that he was very impressed by the fact that there seemed to be a good scientific basis for hypnotism. He asked me if I would like to join him at Stanford and jointly start a laboratory.

"Before doing so, we both spent a year at the Center for Advanced Study in Behavioral Sciences, located in Palo Alto. Jack and I spent most of that time working on the details for the laboratory, what he and I had thought of doing, to see if we could work together.

"I think, at that time, about 10 years of research was mapped out. . . . But the first thing we both agreed was necessary was some kind of good instrument to measure suggestibility, to measure depth."

On Failing to Remove Suggestions: "The assumption. . . . was that if a person did not respond to a suggestion, the suggestion did not have an effect on him. So, for example, if you said to a person, 'You can't lift your hand from your lap because it is getting too heavy, it's getting heavier and heavier, and you really can't raise it,' and someone raises his hand, you say to yourself, 'Okay, the suggestion has failed, so we don't need to bother doing anything more about it.'

"But, what I discovered, quite by accident, was that there nevertheless was an effect; if you didn't remove the suggestion either by asking the person to pretend or telling him, 'Now, your hand is quite normal again, it doesn't feel heavy, and so on,' what happened was that an effect could still be there.

"In one case, what happened with a female subject is that somehow in the night the suggestion took effect and when this young girl woke up in the morning, she found she could not lift her hand from the cover of the bed.

"That was, to me, rather traumatic; it made me take notice and think, 'Hey, what happened? What goes on?' So, I went back over the data and realized that she had broken every suggestion [during the test], but they had not been removed [afterwards]."

On Using the Scales in Clinical Contexts: "In clinical practice, I do not see that the scales are particularly useful unless you want to be rigorous. Because, for one thing, a good clinician, a good hypnotist, is going to very quickly get a good feeling for what the patient can do by just watching how the patient responds, whether he does it like Erickson or he does it in a more traditional fashion. He gets some feedback which will tell him if the subject/patient is capable of developing specific responses under hypnosis.

"The other thing is that they are an intrusion in the clinical situation. They are an element that seems to have nothing to do with therapy. Of course, you can tell the patient that, 'In order to help you, I've got to spend an hour testing you with this instrument.' I think something like the postural sway test doesn't really fit into the framework of clinical work. To me, It seems like vaudeville or night club stuff. I don't feel comfortable doing a postural sway test with patients. I see no reason to do it. I used to do it way back when I first started out, but I found I didn't have to do it.

"Anything else I'm going to find out would be in the course of working with the patient. If the patient can develop amnesia, I'll find that out presently. I start giving suggestions for it under the hypnotic state. Later, by asking questions I'll get some idea of how much amnesia is present. So that's why I say I don't see the use of the scales in that [clinical] setting as desirable."

On Defining Suggestibility and Suggestions: "For me, suggestibility is the capacity to produce responses to suggestion. Okay, that's very broad, so, I also specify that the response must at least be nonvoluntary.

"If the nonvoluntary aspect is not there, you do not have a suggestion. By definition, suggestibility is the capacity to respond to a suggestion, that is, to produce a nonvoluntary response.

"My definition of suggestion is that there must be something nonvoluntary I can establish as taking place or be satisfied it is nonvoluntary. The basic idea in the suggestion also must be fairly directly and clearly reflected by the behavior, either at the level of experience or at the level of actual behavior."

On the Idea of Everyday Trance States: "For me, it is important to distinguish what is hypnosis—to define what it is and to define what it is not—though not necessarily for working with the patient. If we are in a therapy situation, I don't think it is particularly essential to worry about at what point the patient is in a trance state. The important thing to keep in mind is that the patient may go into a trance state, hypnotic state, or whatever you want to call it, and that under those conditions he may be far more affected by what you say. You have to be more careful about what you say, and eventually you may want to be sure that certain things you have said are not going to have an effect on him subsequently. I think you want to be sure the person comes out of that trance state before he leaves your office.

"I don't like the idea of the everyday trance state because I don't think it has been clearly demonstrated that there are everyday trance states. If there are, I think the question obviously is: Are they a hypnotic state or not?

"I'm willing to say that people go into altered states of awareness. There are all kinds of altered states of awareness, and I think that of all the altered states of awareness that exist, there is a certain class of these states that probably we can call trance states. I don't think all altered states of consciousness should be called 'trance,' however. Certain trances are hypnosis. Others are probably not. Likewise, I believe that hypnosis can probably be identified with a class (really a subclass) of trance states and that while one can probably say that hypnosis is a trance, one cannot say that all trances are hypnosis."

On the Skills of a Good Hypnotist: "What I do depends a lot on what's going on between me and my subject. And if I'm in a clinical situation, I think it takes a great deal of skill to succeed. One way I know it takes a great deal of skill is because I can sometimes feel myself tired out by the time I have spent two or three hours working with someone. I will be so concentrated on them, thinking about what's going on, watching, observing, feeding back and getting some feedback, reacting to it, and so on.

"The really skilled people—good hypnotists—are quite skilled. They have skills that are other than just giving a suggestion. They have skills in interpersonal relations, ability to empathize, to establish rapport. It is hard to specify the skills, but they are all there, such as observing what the person is doing, keeping that in mind, integrating that into what is going on and so forth. Milton Erickson was marvelous at those things and that is why he was so good. He had some real skills."

Source: Personal Communication, 1988.

MISCONCEPTION: ANYONE WHO CAN BE HYPNOTIZED MUST BE WEAK-MINDED

Since virtually all people enter spontaneous, informal trance states regularly, the ability to be hypnotized is not reliably correlated with specific personality traits. This particular misconception refers to the all-powerful Svengali image of the hypnotist, and is based on the belief that in order for a hypnotist to control someone, the individual must have little or no will of her own.

Modern "scare stories" about evil hypnotists who control people and force them into doing terrible things play on this misconception. As discussed earlier, the average person does not understand how the hypnotized person can be in control of herself while demonstrating unusual behaviors at the direction of the hypnotist.

Each person has a will, but some people choose not to exercise their capacity to make choices, giving the responsibility for themselves to others to manage. Such individuals assume a "victim" role relative to others. The label of "weak-minded" is quite inappropriate for such persons. Rather, by recognizing "control" as an issue for all persons, one can better respect the individual's choices, including choosing not to choose, and assist the person to recognize her inner resources that can be utilized for change. Strength of will can be used by anyone to any degree to either work with or against the clinician. If rapport is established, the context is appropriate, and the desire is present, the skills of the clinician can be used to effect meaningful trancework.

To counteract the hindering effect this particular misconception has had on the hypnosis-seeking public, many practitioners have made the claim that persons with higher intelligence and greater ego strength will be better trance subjects. Studies performed to test these ideas are ambiguous in their results and lose their worth in trying to make generalizations about highly subjective experience. (How do you define and then measure ambiguous traits such as intelligence? Will? Ego strength? Trance?) There is a potential value, of sorts, in making the claim that intelligent people do better as hypnotic subjects than their less intelligent counterparts. The potential value lies in the hope that the client will view herself as intelligent and so will respond more readily. The other side of the coin, however, is that the person is seeking help at a time when her self-image is not particularly good from having attempted to cope with her problems independently and been unsuccessful in resolving them. If a clinician sets a client up to respond positively on the basis of intelligence or any other seemingly desirable personal characteristic, and then the person has a less than satisfactory experience with hypnosis, the person may use the experience to validate her negative feelings about herself. This is only one example of how a well-meaning clinician can inadvertently do damage to a client. Rather than trying to get the subject to identify with and become the model subject, the clinician can better employ his skills in accepting what the client offers and using it as the basis for further hypnotic interaction.

MISCONCEPTION: ONCE ONE HAS BEEN HYPNOTIZED, ONE CAN NO LONGER RESIST IT

This misconception refers to the idea that a hypnotist controls the will of her subject, and that once one "succumbs to the power" of the hypnotist, one is forever at her mercy. Of course, nothing is farther from the truth, since the hypnotic process is an interaction based on mutual power, shared in order to attain some desirable therapeutic outcome. If a client chooses not to go into a trance state for whatever reason, he will not. The nature of the hypnotic process is *always* context-determined. Even the most responsive clients can refuse to follow the direction of a hypnotist if they choose to. Prior experience with hypnosis, good or bad, is not the sole determining factor of whether hypnosis is accomplished or not. The communication and relationship factors of the particular context where hypnosis is performed are the key variables that will determine the outcome.

One of the sources for this misconception is the stage hypnotist's use of "cues," specific words or gestures that have become associated within the subject to the experience of entering trance, allowing him to reenter trance almost instantaneously. From the perspective of the audience, the hypnotist's use of a simple word or gesture to rapidly induce trance is yet another dramatic demonstration of the hypnotist's power. In clinical practice, it is often convenient to establish a cue to make subsequent inductions swifter and easier, but the power does not reside in the cue itself. Rather, it is the individual's willingness to respond to the cue that makes the cue viable as a trigger for the trance state. Should the subject be given the cue and choose not to enter trance, he will not. The cue, or rapid induction signal, is only effective when the client chooses to respond to it by entering trance. Beginning or ending the trance state is in the client's control.

MISCONCEPTION: ONE CAN BE HYPNOTIZED TO SAY OR DO SOMETHING AGAINST ONE'S WILL

This is probably the most argued issue in the entire field of hypnosis. It raises many complex issues, and consequently I have elected to devote a more elaborate discussion of these issues to later chapters. Suffice it to say here that in my experience the relationship between clinician and client is one of mutual responsibility. The clinician offers communications which the client is in a position to accept or reject. Of course, this is too simplistic to be entirely true, but until the later discussions of the dynamics of influence, it is true enough to serve as a generalization the exceptions to which are situations atypical of therapeutic environments.

The capacity to influence people to do things against their will exists. There is little room for doubt that people can be manipulated negatively to do things seemingly inconsistent with the person's beliefs and attitudes. To put it simply, brainwashing exists. However, the conditions necessary to effect such powerful influence do not correspond to the typical therapeutic encounter. In other words, controlling a person is possible under certain conditions, but those conditions are not in and of themselves hypnosis, and are quite far removed from the trancework promoted in this book. Further discussion of these issues is contained in the chapters entitled "Human Suggestibility" and "Mind Matters."

MISCONCEPTION: BEING HYPNOTIZED CAN BE HAZARDOUS TO YOUR HEALTH

This misconception is a strong one in raising fears. In fact, there is some basis for concern about the use of hypnosis, but the concern should not be about the experience of trance harming anyone. Rather, the concern should be about *who* practices hypnosis. Hypnosis itself is not harmful, but an incompetent practitioner can do some damage through sheer ignorance about the complexity of each person's mind or through a lack of respect for the integrity of each human being.

The process of formal hypnotic induction is an absorbing process in which one's concentration is directed—to an idea, to a voice, to an internal experience, but always to something. There is a slowdown of physiological functions (e.g., breathing, heart rate) and typically the body is lethargic. Such physical responses are healthy, reducing stress and discomfort. Many people do not recognize the amount of stress they carry within themselves until they experience the comfort of trance. Then they are able to distinguish more clearly their internal states and develop greater control over their degree of tension. Persons suffering from hypertension are able to get a great deal of physical benefit from hypnosis. Hypnosis is physically beneficial to any client, though, not just to hypertensives. Trance experiences highlight the extraordinary amount of self-control possible, even of physical processes generally regarded as involuntary.

In terms of potential emotional harm, it is not hypnosis that may cause damage, but difficulty may arise due to the content of a session or the inability of a clinician to effectively guide the client. The same conditions exist in any helping relationship where one person is in distress, vulnerable, and seeking relief. An inexperienced or uneducated helper may inadvertently (rarely is it intentional) offer poor advice, make grandiose promises, misdiagnose a problem or its dynamics, or simply waste the person's time and money.

Hypnosis often gives the client access to memories and feelings long outside of conscious awareness. The content of such memories may be distressing, as they often are in therapy, and an inexperienced clinician may feel unable or unqualified to handle the client effectively. In such instances, the clinician may have gotten more than she bargained for, although someone else may have been able to use the same information to great therapeutic advantage. The less skilled person has "opened up" another person, but has no capacity to do any real healing. An unfortunate example is one self-proclaimed "hypnotist, healer, psychic counselor" I encountered who attempted to impress me by describing his use of hypnosis with a woman who presented the complaint to him of intense guilt feelings over an abortion she had had. He used hypnosis to have her imagine the fetus was still alive within her and then directed her to have a dialogue with it, even giving it a name, in order to explain to it why she needed to abort it. He thought this would be a good technique for settling the matter, and wondered why such a "reasonable" approach didn't fare too well. She left him feeling worse than when she came in. His thoughtlessness confirmed her worst fears—that she had killed a person with a name and personality.

This type of encounter is a basis for the misconception that hypnosis does harm. Clearly, hypnosis does not cause harm, but ineffective or inappropriate use of hypnosis *can*. Ineffective use of any skill, whether it be surgery, psychological testing, or giving haircuts can hurt someone. Just as dentistry is not dangerous, but a poor dentist is, hypnosis is not dangerous, but a poor hypnotist is. Theoretically, we have governmental agencies for regulating licensure and practice, but, unfortunately, at the practical level it is literally impossible to separate those who are competent from those who are not.

The flip side of this issue and the reason for developing skills in hypnotic techniques is the emotional good that hypnosis can generate. In its ability to give people feelings of self-control and the subsequent increase of self-confidence, hypnosis is a powerful means for resolving emotional problems and enhancing emotional well-being. It is essential that the clinician have enough knowledge and skill to use it toward that end.

MISCONCEPTION: ONE INEVITABLY BECOMES DEPENDENT ON THE HYPNOTIST

Hypnosis as a therapeutic tool does not in and of itself foster dependencies of any kind, any more than other tools such as a behavioral contract, analytical free association, or an intelligence test can. Dependency is a need, a reliance, that everyone has to some degree. To a greater or lesser extent, we all depend on someone for things we feel are important to our well-being. In the helping professions especially, people are seeking help at a time they are hurting and vulnerable. They depend on the clinician to help, to comfort, and to care. The clinician knows that the ultimate goal of treatment must be to help that person establish self-reliance and independence. Rather than foster dependence by indirectly encouraging the client to view the therapist as the source of answers to all of life's woes, hypnosis used properly helps the person in distress turn inwards in order to make use of the many experiences the person has acquired over her lifetime that can be used therapeutically. Consistent with the goal of self-reliance and use of personal power to help one's self is the teaching of self-hypnosis to those you work with.

There is an old saying: "If you give a man a fish, you have given him a meal. If you teach him how to fish, you have given him a livelihood." Teaching self-hypnosis to those you work with is a means for insuring that your clients can continue to work independently and grow in your absence. Furthermore, teaching them strategies for problem-solving along with self-hypnosis can allow for the emergence of a self-correcting mechanism that can assure those you work with that they do have control over their lives. It gives you an assurance that you have done your work well.

MISCONCEPTION: ONE CAN BECOME "STUCK" IN TRANCE

Trance is a state of focused attention, either inwardly or outwardly directed. It is controlled by the client, who can initiate or terminate trance as she chooses. It is literally impossible to become "stuck" in a state of concentration. Can you imagine getting "stuck" reading a book?

A source for this misconception is the infrequent occasion where a clinician has given suggestions to the client to "wake up" and the client remains in trance. The inexperienced hypnotist may get anxious or even panic when the individual does not respond to direct suggestions to open her eyes and return to her usual "waking" state. In such situations the subject is not "stuck," but chooses not to terminate the trance state for at least one of a couple of reasons. Either she is comfortable where she is or she is still working on completing the experience. The best thing to do is offer an open-ended suggestion that the client can bring herself out of trance when she wants to—and then leave her alone to do so! In time, usually a short time, the person will arouse and return to her typical "waking" state. Never can someone *not* return, so this is one issue you need not lose sleep over. Respect the choices of the person in trance. If she does not follow a suggestion, there is a reason for it, so don't press your wants; let yourself go with the flow.

MISCONCEPTION: ONE IS ASLEEP OR UNCONSCIOUS WHEN IN A TRANCE STATE

Trance is *not* sleep! The experience of formally induced hypnosis resembles sleep from a physical standpoint (decreased activity, muscular relaxation, slowed breathing, etc.), but from a mental standpoint the client is relaxed yet alert. Ever-present is *some* level of awareness of current goings-on, even when in deeper trance states. In the case of informal, spontaneous trance states, awareness is even more marked since physical relaxation need not be present.

Much misinformation has been circulating for years about hypnosis being comparable to learning while asleep. Research indicates one does not learn while asleep, though one can learn while in the transition phases, i.e., while falling asleep and awakening (midpoints between being asleep and awake are commonly called "twilight states").

A source of this misconception is the word "hypnosis" itself, a word derived from the Greek word "Hypnos," the word for sleep and the name of the Greek's God of Sleep. The word hypnosis was coined by James Braid in the nineteenth century and has been used to describe trance and trancework ever since. Since hypnosis is not sleep, and even the client in deep trance is oriented to external reality to some degree, use of phrases like "sleep deeply" are not relevant to the client's experience, and so should not be used.

MISCONCEPTION: HYPNOSIS ALWAYS INVOLVES A MONOTONOUS RITUAL OF INDUCTION

When considering the communication aspects of hypnosis, one can appreciate that trance occurs whenever someone turns his attention to ideas and feelings triggered by the communications of the guide. When one is processing information, one is gathering information through any or all of the senses and integrating it into one's experiential framework. If I say to you, "Don't think of how your right hand feels," I know you will take these printed words and attach them to some experience in order to make meaning of them. Otherwise, these words are just ink spots on a piece of paper. And in so doing, you will become aware of your right hand, to some degree. For as long as your attention is directed in an absorbing way either inwardly on some subjective experience or outwardly on some external stimulus (which, in turn, creates an internal experience), you are in trance.

Trance does not have to be formally induced to occur. Likewise, the various trance phenomena can (and do) occur routinely outside of formal trance experience. You may recall the earlier description of everyday anesthesia such as when you were intensely involved in doing something, and only afterwards noticed you were injured or bleeding. People don't usually think of this as a trance experience, which is basically why people have come to think of trance in a limited way, as only a state much different from a "normal" state.

Communication has conditioning properties, and whether used in the form of a monotonous ritual of induction or in the form of any offhand remark, it has the capacity to influence others' experience, and thus be hypnotic in effect.

MISCONCEPTION: ONE MUST BE RELAXED IN ORDER TO BE IN TRANCE

Trance has been defined as a state of concentrated attention, one that varies in intensity according to context. Also mentioned earlier was the idea that spontaneous trances occur continuously while conversing, reading, and in countless other instances where one's attention is fixed. One can be anxious, in suspense, and still be focused, as in "glued to a mystery." Thus, physical relaxation is not a necessary prerequisite for trance to occur. In a larger perspective, trance states are the basis for the realities we accept as real in our lifetimes. This "reality" includes our world views, values, views on right and wrong behavior, and emotional makeup. Someone who convinces herself to be phobic around dogs is using all the principles of self-hypnosis to create a negative reality needlessly.

In clinical practice, relaxation is usually a part of the intervention, since it is comforting and soothing. Relaxation often makes it easier to enlist cooperation on the part of the client, as most clients want or expect it as part of the process. Relaxation also makes access to the client's unconscious easier. Furthermore, relaxation can highlight the differences between the trance state and the usual "waking" state, convincing the client that she has, in fact, experienced an altered state of consciousness that fits her expectations of what hypnosis "should" be like.

Relaxation as a part of the hypnotic process is especially useful for the treatment of anxiety and stress-related disorders, as well as for alleviating the stress associated with any change. Many people literally do not know how to relax, and helping your clients attain this skill can have a huge impact on them.

MISCONCEPTION: HYPNOSIS IS A THERAPY

Hypnosis is not a therapy. Rather, it is a therapeutic tool that does not align itself with any one theoretical or practical orientation. I have always been amused that whenever I state that I use patterns of hypnosis in my work, my professional peers smile and think they know what I do. Few of them actually do. What one clinician who uses hypnosis does with it and what another does with it may be as different as night and day. Anything that involves trance and suggestion has been called "hypnosis," unfortunately, and the countless variations possible in the use of trance and suggestion formation get lost under the generic label. Learning techniques and principles of hypnosis is much like learning a language. You learn a common set of rules, words, and structures, yet you will still inevitably express yourself in your own unique way.

Hypnosis is a part of every psychotherapy, and for that matter, a part of every interaction in which one person influences another. It is not a therapy, but is a means for allowing phenomena that seem accidental and random (like the "everyday anesthesia" mentioned earlier) to happen in a more deliberate and systematic way. Furthermore, hypnosis as a tool increases the likelihood of the therapist's communications being absorbed in a meaningful way.

Hypnosis as a therapeutic tool is ever-changing with the context in which it arises, and must therefore be adapted to the individual needs of the client and situation. A basis for this misconception under consideration is the incredible over-standardization of hypnotic procedures some hypnotists promote. Many books on hypnosis advocate verbatim use of prepared scripts that have been written for general problems such as overweight, smoking, etc. In other words, if you encounter a smoker wanting to stop, you are encouraged to turn to page such-and-such of their hypnosis book and then read the anti-smoking set of suggestions to the client after you have induced him in hypnosis from the induction script on a previous page.

Use of scripts robs hypnosis of its real potency, the strength derived from the recognition and use of each individual's unique experiences and needs. Spontaneity is essential for best results, and even when a therapeutic strategy is worked out beforehand, a skilled clinician will still incorporate the spontaneous responses of the client into the procedure. The use of scripts is *not* what effective use of hypnotic communication patterns is about; they promote the misconception that hypnosis in clinical practice can be standardized and that each client is identical as long as they have the same presenting complaint. The dynamic and spontaneous nature of skilled applications of hypnosis is what makes it so complex and demanding an ability to acquire.

MISCONCEPTION: HYPNOSIS MAY BE USED TO ACCURATELY RECALL EVERYTHING THAT HAS HAPPENED TO YOU

There is a great need for clinicians to understand how memory works in order to best utilize this most important aspect of the individual. Some have compared the mind to a computer in which every memory is accurately stored and is available for eventual retrieval. The computer metaphor is an inaccurate one, however. The mind does *not* take in experience and store it in exact form for accurate recall later. In fact, memories are stored on the basis of perceptions, and so are subject to the same distortions as perception. People can "remember" things that did not actually happen, they can remember selected fragments of an experience, and they can take bits and pieces of multiple memories and combine them into one false memory. Memory, simply put, is not reliable; if you are looking for "truth," you are unlikely to find it in memory. If you are interested in how someone represents and accesses past experience, which is essential in psychotherapy, then appreciating that the memory seems "real" to the person is the main point.

An additional point is that not all memory is stored. Short-term memory means exactly that—some experiences are so brief and transient that they are not incorporated into longer-term memory. These will not be retrievable.

The fact that memory is not reliable is significant in doing therapy with hypnosis. Much more will be said about this in the section on age regression in Chapter 17.

CLOSURE ON MISCONCEPTIONS

How you conceptualize hypnosis and the mind will determine almost entirely what limits you place on your use of hypnosis as well as what limits you will place on your clients. At this point, I hope, you have a clear understanding of some of the characteristics of trancework, and are ready to begin exploring some of the dynamics of communication and influence relevant to your use of hypnotic patterns in your interactions with others.

There is no substitute for experience. Only experience in using words and gestures in varying styles will demonstrate to you clearly how the exact same sequence of words will elicit very different responses in the various people you work with. Allow yourself to experiment (using good judgment as a guideline, of course) and notice the outcomes you get. I am certain you will be able to please yourself in adding new choices to your current range of clinical interventions—a very positive outcome, don't you think?

For Discussion

1. When might a client's misconceptions about hypnosis be an asset to the clinician? A liability?

2. Why do treatment approaches become standardized? What are the advantages and disadvantages of standardization?

3. What is a "power struggle"? Why do they arise? Can they be prevented? If so, how?

4. What types of people do you think would be harder to hypnotize than others? Why do you think so?

5. How might a clinician inadvertently encourage dependency in her clients? What may be the underlying motivations?

6. What is the basis for the statement that a person's emotional problems may be as much a consequence of hypnosis as the solutions? How is "reality" determined?

Things to Do

1. Take peers on a "trust-walk" in which you lead them around while they have their eyes closed. What feelings do they become aware of?

2. Interview hypnotists in your area and ask them what percentage of people cannot be hypnotized. What reasons do they give?

3. Find books that contain entire scripts for interventions and choose a script of particular interest to read closely. What sort of person would this script be ideal for? What sort of person would the script be terrible for? Why?

5

Conceptualizing Hypnosis

How one conceptualizes hypnosis has profound implications for its potential applications. Over the decades there have been many perspectives, often differing sharply, on what the mysterious force called "hypnosis" is all about. Each of these perspectives has played a role in both the upgrade and downgrade of hypnotic understanding. I think most scientists have developed an awareness for the paradoxical effects of developing a theory, for theories both illuminate and confound the subject under consideration. Theories illuminate understanding by helping one to discover meanings and relationships in an otherwise apparently random universe, and yet theories can often confound by limiting one's observations to only what the theory allows for. Very few, if any, single theories can entirely explain a given phenomenon.

With something as complex as the broad range of subjective experiences available in hypnosis, the inadequacy of a single theory becomes glaringly apparent. The energy some researchers expend in attempting to fit their observations into a theoretical framework they have adopted is energy that is misdirected. The complexity of the subject of hypnosis and the even greater complexity of the human being capable of hypnosis are so vast that it seems improbable (perhaps even undesirable) that a single theory will evolve to explain its origin and character.

Fortunately, the baby doesn't have to be thrown out with the bath water. My comment on the inadequacy of a single theory's ability to account for all hypnotic phenomena is really a comment in favor of believing a little of everything, and all of nothing. The theories of hypnosis that have been developed over the years are each useful in their own way for describing one or more aspects of hypnosis, but none can be considered the final word in describing the process or experience of hypnosis.

In the remainder of this chapter is an identification and discussion of some of the more useful theoretical perspectives on the reality of hypnosis. You are encouraged to think critically about each model and to consider the phenomena of hypnosis from the individual perspective of the clinician, the individual perspective of the client, and then finally as a result of the interaction of the two.

HYPNOSIS AS A PERMISSIVE STATE

In this older, more traditional theoretical perspective, the emphasis is on the passive nature of the client, whose position is defined as one of responding to the direction of the clinician. In past literature on hypnosis, a hypnotist was described in terms of the degree of her authoritarian or permissive approach to the hypnotic subject (discussed in greater detail in Chapter 12). An authoritarian practitioner is characterized as one who is direct and commanding. The stage hypnotist is a classic example of the authoritarian approach, evidenced by such common direct suggestions as, "You are going to go deeper asleep when I snap my fingers. . . . When you open your eyes you will laugh uncontrollably as if you were viewing the funniest movie you have ever seen. . . . When I clap my hands, you will stutter and be unable to say your name . . ." (clever stuff, isn't it?).

The authoritarian approach of most traditionally oriented clinicians is the basis for this theory's description of the demeanor of the client as a passive, permissive one. Specifically, a permissive client is characterized as one who permits the clinician to direct his experience, seemingly expressing no will of his own. The client is expected to respond as completely as possible to the guidance of the clinician, and because of the secondary, reactive role in the relationship, the client has been viewed as a passive receptacle for the authoritarian clinician's suggestions. An inability of the client to respond to the clinician's direct suggestions to the clinician's satisfaction is the basis for what has been deemed "resistance" in the model. If a clinician adopts a permissive style in guiding the client, a style that is less direct and demanding, this "permissive state" theory of hypnosis is no longer as plausible, because a more active role is required on the part of the client than the mere obedience to authoritarian suggestions.

The "permissive state" theory contains some truth, but is mostly fiction. One can view the quiet, cataleptic (fixed, unmoving) client as a passive receptacle for suggestions. One can view the formation and verbalization of suggestions on the part of the clinician as an active process. On the surface, the hypnotic interaction may seem to be one of the clinician being the active one and the client the reactive one. Is the client really limited to a passive role, however? Discussed in an earlier section was the idea that if one allows another person to guide one's experience, the one in control is the one who has the power to "allow" the actions of another. The role of the client, therefore is *not* a passive one. Rather, it is an active one in the sense that it is the client's responsibility to respond, in whole or in part, to the suggestions of the clinician. A response is inevitable, since even no response is a response!

Furthermore, the more recent developments in concepts of hypnosis emphasize the need of the clinician to flexibly follow the leads of the client, rather than the client obediently following the arbitrary leads of the clinician. The client, in this view that arose from the need to explain the apparent ease with which authoritarian hypnotists obtained cooperation, has the responsibility of adapting himself to the suggestions of the clinician. Adapting one's self to authoritarian suggestions and finding a way to make them meaningful is not a passive state at all. How does a hypnotist counting down from 10 to 1, for example, cause one to enter trance, unless the subject is working hard at making such arbitrary suggestions meaningful?

It can be kept in mind that if the clinician offers suggestions that are unacceptable, the permissive client can passively refuse them, in essence "doing nothing," a condition the authoritarian clinician is likely to call "resistance." The client's role is in many ways an active one of making use of the clinician's suggestions when and if those suggestions are appropriate and can be meaningfully utilized. The paradox inherent in this theory is the active role of passivity.

HYPNOSIS AND ROLE-PLAYING

There is a considerable amount of confusion and speculation over whether there really is a condition of human experience that can be called "hypnotic trance." Graphs of brain waves, measurements of biochemical changes in the body, and objective readings on the activity of the nervous system are ambiguous at best in helping to define the trance condition. The nature of trance is extremely subjective and, to date, has been resistant to objective measurements. Thus, there are some theorists (Sarbin & Coe, 1972) who have adopted the perspective that hypnotic trance as a separate and unique entity of consciousness does not really exist at all. In their view, there is a trance only when someone is willing to role-play one. In other words, the client does not actually enter a dimension of consciousness that differs appreciably from any other. Rather, the person plays the role of what a hypnotized subject is supposed to look and act like, and carries out the hypnotist's suggestions on that basis.

In this view, it is assumed that the client has prior knowledge of what a hypnotized person's behavior pattern is like, and that hypnotic behavior is reproduced on that basis. Even in the event that a person has no prior knowledge of how to behave when hypnotized, she can respond to the leads of the hypnotist, essentially "playing along."

Support for this perspective comes from a variety of research, typically involving a group of subjects who are instructed to behave "as if" they were hypnotized and mixed with a group of subjects who were formally hypnotized. A number of "experts" in hypnosis were challenged to discover which individuals were and were not truly hypnotized. Subjects who role-played hypnotic behavior were extremely convincing and were able to successfully confound the experts. It is not particularly difficult to appreciate the elements of truth in this perspective; imagine someone holding a gun to your head and saying, "I am going to poke you with a safety pin and if you so much as flinch I'll pull the trigger." Most probably, you would be highly motivated to immediately develop a means for withstanding pain that defies objective measurement, but is present nonetheless. Likewise, if someone offered you a huge sum of money, or something else that you find rewarding, to motivate you to demonstrate some feat normally beyond your means, it probably wouldn't surprise you much to discover capabilities you did not know you had. From my perspective, such self-motivation and self-preparation are the essence of self-hypnosis.

Role-playing hypnotic behavior is a large element in the stage show process. Subjects may not feel hypnotized in the way they expected to experience some altered state, but because of the flow of the stage process, they are likely to go along and conform to the demands of the role. One of the classic techniques of hypnosis plays on this, called the "As if" technique in which a person is asked to act "as if" she can do the thing she feels unable to do (e.g., relax, go into trance) long enough to actually do it and experience what it's like to do it. The issue then becomes one of whether it really matters if the action is real or a pretense if the outcome is the same regardless of the intention. In other words, if a client is not really hypnotized, but acts as if she is hypnotized well enough for the clinician to get whatever hypnotic responses are desired, then does it really matter that the person doesn't feel genuinely hypnotized? Frequently, stage show hypnotists will ask their subjects at the end of the show whether they were hypnotized, and the most common response is a hesitant, "I don't think so." Yet that same person just a few minutes ago was responding enthusiastically to the suggestion to hallucinate the nudity of the entire audience, the suggestion of an inability to remember her own name, and other such "entertaining" suggestions.

Role-playing has long been recognized as a way of engrossing a person by letting her lose herself to the role. Many therapeutic strategies involve role-playing as a way of rehearsing positive responses in troublesome situations. Initially, the person typically feels self-conscious and uncomfortable in the role, but gradually adapts and is soon immersed in it. If you have never seen this kind of phenomenon, perhaps you can use your own experience as an illustration. Can you recall a time when you were in a bad mood, perhaps even depressed, sitting around your house when the doorbell rang unexpectedly? After you wondered to yourself, "Who could that be?" you answered the door and there was a friend of yours just coming by for a casual visit. Charitably, you decided you didn't want to depress this person by being in a poor humor, so you began to act "as if" you were in a semidecent, or perhaps even good, mood. Did you notice that after a brief while you genuinely were in a good mood? Almost everyone has had this kind of experience, and it is a useful example to illustrate the power associated with playing a role.

Playing a role can change behavior quite dramatically, a point long recognized. At the turn of the century, the philosopher and psychologist William James asked the question, "Does a person smile because he is happy, or is he happy because he smiles?" In some powerful research done by psychologist Philip Zimbardo at Stanford University (see Aronson, 1984), a mock prison was set up in the psychology building, and a group of student experimental subjects were divided into "guard" and "prisoner" roles. The results of the experiment were both startling and dramatic. A mentality associated with the role evolved, with guards becoming abusive and even brutal, and prisoners becoming passive, obsessed with escape, and ultimately depressed and agitated. Role behavior became so intense, the experiment had to be called off for everyone's well-being.

Role-playing as a theoretical perspective on the phenomena of trance is useful up to the point where the experience becomes a unique and genuine state of mind and body called trance. To claim that the *entire* experience of trance is role-play is to deny the genuineness of a special subjective experience called "trance" (for lack of a more precise term). A subject may begin by playing at trance behavior, but at a certain, idiosyncratic point along the way, a true trance experience begins. Role-playing involves a conscious effort to adhere to the behaviors scripted by a role. Until the role has been played, or rehearsed, enough times to allow unconscious identification with that role, role-playing trance is an experience occurring largely on the conscious level. Consciousness is limited (how many things can you pay attention to at one time?); the unconscious mind is much less so. When responses become unconscious, the role-play is over and a true trance state begins.

The role-playing perspective accounts for many aspects of hypnosis, but is not entirely satisfactory in its restrictive limit-setting on the experience of hypnosis.

HYPNOSIS AS AN ALTERED STATE OF CONSCIOUSNESS

The experience of trance has also been conceptualized as an altered state of consciousness (Tart, 1969). In this perspective, the trance state is considered to be a unique and separate state of consciousness, relative to one's "normal" state of consciousness. The trance state, in this view, is a state that is artificially created by the trance induction process, which alters the person's consciousness through the narrowing of attention to the offered suggestions.

This view has historically been a popular one because of its recognition that people in trance can experience things beyond their usual capacity. The idea of an altered state of consciousness allows for that possibility, and also allows for the variable proportion of people who can experience such a state as described in susceptibility statistics.

More recently, however, the view that the trance state is *not* an altered state of consciousness has come into vogue for a couple of reasons. First, when trance is defined as a state of concentrated attention and trance phenomena (such as age regression) are found in everyday experience, the trance state is no longer a separate, artificial, and distinct entity in consciousness. Rather, it becomes a natural and routine experience of every person's mental processing. Second, the term "altered state of consciousness" is, like "hypnosis," very imprecise. Consciousness is a subjective experience. What is "normal consciousness" relative to an "altered state of consciousness"? Aren't I altering your consciousness with each word, each page you read?

WAIT! Think of a purple elephant with green ears! Did I just alter your consciousness? How much? Any time your awareness is shifted from one stimulus to another, your consciousness has been altered.

The question, then, is this: If trance is an altered state of consciousness, what is it altered *from?* Yet, the trance state that arises from formal hypnotic interaction in which a hypnotized person experiences her body as numb is not her everyday experience of herself. Clearly, *something* has changed, but what changed and how it changed remain a mystery. It was pointed out in the previous section that attempts to objectively measure the existence of the trance state on chemical and electrical levels have been less than successful. Thus, the view of trance as a distinct state of consciousness altered from "normal" consciousness is useful in accounting for the greater control of hypnotized persons over their experience, but its usefulness diminishes with the lack of recognition of the naturalistic, everyday dimensions of the trance experience.

THE REALITY-TESTING VIEW OF HYPNOSIS

Can you estimate how far it is from where you are sitting to the nearest door? About how far apart are your hands from each other right now? What direction is that sound you hear now coming from?

These questions are answerable by you because you are able to use your visual, auditory, and tactile senses to gather information from the world around you. Consciously, but more so unconsciously, you are continually engaged in the processing of huge amounts of sensory input flooding your nervous system that tells you where you are relative to your immediate environment. Information is continuously coming to you through virtually all of your available senses, and all of these tiny bits of information give you a sense of where your body is, what position it is in, and how it is distanced from objects and outside experiences near and far. You are probably not consciously aware of the sensations in your left shoulder until I draw your attention to it. Yet your shoulder (its nerves) is processing information, such as the gentle rub of your clothing against it, and that information is available to your unconscious mind for whatever purpose it may serve there.

Obtaining feedback from our senses about the world around us is a process called "reality-testing." Proponents of this view claim that people are continually reality-testing in order to preserve personal integrity and alleviate the anxiety of uncertainty in not knowing our position in the world. This process is generally so unconscious we take it for granted.

However, if you have the experience of working with psychiatric patients deemed psychotic, you will often find them desperately engaged in reality-testing. In such patients, reality-testing is evidenced in such activities as feeling the walls for guidance as they walk, touching you repeatedly as they speak to you to make sure you are "real," touching themselves to assure themselves that they exist, and repeating simple cause-effect behaviors such as opening a door to show themselves they can affect their environment.

The process of sensation is simply the neurological response to a stimulus and is purely a biological phenomenon. Perception, however, is the interpretation of the neurological experience, the meaning attached to a sensation. A person's perception is a person's reality. The role of perception on experience is so profound that it literally cannot be overstated. Your perception of events is the determining factor in the course of action that you take. A false perception about a person or situation leads to a very different response than a more accurate perception might. A good example of this point is in the world of political sabotage. Planting misinformation with a governmental representative that is perceived by him to be accurate information can have disastrous results! The television show *Mission: Impossible* was an extremely clever one that illustrated this point well. It involved a group of highly sophisticated government agents whose job it often was to deceive enemies with misinformation. In the process, they would let the enemy think he was clever in his wiretaps and break-ins, letting him obtain misinformation carefully constructed to seem plausible. Then, on the basis of the misinformation, the enemy spy would inevitably do something to assist the "good guys." The point of this show, the point of psychotherapy, the point of selling a product, is to provide information to others that will be perceived by them as a basis for doing something desirable. This is one perspective on therapeutic influence.

The reality-testing view of hypnosis theorizes that when someone is first entering and is then in a trance state, the person's ongoing process of reality-testing is markedly reduced. When someone suspends the process of obtaining feedback from the world around her by focusing inwardly as is characteristic of most trance experiences (trance can also be externally focused, usually the case in being the hypnotist), the person is no longer oriented to anything other than internal experience. The suspension of objective reality-testing frees the person to accept whatever reality is provided for her. The provided reality, like any perceived reality, whether true or false, will determine the quantity and quality of behavioral and emotional responses.

Living in San Diego as I do, and as the majority of my clients do, I can do hypnotic processes such as one involving relaxing at the beach if I care to, since most people here are familiar with that experience. The process might involve incorporating all the sights, smells, sounds, tastes, and tactile experiences associated with being at the beach into the process in such great detail that the client can genuinely feel as if he is really at the beach. In this kind of a trance process, the reality of being in my office several miles away from the beach is suspended long enough to accept suggestions related to the "realities" of being at the ocean. The degree to which the client is successful in letting go of the need to have an objective reality immediately at hand (a need whose strength is directly proportional to the person's degree of insecurity) is the degree to which the person can accept the provided experience.

Reality-testing concepts relative to the experience of hypnosis are, in addition to other models, useful in helping to explain trance phenomena. Understanding the role of perception on one's range of possible behaviors, thoughts, and feelings is fundamental to successful trancework.

THE CONDITIONING PROPERTY OF
WORDS AND EXPERIENCE

Three of the most advantageous properties of having evolved consciousness for us as a species are our ability to reason, ability to learn on multiple dimensions of experience, and ability to communicate about experience. The complexity of the human mind permits us to have experience both on conscious and unconscious levels. More importantly, we can learn from our experiences on multiple levels, and rely on those learnings to guide current and future behaviors. Perhaps more importantly still, we can communicate about those learnings to others.

Many animal species communicate; complex behaviors such as competition for social position and such dynamic needs as territoriality are examples of routine communications in the animal world. In recent years, interspecies communication has been attempted between human and dolphin, human and ape, and humans and other species. These attempts at communication have had marginal success, due in large part to the limited capacity (according to the human perspective) of animals, evidenced in their inability to invent symbols, using only the symbols provided for them. Evolution has allowed us to attach words to experience and thus represent experience abstractly. Instead of our communication concretely being tied to a current need or experience, human communication is abstract, allowing us to communicate about things that occurred millions of years ago or speculate about things yet to come centuries from now.

Language and communication will be discussed repeatedly in various forms throughout this book. When we seek to provide a theoretical perspective for the various phenomena of hypnosis, the recognition of the role of words as symbols of experience is absolutely crucial to the attainment of sophistication with hypnotic techniques.

You are reading this book, this page with lots of black inkmarks in various configurations. The patterns of configuration form what you have come to recognize (from years of learning and experience) as words. As you read each word in a fixed left-to-right sequence, you are taking the words and attaching them to your experience of what they represent to you. The words on this page don't mean anything at all to you *until* you attach a meaning to them, and the meaning can come from nowhere other than your own experience of having learned what experiences the words represent. Without your attaching meaning to the words, the words on this page are just like inkblots that are meaningless. When you see the lines and squiggles of written words or hear the sounds of words from a language that is unfamiliar to you, those markings and sounds are meaningless because you have no internal frame of reference for them. The important point is that *you use your own individual experience in attaching meaning to a word.* Therefore, the same word will mean different things to different people. The more abstract a word, the more this is true.

Exercises suggested throughout this book will make this point clear to you, but you have probably already had experiences in which your interpretation of a word or phrase differed from another person's interpretation sufficiently to make you wonder whether that person was from this planet. The differences in interpretation among people account for most communication problems in whatever context problems exist. In the practice of hypnosis, the clinician must be sensitive to the words and phrases she uses because of the idiosyncratic nature of interpretation. The phrase that works well in helping you attain trance may be like fingernails on a chalkboard to your client. The word that fits well for your understanding of an experience may represent something entirely different to your client.

Words are conditioned stimuli representing internal experience. Gestures are also conditioned stimuli arising from certain experiences. People are individuals, each communicating in his or her own way. Thus, meaningful communication allows the clients to interpret and respond in their own unique ways.

The theory of hypnosis regarding the conditioning property of words and the experiences words represent is a powerful one in explaining hypnotic experiences. The process of attaching words to experience in linguistics is called "transderivational search," and has been a subject of considerable study in that field. How experiences create habitual response patterns has been described in numerous places, and generally operates on various principles of learning and reward structures. Basically, people do what they are reinforced (rewarded) for doing; the reward may be the comfort of familiarity from having done something the same way before (even if it appears to be a useless or harmful behavior), the favorable reaction of people nearby, the attainment of a goal, and literally countless other possible reinforcements.

Responses may be conditioned, "wired-in" so to speak, on the basis of a single experience. Behaviors have emotional counterparts and emotions have behavioral counterparts and physical responses occur with each, thus creating the holistic nature of the mind-body relationship. In hypnosis, the conditioning property of words and experience is apparent both in the process of transderivational search the client undergoes (in attaching the clinician's words to experience), and the resulting physical, emotional, and sensory changes that occur while the client is mentally absorbed. These changes, subtle but present, occur quite naturally all of the time, but are accentuated in hypnosis. When listening to someone describe the pleasure they had in eating at a good restaurant, why do you get hungry, salivate, and want to go to that restaurant at the first available opportunity? The experience of transderivational search involves you in attaching their words to experiences of pleasurable eating, and while your mind is absorbed to whatever degree, you react to the mental experience on motoric, sensory, and affective levels automatically and, to a large degree, unconsciously.

The motoric, or physical, response is called an "ideomotor response," and is a basic feature of hypnotic processes you will be exposed to later. The ideomotor response is one of several automatic responses collectively called the "ideodynamic" responses. Automatic sensory associations are called "ideosensory" responses, and automatic emotional associations are called "ideoaffective" responses.   (continued on p. 63)

FRAME OF REFERENCE: DAVID B. CHEEK

David B. Cheek, M.D., is one of the original pioneers in the medical applications of hypnosis. Cheek has had many decades of experience in developing and using hypnotic techniques in numerous ways, some quite nontraditional. Cheek's development of ideomotor questioning techniques has led to some highly controversial positions relating to the nature of human memory and information processing. For example, Cheek asserts that the unborn child and the young infant are capable of reacting to and storing experiences that can have emotional impact throughout life. Cheek has written extensively on the use of hypnosis and ideomotor questioning techniques to retrieve memories of such experiences, patterns which defy more traditional views regarding memory. He has also written a great deal on the ability of surgical patients to hear and be aware of ongoing events during their surgeries while under the influence of anesthesia. Cheek's investigations of the unconscious mind's relationship to nonverbal and somatic memory storage may have profound implications for a better understanding of the mind-body relationship and healing.

On His Early Interest in Ideomotor Signals: "Leslie M. LeCron was the first to introduce me to the idea that we can tap into information having to do with the beginnings of human physical and emotional problems by setting up unconscious muscular movements to answer questions. His first explorations were with the movements of a Chevreul pendulum as described in Beaudoin's book about Emile Coue. Instead of having a pendulum seek out letters of the alphabet as is done with a ouija board planchette he asked his subject to think consciously, 'yes-yes-yes' until the pendulum chose one of four repetitive body movements to symbolize a 'yes' response. He had his subjects get a 'yes,' a 'no,' an 'I don't know' and an 'I don't want to answer.'

"As with all consciously repeated actions, we tend to relegate the mechanism to unconscious associative levels. This happens when we learn to drive a car, learn a new dance step or study the touch system with typewriting. LeCron asked the subject to watch the pendulum as though someone else were holding it; to avoid thinking consciously what the answer would be. By asking about successively earlier beliefs about the origin of a problem he would locate the first moment his subject thought trouble was starting. If there were no earlier conditioning experiences he asked the subject to have an unconscious response to the question, 'Now that you know this, can you be free of the trouble it caused?'

"He was in this way searching for the first experience that set up unfavorable emotional or physical patterns of behavior and helping the subject decide from mature perspectives whether or not the behavior needed to continue. The pendulum was used with unhypnotized subjects. They usually slipped into a light trance as they became interested in the responses. Then he would gently remove the pendulum, ask the subject to close his eyes and select finger movements for the same responses.

"Neither LeCron nor Milton Erickson mentioned ideomotor responses in the 1954 workshop that I attended. Later, I learned that Erickson had experimented with symbol ideomotor responses as early as 1929 but gave them up in favor of watching the total picture of behavior as he worked with his patients. He was using imaginary 'crystal balls' into which the subject could look and see important events. He did not like the Chevreul pendulum as a divining instrument. He stopped using hallucinated crystal balls also because both modalities smacked too much of 'hocus pocus.' Erickson was such a gifted, intuitive person that he needed no 'gimmicks' like the pendulum to learn about his patients.

"LeCron, on the other hand, felt that there would probably never be another Erickson. He felt he needed to teach physicians, dentists and psychologists easily learned, simple techniques to use in their work. He felt the ideomotor signalling was a priceless tool. I agreed with him on this after seeing how rapidly his subjects could zoom in on meaningful, imprinted experiences that had caused maladaptive behavior."

Imprinting: "Repeatedly his demonstration subjects in our workshops would lead him to a birth experience or to a traumatic anesthetic experience. I had never been able to tap these areas of information although all my obstetrical and surgical experience suggested that these were important, untouched periods of experience. Something said or done in association with great physical or emotional stress seemed to *imprint*, or stamp in the behavior evoked by that experience. Later, more or less similar stimuli would reawaken and stimulate the patterned behavior. Simple reassurance and consciously suggested improvements were *not* associated with the same epinephrine secretions. They had no power to replace the imprinted effect.

"My experience using hypnosis between my dawning interest in 1943 and the time I joined LeCron in the 'Hypnosis Symposiums' in

1956 had suggested that head movements, for example, often seemed to contradict the verbal statements of my patients, regardless of whether they were in hypnosis or not. One obvious example was given me by a patient who came to me for an infertility problem. For five years, she had been trying unsuccessfully to get pregnant. In my initial interview I asked if she had wanted children when she was first married. Slowly she shook her head from side to side as she answered, 'Oh yes, doctor, I have *always* wanted children.' After two years of unfruitful exposure to my gynecological efforts she gave me the reason for those head movements as she was recovering from a pentothal anesthetic. The same question was answered with, 'No, because I was born too soon.'

"We found that her sister had angrily shown her that she had been born three months after the date of her parents' marriage, documented on the flyleaf of the family Bible. The information she later discovered was in her sister's handwriting. Her mother had not made such a foolish documentation. This woman became pregnant a month later. I delivered two of her three children that came after resolution of this traumatic imprinting."

Is Early Life Reporting Controversial?: "My beliefs about very early life imprintings and subsequent verbalized reports have seemed controversial because people cannot accept the idea that a baby can imprint on language that it could not possibly have learned during prenatal life. To that I can say the mechanism is comparable to understanding the noises associated with an exciting Chinese lecture that was unintelligible at the time but understandable later after listening to the tape recording and studying the Chinese language. Unborn babies feel maternal hormones associated with emotion and register the subjective impressions associated with the auditory and postural stimuli. The newborn infant whose mother is drugged to the point that she cannot say anything to her baby feels rejected and may never believe a maternal show of love later when she is fully conscious.

"In response to the complaints I add that I do not accept as valid any report that has failed to meet my criteria.

"There has to be an initial physiological expression that something important has happened. This must precede the ideomotor signal from a higher associative level in the nervous system. The patient is unaware at the higher associative levels reflected by verbal communication until after there have been repeated reviews of the event at physiological and skeletal muscle levels."

The Hierarchy of Memory Traces: "You see, I am talking about evolutionary processes here. All sensory stimuli register at the most primitive part of the brain, the brain stem and its Reticular Formation that surrounds the brain stem. The Reticular Formation, or Reticular Activating System (RAS) seems to decide what is meaningful, what should be relayed higher up and what could be suppressed as unimportant. Biological stresses seem to relate to right brain activity having to do with survival. They take priority over pleasant, nourishing left brain impressions. Here is the reason why the original concept of a trauma theory of neurosis as conceived by Breuer should, I believe, be resurrected if we are to deal effectively with the therapy of physical and emotional distress."

On Imprinting in Humans: "The term imprinting, as understood by ethologists, relates to birds and lower mammals. It has not usually been associated with human experience until LeCron and I put it into the book we wrote together, *Clinical Hypnotherapy,* in 1968. I feel that human imprinting can occur at any time in life and depends on the proximity of epinephrine outpouring with a stimulating, threatening event. Like the imprinting first described by Konrad Lorenz, human imprinting does not fade with the passage of time. Behavior that has become imprinted at a time of stress will not be dislodged by experiences tending to contradict the first, fixed impressions. I believe this is the reason we have more than 400 therapeutic modalities. People can reassess early imprintings and change behavior constructively if their therapist really projects his or her belief that what is being applied as a treatment will *really* work. The *affect* of a trauma may change with any of the modalities of treatment but the original imprinting will remain unchanged. I have tried often to mentally excise an imprinted traumatic experience and replace it with something else. I can do it at verbal levels of communication but when I later ask for an ideomotor review of the experience I get the real rather than the suggested replacement. This is why we need to explore the world of unborn infants and their reactions to birth stimuli if we are to materially influence human maladaptive behavior. We have to release our biases in order to do this. We cannot learn unless we have the tools for searching. These are the reasons I am committed to the value of ideomotor search and treatment methods."

On Milton Erickson: "I feel that Erickson was a genius and a teacher's teacher. Many of the things I heard him say had a profound effect on my thinking without my realization of the fact. I would later find some essential 'truth' that I believed must be original with me only to realize with a shock, 'Why, that comes from Milton. Now I remember!'

"Erickson often shocked people who watched him work with a subject. They would be horrified about his obvious coercions and manipulations without realizing that he was forcing the subjects to find ways of getting around the problems he gave them. He had enormous respect for the dignity of his subjects and for his patients yet they frequently were disturbed by his methods of showing this respect.

"Erickson showed us that we go into hypnosis when we are reviewing any sequence of events. This is the essence of most induction techniques. He and Elizabeth, his wife, showed us that people carrying out a post-hypnotic suggestion re-enter hypnosis in order to carry it out. He taught us that we only have a certain amount of attention to spend on anything. He taught women how to ignore the distress of hard labor by getting out of their body and sitting across the room while their body had the baby. He projected the woman who wanted a sterilization into the future a few years hence to see how she is feeling having had the operation and then how she feels having held on to her ability to have a pregnancy. He always maintained that hindsight was better than foresight. He taught me that this projection into an imaginary future of feeling well and unafraid of trouble was a valuable way of discovering hidden causes of resistance to therapy. He taught us all that pain is something that can be manipulated in a meaningful way if we have trouble eliminating the pain entirely. By making pain more severe for shorter than usual periods or having it when it does not matter very much the patient is learning about the built-in power we all have. I will not forget the teachings of Milton H. Erickson. His voice goes with me."

Source: Personal communication, 1989.

The relationship of mind and body is an incredibly close and powerful one. How the medical establishment was able to successfully separate mental involvement from physical treatment for so long has continued to be a mystery to me, but I am greatly encouraged by the movement towards a reintegration of all the human resources available to people in the process of healing.

Transderivational search and ideodynamic processes are deceptively simple but highly sophisticated characteristics of communication in general and hypnosis in particular. The role of individual experience in attaching meaning to words accounts for a great deal of the individuality and uniqueness of each person's response to hypnosis. This model does not, however, consider any of the relationship dynamics that are inevitably a part of all hypnotic work.

HYPNOSIS AS AN INTERACTIONAL OUTCOME

In more traditional views of hypnosis, the induction of trance was something a hypnotist "did to" a subject. In a standardized, nonindividualized approach, inducing hypnosis was something a subject did to himself in response to the depersonalized approach of the hypnotist's suggestions. In the utilization approach, responsibility for the experience of hypnosis is a shared one between clinician and client. Trance, in this view, is a result of a meaningful interaction between clinician and client in the sense that they must be attentive and responsive to each other. The clinician, to be successful, must be responsive to the needs of the client and tailor her approach to those needs if the client is going to be at all responsive to the possibilities for change the clinician makes available. The relationship is one of mutual interdependence, each following the other's leads while, paradoxically, at the same time leading.

The idea that the participants in the relationship are both leader and follower is a key point in this theoretical perspective. Based, in part, on the methods of Milton Erickson, this perspective views the process of hypnosis as a process of "accepting and utilizing" a person's behavior. A client's behaviors and/or feelings are fed back to her verbally and/or nonverbally, thereby creating a sense in the client of being understood—the essence of rapport. Tied to verbalizations of what she is experiencing as true are suggestions of what can be true to her. Instead of imposing on clients the clinician's belief system of what they should do, the possibility is made available to them of something they can do in their own way and at their own rate.

More will be said later on this idea of accepting and utilizing client behavior, but the important point here in describing this theoretical perspective is that hypnosis is considered a natural outcome of a relationship where each participant is responsive to the sensitive following and leading of the other. Other relationship variables that will be specified in the chapter on "Human Suggestibility" are very important to consider as well, but the view of trance as an outcome of a special relationship is a useful one in its ability to emphasize the integrity of each person. Thus, the generally undesirable approach of imposing one's beliefs and values on one's client is avoided to whatever degree is humanly possible (I think it is impossible to entirely avoid the sharing of one's values, and I also believe that, in some cases, it is *very* desirable to openly make one's values available to the client as a model to consider).

The interactional view emphasizes responsiveness and respect for the client, which is ideal in therapeutic contexts. However, clearly these factors need not be present for hypnosis to occur. After all, the stage show hypnotist has no special personal relationship to his subjects, and is certainly not sensitive or responsive to their unique personal characteristics and personalities.

OTHER THEORIES

Beyond the five theories presented and discussed in this chapter thus far, there are other theoretical perspectives worthy of brief mention. One is the Neo-Dissociation theory of hypnosis (Hilgard, 1973), in which the trance state is conceptualized as a dissociated state where the unconscious mind is capable of functioning more autonomously than in the "normal" waking state. Another perspective is the psychoanalytic perspective, in which the trance state is characterized by "primary process" thinking, and the trance subject is considered to be in a regressed state in which she responds to the hypnotist (through "transference") as a parental (or similar authority) figure.

Another recent theoretical perspective considers the existence of the trance state and the various hypnotic phenomena as a result of hemispheric asymmetry (Watzlawick, 1978). The two brain hemispheres each have some specialized functions, and hypnosis is thought to be caused by the distraction of the typically dominant left hemisphere while accessing the typically nondominant right hemisphere.

Another theoretical position is the idea of trance as a natural consequence of the ultradian cycle (Rossi, 1982), the biological cycles of alternating attentiveness and relaxation that physiologically occur about every 90 to 150 minutes. The natural, everyday trance state occurring for biological reasons can simply be amplified by the observant clinician, in this view.

CLOSURE ON PERSPECTIVES

Having now discussed some of what I consider to be among the most useful explanations for the experience of hypnosis, it is my hope that you have an appreciation for my earlier comments about the applicability of aspects of each, and the inadequacy of any single one as a means for understanding hypnosis. As you get more involved in the actual use of hypnotic techniques, you will discover that the complexity of people and the diversity of responses necessitate your keeping an open mind about the specific elements of each model that seem to be operating in an interaction at any given time. The greater the flexibility you have in making use of the many models there are to work from, the better the response you will get to the work you do.

For Discussion

1. How do one's expectations affect one's ability to observe objectively?

2. What is your reaction to the often-used analogy between the human mind and a computer? Do you believe the mind is "programmed" and that a person needs to have "old tapes erased" when undergoing change? Why, or why not?

3. What is "normal" consciousness? Do you experience altered states of consciousness? When? What defines it as an altered state?

4. How do the transderivational search and ideodynamic processes necessitate careful word choice in doing trancework?

5. What is your concept of holistic health treatment? In what ways do you acknowledge the mind-body relationship in your work?

6. What is "personal integrity"? As each class member gives their definition, what do you discover about the variety of experiences attached to an abstract term?

Things to Do

1. Do a role-play in which you and your partner both (in turn) pretend to be deeply hypnotized. What do you experience?

2. Contact health care providers in your area who identify themselves as "holistic" in approach. What do you discover about the variety of approaches called "holistic"?

3. Choose a role to play for a day. For example, if you are basically shy, play the role of someone very outgoing. If you are basically assertive, play the role of someone passive. Whatever role you choose to play for a day, really stay in the role, but make sure it is a safe one to do! What do you discover about the role? How does it affect your perception of yourself?

6

Contexts of
Hypnosis

One of the questions I am most frequently asked by others when they discover my involvement with hypnosis is, "Can hypnosis be used in the treatment of such and such?" I used to think that I should be able to cite a variety of literature to support my eternally affirmative response, but I have changed tactics in recent years. Now I am much more likely to respond to their question with such questions as: Do you think there is any mental or emotional involvement with that disorder you are asking about? Do you think one's attitude or belief system plays a role, however major or minor, in the experience of the problem? Are one's feelings, personal needs, or self-image a factor in the way that particular physical and/or mental health problem is experienced?

In asking virtually hundreds, if not thousands, of people these types of questions, I have never yet had anyone respond "No, the mind is not a factor at all." Sometimes, I worry that I may one day run into someone who believes their mental and emotional makeup has no effect on their experience of life, including physical symptoms, but I'm sure that after I get over the initial shock I will be able to give that person some demonstration of ways to use the mind for self-control previously thought of, in his view, as impossible. In the meantime, most people seem to have an intuitive understanding that the holistic nature of human experience is one including a powerful mind-body connection. The mind affects the body's physiology, and one's physiology affects one's mental experience.

Unfortunately, while most people can accept this point with relative ease, they often tend to think of this relationship as a one-way relationship in which the person's mental makeup can cause him or her to be physically sick, evidenced in the psychophysiological disorders. The relationship between lifestyle and disease is commonly acknowledged, with stress symptoms (e.g., ulcers, migraine headaches) rampant in our society. If the mind can cause sickness, why can't it also cause wellness? It is encouraging that varieties of hypnotic techniques, including visualization, have been used with considerable success as adjunct treatments in the intervention of physical disease.

Essentially, my response to the question of whether hypnosis may be used in the treatment of a particular disorder, whether mental and/or physical, is one promoting the idea that hypnosis can be used as a tool in the treatment of *any* human condition in which a person's attitude is a factor. Thus, even if the disorder is genuinely an organic one, a physical injury for example, the person's mental resources can be enlisted to aid in managing the subsequent discomfort a little more easily, and to enhance the recovery process. In physical disorders in which there is no known path to recovery, hypnosis can ease the discomfort, allow some rest, and lessen the associated emotional trauma. Hypnosis may not ever facilitate a cure, and often does not, but it *can* assist the person on a variety of levels in meaningful ways.

A person's mental involvement in the various psychological disorders is far more readily apparent, and seems to be the basis for more widespread acceptance of hypnotic principles and techniques among psychotherapists, who comprise the majority of participants in my training programs to date. Hypnosis can be very useful in altering one's perceptions and thereby helping one surpass the hurtful limitations people invariably impose on themselves.

Wherever there is involvement of the person's mind in a particular problem, which is *everywhere* to one degree or another as far as I can tell, there is some potential gain to be made through the application of hypnotic patterns. With that point in mind, let us consider specific contexts where the tool of hypnosis may be used to facilitate desired outcomes.

STAGE HYPNOSIS

Stage hypnosis is the application of hypnotic principles and techniques for the purpose of entertaining an audience. It is usually found in night clubs, state fairs, parties, and other similar contexts where entertainment is desired. I have shared my distaste for the stage show uses of hypnosis. In the stage context, hypnosis appears to be a method of mind control bordering dangerously close to brainwashing. People are encouraged to look silly (with their permission, of course), and audiences typically have a difficult time understanding how the entertaining routines in the show can possibly be used in a professional context for therapeutic purposes. Consequently, hypnosis is not considered as a serious treatment alternative, and the consumer is inadvertently robbed of a viable treatment option. It is also true that some people know better, and actually become attracted to therapeutic hypnosis as a result of exposure to stage hypnosis, but such people seem to be in the minority, in my experience.

MEDICAL HYPNOSIS

Traditional medicine has long recognized the "placebo effect." In some instances, a patient's belief that she is getting an active drug when she is really getting no drug at all, only a sugar pill resembling a drug, will cause the same therapeutic effect as if the patient had been given an active drug. A person's expectations and attitudes can have profound effects on mental and physical experience. With this recognition is coming a growing use of hypnosis and hypnosis-related techniques. The quantity of literature describing the applications of hypnosis to medical problems is growing quickly, and for specific applications you are encouraged to refer to the various scientific hypnosis journals in which such research is published. Some of these are mentioned in the final chapter.

In general, hypnosis can be a useful adjunct to more traditional medical treatments for several reasons, the first of which relates to the discussion at the beginning of this chapter regarding the mind-body relationship and the role of the mind (attitudes and related emotions) in medical disorders. "Miracle cures" that defy current medical understanding, which have evolved out of a patient's refusal to give up, are not uncommon in the literature; why not encourage—or at least permit—"miracles"? Why place limitations on the patient that she would not place on herself?

A second reason for making use of hypnosis is because of its emphasis, by its very nature, on the responsibility of each person for his own health and well-being. Use of hypnosis gives people a direct experience of having some control over their internal experiences. I have worked with many people who actually cried tears of joy in a session for having had an opportunity to experience themselves as relaxed, comfortable, and positive when their usual experience of themselves was one of pain and despair. Finding resources within themselves they never knew they had was a dramatic experience, and allowed them to take on a new and higher level of responsibility for themselves and their own well-being.

Specific applications of hypnosis in medical contexts are greatly varied, but can generally be described as a way of attaining a significant degree of control over physical processes. One possibility is the reduction or elimination of pain without the use of medication. Anesthesiologists, for example, seem to be developing a greater appreciation for hypnosis because of the opportunity it affords them to reduce the amount of chemical anesthesia used. Consequently, the potential dangers associated with the use of chemical anesthesia are reduced. Such medication reduction is an attractive possibility to these and other physicians who would like to curtail patients' reliance on medications in their interventions. Pain management is one of the more sophisticated uses of medical hypnosis, and is applicable to the patient in both chronic and acute pain. Pain management techniques can be used before, during and after surgery, to facilitate easier childbirth, and to help manage physical trauma of any sort. Methods of hypnotic pain management are generally very sophisticated, and you are advised to have a very strong background of education and experience in hypnosis before working with such cases. Working with patients in physical pain presupposes appropriate medical licensure or appropriate medical supervision in *all* cases.

Hypnosis is commonly used in the treatment of stress disorders, and is considered to be a most effective treatment. Teaching the medical patient techniques for preventing negative stress wherever possible, techniques for identifying stress well before it reaches a level where it is likely to cause debilitating symptoms, and techniques for relaxing and managing stress positively are all elements in teaching a hypertensive patient to manage her condition positively and responsibly.

Hypnosis in the treatment of serious diseases, as an adjunct, *not* a replacement, for more traditional approaches, has demonstrated the necessity of addressing the emotional needs while using the mental resources of the patient as a part of treatment. This is true even for diseases that seem, and probably are, entirely organic in nature. The exact mechanism whereby a doctor can mumble a few hypnotic phrases and effect changes in the patient is unknown, but the answer is thought to reside in the immunological system of the person. Current research in this area suggests that a person is more likely to develop a serious disease during or after a highly stressful period in their lives. Stress is thought to reduce the capacity of the body's natural defenses, the immunological system, and the disease organisms are able to multiply in the weakened person. Hypnosis is thought to strengthen the body's immunological functions and assist in the fighting off of the disease. Much research still needs to be done to discover solutions to the mysteries of the mind, but the lack of precise explanations for mechanisms of action should not inhibit the use of techniques that can assist in the healing of a human body. Hypnosis can assist in the recovery process, and can be another tool in the physician's repertoire to share with her patients. Hypnosis doesn't replace other treatments—it adds to them.

There are a couple of issues here that need to be touched on. The first concerns the responsibility of a patient for her health; the idea here is to encourage a patient to use all of her resources to help herself, *not* to blame the patient for her condition. One of the most distressing (to me, at least) things to arise from the recognition of patient responsibility is when the doctor or other well-meaning health professional further burdens the patient with responsibility for her illness. It's not bad enough the person is sick, she is also told she caused it, and is even asked why she did this to herself! No, this is not the intent; responsibility is positive, blame is not. Helping the person to feel guilty about having made herself sick is an unforgivable outcome of a careless interaction.

The second issue, and I hope you already know this, is one related to the use of hypnosis in the treatment of medical problems. Specifically, unless you are a physician, or have the proper training and credentials to treat a person's physical disorders, you are working out of your field and are inviting trouble for both you and your patient. If you want to assist someone in the treatment of a physical disorder, it is imperative from an ethical, legal, and humane standpoint that you have the support and involvement of the appropriate medical practitioners. Do not assume, for example, the patient with migraines is "just stressed." With that symptom, and any others, the patient should have had a thorough physical examination, and you should have a medical backup. Call the patient's doctor, and ask if your treatment plan will interfere with hers, at the *very* least. Rarely, if ever, will it interfere and treatment can be coordinated. Knowledge of medications the patient may be taking and the physical impact of his symptoms is essential to effective suggestion formulation. The use of hypnosis in diverse medical contexts is a tribute to the power of the unconscious mind; the examples of potential applications cited in this section are just the tip of the iceberg for a huge range of possibilities.

DENTAL HYPNOSIS

The powerful mind-body relationship evidenced in medical applications of hypnosis is also evident in dental applications. Many of the desired outcomes sought in medical contexts are also desirable in the dental setting because of the physical nature of dental work. Physical parts of the body (i.e., teeth, gums, and associated structures) are under treatment. Furthermore, attached to every mouth under treatment is a human being whose attitudes about the work being done, the dentist, and her self (self-image) will affect the outcome of the intervention.

Dentists are aware, perhaps acutely, that most dental patients do *not* mark their calendar months in advance of their appointment and wait with eager anticipation for the big day to arrive. Far more common is the patient coming for treatment who can be described as somewhere in between mildly reluctant and terrified.

Hypnosis as a means of effectively communicating with the patient on her level, whether trance is formally induced or not, is a handy tool in the dental context. Helping a patient reduce her anxiety about receiving dental treatment with a few well chosen statements can make a huge difference in the outcome. Furthermore, one good dental experience can skillfully be used as a prototype for future dental experiences. The person may not eagerly await the next appointment, but she won't have to live in dread, either.

A second good use of hypnosis in dentistry involves the use of pain management techniques. Many people either cannot or choose not to use chemical anesthesias (or analgesias) such as Novocaine or Nitrous Oxide, and prefer to rely on their own resources when undergoing dental treatment. Hypnosis techniques for creating the experience of analgesia or anesthesia allow the patient to reduce to a more easily managed level the degree of discomfort experienced, and many are able to eliminate the discomfort altogether.

A third use of hypnosis in dentistry is for its ability to assist in directing the flow of blood. With proper techniques, ones that really fit well with the patient's experience of himself, hypnosis can reduce blood flow to the area under treatment. The result is a less traumatic experience for the patient and greater clarity for the dentist in seeing what he is doing.

Another use of hypnosis in the dental context is for the enhancement of the healing process following treatment. Use of hypnosis techniques involving the imagining of healing (e.g., images, feelings, and sounds associated with rebuilding, repairing, and strengthening) can both shorten the recovery period and allow greater comfort during that time.

Many dental practices could easily incorporate hypnosis into treatment through the use of generalized relaxation tapes the patient can listen to (through headphones) during the dental procedures. Of course, better responses occur with more individualized approaches, but unusual is the dentist who has the time, interest, and means for the greater involvement in hypnosis such a practice would require.

HYPNOSIS IN THE FORENSIC SCIENCES

Hypnosis has frequently been used in the course of police work. Generally, hypnosis is used as a tool to assist in investigative processes, but is also applicable in helping reduce the trauma to a person involved as a victim or a witness to a crime.

As a part of the investigative process, hypnosis may be used to facilitate a person's recall in an attempt to recover details of the crime the person could not consciously remember. Often, a person's conscious mind is so absorbed in feelings (e.g., fear, fascination, confusion) during the experience of witnessing or being victimized by a crime that conscious memory is poor. Because of the dual nature of the human mind (i.e., conscious and unconscious), memories and details that may have been repressed or else simply escaped detection by the conscious mind may not have escaped the person's unconscious mind. A number of famous, or perhaps infamous, criminal cases have been solved through hypnotically obtained information, one such case being the "Chowchilla Kidnapping" case in which a school bus driver and his bus full of students were kidnapped in the small town of Chowchilla in Northern California. Three men commandeered the bus to a nearby rock quarry where it and the people inside were buried, and a ransom demand followed. The bus driver managed to escape, and the children were soon rescued. Dr. William Kroger, a long-time contributor to the field of hypnosis, was called in to use hypnosis with the driver, who was then able to recall the license plate number of one of the kidnappers' vans. This hypnotically obtained information led to their arrest and subsequent conviction for the crime. (continued on p. 77)

FRAME OF REFERENCE: WILLIAM KROGER

William Kroger, M.D., is one of the distinguished elder statesman of the field of clinical hypnosis. Born in 1906, Kroger became fascinated with hypnosis at an early age, and his interest endured throughout his long, distinguished career. Not only did Kroger write the book that was long considered THE book on hypnosis, *Clinical and Experimental Hypnosis in Medicine, Dentistry and Psychology* (1977), but he authored and co-authored many other important works.

Kroger's precedent setting videotapes of surgical procedures done under hypnosis remain landmark events in propelling the young and questionable field of hypnosis onto its current level of acceptability and interest. Anyone who professionally practices hypnosis owes a great deal to William Kroger, whose pioneering efforts paved the way for the field to grow to its current proportions.

On the Origin of His Interest in Hypnosis: "My interest in hypnosis started in 1919. My father had a fur store in Evanston, Illinois. In order to stimulate business, he hired a professional hypnotist to hypnotize a woman as a publicity stunt in order to create interest in the Main Street Businessmen's Association. This, I can see as if it was yesterday. The girl's name was Florina, and she was dressed in purple flowing gowns and veils. And he, with the piercing eyes, approached her and said, 'Florina, sleep!' He stared in her eyes and she fell backwards and they put her in a coffin and buried her in the ground. I was a curious little cuss, and so I went by and paid a nickel to see this sleeping beauty in the ground. She lay there in a vault for two days, and I thought, 'Gee, that's fantastic!' On the third day, they dug her up. 'Florina, wake up!' She opened her eyes, she blinked, she stood up—it was the same thing you'd see on the stage today. So I went around to the kids in the neighborhood and I looked into their eyes and said, 'Sleep!' And to my amazement, half of them fell over. I did the usual things; like I could put pins in their arms, and I'd say, 'Jeez, I could be a doctor some day. This would be great for anesthesia.' So, I didn't realize that hypnosis was anything more than a stage tool until I got to Northwestern University. At Northwestern University, I met the late Dr. J.D. Morgan, whose book you may be familiar with on abnormal psychology. We had several lectures on hypnosis, and I said, 'My God, this is a scientific tool!' "

On Early Prejudices Against Hypnosis: "I was the only doctor who was using hypnosis in the Chicago area. I was laughed at, ridiculed, vilified, and abused, and made to walk seven steps behind everybody else like I was a leper. I was persecuted by the Illinois State Medical Society for an exhibit. They were just against hypnosis, [even just] the word. . . .

"The difficulties I went through. . . . You don't know how difficult it really was! [For the first movie ever showing thyroid surgery done with only hypnotic anesthesia] . . . it was an historic moment. First one in the world, and we pulled it off! [The medical director] was sitting downstairs in his office, getting a 'blow-by-blow' description of how the surgery was going, hoping it was going to fail [because hypnosis was involved].

"Individuals who have never gone through things like that can't understand it. See, today hypnosis has some respectability, but in those days, they said, 'Walk seven steps behind me, you're a leper!' They didn't want to associate with me; they said, 'You're a hypnotist.' "

On "Trance" and Hypnosis: "Most people refer to it as a 'trance.' It's not a 'trance.' To me, that term is like fingernails scratching on a chalkboard. That's the most ridiculous term for it. [Hypnosis] is a state of increased awareness. If you're more aware, whatever you hear is going to sink in better. If it sinks in better, you get a better response, whether it's hitting a golf ball or having an erection. As Bernheim said, 'There is no hypnosis, only suggestion.' That's how I conceptualize it. I conceptualize it in terms of neural science concepts as a method of transmitting a message in a minimal noise environment. If the signal to noise ratio is reduced, the message is clearly received.

"No other living system can do [what humans can]. Ideas have representations and names. You can't say to a dog, 'Go to the toilet.' He doesn't understand 'toilet.' But a human can—and that makes humans unique, because they can manipulate symbolic communication. The cortex is uniquely different in a human than in any other living system. And it's that cortex that you get out of the way (in terms of its criticalness) that allows you to induce a feeling of belief. So, what is hypnosis? It's the induction of conviction. All these guys talk about 'hypnosis is this and that'—it's a very simple thing that's [been made] complex, enormously complex."

On Inductions and Beliefs: "Now, an induction technique is an interesting study on feedback control. I'd say, 'You are looking into my eyes, your eyes are getting heavy.' They're not getting heavy because of what I'm saying. They're getting heavy because of the fact that he is gazing up at the ceiling. But the subject imputes to you a magical omnipotence, and he says, 'My God, my eyes did get heavy! This guy's got power!' If he accepts A, B, C, and D suggestions, then he'll accept X, Y, and Z ones. All the time you say, 'You are a good hypnotic subject and yes, that's why that happened.' And all the time, it had nothing to do with what the operator was saying, it had more to do with restructuring his beliefs."

On Cybernetics and Hypnosis: "I'm going to continue to emphasize the cybernetic principles of feedback systems relative to theories of hypnosis, as well as some of the very important neuropsychophysiological aspects by making the computer analogies. The brain functions like a computer. I'm not saying the brain *is* a computer—I'm only saying I think we can better understand the brain's chemical qualities and neurophysiological mechanisms in terms of cybernetic principles and feedback mechanisms. This is described more fully in my book, *Clinical and Experimental Hypnosis in Medicine, Dentistry, and Psychiatry* [*1977*]."

On Milton Erickson: "Erickson contributed a lot, but his stuff will have to be put in the proper perspective. A lot of the significance of his work has perhaps been carried a little bit too far. Erickson might come out of his grave and ask, 'Is this me?' I think he deserves all the accolades but I think he's been misinterpreted. Erickson was a very modest man; he was never looking for self-aggrandizement. I attribute the success of his techniques to a profound knowledge of human nature, a solid eclectic psychology on the nature of everyday living. He could take a patient into his heart; that was his secret, the patient could feel the empathy. It wasn't so much what he did, but it was that feeling the patient had in knowing that he cared. And then he could structure the therapy appropriately."

Source: Personal communication, 1987.

As of this writing, the use of hypnotically obtained testimony in the courtroom is embroiled in controversy. Experts are at odds over the issue of whether hypnotically obtained testimony is valid because of the unknown effect of hypnosis on memory. On one side of the issue are those who claim that the information obtained from a hypnotized person is as usable and reliable as any other information, and that hypnosis does not necessarily distort memory. On the other side of the issue are those who claim that hypnosis alters memory, that the hypnotized witness can lie while in hypnosis, and is likely to fill in missing details either with fantasy material or with information contained in the subtle leading questions of the investigator.

The issue is really one concerning the nature of memory. In a sense, both views on hypnosis and memory are correct. The conflict is a pseudoconflict, a conflict arising because of its "either-or" nature, which is not a useful dichotomy in this case. All human memory is a distortion of experience—an internal representation of an event. The process of experiencing and then remembering is regulated by previous experiences and inner makeup. Variables affecting memory include: one's values of what is important to notice; mood; internal or external focus; expectations; previous experiences in similar situations; and a variety of other factors that must be considered.

Memory, whether in a formally induced trance state or whether in the less specific trance state called "life," can be reliable to a large extent, such as in "objective" experience when many people reach agreement on the object of observation. Likewise, memory in or out of trance can distort experience because of all the factors described earlier that comprise one's personal unconscious. Why else can 10 people (presumably not in trance) on a corner all see the same accident and their reports to the police comprise 10 different versions?

Hypnotically obtained information should be considered in the same way as information obtained by any other means. It should be considered, evaluated, and substantiated by other means. If one has a motivation to lie, hypnosis has no preventative powers. If one must distort or misrepresent an experience, it won't be because of hypnosis. One doesn't require formal hypnosis to fill in gaps or rely on others' leads; these processes are ongoing in all human beings.

The other common use of hypnosis in the forensic context is to help alleviate the stress and distress in having witnessed or been victimized by a crime. A skillful practitioner can help lessen the trauma by easing the person into a different frame of mind, either by helping the person shift her focus away from what has happened to another experience, or by helping the person shift from one uncomfortable dimension of the experience to another that is relatively neutral (neutral at least, but positive if possible). The things one concludes and the things one says to one's self after a traumatic experience play a huge role in the rate and degree of recovery.

Special consideration for the emotional state of the person who recalls details of the trauma must be an integral part of the use of hypnosis in the forensic sciences. Mechanisms to assure the emotional security and well-being of the person must be part of the process, for being left alone to carry the hurt of memories brought out hypnotically is otherwise one more trauma for an already vulnerable human being.

HYPNOSIS IN EDUCATION

Teaching and learning are highly refined skills which require a great amount of information processing on multiple levels. Teaching is a learning experience—learning how to capture students' interest and attention (a skill necessary for trance induction, not coincidentally), learning how to present information in such a way that the student can use it (a skill necessary for trance utilization, not coincidentally), and learning how to allow students to become self-sufficient learners (a skill necessary for consolidating trance results, not coincidentally), so they may be competent and motivated to learn in the absence of the teacher. Whether a teacher is teaching preschoolers or doctoral candidates, effective teaching involves these steps paralleling hypnotic patterns.

Learning is a multiple step process. For the sake of simplicity (learning theory is a complex world in its own right), effective learning must include the following steps: First, there must be some degree of attentiveness to the material to be learned. Second, there must be some method for bringing the material from the outside world into the internal world. One's senses (e.g., sight, hearing, etc.) are the means for gathering information from the world around us. There is nothing we experience of the external world that does not enter our conscious or unconscious mind through one or more of our senses. Which sense is the dominant one at a given time determines, to a large degree, how much and what kind of information can be acquired. For example, a high level of awareness for one's internal *feelings* while trying to memorize a set of graphs or charts (external visual information) is likely to result in ineffective learning. Third, there must be some method for organizing the information internally as it mingles with previously acquired information while simultaneously building a framework in which to incorporate future learnings. Fourth, and last, there must be some method for being able to retrieve the information from within as necessity dictates.

Hypnosis as a tool has frequently been used to assist in the learning process both by enhancing concentration and diminishing anxiety. Anxiety can interrupt any of the above steps (e.g., "going blank at exam time") and poor concentration can distract one from adequate exposure to the information as well as disrupt its internal organization.

Many creative teachers at all levels are using hypnosis in their teaching, guiding students with relaxation procedures, for example. Many students are developing themselves with self-hypnosis exercises, learning to manage anxiety and increase their ability to notice and organize their subject of study. Hypnosis in the educational context, whether formally or informally used, can enhance both teaching skills and student performance.

HYPNOSIS IN BUSINESS

In the business context, formal hypnosis in the sense of overt trance induction procedures is less applicable than is the use of the informal or spontaneous trance. Communication that influences is the guiding definition of hypnosis in this book, and in the business context the principles of effective communication can either make or break a company. Discussing specific communication skills is the subject of later chapters; suffice it to say here that for the businessperson who is able to communicate her ideas in flexible ways to those she interacts with, there is a greater likelihood of success at all levels. Communication skills in such interactions as the presentation of a marketing plan, the handling of a troublesome employee or supervisor, the job interview, performance evaluations, job standard clarification, the creation of a desired work atmosphere, and the many other dimensions of the business world are all ultimately interpersonal interactions where communication and influence inevitably occur. The issue is not one of whether one communicates and influences, impossible *not* to do, but rather one of whether the communication patterns that exist influence participants in a desirable way. In the business consultations I do, identifying rigid and dysfunctional communication patterns and replacing them with more flexible approaches helps enhance the business on multiple levels. I don't call my interventions "hypnosis" while there, but hypnotic patterns are rampant in my recommendations.

HYPNOSIS IN SPORTS

Engaging in athletics with any degree of intensity involves a large measure of physical control and mental concentration. Hypnosis as a tool can provide both with an extraordinary amount of efficiency.

For the athlete, having precise control over one's body is essential to outstanding performance. Athletes often describe what they call "muscle memory," the body's keen awareness of how each limb, each muscle must be positioned in order to perform successfully. The physical control through the amplification of the mind-body relationship can help an athlete push his body to the limit of his talents. The requirement for intense concentration is obvious, and hypnosis as a technique for narrowing one's attentional focus to the task at hand is a powerful tool to have available.

One of the most famous examples of hypnosis helping an athlete is the story of Rod Carew, one of baseball's best. Carew had suffered an injury, and though technically the injury healed, there was still some lingering pain and a lot of self-doubt. After consulting a hypnotist, learning and practicing self-hypnosis, Carew came back to the best season of his career, batting nearly .400 and winning the league's Most Valuable Player award. Hypnosis gave him access to more of his own, natural ability.

In addition to building concentration and physical control, hypnosis can help in better managing the tension inherent in competing. Furthermore, building positive expectations and positive communication with one's self through self-hypnosis can enhance performance dramatically. Often, the troubled, slumping athlete has mental images of failure, which all too easily get translated into real failure. Building positive images through hypnosis and self-hypnosis can turn an athlete's performance around completely. Certainly, hypnosis does not provide extra talent to the athlete; it simply amplifies the talent the athlete has, giving him access to as much of his talent as possible. A lot of athletes appreciate that, as you can well imagine.

HYPNOSIS IN PSYCHOTHERAPY

Being a psychotherapist by training and in practice, I have developed a profound appreciation for the possibilities hypnosis as a tool has to offer in the treatment of behavioral and emotional problems. Hypnosis as a part of therapist training programs seems an essential need, yet only a handful of formal programs offer the opportunity to develop expertise in hypnotic skills. Most people who become knowledgeable in hypnosis do so through involvement with workshops and seminars organized by private practitioners and professional hypnosis societies.

The interesting thing about the omission of direct hypnosis training in many schools is that they are teaching hypnosis indirectly anyway. Every psychotherapy involves influencing a troubled person in some way so the person may feel better. There are countless approaches for helping others to grow, adapt more successfully to the demands of life, or carry out whatever you think therapy should do. Each of them can show positive results, too. What are the elements of each approach that influence the person seeking help to change? Whatever model for conceptualizing the human condition you might work from, clearly you are attempting to influence another human being's experience in a way that is beneficial. The way you do this, regardless of what you say or do (which is the difference in content from approach to approach), is through *communication.* How do you know where to step in and offer help in this client's world? Only from the way the client communicates about her world can you come to know enough of it to discover where and how much to intervene. Only through the way you speak (including what you say and what you don't say) and move can you effect a change in another human being. The client seeking psychotherapy cannot *not* respond to your communications; the sophistication of a good therapist is getting the desired, therapeutic response.

Whatever therapies a clinical training program offers will indirectly include hypnosis because every therapy includes hypnosis. Hypnosis is influential communication. Even the classic hypnotic phenomena (such as age regression and dissociation) described in a later chapter are evident in every therapy, but the concepts and uses for those phenomena are typically not taught because of the narrowness of what a given therapeutic model allows itself. For example, I remember my frustration when studying psychoanalysis at my very analytically-oriented undergraduate college in learning that if someone got better in less than two years of intensive analysis it was to be considered a feature of the illness called a "flight to health." Narrow, inflexible thinking, to say the least.

When one studies numerous psychotherapies, elements of classic hypnotic phenomena can be found in each. Training in hypnosis, of which this book is only a part while experience with the uniqueness of each person is the greater teacher, provides an appreciation for the dynamics and techniques of influence that assure a greater flexibility than any single approach can ever offer. A willingness to develop many skills based on a variety of perspectives assures a greater likelihood of success. *All* of the various therapeutic approaches work. The skill is in knowing what will work with *this* specific person.

Hypnosis is a tool, not a therapy. Consequently, you do not face an "either-or" conflict. It is not competitive with beliefs in psychoanalysis, behaviorism, Gestalt principles, client-centered approaches, or any other perspective. Hypnosis is not a theory; instead, it works at the communication level at which your theories and ideas for intervention are transmitted to your client. It is a means for having more systematic control over your communications and having a greater flexibility in dealing with that person you are trying to help who is unlike any other person you have ever worked with.

The main advantage of using hypnosis in psychotherapy lies in its ability to use the many extraordinary resources of the unconscious mind. The unconscious mind contains a lifetime of experiences and learnings, and is a resource that must be used with a proper amount of respect and appreciation. The person seeking help has already tried to consciously change (e.g., through willpower or self-understanding through self-help books) and has not been able to, which is why you are seeing him in the first place. The conscious mind is not where that person's strength is, nor is it where that person's needs and desires can be met most efficiently. Rather, it is in the unconscious mind where one will find people's motivations, assumptions about life and people, weaknesses and strengths. Hypnosis simply permits greater access to the unconscious mind's resources that may be used to assist this client in making a desired change. Feelings, values, behaviors, memories, understandings, all the perceptions that guide the client's choices are subjective and thus can change. Trying to change someone's ideas about himself on only a conscious level ("let's sit down and talk about this . . .") is one way of assuring a longer therapy. Imposing one's theoretical perspectives and one's own values is another.

Hypnosis that involves simply inducing trance formally and then giving suggestions directly related to the problem is the most superficial and least sophisticated use of hypnosis. Telling someone in trance who wants to feel better about herself the old traditional hypnotic phrase, "Everyday in every way you are getting better and better" is an insult to the intelligence of a client, not to mention a bore to the clinician. This kind of hypnosis is used on a symptomatic basis, and is the kind of hypnosis almost all lay hypnotists practice and even many psychotherapists use. It can and will be effective with a certain percentage of people; of course, there are some people who will change when you look at them harshly and say in a stern voice, "Stop doing that!" simply because they are ready to change. Since a symptomatic approach can and does work with many people, it is a viable choice to use in some therapies. Be aware, though, that this is only a small fraction of what hypnosis is and how it can be used.

More complex and more skilled use of hypnosis involves the use of techniques aimed at resolution of deeper conflicts (taking the symptoms with them) or else it is not truly a success. This kind of hypnosis involves more of an interactional approach and works on multiple dimensions of the individual. Memories in the form of powerful learnings from the client's unconscious mind can be used skillfully to make available to the person the resources she requires to handle her life in the desired way. Clarifying misperceptions of early or recent experience, learning creative and positive ways to meet one's own needs, helping a person to discover within herself the many fine abilities she has had all along but never knew how to use are all general outcomes that may be accomplished by integrating hypnosis into the psychotherapy. Later discussion of hypnotic phenomena will clarify when a particular hypnotic procedure might be a useful means of therapeutic intervention.

The flexibility of hypnosis as a tool allows clinicians to use it as superficially or as intensively as deemed appropriate. How one ultimately incorporates hypnosis into one's practice is determined by the assumption one makes about people. A view of people that appreciates each person's uniqueness would preclude one from approaching each client in the same way. To diagnose and categorize, and then treat the category rather than the person in a "cookbook" manner is undesirable. Likewise, a view of people that assumes all people seeking help are "sick" and need to be made "well" would preclude one from making use of the wealth of their resources that would be available to another clinician who views people as uniquely special and potentially powerful in their ability to make use of their resources for growth.

Use of hypnosis in the context of psychotherapy is a potent means for facilitating the client's movement towards a more satisfying existence. Practice with hypnotic techniques will demonstrate to you repeatedly the diversity of people, and that is one last great reason for its use; you will grow a lot, too!

In whatever context one chooses to apply hypnosis, one cannot help but notice that the increased flexibility and sensitivity one demonstrates toward others is responded to by them with appreciation.

For Discussion

1. Why do you think the mind-body relationship has been a divided one in Western society? What impact has this division had on people's attitude about health care?

2. What does "responsibility for one's health" mean? Do you agree or disagree with those who claim that all sickness is psychogenic? Why or why not? If you get a cold and people ask you, "Why do you let yourself get sick," how do you answer? Is it a reasonable question?

3. What ways can you think of to apply hypnosis in addition to those mentioned in this chapter? How might you encourage people working in that specific area to employ hypnotic methods?

4. Are there any contexts in which hypnosis should *not* be used? What is the basis for your response?

5. What are the implications of calling hypnosis a "tool" and not a "therapy"?

Things to Do

1. Review recent issues of the *American Journal of Clinical Hypnosis* and the *International Journal of Clinical and Experimental Hypnosis* in order to discover the many ways hypnotic patterns are clinically used. These journals are likely to be available at the university library.

2. In your chosen field, what are the assumptions you find the most limiting? Make a list of what things are and are not possible in your field as a direct consequence of these assumptions. For example, psychoanalysis does *not* allow for a rapid cure. How do you overcome such limiting assumptions?

3. Visit a book or tape store that sells motivational tapes employing standardized hypnosis. How many different applications of hypnosis do you find? Ask the salespeople about these tapes and people's reactions to them. What impression do you form?

7

Human Suggestibility

The field of social psychology offers a number of valuable insights into the dynamics of interpersonal influence relevant to the use of hypnosis. Social psychology as a field evolved out of the recognition that people will do things when they are alone that they will not do if even just one other person is around. An individual's behavior changes in the presence of another individual, often in systematic and predictable ways. Social psychology's task as a field is to identify what kinds of interactions between people cause specific types of behavior, and has as its ultimate (and idealistic) goal the establishment of organizations and environments that will maximize positive behaviors in individuals. Interpersonal influence has been studied in a variety of ways and contexts, yielding a substantial amount of information that I think is extremely valuable in describing many of the dimensions of the hypnotic relationship. Some of these dimensions are conscious, while many are unconscious factors in the relationship; recognition of these factors may allow for a greater diversity in their applications. Let's take a look at influence in specific contexts.

THE INFLUENCE OF ADVERTISING

In America, billions of dollars are spent yearly on advertising. Does all that advertising work? To the corporations who budget hundreds of millions of dollars annually for television commercials and radio and magazine ads, the answer is clearly "Yes!" Advertisements filter into our brains and influence our buying habits. Why do you buy the products you buy when you shop? How did you arrive at choosing one brand over another? Why do you usually feel like you are making a sacrifice when you buy the cheaper house brands or plain wrapped brands instead of the brand you really want (because of its greater attractiveness)?

Advertising as an industry makes great use of hypnotic techniques to influence you to buy a product. Advertisers begin by creating a need for a product (for many centuries, bad breath or body odor was not on the forefront of people's consciousness), using techniques such as promoting identification with the person in the ad so that you'll solve your problem by using the product in the same way she modeled for you, and finally strengthening your buying habit by rewarding you for having made such a fine choice. Ads try to generate feelings or recognitions that will be tied to the product, that induce you to purchase one brand over another. The entire field of advertising is much more complex than this brief description may suggest, but the point here is that advertising uses words and images in a way that is intended to influence your buying behaviors. And it works! An ad may last only a few seconds, or as much as a minute on television, for example, and that ad time costs a bundle.

Most people don't pay much conscious attention to the commercial, but let their attention drift to other places. Where does the commercial go? It goes into the unconscious, where a feeling of recognition can be triggered when seeing the product in the store. Social psychology has shown in many different studies that the more familiar an item is, the more positive regard one has for it (familiarity is positive; for example, when you are in an unfamiliar location while traveling, you may be relieved to see a McDonalds hamburger restaurant). In conscious experience, repetition is boring, but the unconscious mind thrives on it and reacts to it.

Every day, human beings are bombarded by thousands, and by some researchers' estimates hundreds of thousands, of messages. Each message is, in a sense, an advertisement—some overt (such as television commercials, radio commercials and the like), some covert (such as when your friends comment favorably on a particular restaurant). Each interaction you are involved in will influence your experience in some way, whether the interaction lasts only a moment or many hours. Can you think of any interaction in any context in which one person is *not* influencing another? In your internal dialogue, is there anything you can say to yourself that *doesn't* affect you in some way?

In recognizing that every communication has a capacity to influence, it becomes especially interesting to consider the dimensions of human beings that make the capacity to be influenced a factor in all relationships. The hypnotic relationship is only one particular context where this factor called "human suggestibility" operates.

Therapeutic intervention involves influencing other persons sufficiently to alter their experience of themselves. Therapy in *any* modality requires guiding the client from a state of distress and dissatisfaction with some portion of his experience to a new, more satisfying and useful way of living. Therapy requires the development of a more adaptive means for coping with life. Whatever form therapy takes, from pills to pillow fights, the client is learning to experience himself in a new way, one that allows for greater flexibility and inner satisfaction. How does a therapist do this? What is it a therapist says or does that influences the client in this way? Is this ability to influence a property of the therapist? Certainly the therapist's skill and knowledge are a factor. Is the ability to be influenced a property of the client? Certainly a motivation to change and a willingness to grow are factors. Is inducing change in the therapeutic context (or any other context, for that matter) an interaction of the two? The relationship between hypnotist and client (or you and your friend, or a barber and his customer, or a talkshow guest and the audience) is one that involves the unique characteristics of each party relating to the other. The characteristics of each affect the other, and an outcome of some sort is inevitable.

What is suggestibility? It is an openness to accepting new ideas, new information. As this new information is acquired, depending on its subjective value, it can alter the person's experience anywhere from a little to a lot. In the therapeutic interaction, the person to be influenced is, to some unknown degree, suggestible and wants to acquire new information or experience that will allow him to alleviate distress. The person is unhappy with some aspect of himself, and consequently is seeking help from someone else who might be able to say or do something to make a difference. Very few, if any, people are completely non-critical in accepting information, and so there is a recognizable difference between suggestibility and gullibility.

Suggestibility as a trait exists because of each human being's recognition that he or she is limited; no one person knows all there is to know about himself, or others, or any given subject. No matter how knowledgeable one is in an area, information is incomplete. As far as human beings developing what has been called "total self awareness," that is an idealistic impossibility. For as long as each person has an unconscious mind, there will be parts of each person that are "unconscious." As soon as one becomes aware of something, it is not unconscious anymore.

THE NEED FOR CLARITY AND CERTAINTY

When people experience uncertainty, both social psychology and common sense have taught us that other people become very important as sources of information. The old saying, "When in Rome, do as the Romans do," reflects the reliance on other people's judgments and behaviors as models of what to do when faced with uncertainty of what is proper. I wonder whether you can recall a situation you were in that was new to you, and how uncomfortable you felt because you really weren't sure whether you were doing things in the proper way. How much did you rely on others to guide your behavior? Almost everyone has had an experience like that. Of course, there is no assurance that the others are behaving properly, but at least you're not alone! The old Candid Camera television show was one that played on this theme by deliberately confusing people and enjoying their confusion as they would try to figure things out, desperately trying to make sense out of a nonsensical situation. This recognition of human nature, specifically the discomfort of confusion, is the basis for a very sophisticated hypnotic technique called, appropriately enough, the "Confusion Technique." This technique is described later.

Using this principal, it seems likely that a therapist will have some influence arising from the client's belief that she is mismanaging some portion of her life apparently outside of her control. Attempts at self-correction have failed, and the person then seeks out someone more knowledgeable than herself to learn from. The person who is sought out is a function of her own value system; some people would rather talk to a hairdresser than to a doctor, some would rather confide in a co-worker than in a psychologist, and still others would rather write a letter to "Dear Abby" than talk to anyone at all. Many people have a self-imposed stigma about seeking help for their problems, perhaps because of pride or ignorance. The point here is that some persons invest power in someone else who is apparently more knowledgeable than themselves. Their uncertainty turns them to others for an explanation or advice.

If one has attempted change and failed (who hasn't?), the suggestion may be accepted that one who is professionally trained in such matters will be able to help. The helping professional is more of an authority on a personal problem because she has been trained to recognize causes and treatments. The person seeking help has already accepted his own ignorance and power-lessness about the situation, and with a strong sense of hopefulness the therapist is looked to as the person who can make the hurt go away.

The quality of the relationship between the hypnotist and the subject has been referred to as a primary basis for the trance experience. This relationship is composed of multiple intangible variables, discussed throughout the remainder of this chapter.

THERAPIST POWER

When a person comes in for help to deal with a distressing problem, that person is making an investment in the therapist as a person of authority and, hopefully, a source of cure. Power is not typically something the therapist has in and of herself; rather, it is an acquired property from the person's reaction to her. A controversial experiment on power was done by Stanley Milgram (1974) several decades ago that illustrates quite dramatically how much power can be given to a person in a position of authority.

Milgram's experiment was actually done in a variety of ways, but each essentially involved deceiving naive experimental subjects, leading them to believe that they were involved in an experiment on learning. Directions were given to the naive subjects and to confederates (accomplices) of the experimenter that the purpose of the study was to discover whether the use of punishment, in the form of electrical shocks, would increase a subject's ability to learn word pairs. Naive subjects would be teachers, and confederates the learners. Teachers watched as the learners were strapped into a chair and hooked up to the shock-delivering electrodes. Then they were placed in a nearby room and positioned in front of the shock generator. Teachers were then instructed to deliver to learners a shock of increasing intensity with each incorrect response. Teachers were convinced that the learners were getting shocked, and as the shock levels escalated, the shrieks and pounding on the wall were further evidence that learners were truly being shocked at their initiation. In reality, learners were not being shocked at all. Most subjects in the teacher position were very anxious and reluctant to let the experiment progress, often turning to the experimenter for guidance. The experimenter's job was simply to say "You must go on. The experiment must continue."

More than 50% of the teachers delivered the highest shock level, at a point on the machine *past* the point labeled, "Danger: Severe Shock" and past the point where the learner became silent and may have been dead, for all the teacher knew. This experiment was based on the "obedience to authority" phenomenon that was evident in the Nuremberg War Crimes Trials following World War II, when many Nazis charged with atrocious crimes claimed as a defense that, "I was just following orders." If the person perceives that there are no viable alternatives open to her, she will follow orders even if destructive. Some subjects in Milgram's experiment, when told "You have no choice ... you must continue with the experiment," planted their arms firmly on their chests and said "I have a lot of choice, and I refuse." Such subjects were in the minority, however. By and large, the phenomenon of obedience to authority is observable in many contexts—business, education, even some intimate relationships are built on a markedly disproportionate balance of power.

Where does this power come from? The status of the therapist is one factor, her perceived expertness another. Probably the greatest power, however, comes from the role the therapist is in; the therapist-client relationship is generally not, perhaps never is, one of equals. The person coming in for help must divulge personal and sensitive information to a person about whom he knows very little—only professional status, and, for the more inquisitive, training. The client is in a position of revealing his problems, inadequacies, and fears to a person who seems to be going through life successfully and carefree for the most part. This is more or less true depending on the amount of self-disclosure an individual therapist feels comfortable in doing. Sometimes too much self-disclosure can hurt the relationship, other times not enough. Regardless, the relationship is characterized by the therapist being the expert, the authority, and a client's uncertainty or inability to detect personal choices can easily induce obedience to authority.

There are at least five different types of power: 1) coercive (derived from the ability to punish), 2) reward (derived from the ability to give benefits ranging from monetary to psychological), 3) legitimate (derived from position, including elected and selected positions), 4) expert (derived from greater knowledge in an area), and 5) referent power (derived from personal characteristics, such as likability or amiability). All five of these powers are operational in almost any context, to one degree or another, but are especially prevalent in the therapeutic context. The role of therapist can be a powerful one. The capacity for influence in using principles and techniques of clinical hypnosis must lead one to consider the dimension of power in relationships if one is to use power sensitively and with absolute respect for the integrity of the client.

THE NEED FOR ACCEPTANCE

The person seeking help, or information, is feeling deficient or incomplete in some way. A basic need people seem to have, which is the cornerstone of society, is other people. When one combines the feeling of deficiency with the need for others, the need for acceptance begins to emerge. One of the largest fears in the mind of the typical client coming in for help is, "If I disclose myself to you, with all my fears, doubts, and imperfections, will you like me and accept me? Or will you find me weak, repulsive, and somehow less than human?"

One of the more interesting pieces of research in the literature of social psychology is the work of Solomon Asch on conformity (see Aronson, 1984). Asch brought in three confederates to interact with a lone naive subject for an experiment on perception, or so he said. In reality, the experiment was one studying the dynamics of conformity, defined as a person changing behaviors, beliefs, or attitudes in the direction of others around her.

Asch presented a series of different sized lines, A, B, and C, and a fourth line, X. The task of the group members was to identify which of lines A, B, and C was closest in size to line X. The task was a very easy one—lines were generally of distinctly different sizes and the discrimination was simple. The first rounds, by design, found all four subjects in agreement. In later rounds, though, the confederates had been given instructions to give an obviously incorrect answer, generating a great deal of uncertainty in the naive subject. These same people who only a few moments ago were viewed as reliable now are giving answers that seem wrong! The typical naive subject was so confused that when the other three subjects all agreed on an answer that seemed wrong, the subject conformed and also gave that answer! Through earlier trials of total agreement, a group identity had formed, a group belongingness and agreement filling a very basic need of people. To disagree and act as non-conformist was too uncomfortable a prospect for many of Asch's subjects to bear. A basic principle guiding relationships according to the literature of social psychology and verifiable in your own experience is that similarity is rewarding, dissimilarity is punishing.

The need for acceptance and the need to belong are also factors present in the hypnotic relationship. Avoiding confrontations with the authority, doing things to please her (ranging from generating therapeutic results to knitting her a sweater), conforming to her language style, values, and theoretical ideas are all ways this need can be discovered within the therapy relationship. Relative to the discussion on power, this is where reward power becomes a considerable force in the process.

EXPECTATIONS

The role of expectations on experience is a profound one that has been demonstrated in numerous places and been called by many names. Probably the most widely used term is "self-fulfilling prophecy," describing the likelihood that what we expect to happen will happen, and, conversely, what we don't expect to happen will not.

When someone comes in for help, or for information, typically that person has an idea of how things are going to turn out. The idea that a person has about his future experience guides his present experiences in that direction. The more emotional investment the person has in that expectation, the less likely he is to experience anything that contradicts it. For example, if I have the idea that this problem I'm trying to solve is hopeless or unsolvable, potential solutions people offer me go untried, allowing my problem to remain unsolved, and unsolvable. This kind of process is called a "calibrated cycle" in the world of systems theory, and essentially it describes a mechanism whereby people can work very hard at staying the same.

A model of the condition called "depression," which all people experience on occasion, was developed by Martin Seligman a number of years ago which he called "Learned Helplesssness" (Seligman, 1975). Seligman's model describes the calibrated cycle of depression in a very useful way. His research, described here simplistically, involved giving rather painful electric shocks to two groups of dogs (a variation was later done with humans); one group of dogs was harnessed and could not escape the pain, while the second group of dogs was free to run away and escape the shock. The dogs were then placed in a large box that had a divider in its middle and wiring to deliver electric shocks on one of its halves. When shock was delivered to the dogs that had been shocked previously but were free to run away, the dogs taught themselves to jump over the divider to the safe side and escape the pain. When the dogs that had been harnessed were shocked, though, they would stand there, passively taking the pain, and do nothing to escape. In this situation the dogs were just as free as the others to escape hurt, but because of their prior learning experience that nothing could be done to escape pain, they did not even try to help themselves. When the researchers would grab the dogs and literally drag them to safety repeatedly, the dogs still did not learn to escape. They were depressed, with all the accompanying symptoms. Only after hundreds of trials did the dogs learn to escape.

(continued on p. 95)

FRAME OF REFERENCE: MARTIN E. P. SELIGMAN

There is virtually no possibility of taking even an introductory psychology course without being exposed to the work of Martin Seligman,

Ph.D. Seligman rose to fame at a relatively young age for his innovative work on what eventually became his "Learned Helplessness" model of depression. He observed that laboratory animals and human beings exposed to aversive, uncontrollable stimuli often developed what appeared to be signs of clinical depression. These observations have led to countless studies, reformulations, and, most importantly, deeper understanding of one of the most common disorders clinicians are asked to treat.

On His Research Beginnings: "When I got to graduate school at the University of Pennsylvania, what I was looking for basically was something that may be a model of some form of human suffering. When I saw dogs lying down in a shuttle box and not doing anything (even though there was an electric shock there), and even though the people around me, who were into learning theory at the time, were treating that as an annoyance, that seemed to me to be a phenomenon that modeled human suffering. I understood that it might be brought to bear on human suffering. So, I spent the next few years of my life trying to understand learned helplessness in dogs and rats."

On Helplessness and Depression: "I remember the first time someone told me about depression. Jim Geer, who is a behavior therapist, looked at my dogs one day being helpless, and he said, "Marty, that's depression." I said, "What's depression?" You know, in the mid-1960s, it was an unfashionable category. So, about that time I got to know [Aaron] Beck and his view of depression, and then began to think about helplessness as an explicit model of depression. But, helplessness to me didn't map exactly into depression, because there was a lot of depression it didn't cover and there were a lot of other things it didn't speak to; two of these were achievement (because giving up is so important there) and physical health. In the early 1980s, I started to work on achievement and health: attributional style, helplessness as a predictor of achievement, and as a predictor of immune response and physical health."

On Prevention: "I view the role of the clinical psychologist as possibly undergoing a radical change over the next 20 years. [I think] clinical psychologists will less and less take people who are already sick or who already have a problem and make them better, and more and more will take people who are well and arm them with tools preventatively. Thus, when these people face the slings and arrows of life that produce depression, for example, people will be better armed against them. Now, I'm talking prevention and I'm talking specifically for the set of things that helplessness and depression impact; so, I'm talking about depression, suicide, poor achievement, and physical incompetence.

"Jonas Salk, on the 30th anniversary of the first trials of his vaccine, said if he could do it all over again, he'd still do immunization, but he wouldn't do it biologically. He'd take the tools that have been learned in the therapeutic endeavor in the last 20 years and apply them to young kids and use them preventatively. I agree with him."

Source: Personal communication, 1988.

Seligman's research is a fine example of how people can so convince themselves they are helpless that they cannot recognize any possibilities not accounted for in that view.

A less serious example of the same phenomenon is one that almost everyone has experienced. Have you ever looked for something, really searching hard for it, only to discover later that you have been looking directly at it all along but didn't see it because it wasn't where it was supposed to be? One's expectations clearly do affect one's experience.

Expectations can either work for or against the attainment of desired outcomes. Persons seeking you out because they have been referred by someone you impressed are coming in with a positive expectation about you that will work in your favor, increasing the likelihood of your being able to impress that person, too.

Expectation is crucial to outcome in any healing process. The role of beliefs in cultures considered primitive by our standards is evidenced in the power of witch doctors and practitioners of voodoo. A strong belief that sticking pins in a doll with your likeness can hurt you is very likely to generate some interesting effects when someone does so. On a more sophisticated level, many of the things that are considered basic to a professional practice are intended to build positive expectations on the part of the client. Why hang your diplomas on a wall? Why print business cards with a fancy title? Why adopt a professional demeanor other than to instill confidence?

Many hypnosis rituals out of the older, traditional model are geared specifically to building positive expectations in the subject that she can have, or is having, the experience of trance. Many of the tests associated with susceptibility measures discussed earlier are present solely to convince the subject that she has experienced some altered state. For example, when a subject is given suggestions for being unable to open her eyes ("eye catalepsy") and then is challenged to do so, if she passes that test by being unable to open her eyes, then she is convinced she is in a trance state. This creates a greater receptivity to further suggestions of the hypnotist.

Building expectations in clients can be done in a variety of ways: through one's mannerisms, dress, furniture, reputation, promise of results, attitude, and others. I know of one therapist, for example, who tells all new clients who call that his schedule is booked up solid and he cannot see them for two weeks (even though he really does have time for them). His belief is that by making the client more anxious to come in, he will instill higher expectations in them because he is so busy and therefore must be good. Social psychology has shown that the harder a goal is to attain, the more valuable it is perceived to be. This practical therapist uses that strategy to build up expectations of his potential value.

For therapists of extraordinary reputation, the reputation often makes their job remarkably easy. During the later years of Milton Erickson's life, for example, people came from all over the world to experience him and his techniques. Many of them came hundreds or thousands of miles to be put in a trance by him, and into trance they went!

What it takes to build positive expectations in a person varies from individual to individual. Skill in finding out what a person needs in order to build positive expectations can be a real asset to getting the therapeutic process going.

THE NEED FOR INTERNAL HARMONY

Often when I flip through magazines, I am astonished by the claims made by many products advertised for sale through the mail. There are weight loss products that guarantee this product is so good that one can lose weight just by looking at it (slight exaggeration); there are books for sale that assure you of being able to acquire the dynamic personality that will get you into the most elite social circles (and even how to "use hypnosis to pick up girls"!); there are products for sale that promise to clear up your skin, grow your hair, cure your arthritis, improve your vision, turn your house into a showcase, liven up your hamburger, and on and on . . .

Who buys these things? Who is Bill K., and who is Mary R., who are both quoted in almost every ad as saying how this product gave them a reason to go on living?

Actually, this is a modern version of an old theme. Now the testimonials are in print as a part of the advertisement, to show you, the skeptical buyer, that real people not unlike yourself have purchased this product and experienced peace with the universe as a result. One hundred years ago, the medicine show was a con man traveling in a covered wagon from town to town, with a confederate (or two) sent in advance, who would publicly purchase a bottle of the "Doc Marvel Health Tonic" and experience relief from every known ailment. Others wanting similar relief would purchase the tonic; mysteriously, they would feel better, too.

Certainly, the person's expectation, a placebo effect, is at work in such instances, but there is also another factor to consider in operation here: the need for internal consistency, or harmony, based on Leon Festinger's "cognitive dissonance" concept (1957). Human beings have a desire to alleviate confusion and contradictions within, and can do so by omitting contradictory bits of information or by twisting such information around until it all fits comfortably. People have a strong desire to feel certain, and when in an uncertain frame of mind, perhaps because of the novelty of the situation, they will turn to others to find out what is proper. The more the explanation fits their personal needs, the more easily the explanation is taken in at a deeper level. There was an old gold miner once, the story goes, who came in off the dusty trail and went into the town saloon. He was very excited and bursting with pride as he showed all the townsfolk the huge diamond he had just purchased from a stranger passing through. When the local jeweler got a good look at the fist-sized rock, he said "Old Man, what makes you think this here's a real diamond?" The old man said "Damn well better be or I been cheated out of a buck and a half!"

In an illustrative piece of research by Schachter and Singer (1962), the point about uncertainty and turning to others to explain one's feelings is made clear. When one is chased by a bear and experiences a rapid pulse and heart rate, one can easily attribute the changes to fear. What if one experiences those effects, but has no apparent explanation for why? Schachter and Singer's experiment involved injecting subjects either with epinephrine, a synthetic form of adrenaline causing physiological excitation, or with a placebo. Subjects were told they were receiving a vitamin supplement. Some of the subjects were told they would experience an increased heart rate as a side effect of the drug, but other subjects were not told. For those subjects who were not told of the side effects of the epinephrine, what were they to conclude when their hearts started to pound in their chests and their hands began to shake? Because they did not know what to make of it, they incorporated within themselves the reactions of those around them.

Confederates of the experimenter were introduced into the experiment, and subjects were told that this subject was also given an injection of the vitamin supplement. The confederate had been given instructions on how to behave—in some instances as if euphoric, in others angry. Experimental subjects, uncertain as to the cause of their reactions, behaved in the same manner as the confederate. When subjects were certain of the cause of their reactions, the behavior of those nearby had little or no effect.

The ambiguity of subjects' feelings led them to adopt others' perspectives. Relative to hypnosis, the experience of hypnosis is a subjective, often ambiguous, one that sometimes leads the client to ask, "Was I hypnotized?" If you choose to answer directly by saying something like, "Yes, did you notice the change in your breathing, and the changes in your . . . ," most likely the client will adopt your perspective of the interaction as his own!

The need for cognitive consistency surfaces as a need, more or less depending on the individual, to have some benefit from having paid for and received professional help. When people invest money, hope, and time in something, they desperately want it to work, even if "only a little." There is the need to justify the investment to themselves. This need is evident in the testimonials of people who have bought products that are virtually valueless, whose benefit was derived solely from their own expectations.

Of course, the flip side to this is the role of expectation and cognitive consistency when the person views herself as a hopeless case, and will go to great lengths to prove it. Some people, like the ones who go on stage to prove they cannot be "hypnotically controlled," have a need to prove their commitment to failure. The patient who has been to every doctor in town and is proud of her inability to be helped is a perfect example; the client who spends years in psychotherapy going from therapist to therapist is another.

Testimonials in ads are sometimes a deceptive ploy, made up by the advertiser. Often, however, they are the true feelings of a consumer who attributes great power to the useless product. After all, it cost $4.98, plus tax. And mailing.

COMMUNICATION STYLE

The style of communication is a significant factor in suggestibility. By communication style, I refer to the manner with which you convey information to your client. There are many different styles, each having a different impact on how receptive the person will be to the information you present.

Widely utilized are the five communication styles prominent family therapist Virginia Satir (1972) described:

1. *Placating*—a self-sacrificing, always-trying-to-please "yes-man" kind of style in which the predominant message is one communicating no self-worth.
2. *Blaming*—a fault-finding, bossy, superior-acting dictator, whose predominant message is one communicating unquestionable right.
3. *Computing*—a very reasonable, cool and calm person with a sophisticated rationale for everything, no apparent feelings, and whose predominant message is one of unfailing logic.
4. *Distracting*—an irrelevant, tangential and off-the-mark person who goes nowhere while sidetracking everywhere. The predominant message is one of not fitting in.
5. *Leveling*—a sensitive and understanding response, carrying acknowledgment and a willingness to resolve the issues at hand. The predominant message of the leveler is one of openness and a desire to reach a worthwhile goal at the expense of no one.

(continued on p. 101)

FRAME OF REFERENCE: VIRGINIA M. SATIR

Is there a psychotherapist anywhere who is unfamiliar with the work of Virginia Satir, A.C.S.W.? For four decades, Satir was central in the development of the field of family therapy. Her often simple, but never simplistic, views of the family and its effect on health, illness, and self-esteem have virtually revolutionized concepts and techniques of psychotherapy. Satir's intense belief in the inherent positive capacities of humans led her virtually all over the world sharing her vision. Everywhere she went, she was appreciated and admired, and it is obvious that her message of "community" was and will continue to be a timely one.

On Pathology: "The standard for professionals in mental health was to practice in terms of psychopathology. I wasn't doing that—I felt it was a dead horse. Freud was one of my heroes as far as his willingness to go out on a limb and find some things which we needed to know which are in our insides. We carry the seeds for our direction and our destruction or construction, and that was a different notion from when we were at a place where we didn't know that so we thought everything came from the outside. The psychoanalytic model, per se, I know it well. I was taught it, but because of its emphasis on the pathological, it was limited in what it could do to help."

On Health: "That's going against the grain—to work on health. Some say that's only 'soft' when you work on health. People miss the whole point that what grows in your garden is where it's fertile. If there are dead spots in your garden, you help by making them fertile, adding some things to them. I knew that that was an important thing, and I knew that that would break the back of our current pathological thinking if enough people got there. Then we'd have in this world a whole lot of people trained to be mental *health* practitioners."

On Growing: "I think that growing pains are always present and they are often hurtful. We've gone through a lot of growing pains, and while there are still a lot of people who are looking for the one 'right' way, that is diminishing. We are more apt to listen to other people, and I think that's a good thing. What we have to learn is how we can feel a sense of our own grounding without at the same time wearing blinders— and I see a lot of that changing. I can only approach this with hope."

On Family Systems: "I was talking about the fact that there is no one to blame. There are actions, reactions and interactions, which is what a system is as opposed to a linear model. That's how a family works— there is no one to blame. You, the husband of the family, you're doing what you learned. You, the wife in the family, are doing the same thing, and you are not doing it out of perversity, you're doing it out of the best that you know. Instead of seeing things as only linear, you know they are all related and it's a systemic organization rather than a linear one. There is no such thing as a single variable. Well, it takes a long time for that to move. I see that as so basic to our present century's knowledge, as basic as the knowledge that the world is round instead of flat."

On Milton Erickson: "I was scared to death of hypnosis, because for me it was a form of control—that was because of my ignorance, but nevertheless, that's how it was. When Milton came, I saw him make motions and I watched him in groups and it was frightening. So, I didn't do much with him; I got out of the room when he came—I was scared! Later [I began to like him] as I came to know him a little bit more. Maybe Milton changed too, I don't know. But I know that in the last years of his life, I understood something about him that I hadn't understood before. Whether it was true before or not, I felt in the last years of his life that he was a kind man and that he really wanted to help people and that his motivations were human and loving."

Source: Personal communication, 1988.

The Satir categories (on p. 99) are useful for describing general positions one might take in an interaction. If a hypnotist wants to get a message across, the hypnotist must consider what style of communication this person is likely to respond to in the desired way. Should the interaction be one of rationality and reason, or would an emotional appeal perhaps work better? Should the techniques used be direct or indirect? Should the position adopted be a supportive one, or a confrontive one? Would it be better to be demanding of this person, or nondemanding? Will an incongruent message ("mixed message") have greater impact, or a congruent one?

The structures of suggestions are dealt with later; suffice it to say here that there are a variety of ways to approach another person, and no one style is going to be effective in all instances.

CONCLUSION

Each of the factors of human suggestibility discussed in this chapter is only a piece of the pie—to be considered as a part of the hypnotic interaction but not its sum total.

There are no set rules about what makes for the most influential communication. What appeals to one person will not appeal to another. Some people appreciate and seek out professional help, others would rather seek out the advice of a friendly neighbor. Some people want to be told what to do in a step-by-step fashion and follow such directions happily, others fight such directions and want to be left alone to figure things out for themselves. Some respond better if they have to go through demands to reach a goal (e.g., a therapist with a waiting list is a frustration to a new client who may perceive that therapist as better when she finally does get to see him), while others won't even consider putting up with such demands (if faced with a waiting list they'll just see another therapist). Some require scientific evidence for everything they hear, others are suspicious of science and of those who promote its beliefs. Some open up to the ideas of others when confused, others close off and resolve the confusion within themselves even if with misinformation.

In order to be truly influential, discovering where (*not* whether) a person is open to suggestion (and everybody is at *some* level) is the task of the clinician. It is the suggestibility of each individual that makes change possible, and allows growth to take place. The process of discovering what your client wants and how to best reach him is the process of acquiring rapport, arising when your client feels you have an understanding of his experience. Principles of suggestibility discussed throughout this section have addressed better ways to attain an understanding of and a rapport with the people you encounter, regardless of context.

For Discussion

1. What commercials seem to have the most impact on your buying behavior? What makes them so influential?

2. What products or services do you feel almost entirely ignorant about (for example, car repairs, dental work, etc.)? How does this affect your role as a consumer?

3. Do you think Milgram's experiment on "Obedience to Authority" would have the same results today? Why or why not?

4. Describe an example or two of times when you gave in to peer group pressure. How did you feel? What penalties did you think you'd face by not conforming? Did you have control of yourself?

5. Describe an example or two in which you obeyed an authority when you thought he or she was wrong in demanding what was asked of you. Why did you obey? How did you feel at the time?

6. What impresses you? How does someone create positive expectations in you?

7. How does a therapist have each of the five powers described in this chapter?

Things to Do

1. Interview a number of physicians in regard to their ideas about the "placebo effect." What is their description of the phenomenon, and how do they account for it? What kinds of cases, if any, do they employ it in?

2. List some of your most valued characteristics. How do you react when you are given feedback that contradicts your beliefs about yourself? Does your belief change? Why or why not?

3. List the feelings or situations in which you find yourself most responsive to others. How might you say things or do things that would create these same feelings in someone else?

8

Mind Matters

How successful you are in applying hypnotic patterns is largely dependent on how well you are able to structure and transmit messages that are meaningful to the receiver. Prior to structuring and transmitting a suggestion, you must determine what you want the suggestion to do—what kind of response or experience it is intended to facilitate in the client. Then you can determine what specific approach to use on the basis of your assessment of the client's needs and personality. There are many ways to structure almost any message, and these structures will be explored in detail later.

Knowing what you want to accomplish in a given interaction is the best of all starting points in formulating suggestions, but simply knowing what you would like to accomplish is not enough. There must be a viable means for attaining the desired result. For example, if you want to help a client extricate herself from a destructive relationship that she wants to leave yet feels unable to, that may be a worthwhile therapeutic goal. How can you say or do something to the client in such a way as to allow her to find the resources within herself to make it possible to leave? There are probably hundreds of different ways for you to communicate your intent to the client—how do you know which approach will have the desired impact?

Many points regarding human nature were raised earlier in order to encourage awareness of the many factors you must necessarily take into consideration when choosing a structure and style for your suggestions. Adequate understanding of the dynamics of interpersonal power, conformity, cognitive dissonance, self-esteem, and other such variables can help you choose an approach for a given client that is more likely to succeed. In this chapter, characteristics of the mind relative to the processing of hypnotic suggestions will be discussed. Familiarity with these characteristics can further increase the likelihood of choosing an approach that can succeed.

What is "suggestion"? In the traditional perspective, a hypnotist's communication had "the power" to cause unusual experiences in the suggestion's receiver. We know now, of course, that only a small part of "the power" is in the words spoken. The word "suggestion" is not inaccurate to describe the communication patterns of hypnosis. "Giving a suggestion" is simply the offering of a piece of information to someone else (heterosuggestion, heterohypnosis) or to one's self (autosuggestion, autohypnosis). "Suggesting" is the act of offering information, and except for the Godfather's offer that can't be refused, *any* suggestion can be either accepted or rejected. The skill of a good hypnotist is in her ability to maneuver the client into a position of accepting the suggestion, or at least a position of not rejecting the suggestion (thus a passive acceptance that can serve as a basis for accepting later suggestions that may be more actively responded to).

Communication in any context has multiple components. Even at this simplest level of analysis, the quality of the relationship between these two components can determine how a message is received and interpreted. For example, if I say the words, "I would like to be open with you in discussing this matter" while I simultaneously cross my legs, fold my arms across my chest, look away, and hunch over, my guess is most people would tend to doubt the sincerity of my words. Such a contradictory message is called an "incongruent communication," or, more commonly, a "mixed message." Congruity of communication is one factor to take into account when formulating and responding to communication. How can one send or receive and respond to messages that are contradictory on verbal and nonverbal levels? The answer to that question has to do with the very nature of the human mind.

A most significant factor in hypnotic communication is the response of the conscious and unconscious minds to a message. The communications one is exposed to may be experienced to some degree on a conscious level where they are processed in a characteristic fashion. The same communications, however, are also simultaneously processed at an unconscious level in a different fashion. Much of what one experiences in one's interactions does not get processed at the conscious level at all; in using hypnotic patterns, suggestions are deliberately formed in order to convey meaning to the client's unconscious mind while her conscious mind is preoccupied elsewhere. Acknowledging the differences between conscious and unconscious characteristics is immediately relevant to the formulation of effective suggestions.

CONSCIOUS AND UNCONSCIOUS CHARACTERISTICS

One of the great events in the evolution of the human species, so the story goes, was the development of consciousness. There are those who claim other species besides humans have consciousness, too, but it is of interest here to discuss only the human mind. The fact that human beings have both conscious and unconscious minds makes for a very interesting set of capabilities. The use of sophisticated tools, the creation of civilization, and the large degree of mastery over the earth are ample evidence of human mindpower.

The conscious and unconscious minds have a different set of functions, but also share a considerable number of functions between them. The overlap allows them to work together, while the differences can and often do surface in internal conflict. The conscious mind is defined as that part of the mind that allows you to be aware of things; whenever you pay attention to something or when you are aware of noticing something, you are conscious of it. The things in one's immediate awareness are in one's conscious mind. The conscious mind has the ability to analyze things, to reason, and to make judgments about what is right or wrong. It is the conscious mind that very rationally (or so it rationalizes) decides what is possible to do and what is not possible to do. Consequently, the limitations in one's life are limitations based on the conscious mind's critical appraisal of experience. A person tells herself she would like to be able to assert herself, for example, but she tells herself she "can't." In terms of suggestion formation, if a suggestion is given that causes enough conflict within the client for her to notice the conflict, she is most likely to respond to it by rejecting the source of the conflict, namely the conflicting suggestions. Bypassing the client's conscious mind and its critical nature is fundamental to successful utilization of the more complex trance phenomena.

The conscious mind, powerful and wonderful as it is, is also the most limited part of us. How many things can you pay attention to at one time? Can you read this sentence, understand it, and also be aware of the sensation in your ring finger? Or not until I direct your attention to it? Awareness is limited to a very few things at a time, and if too much comes in at one time, the mind selectively attends to whatever is given high priority based on personal values, motivation, experience, and other such factors. Selective attention is a characteristic of hypnosis in the client's focusing on the clinician's communications. Beyond the hypnotic interaction, selective attention is a general characteristic of human information processing. One cannot pay attention to everything at once, and so the world is reduced to a manageable level through the conscious or unconscious selection of focal points. Communication to absorb and occupy the client's conscious mind is the starting point in the hypnotic interaction; such communication is called an "induction."

The unconscious mind is that part of the person that is a reservoir of all the experiences acquired throughout his lifetime. One's experience, learnings, manner (drives, motivations, needs) for interacting with one's world, and one's automatic functioning in countless behaviors each day are all evidence of unconscious functions. The unconscious mind is, in contrast to the conscious mind, not as rigid, analytical, and, most importantly, limited. It responds to experiential communications, is capable of symbolic interpretation, and tends to be global in view.

While a hypnotized client has her conscious mind occupied, absorbed and focused through the process of selective attention, she is still processing information at an unconscious level. The conscious mind is either unaware of it altogether, as in deeply dissociated states called "somnambulism," or has some limited degree of awareness but is not responsive to it by choice. For example, assuming your attention is selectively focused on what you are reading here because you are interested in learning about hypnosis, your consciousness is involved in the reading process. If you are engaged in what you are reading, then you are either unaware of the routine things occurring around you, or you have some awareness of them but choose not to respond to them because you do not want to be distracted from reading. If someone else is nearby and calls you by name, for example, perhaps you do not hear her at all. Or, perhaps, you hear her in the "back of your mind," but are too involved in reading to respond; you'd rather not divert your attention. And when she finally calls you for the fourth time and says, "Dammit, I'm talking to you!" you have an experience of awareness inside indicating to you that you have heard her all along!

UNCONSCIOUS PROCESSING

Just because a person is not aware of taking in information doesn't mean the person hasn't internalized any. Information that is integrated at an unconscious level can be as powerful as information that is processed at the conscious level, and often more so. While a client is in a trance state, her conscious mind will inevitably wander about from thought to thought, and for those periods of time that can be long or short, the client's unconscious mind continues to take in the clinician's suggestions, and is still quite capable of responding to them. Generally, the client will not remember the suggestions (amnesia), but they are at work in her unconscious mind nonetheless. Interestingly, many times clients of mine will come back, or call, quite some time after our therapy session and describe to me "new" insights and learnings that have caused a beneficial change in their experience of themselves. When they tell me what they've realized, almost word for word it will be things I said to them while they were in trance. The important learning is experienced as arising "spontaneously." I never point out my role, though, for their learnings and changes belong to them.

The unconscious mind can process information at a more symbolic, metaphorical level than the conscious mind. While the conscious mind is occupied with rationally analyzing the words, it is the unconscious that is more concerned with meanings. This is the basis for the multiple level nature of hypnotic communication—using wording and phrasing of suggestions to appeal at one level to the client's conscious mind by matching its understanding of things, while simultaneously providing possibilities of new understandings to the unconscious mind. The mechanisms for doing so will be described in detail in later chapters.

THE UNCONSCIOUS AND SYMPTOM FORMATION

The metaphorical nature of the unconscious mind may be more easily understood when we consider the nature of symptoms. How does a person develop a particular symptom? Why do two different people under similar stresses react with different symptoms? Symptoms may be thought of as metaphors for the client's experience. For example, a man who feels helpless or victimized in an intimate relationship, in my experience, is a man more likely to develop an erectile dysfunction than a man who does not feel helpless. "Impotent" literally and metaphorically means powerless. When the relationship dynamics change so that the power is distributed more evenly in the relationship, the impotence can stop being a problem. In this example, the symptom is not just a symbol of what is happening within the person, but is symbolic of the relationships he forms in which that symptom arises.

Most clinicians I have encountered acknowledge quite readily symptoms as metaphors for the client's experience. Their use of that information, though, has generally taken the form of trying to provide the client with insights about his unconscious needs. In short, they try to force unconscious information into the client's consciousness; it seems to me, though, that if the client wanted it there, his unconscious would have allowed him that. Furthermore, if the client doesn't make the transfer of the unconscious information the clinician wants brought into consciousness, the client's lack of insight is deemed uncooperative. In fact, he's really just protecting himself. Unless the clinician is willing to outright admit that he is imposing his own values onto the client, the clinician can respect the client's desire to keep information unconscious. The clinician's role is not necessarily to impose his solutions on the client, but rather can be to help the client find his own solutions in a way that is acceptable to him. Realistically, imposing one's values and beliefs on the client is an inevitable byproduct of the therapeutic relationship, but it is to be minimized, in my opinion, while maximizing respect for that person's integrity.

Understanding the unconscious, metaphorical nature of the client's symptoms leads to a different level of appreciation for the makeup of the person, and it suggests an alternative to the very rational, cognitive, intellectual approach of many psychotherapies. The symptom is formed at an unconscious level. No client I have ever experienced has made a conscious decision to have a problem. I've never heard anyone say, "Gee, I think I'll develop a migraine headache since things are a little slow today," or "Well, I wonder how it will spice this day up some if I develop hysterical paralysis." No, these and other symptoms are byproducts of the person's unconscious mind.

Just as symptoms are symbols of experience, they are often coping mechanisms that may have made a great deal of sense in the context in which they arose. For example, what better way to prevent intimacy and all its associated risks than to develop some symptom, such as depression or non-communicativeness, that prevents it? The symptom isn't a symptom, though, until the person has the experience of wanting intimacy, and then discovers she is unable to attain it. Then is when it is identified as a problem, and what once served a useful purpose is now a hindrance to happiness.

The unconscious mind's contribution to a person's experience highlights the need to be able to communicate with the unconscious; hypnosis is the most effective tool I know of for this purpose. If the symptom is unconscious and metaphorical, why should the treatment only be conscious, rational and intellectual? It seems apparent, to me at least, that a conscious approach is valuable to some degree and in some contexts, but a therapy that appeals to the unconscious can often be of greater value.

TREATMENT AT AN UNCONSCIOUS LEVEL

If the symptom is metaphorical, so can its treatment be. The opportunity to communicate through a variety of mechanisms (detailed in the later chapter "Structuring Suggestions") with the client's unconscious mind is a more respectful approach to addressing her needs without having to confront her conscious fears and limitations. Furthermore, such communication is more respectful of her personal integrity because it operates in a way that does not force the clinician's values into her conscious mind through cognitive restructuring. Rather, such communication allows the client the opportunity to keep unconscious whatever she wishes to, and likewise to make conscious what she cares to. Often, a client will open up with information from the unconscious at opportune moments in the therapy simply because the clinician has not been demanding (i.e., threatening), and the client's unconscious has now made the choice that she is ready to deal with this information.

For many people, this is where the misconception about hypnosis having the ability to make people say or do things against their will comes from; information comes out that they did not consciously expect to discover or release, yet the client's unconscious mind has made a choice that "now is the time and this is the place" to finally unload useless baggage. My belief after years of having people come out with unexpected but powerful information in this sort of way is this: It takes control to lose control. It takes a trust of one's self and a trust for the person and place, *a lot of* control therefore, to let one's self let go of one's emotions.

Perhaps this story will illustrate the point I am making. When I first began training in hypnosis (under a skilled clinician by the name of Neil Simon in Ann Arbor, Michigan), I worked with a woman who had come to the office to quit smoking. Helping someone to stop injuring themselves through the inhalation of toxic gases is not a particularly difficult procedure in most instances, and is generally the kind of intervention that is brief and superficial in nature. Inducing trance went smoothly, and as I began to utilize her trance state for her stated purpose, an ambulance happened to go by, its siren blaring. For a moment that seemed an observable eternity to me, she stopped breathing, her face went white and then red, and her body tensed up everywhere. A moment later, she began crying hysterically, for she was certain that her son who had been killed in the Viet Nam War years ago was in that ambulance that had gone by. Her emotions were very intense, and while I was not expecting the session to be an intense one of this type, I was aware that this woman had made a choice. She needed to resolve her grief and anger, and in this case her smoking was apparently of secondary importance to her. She made the choice to resolve her grief in my office with me. Apparently, she trusted me enough to give herself the opportunity to relieve her hurt with my guidance. Unexpected as her emotional release was, is that losing control or using control? Certainly, she had heard ambulances in recent years without reacting that way. Why did she react that way at that moment and in that context other than to use the opportunity to feel better, to grow?

In supporting her, guiding her, encouraging her, and helping her gain a perspective on her loss and her responsibilities to herself, what started out as a session for stopping smoking became a turning point in her life. She was not out of control nor was hypnosis forcing her to reveal something against her will. Rather, it was a choice to acknowledge feelings that had been buried along with her young son. How and why she made that choice (was it my age, my name, my height, or some other unconscious association?) is not known, nor was it necessary to know. The point is, the client's unconscious mind is capable of making choices, and those choices should be respected.

In Paul Watzlawick's book *The Language of Change* (1978), he described eloquently the need to communicate with the unconscious mind of the client in order to be as influential as possible in altering her experience of herself. Rather than the intellectual, computer-like jargon that appeals to the limited conscious mind of the client, language that is descriptive, emotional, and appealing to the senses is language that will make greater contact with the client's powerful unconscious mind. More will be said on this later; suffice it to say here that the unconscious mind of each person is a most powerful, competent, and resourceful dimension of the total person. The strength of hypnosis lies in its capacity for helping the client gain greater access to the dormant resources she has within herself.

FRAME OF REFERENCE: PAUL WATZLAWICK

For those therapists who are knowledgeable about systemic viewpoints of psychotherapy, the name Paul Watzlawick, Ph.D., is already very familiar. Watzlawick and his colleagues at the Mental Research Institute (MRI) in Palo Alto, California, have been at the center of the revolution in thinking about relationships and psychotherapy for nearly three decades. The many books Watzlawick authored and co-authored with his colleagues are considered to be among the most elaborate and lucid descriptions of the nature of hypnosis and strategic psychotherapy, including such well known titles as *Change* (1974), *The Language of Change* (1978), *How Real is Real?* (1976), *Pragmatics of Human Communication* (1967), and *The Situation is Hopeless, But Not Serious* (1983).

On Joining MRI and Shifting Perspectives: "The Bateson group was outstandingly interesting and I decided to go to Palo Alto for six months, maybe a year, and see what they were doing. . . . This has now been 27 years! When I got there, the Bateson group had already brought out their most important contribution—the double-bind theory. . . . Haley had written some of his very revolutionary books. Jackson was doing a kind of therapy that left me speechless, because it was so elegant and so 'here and now' oriented; he worked with a minimum of history. Then I had not yet met Erickson, but Jay Haley and John Weakland had been to Phoenix many times, had interviewed, worked with, and watched Erickson, and brought back the idea that if you can get people to behave differently then they may find different ways of coping with their problems, without necessarily arriving at an insight.

"I slipped into this 'cybernetic' thinking. It made sense to me immediately. Needless to say, there was a difficult period of adaptation, giving up the Jungian view with its emphasis on the intrapsychic and coming over to a view that from a Jungian or even a Freudian point of view is terribly superficial because it does not go into the causes. But it was less difficult than I would have imagined. It aroused my interest. Bateson had a marvelous way of getting people to see things in his new, systemic interactional way . . . and then to see Jackson work and bring about change, to see Jackson do therapy within the first 10 minutes of the first interview, that really was amazing."

On "Truth" and Results: "I would say that to assume that human problems arise in relations rather than intrapsychically, to me, seems the more useful, effective approach. It doesn't mean that it is 'true,' in any metaphysical sense. The goal of science can only be the development of useful methods for a given purpose. If it works, then it is all right. Now, the moment I say this, someone will immediately accuse me of a crass utilitarianism, that it is immoral to concentrate only on outcomes, etc., for very much the same reason that Erickson was accused of being a manipulator who tricked people. Sure, if you take the moral stance, that you should never say something you don't believe, then you can never use a reframing, because you are saying something you may not 'really believe.'

"Every medicine can also harm. This is no news. It is well-known in the medical field, especially, that that which helps one person can harm another person. Anybody who comes for help, on the other hand, signals not directly, but indirectly, 'Change me ... do something with me to get me out of my predicament.'

"Therefore, any act of helping is, if you will, manipulation. What else? If I pull a drowning man out of the water, jump after him and save him, I have manipulated him. There is no question but that those paragons of morality will say, 'Oh no, this is different, and in that case, it is all right.' If I use a reframing, why am I untrue at the moment? Bear in mind the absolute destructive potential of so-called 'truth.' What these people usually demand of us is that we never say anything we don't really believe. This is hypocrisy in its own right, because it is based on the assumption that whatever wells up from the depth of my being is 'the truth.' Bloody nonsense!

"If I claim to be a therapist, and therefore a helper, then the parameters of my endeavors or the whole purpose of my activity is to help. Helping presupposes certain actions that are helpful. For me, this is the ethics of my profession, not to harm."

On Observing the System: "I prefer to see the so-called [family] system in operation in my office. I may then continue seeing only one person, but that's the person who, from my understanding of how the system functions, seems to be my best, most promising entry into the system. He seems to be the one who is most likely to be willing to carry out something. In the case of the delinquent, rebellious teenager for instance, I know that I am not going to get very far with him sitting there. I want to see how he behaves, I want to see how the parents react to his behavior, but very often, after a session, I think, now I got a certain idea of how this system functions and keeps itself in trouble."

On Milton Erickson's Therapy Tasks: "I believe that where Erickson asked for some potentially dangerous behavior, or gave prescriptions that seemed to be potentially dangerous, with his enormous intuition and with his clinical experience, and with the humanity of his approach, he had reason to believe that with this particular person, he could afford to do this. In our case, not being Erickson, we believe that the nature of our interventions seems outlandish only to the outside observer. What we take into account before we make an intervention is the attempted solution. This is the cornerstone of our approach. We try to find out what people have done so far in order to deal with their difficulty. And we know that they wouldn't sit in our office if that particular problem-solving behavior were successful. As you look at what they are doing, you find this is the very thing that feeds into the maintenance of the problem."

On Erickson's Critics: "He is bound to be criticized by people who, basing themselves, for instance, on a psychodynamic model, will say, this is cosmetic, superficial symptom-removal. What about the underlying conflict that is not touched upon? They're saying he is wrong, because 'in our view, this shouldn't be done.' But, that's the very thing that I am trying to oppose—the idea that 'I have found the truth, and therefore everybody else who doesn't see it the way I see it is wrong.' "

Source: Personal Communication, 1987.

IN DEFENSE OF THE MIND

The fact that information can be and often is processed without conscious awareness is a major factor in the fear many have that destructive or harmful information from the hypnotist is going to get in at an unconscious level and wreak havoc in the individual. What most people have not yet developed is an appreciation of the mind's uncanny ability to protect itself. Every student of psychology, and anyone who has spent some time in the company of other people, learns about the classic defense mechanisms people employ to ward off threats from entering consciousness. The classic defenses such as repression, projection, rationalization, sublimation, and all the others are unconscious coping mechanisms; no one consciously says, "I can't accept responsibility for my feelings so I think I'll attribute these feelings to that person over there" (e.g., projection). The defenses are unconscious, and are rooted in the person's need for self-esteem and the desire to avoid internal conflict if at all possible. These defenses are certainly relevant to hypnosis, and can demonstrate my point about the safety of the unconscious mind. Its safe nature is further illustrated by other factors, described next, that maintain the mind's ability to function normally.

In describing the selective nature of attention, I made the point that one's motivations and priorities help determine what one will consciously attend to. At the same time, of course, one is also determining what *not* to pay attention to. The conscious mind cannot process more than a few things simultaneously, and although the unconscious mind is not as limited in its abilities to process input, it also has an upper limit. It can't process *everything* all at once.

In order for the mind to function in a healthy way, it cannot handle too much stimulation, a condition often called "sensory overload." There are neurological limitations of the human body, and when the mechanisms that reduce the huge amounts of stimulation of a whole universe of energy to a level manageable for the fragile human being fail, the results can be disastrous. Some of the psychoses are illustrative of what happens to an individual who cannot filter out the overwhelming amount of sensory stimuli in an environment considered routine to "normal" others. Selective attention is a necessary coping mechanism. This is one reason why anyone who can focus, even a little, can experience hypnosis meaningfully.

Likewise, too little stimulation of the senses, a condition called "sensory isolation" or "sensory deprivation," is also an unhealthy condition for the mind. Normal functioning requires continuous stimulation of the senses; when such stimulation is absent for extended periods of time, the mind is quite likely to manufacture its own in the form of hallucinations. The unconscious mind has a defense for this condition as well: It's called "boredom," an unpleasant internal state that motivates one to seek stimulation. The nature of the mind relative to amounts and kinds of stimulation is a relatively recent area of inquiry. John Lilly (see McConnell, 1983) pioneered research in this area with his intriguing research in sensory isolation several decades ago, and the isolation tanks ("samadhi tanks") that many "New Age" help centers are using in the treatment of emotional problems are a direct spinoff.

Related to sensory isolation is the "brainwashing" phenomenon, since isolation for extended periods of time is a typical first step. When one is removed from all that is familiar and is craving sensory input from virtually anywhere, inputs that would be ignored in a routine environment can have a profound impact. The mind's need for just enough but not too much stimulation carries with it some serious implications. Some practitioners are using such techniques as sensory isolation coupled with subliminal suggestions, the effects of which are not yet fully known. What is known is that in extended periods of sensory isolation, suggestions can have a far more profound impact. Such "therapy" is dangerously close to brainwashing, and is not to be considered in the same realm as clinical hypnosis, an interpersonal process of influential communication in the context of an intense, cooperative, caring, therapeutic relationship.

Except under extreme conditions, the mind has the ability to protect itself from threats, sensory overload and sensory isolation. The unconscious mind is not a danger to the person; rather it has the potential to be a safe haven for one's inner self. For example, while one gets lost in thought while driving, a common experience, one's unconscious mind still operates the vehicle safely; the conscious minds pays attention only when some unusual situation arises that requires its attention. In defense of the mind is the mind.

In the practice of hypnosis, you will discover that access to a person's unconscious mind gives you information, but not power. If a suggestion is unacceptable, the unconscious will not take it in. It is universal in the practice of psychotherapy that a client consciously wants to change, but some unknown or inadequately addressed unconscious need prevents the change from occurring. Even though the client is consciously dissatisfied and uncomfortable with the problem, the unconscious may have that symptom there for some reason. Assistance comes in the form of developing a better means for adapting, one that doesn't cause the client pain. If the suggestion is acceptable to the unconscious, establishing a more positive association in the person, then change can take place.

As a final point about this issue of the mind's ability to protect itself, it seems to me that if there were a group of powerful humans called "hypnotists" who could control others through manipulation of the unconscious mind, hypnosis would be a uniformly successful tool in practice. It isn't.

THE DUALITY OF THE MIND

Characterizing the dual nature of mental functioning as "conscious" and "unconscious" has been abandoned by many in recent years in favor of characterizing mental functions by brain hemisphere. The two major hemispheres of the brain naturally have many common functions but are popularly characterized by their differences.

The left hemisphere of the brain corresponds roughly to consciousness. The left hemisphere, sometimes called the "verbal hemisphere," is responsible for the majority of speech functions. It is also often called the "logical hemisphere" because it is thought to contain the reasoning, analytical, and intellectual functions. Its focus on detail makes it more likely to "see the trees and not the forest," as the saying goes.

The right hemisphere of the brain corresponds roughly to the unconscious. The right hemisphere is often called the "silent hemisphere" or the "intuitive hemisphere." The right brain is said to contain a person's intuition and creativity, and is thought to operate on a more symbolic level than the left brain. Thus, the appreciation of and ability to create art and music are considered right brain functions. The right brain is said to contain the person's world view and self-image, and is more likely to get the overview of things—"seeing the forest and not the trees."

The process of hypnosis in this "left-brain—right-brain" scheme of things is characterized as distracting and occupying the left hemisphere of the client while utilizing the resources of her right hemisphere. Language that is sensory based, descriptive and emotional, is more appealing to the right brain, and is the basis for Paul Watzlawick calling such language *The Language of Change* (1978).

CONCLUSION

However one conceptualizes the mind, there is a duality present, with each component having some unique characteristics and with each offering its own contributions to subjective experience. Hypnosis as a tool is extremely useful in its ability to utilize more of the client's mental resources than other approaches typically do. Due to the enormous complexity of the human mind, and because of the extraordinary uniqueness of each human being, respect for the personal power and integrity of each person is not just desirable, but mandatory.

For Discussion

1. Why do people transmit messages incongruously? Is it safe to assume they are being deceptive in doing so?

2. How do you characterize the differences between the conscious and unconscious minds?

3. Our society has been called a "Left Brain" one. Why do you think it has been characterized this way? Do you agree?

4. Do you trust your unconscious mind? Why or why not? Do you trust your conscious mind? Why or why not?

5. What do you think of the use of sensory isolation coupled with subliminal messages as a therapeutic intervention? Why do you hold that opinion? What potential dangers, if any, can you anticipate arising in this approach?

Things to Do

1. Research the functions of the left and right brain hemispheres. Which functions overlap? Which do not?

2. Have one person talk to you for a minute, then two people simultaneously, then three simultaneously, and so on. At what point do you feel overwhelmed in trying to attend to each? What can you conclude from this exercise about the mind?

3. Make a list of 10 common disorders, and then make a list of underlying feelings or motivations the problem may be metaphorical for. For example, a weight problem may be viewed as a person surrounding herself with fat for protection against some threat. How do you know your interpretation of a symptom is really what that symptom is about?

9

Susceptibility
to Hypnosis

One of the oldest yet still most frequently asked questions in the field of hypnosis concerns "hypnotic susceptibility." What sort of human being is susceptible to the condition called "trance"? Traditional considerations of susceptibility, and even use of the word "susceptibility" itself, can leave one with the impression that hypnosis is some sort of disease some special type of person, for better or worse, is prone to get. The issue of who can be hypnotized (and, likewise, who cannot) is one that has been researched and written about in numerous publications, both scientific and otherwise, by some of the most respected people in the field. Such research has uniformly described personality types and other characteristics (e.g., intelligence) of subjects that predispose them to favorable or unfavorable responses to formal hypnotic inductions. Many studies have also published statistical breakdowns of the general population into percentages of people who can be hypnotized to various depths of trance as well as those who apparently have no unconscious mind (at least not one the researcher can find), and thus cannot be hypnotized at all.

The susceptibility issue was touched on briefly in the earlier chapter dealing with misconceptions about hypnosis, specifically in the discussion of the misconception that "only certain kinds of people can be hypnotized." This chapter expands on that discussion of susceptibility in order to allow the clinician a greater degree of certainty in her work that the client she is working with can indeed experience hypnosis meaningfully.

TRADITIONAL VIEWS ON SUSCEPTIBILITY

Many researchers consider susceptibility to hypnosis as a personality trait comparable to other personality traits. In this view, it is unclear whether

119

one is born with a high, low or absent "hypnotic susceptibility" gene structure, or whether this trait is acquired as a learned phenomenon through the socialization process. Regardless, in this view the presence or absence of the hypnotizability trait is a condition that remains relatively stable over time. In other words, if a person lacks responsiveness to the formal hypnosis induction procedure, that person is deemed a poor subject apparently unable to respond adequately to hypnosis. Further research studies on the reliability of this conclusion support it: Poor subjects remain poor over time (in repeated attempts to induce hypnosis in the same person with the same procedure) and good subjects remain good over time.

Research demands standardization. Every research subject, regardless of whether it is in research on hypnosis or research in some other area, must experience the exact same procedure in order for a study to be considered scientific (i.e., controlled, replicable). In standardizing hypnotic inductions, the process must be the same: The timing, the hypnotist's voice dynamics, the degree of formality of the relationship between researcher and subject, the recording of responses to the procedure, the place, the lighting, and virtually every other variable must be carefully controlled. Consequently, a large number of research subjects are exposed to the same hypnosis procedure, then are given a test to determine their degree of responsiveness. The resulting statistics are published as evidence of the degree of hypnotizability of the general population of which the research population is a sample.

The emphasis throughout this book is on the clinician's need to individualize the hypnosis procedure to the individual requirements of the client. From this perspective, such research statistics on hypnotizability not only are useless (except in the research context in which they originated) for assisting one in determining an approach to a particular client, but can actually be *detrimental* to the clinical practice of hypnosis. You can recall the practitioner referred to earlier who viewed clients' hypnotizability as a "tryout for the choir," with an expected failure rate of about 50%. Expecting a percentage of people to be unresponsive will most certainly assist one in helping them attain that outcome. Worse yet, the failure to achieve trance will be considered a property of the client rather than a shortcoming of the clinician!

Elsewhere in the traditional literature on hypnosis, one can find discussion of other dimensions of hypnotic susceptibility that are more descriptive than mere statistical averages of responsiveness to standardized procedures.

Such dimensions include age, intelligence, mental status, self-esteem, degree of imaginative skill, and relationship factors between clinician and client. Each dimension will be discussed from both a traditional and utilization perspective.

AGE AND HYPNOTIZABILITY

Much of the traditional literature promotes the idea that children, especially around the ages of seven to nine, are the best hypnotic subjects because of their active imaginations and willingness to follow directions. Other literature contradicts this, claiming that children's lesser ability to concentrate and their smaller reservoir of personal resources cause them to be poorer subjects. In my experience of working with children, I have found children to be excellent hypnotic subjects, each in his or her own way. Children have much more complexity and awareness than many adults give them credit for, and a sensitive clinician can look for the interests and resources of a child and make use of them just as effectively as in working with an adult.

One of the most common reasons why some practitioners come to doubt the responsiveness of children to trance is because of the active nature of many children. As will be discussed later, adults generally inhibit voluntary activity when in trance, but children often fidget and appear restless even though they may be very involved with the clinician and what he is doing. If one has an inflexible expectation of how a client in trance must look and behave, as many of the more traditional practitioners do, a fidgety child will be viewed as unaffected by hypnotic procedures. Sometimes, perhaps much of the time, a procedure with children can encourage and make use of the child's energy by engaging him in some activity (e.g., a game) that distracts him from what the clinician is really wanting to communicate. Demanding inactivity as evidence of trance is an imposition on the child with an active nature, and simply is not necessary for one's communications to have a meaningful effect at an unconscious level.

Observation of the child's interactions with his parents and siblings can provide a great deal of useful information about the kind of relationship (i.e., friend, ally, teacher, doctor) one may build with him in order to best influence him. Knowledge of his interests and emotional needs will also help one discover the best avenue of intervention. An extraordinary example of the utilization approach to a child's problem is one of Milton Erickson's cases described by Jay Haley in *Uncommon Therapy* (1973). A young boy with the problem of enuresis was literally dragged in by his parents to see Dr. Erickson. Alone with the child in his office, Erickson angrily muttered aloud about the audacity of those parents to order him to cure the boy's enuresis. The boy was entranced by this strange doctor's unexpected raving against his parents, whom he was pretty angry with, too. When Erickson then said he'd prefer not to deal with the bedwetting at all, he shifted the conversation to talking about the muscle coordination necessary for the sport of archery. By talking about the development of muscle control, Erickson was able to indirectly offer suggestions for establishing control of the bladder muscles. Erickson's intervention was a successful one that started out by utilizing the boy's anger, first forming an alliance with him against his parents, or so it seemed.

Age has been a factor in traditional views of hypnotizability in another population: the newborn. Some writers have claimed newborn babies are not hypnotizable. Why anyone would want to induce hypnosis in a newborn has always been and continues to be a mystery to me, but apparently some clinicians think it important. Even newborns are capable of trance, however, evidenced by the intensity with which many babies stare at the mobiles hanging over their crib.

In general, age is a relatively minor consideration in assessing capacity for trance. Age *is* a factor in determining the best method for trance induction and utilization because of the need to do trance processes that are appropriate to the age and background of the client.

INTELLIGENCE AND HYPNOTIZABILITY

Studies on hypnotic susceptibility have often suggested that the more intelligent the person, the better the hypnotic subject she will be. Such studies have been remarkably ambiguous, and if there is a positive correlation between intelligence and hypnotizability, it is believed to be because of the positive relationship between intelligence and ability to concentrate.

Often, a fact is confused with its practical application. One might suspect this is the case in the relationship between intelligence and hypnotizability. Many practitioners make the statement to a client or a stage show audience that "the more intelligent one is, the better a hypnotic subject one is; only morons can't be hypnotized." People noncritically accept this as fact because of the hypnotist's expertise, but the statement is made for a purpose unrelated to the desire to provide objective information about hypnosis. Rather, the statement is made for the purpose of getting the subject to cooperate; hopefully the subject wants to view herself as intelligent, and in this instance intelligence is defined as being responsive to the hypnotist's suggestions. Many practitioners make the statement relating hypnotizability to intelligence routinely in order to build cooperation. They overlook the fact, though, that many people, especially when seeking help for personal problems while feeling bad about themselves, don't view themselves as intelligent at that point in time. They can then use a failure with hypnosis to confirm their lack of intelligence to themselves. This is one more of the potentially damaging aspects of stage hypnosis, a context where many people are told, "Only morons can't be hypnotized." "Unsuitable" subjects are dismissed, and are left alone to conclude they are somehow mentally deficient. The same problem can exist when such statements are made carelessly in the clinical situation. The value of the statement relating intelligence and hypnotizability in generating responsiveness is questionable, and in many instances its use is best omitted.

Traditional views of hypnosis, based on the assumed relationship between intelligence and hypnosis, have stated that hypnosis cannot be used with mentally retarded persons. In reality, depending on the degree of retardation, specialized techniques *can* capture a mentally retarded person's attention and, thus, their responsiveness. Such techniques might involve massage, simple physical care like bathing, and especially playing. Approaches should be molded to the capacity of the individual. Formulating goals and approaches that are consistent with the person's abilities is more the challenge in such special cases than is inducing trance.

MENTAL STATUS AND HYPNOTIZABILITY

For a number of years, I worked on a psychiatric inpatient unit with patients "out of touch with reality" in varying degrees along a continuum ranging from mildly thought-disordered to extremely psychotic. Patients were given large doses of major and minor tranquilizers, mood elevators, electroconvulsive treatment (ECT), and a wide assortment of other treatments intended to help them carry on their most basic daily functions. I had been utilizing techniques of hypnosis for over five years before I began working on this unit, but virtually none of my experience had been with anyone deemed psychotic. When joining the staff and describing to others my experience and understandings about people from working with their unconscious resources, I was asked by the medical director to solemnly vow never to use hypnosis on the patients because of its potential to precipitate hysteria in them, an unfounded misconception carried over from Freud's day, yet still commonly taught in psychiatric training programs. My response was agreement not to use hypnosis, "but would it be alright for me to teach patients skills in relaxation, mental imagery, and other forms of self-management?" "Yes, that would be fine, just no hypnosis, please." Well, I confess I am not particularly fond of the word "hypnosis" anyway, since it has come to mean so many different things as to be almost meaningless. As long as I could use techniques to help patients rely less on medications and their doctors, I found the arrangement I had made a comfortable one. A rose by any other name....

I had been taught in traditional circles that psychotic persons cannot be hypnotized. Even in the most recent of hypnotic texts dealing with the subject, psychiatrists have said that they are likely to rediagnose someone labeled psychotic if the person is found to be hypnotizable. My experience and the experience of Milton Erickson, Jeffrey Zeig, and many others working with the more flexible utilization approach have suggested that some psychoses can be penetrated, circumvented, controlled, or therapeutically used in hypnotic interactions. Erickson, in particular, published a number of articles on the subject of hypnosis with psychotics, and many examples of his work appear in other books about him as well. When one teaches such patients formal, concrete relaxation procedures, makes contact with their idiosyncratic views, appreciates the manipulative aspect to much of the psychotic's behavior and removes the payoffs when possible, and metaphorically intervenes, psychotic patients can and do improve.

A psychotic's symptoms can in and of themselves be viewed as a communication—a metaphor for his inner conflicts and self-concept. The systems theory concepts of the Palo Alto Research Group, including such notables as Jay Haley, Gregory Bateson, Paul Watzlawick, Don Jackson, Richard Fisch, and John Weakland, provided the perspective that a symptom is a communication, one that reflects the relationship between the identified patient and his circle of contacts. The communication of the patient, the psychotic symptom, is on a metaphorical level; so can its therapy be metaphorical, and thus qualify as an indirect hypnotic communication. Psychosis is a result of an inability or an unwillingness to face "reality" directly, and so skilled indirect communications are a viable therapeutic alternative in their lesser likelihood to generate resistance, whether in psychotics or in "normals."

Much of the traditional literature that promotes the idea of psychotics' inability to be hypnotized will give the reason for their lack of responsiveness as an inability to concentrate. It is claimed they are unable to attend to the hypnotist's guidance due to their hallucinations, delusions, and confusion. However, individualized techniques that allow for the building of trust (rapport), that don't make too many demands too soon, and are indirect enough to not arouse fear and suspicion can get in and work.

Of course, the degree of psychosis is a variable to consider—I doubt a manic-depressive in peak manic phase, for example, can be affected by a good hypnotist or anyone else. Likewise, cause of the psychosis is a noteworthy factor as well. Drug-induced psychosis is difficult to overcome, for example. Persons with organically induced psychosis such as that associated with aging can respond to some hypnotic techniques successfully. Many older patients suffering senility I have worked with could not remember what they were doing five minutes ago, but can remember with remarkable clarity things that occurred 50 years ago. Regressive techniques to early experiences can have a calming, soothing effect. Likewise, basic care of these and other psychotic patients, such as care given during bathing and dressing, can have very positive effects.

My experience has convinced me that effective use of hypnotic concepts and techniques on psychiatric units with disturbed patients is possible and a potentially effective way for reducing reliance on medications. Use of techniques that really do teach self-control seem far more desirable, in my opinion, than the mixed message typically given the psychiatric patient: "You need to control yourself, so here are some pills." Medication is useful in many cases, but the overprescription of drugs in American society has been observed by many.

Every model has its limitations, its areas where it is ineffective in providing useful answers. Traditional treatments, in the medical model or elsewhere, are called traditional because of their established and fixed boundaries. How much is to be gained when self-limiting boundaries of conventional treatment are suspended in order to allow for the utilization of whatever will work in a particular case? The gain is made in terms of human life.

SELF-ESTEEM AND HYPNOTIZABILITY

Every person one interacts with, in whatever context, has a self-esteem, a value that all people place on themselves in terms of their perceived self-worth. The self-esteem of a person can range from very low to very high. Self-esteem is not necessarily a stable trait that remains fixed throughout one's lifetime; rather it can go up or down with experience. Yet, self-esteem is self-preserving in that it can motivate one to work very hard at staying the same in many important ways. If a person has a poor self-esteem, she is unlikely to take even the smallest risks in her own behalf. New opportunities to grow or to leave behind people and situations long outgrown may be ignored. For example, the person may be unhappy with a certain life situation, but at the same time feel fearful and uncertain about changing it, and thus be immobilized in terms of progress. The person with a high self-esteem, by contrast, is able to take calculated risks, not reckless ones, trusting herself enough to manage the new situations and opportunities appropriately. She, too, may feel fearful about the impending change, but the fear is not so paralyzing that the opportunity for change is missed.

The self-esteem of the client is a major variable in her ability to respond meaningfully to the clinician's communications. It is one's self-esteem that, in part, determines what one views as possible for one's self. The little boy who says, "Mommy, I can't do math," is not likely to be reassured by a simple, "Oh, sure you can." If a communication is not consistent with what the person believes to be true, it is not likely to go far. One of the most enlightening concepts relative to self-esteem and responsiveness to the communications of others comes from the literature of social psychology. In the 1950's, social psychologist Leon Festinger coined the term "cognitive dissonance" to describe the tendency for human beings to seek consistent self-knowledge. If one is faced with internal inconsistency in the form of opposing or contradictory bits of information about one's self, an uncomfortable internal state of "dissonance" arises, and the inconsistency must somehow be resolved. Resolution can take many forms, but all involve either omitting contradictory information or twisting it around until it somehow fits in the desired way.

If you consider the typical cigarette smoker as an example, you find that the smoker may view herself as intelligent, sensitive, rational and having other desirable qualities as well. If you ask this intelligent, sensitive, rational person why she inhales toxic gases voluntarily at great risk to her health, the reaction is likely to be defensive, perhaps even angry. You have presented a question that brings her irrational actions into her awareness, suggesting to her that her way of managing herself is not an entirely sensible one. A typical response is one of rationalization: "I only smoke a few each day. . . . I'd rather smoke than be overweight (as if they are a tradeoff). . . . I plan on quitting as soon as the stress I'm under eases up. . . ." The rationalizations are virtually endless in an attempt to maintain the belief that "smoking is acceptable." The point of cognitive dissonance and its importance for hypnotic communication is that information contradictory to what the person believes to be true is defended against through a variety of means in order to preserve the original belief. A person with a terrible self-image who is told, "You have so much to offer," is not likely to take that message in. The real skill of hypnotic communication is in knowing how to package a communication for someone in such a way as to maximize its likelihood of becoming internalized.

Self-image is directly related to how much control a person feels the need to have at all times. Control as an issue for some people was discussed early on as a factor affecting the outcome of your work with hypnosis. If a client is terrified that he will lose control of himself, a formal, ritualized approach to hypnosis that emphasizes the need to respond obediently will be marginally successful at best. Conversely, if a client's self-image is a strong one and there is self-trust, the client can be comfortable that no one can do anything to him. Rather, he can allow himself to be guided only if he chooses to. For such people, control is not an issue of significance. They don't need to control other people's thoughts and actions, nor do they need to fear other people's attempts to influence them. Such people are confident that they can respond as they wish to.

Self-esteem is an entirely learned phenomenon, not a trait present at birth. Your experiences and, more importantly, the conclusions you draw from those experiences determine what you will view yourself as being capable of. Confronting a client's self-image directly in the form of contradicting it is rarely a successful maneuver in changing it. Typically, the client just gets the feeling the clinician really doesn't understand her.

It is important to know how a client views herself, as well as her experiences and feelings. Virginia Satir has an excellent technique for getting at the person's self-esteem. For example, when a client of hers said, "I'm angry about this situation," Satir was likely to ask, "How do you feel about feeling angry?" Knowing a client's view of her own self-worth can provide a great deal of information about how to present information to her in such a way as to increase its chance of becoming internalized and having value. Whatever the context, the person you are communicating with has a self-esteem, and its significance in influencing the course of an interaction must be appreciated before any meaningful exchange can take place.

Related to self-image is the power distribution of a relationship. How much power one person gives another to influence him is also determined by one's self-image. Some people's self-image is so poor they give power to virtually everyone to even tell them their personal views; others' self-esteem is sufficiently high that they can determine for themselves their own personal values. Adopting others' values and trying to live by them is one certain way to maintain a poor self-esteem.

The client seeking help of any kind in order to treat a personal problem is, one can be sure, not feeling good about her situation. I have never had anyone come to me and say "I really like how badly I'm feeling about this situation." Rather, the person is feeling a mixture of emotions: helpless and depressed about the problem, embarrassed perhaps, hopeful the problem can be eliminated, confused, as well as a variety of other feelings that are all a part of her self-esteem at that time. These feelings all have to be acknowledged, directly or indirectly, and used in order to facilitate change. Attaining the necessary rapport and building on it in order to guide this unhappy person to a happier existence is the goal of clinical work in general and hypnotic work in particular.

IMAGINATION AND HYPNOSIS

Less a factor, but still worthy of consideration, is the imaginative ability of a person. People vary in their abilities to process information; some people are quite concrete and require highly detailed descriptions of experience they have already had in order to experience trance, while others are capable of high level abstraction in which imagination and fantasy can run loose in their minds and generate meaningful experiences for them. How concrete or abstract someone is in their thinking is a factor in responsiveness to hypnosis because of the subjective nature of the experience. There are no rockets that go off, no sirens that sound, no marching bands that come by waving banners that confirm "this is trance!" The trance experience can be a very subtle one, virtually indistinguishable from one's normal waking state, or it can be a very profound, distinct experience characterized by certain sensations collectively identified as a "trance." To the very concrete individual experiencing the subtleties of a light trance, the reaction is often "I wasn't hypnotized . . . . I heard everything you said." The concrete subject should generally be spoken to in parallel concrete terms of verifiable experience. In California hot tubs, for example, people talk about such abstract things as a person's "energy flow," their "essence," their "groundedness," and other nondescript variables that may carry clear meaning to a person with a certain orientation and the capacity for abstraction. However, to a person with a more concrete thinking style or a different orientation, talking to her about "letting her energy flow unrestricted in order to achieve a harmony with the universe" is likely to result in a cosmic failure.

Every person has an imagination and an ability to fantasize, but some more so than others. Some people's imaginative powers are very concrete, others' are more abstract. This is one more variable to consider in formulating one's approach.

RELATIONSHIP FACTORS AND HYPNOTIZABILITY

Rapport between clinician and client has traditionally been considered a major factor in the therapeutic process, and rightly so. Rapport is, by my definition, a positive interrelationship between individuals based on understanding and trust. One has rapport when one's client feels understood, when he feels the clinician has an appreciation for the complexity of his personal experience. Agreement in the form of acceptance is a most valuable means to obtain rapport. For example, when a client says "I'm nervous about being here," the clinician can, with good intentions, respond by contradicting or devaluing the comment and say, "You shouldn't feel that way." A better choice for attaining rapport is one that accepts the client's feelings, such as, "I can understand how this new situation might cause you to feel nervous, and I'm sure you'll soon realize how comfortable you can be here with me."

In the older, traditional methods of hypnosis, rapport was largely based on the subject's responsiveness to the hypnotist's authority. This kind of one-sided relationship may still be considered a viable choice for the hypnotic interaction, but one that seems more satisfying and allows for greater flexibility is the more balanced type of cooperative relationship inherent in the utilization approach. Trance can be viewed as a naturalistic outcome of a special kind of relationship, one of mutual responsibility and accountability. The clinician's leads are determined by the client's leads and vice versa. Trancework is a continuous process of adjusting and readjusting to each other, and at any given moment one or the other might be setting the pace of the interaction. A continuous feedback loop is essential in this approach, with feedback from the client determining the clinician's leads, and feedback from the clinician determining the client's leads. This kind of relationship is one that differs appreciably from those perspectives of the hypnotic relationship in which the client is to obediently follow the leads of the clinician, and failure to do so signals "resistance." Responsiveness to the client allows a clinician to offer suggestions both in a format and at a pace that maximizes the client's ability to respond. The recognition that trance is a naturalistic outcome of this kind of responsive relationship is one that is reflected in the structure of hypnotic suggestions: The tying of what is true now to what can be true later. A later chapter deals with the structure of hypnotic suggestions; suffice it to say here that when a client is given meaningful feedback of a certain type, trance is a result.

Rapport often involves fulfilling the expectations of a client. Finding out what a client wants or expects does not obligate one to meet those expectations. It does, however, put one in a position to choose whether or not one needs to or wants to meet them in order to increase the likelihood of obtaining positive results. Often a viable choice is *not* meeting the person's expectations, but instead finding a way to use those expectations for some other therapeutic purpose.

Other relationship factors that affect the hypnotic interaction are discussed in greater detail in the chapter on "Human Suggestibility," in which the characteristics of people that predispose them to be influenced by others are considered.

HYPNOTIC SUSCEPTIBILITY TESTS

I would be remiss in my desire to be as complete as possible in providing an overview of the field if I did not mention that there are a number of hypnotic susceptibility scales available for use should one desire to. Each of these scales attempts to standardize hypnotic behavior by first inducing trance in a person, and then giving her tests in order to determine her degree of trance depth and responsiveness. The client must inevitably pass and fail the various tests, and the administrator of the susceptibility scale records the test results in order to establish a profile of the person's trance capacities.

The susceptibility scales are subject to the same criticism levied against the standardized inductions: Measuring a person's response to a non-individualized standard indicates virtually nothing about the person's true ability to meaningfully experience trance. Such scales may be useful in doing research for purposes of standardization, but they are impractical for deriving information about how one might approach a given individual in order to form the best intervention for her. For this reason, as well as the following reasons, I cannot recommend the use of such scales in clinical contexts. A second reason for my negative appraisal is my belief that every person is susceptible to the condition known as trance. The task is not to determine *whether* the person is hypnotizable, rather the issue is *how* the trance capacity of the person should best be utilized. Third, each of the scales, with the exception of the Hypnosis Induction Profile (HIP), assumes that if someone can demonstrate "trance phenomenon X," then he is at "trance level Y." This is an erroneous relationship, for people can and do demonstrate hypnotic phenomena regularly in various degrees of trance that, according to the susceptibility scales, can be done only at either lighter or deeper levels. For example, while you are reading a book, often you do not hear the everyday sounds occurring all around you because you are absorbed in what you are reading.

Not experiencing sensory stimuli that are present in your environment is evidence of a trance phenomenon called "negative hallucination," which can be experienced only in deeper trance states, according to some susceptibility scales. Are you in deep trance? Or are you in a trance just deep enough to experience negative hallucinations? Emphasis on trance depth is not, and need not be, important. Only a trance deep enough to get the desired response is necessary. Another reason for avoiding use of susceptibility scales is because of the inevitability of a failure for the client in responding to one or more tests. Why put the client in a position to fail, with its unknown but certainly negative impact on the interaction?

Both of the following scales employ a "phenomenon X-level Y" susceptibility rating:

Stanford Hypnotic Susceptibility Scale (Weitzenhoffer and Hilgard, 1959)
Harvard Group Hypnotic Susceptibility Scale (Shor and Orne, 1962)

Another widely used scale is the Hypnosis Induction Profile (HIP). The HIP is composed of three tests, the most unique being the Spiegels' Eye Roll Test. Capacity for trance is regarded as a genetic or neurological one that is fixed, unchanging in the adult years. The "biological capacity" for trance is evidenced by the degree of elevation of the eyes in their sockets the person is capable of showing as she closes her eyes. The eye roll is thought to be a "biological marker," a natural indicator of trance capacity (Spiegel and Spiegel, 1978). The higher up in the sockets one's eyes are when one can close them, the more hypnotizable one is assumed to be. The person's experiences and resources, self-image, and all the complex variables that cause each person to respond to hypnosis in his or her own unique way are almost entirely negated in susceptibility testing for an eye roll or some arbitrary test like hand levitation.

Susceptibility tests are redundant, time consuming, and yield little, if anything, that a skilled listener and observer wouldn't get from a more personal, spontaneous interaction. Use of susceptibility scales takes responsibility from the clinician to respond to the individual, a violation of the most valued principle of the perspective promoted throughout this text.

SUMMARY

The issue of who is hypnotizable is an important one determining your expectations and subsequently your behaviors in employing hypnotic patterns. The following points summarize the issues associated with hypnotic susceptibility:

- Standardized approaches do not address the individual needs of the client, which is necessary for maximizing effectiveness.
- Clients of all ages can experience trance, formally or informally, with varying degrees of responsiveness.
- Intelligence and hypnotizability may be related, but research in this area is ambiguous. Promoting the idea that an intelligent person is a better hypnotic subject may complicate things rather than help.
- Many persons considered psychotic can be communicated with at an unconscious level; symptoms are often metaphorical communications and can be responded to with interventions on that level. Specialized techniques for the mental condition of the person can yield positive results.
- Self-esteem is a major consideration in hypnotizability; cognitive dissonance as a basic human process leads to the conclusion that suggestions must be consistent with a person's self-image in order to be successfully integrated; self-esteem is related to the need for control and the amount of power and capacity for influence one gives to another.
- People vary in their degree of ability to imagine, and this affects susceptibility to subjective experiences such as hypnosis.
- Trance is viewed as a naturalistic outcome of a special relationship in which clinician and client are mutually responsive to the continuous exchange of feedback.
- Commercial hypnotic susceptibility scales standardize hypnotic behavior according to trance depth or "biological markers." Such tests do not recognize the individual capabilities of a specific person, and thus are viewed as having little value in a highly individualized clinical context.

For Discussion

1. What basis do you think Milton Erickson had for making the statement that "anyone who can be socialized can be hypnotized"?

2. Why do researchers conclude that if *they* can't hypnotize someone, *no one* can?

3. What age related factors should one take into consideration when formulating a trance process? In what ways will an approach to a 60-year-old differ from an approach to a 20-year-old?

4. Is intelligence related to the ability to concentrate? Why or why not?

5. When should one meet one's clients' expectations? When shouldn't one? Why do you say so? What interpersonal dynamics should be taken into account in deciding whether or not to meet the expectations?

Things to Do

1. Obtain and review the various susceptibility tests. What ways, if any, can you discover for their use in your work?

2. If possible, arrange to tour a psychiatric hospital or nursing home. In observing the residents of the facility, can you determine their degree, if any, of susceptibility to hypnosis? Can you specify any approaches that might be effective with them?

3. Make a list of every rationalization you have ever used to maintain a behavior of yours that you would consciously like to change. Can you see "cognitive dissonance" at work? In what ways?

10

The Experience
of Trance

Trance is a highly subjective experience, for no two people experience it in exactly the same way. It is because trance is so highly subjective an experience that attempts to objectify its nature with numerical rating scales and quantified research data have been so limited in their significance. You can recall the earlier discussion about the limited nature of the conclusions that can be drawn when standardization, necessary in research, is applied to hypnotic procedures. The traditional western scientific community has only recently begun to take a look, and a skeptical one at that, at hypnosis as a tool of treatment. Trance states have not been reliably measured chemically or electrically in the human body or mind, and it seems that many clinicians hold the detrimental belief that "if you can't measure it, ignore it."

Appreciating the uniqueness of each person you interact with is a worthwhile goal in general, but if one wants to learn and apply hypnotic patterns effectively, it is a strict requirement. There are certain assumptions that are beyond question and are unfailing in doing trancework. One concerns the uniqueness of each person and all that implies about each person's individual personal history being unlike anyone else's. A second assumption is that each person is going to have his own way of experiencing trance; what associations one's communications will trigger in the client are unknown to the clinician until they are somehow communicated (unless one is a board certified mind-reader). A third assumption concerns the mind-body relationship; whatever the person is experiencing mentally will have a physical counterpart, and vice-versa.

Given these assumptions, presented in this chapter are some of the more prominent general characteristics, both psychological and physical, associated with the trance experience. Appreciating these dimensions of the

---

Table 1. The Experience of Trance

Experiential and selective absorption of attention
Effortless expression
Experiential, nonconceptual involvement
Willingness to experiment
Flexibility in time/space relations
Alterations of perception
Fluctuations in degree of involvement
Motoric/verbal inhibition
Trance logic; reduction in reality testing
Symbolic processing
Time distortion
Amnesia

---

trance experience will be invaluable in guiding your work, for it is these factors that necessitate communicating differently to a person in trance than one might in more routine interactions. Table 1 lists characteristics of "The Experience of Trance."

PSYCHOLOGICAL CHARACTERISTICS OF THE TRANCE STATE

SELECTIVE ATTENTION

If you have ever heard or used the phrase, "He only sees what he wants to see," you have an awareness that human beings can notice what they choose to notice. By implication, humans can also *not* notice what they choose not to. This phenomenon is referred to as "selective attention," the ability to focus on one portion of an experience while "tuning out" the rest. For example, if you like to read with the radio on, the music can drift out of your awareness until a favorite song comes on. At that moment, your attention is turned selectively to the music, and the reading is temporarily suspended from your awareness.

The conscious mind is limited in its ability to pay attention to numerous things occurring simultaneously. One consciously notices only a small part of a total experience. How do you decide which part of an experience to pay attention to? At a concert are you more likely to notice how the musicians look, the words to their songs, or how you feel while you're

there? Which part of the concert sticks in your memory? Why *that* particular part? There are a number of complex factors that determine what works
its way into one's field of attention. These factors include: The degree of
sensory stimulation (how weak or strong the stimulus is); the novelty of the
stimulus; the person's response tendencies (arising from a complex inter-
play of socialization and genetics); the person's motivation in the context
under consideration; the person's mood; and the kinds and amounts of
other sensory stimulation co-existing in the environment.

The Gestaltists, in particular, have paid a great deal of attention to the
perceptual processes involved in awareness; becoming familiar with their
work is encouraged. Suffice it to say here that the process of selective
attention is an instrumental factor in the hypnotic interaction. The client
must gradually selectively attend to the provided suggestions and narrow
her attention to the associations the suggestions stimulate. The client's
focus is generally inward, and so external events may be noticed and
responded to, yet externals account only for a small minority of the client's
attention. The unconscious becomes prominent in its ability to respond to
things outside of the person's attentional field. I have just described a basis
for the next characteristic I will discuss: Dissociation.

DISSOCIATION

While the person in trance has her attention selectively focused on the
suggestions of the clinician and whatever unconscious associations may be
triggered as a result, there is a separation occurring between the conscious
and unconscious minds. The conscious mind is occupied with the trance
process, and the unconscious is actively searching for symbolic meanings,
past associations and appropriate responses. This separation of conscious
and unconscious during the trance experience is accomplished in varying
degrees with different people, and is called "dissociation." The fact that the
conscious and unconscious minds can be divided and utilized as inter-
dependent yet independent entities is the backbone of hypnosis. Facilitating dissociation through one's trancework allows one to have a more direct
access to the unconscious mind's many resources and knowledge of the
inner workings of the client.

Another way of considering the dissociative nature of the trance experience is through the "parallel awareness" during the trance experience. The
client in trance has multiple awarenesses, each operating on a separate
level. One of these levels is a relatively objective one that has a realistic

understanding of the nature of the experience, a part of the person Hilgard (1977) called the "hidden observer." The "hidden observer" is separated (dissociated) from the immediacy of the suggested trance experiences, and can maintain a degree of objectivity about the experience. This dissociative characteristic of the trance state allows the client to attend to and respond to suggestions while at the same time observing herself go through the experience.

For example, my practice is centered in San Diego, where people generally appreciate the fine weather and beautiful beaches. If I do a trance process with a client and suggest to her that she visualize herself at the beach, she can really experience that suggested reality. She may smell the salty air of the ocean breeze, feel the warmth of the sun on her back, hear the calling of the sea gulls floating overhead ... in short, she may really experience the sensations of being at the beach. Yet, there is another part of my client that knows very well she is not at the beach, but is in my office. The dissociation allows her to let her hidden observer fade into the background while she chooses to respond to the suggested reality. The implication of this dissociated state is that even in deep trance the client knows, unless *she* chooses not to, what she is doing and where she is. This is the basis for my flatly rejecting the possibility of hypnosis being used to cause someone to behave antisocially. If someone wants to find blame, hypnosis can be a good scapegoat, but it has no basis in fact.

If a male clinician were to be so unethical as to suggest to a woman in his office that she believe herself to be at home, preparing to take a shower and therefore needing to undress, *she may do so!* But because of trance? No. Some other personal motivation (e.g., loneliness)? Yes. If there were a breed of people in the world called "hypnotists" who could control others, this world would be a slightly different place, don't you think?

The presence of dissociation as a characteristic of the trance state is one of the most fascinating dimensions of doing trancework. It is the most overt means for uncovering the workings of the unconscious mind, and is the basis for many of the classical trance phenomena described later.

INCREASED RESPONSIVENESS TO SUGGESTION

The attentional and dissociational factors described above lead to an increased responsiveness to suggestion. The hypnotic interaction has been defined as a therapeutic and/or educational one for the client, and the capacity for influence is certainly present. The client selectively attends to the suggestions of the clinician, and the suggestions trigger responses and associations within him. Increased responsiveness is evidenced as a greater willingness in the client to be guided by the suggestions of the clinician, probably because of the associated expectation of something to be gained through them. Responsiveness, therefore, is not to be confused with gullibility, or noncritical acceptance. The trance state actually *amplifies* a person's range of choices, including the choice to reject a suggestion that isn't particularly fitting. The increased responsiveness to suggestion is a choice on the part of the client to be guided by someone he trusts and feels is wanting to help him. If the personal, interpersonal, and contextual dynamics are not favorable, responsiveness is nonexistent and the result is what is classically termed "resistance."

LITERAL INTERPRETATION

One of the wreakers of havoc in the beginning phases of working with hypnosis is the trance characteristic of "literal interpretation" of communication. After one makes the inevitable mistakes at first, the mistakes taper off (but never disappear altogether) in terms of the number of times a word or phrase is used that is taken all too literally by the client with an unexpected result. The characteristic of literal interpretation causes the client to react to words at their face value, in spite of what you may have meant. This is the basis for developing a careful approach to clients in terms of your word choices.

Neil Simon, mentioned previously, likes to tell this story reflecting one of his earliest experiences with literal interpretation. In working with a woman wanting hypnotic anesthesia who was to have minor surgery on her wrist to remove a growth, Neil induced trance and suggested that she develop an anesthesia in her arm. She did this quite readily. In order to test her anesthesia, Neil took a pin and gently poked her arm progressively downward from her shoulder. Each poke was met with a comfortable "No, I can't feel that." When Neil poked the back of her hand, she yelled "Ow!" Neil asked "What's wrong?" and the woman responded "You said my arm was numb, not my hand!" Well, Neil knew what he meant—an arm is everything from the shoulder down. To his client, though, an arm is an arm and a hand is a hand and they're not the same! Needless to say, Neil learned quickly to be much more specific about what he suggests.

How a given person will respond to a word or phrase is unpredictable. Remember, the person is using her own frame of reference (i.e., experience, understanding) to make meaning out of your words. The best you can do is use words carefully enough to leave as little room (or as much room, as the case may be) for misinterpretation. Training in trancework with peers allows for the kind of feedback on the impact of words and phrases used that clients are highly unlikely to provide. Finding out which communications facilitated the trance experience and which hindered it are two of the most valuable aspects of small-group training in clinical hypnotherapy.

TRANCE LOGIC

A characteristic of the trance state that is eminently practical in its clinical applications is called "trance logic." This refers to the client's lack of need for objectifying her experience. In other words, the client can accept the suggested reality, however illogical and impossible it may be, as if it were the only reality. If, for example, I want to do an intervention involving the client's currently inaccessible parents (who live in another place or are deceased), I can suggest the client see her parents and interact with them on the issue(s) needing resolution. Trance logic allows the client to accept her parents as there, instead of responding with an intellectual assessment such as, "How can my parents be here when they live in Europe?" Things that don't make much logical sense can make perfect sense to the trance subject willing to engage in trance logic.

Trance logic involves dissociating the conscious logic and hidden observer long enough to allow the suggested reality to impact personal experience, thus deriving its therapeutic potential. Typically, the person engages in some self-justification process to explain to herself how such an experience could happen. Stage hypnotists often illustrate this by snapping their fingers in the middle of the subjects' silly routines and questioning them as to why they are attempting to seduce a microphone (or some equivalent). The stage subjects come up with some very interesting, creative, yet entirely rational responses to explain themselves.

Trance logic is a voluntary state of acceptance of suggestions on the part of the client, without the critical evaluation taking place that would, of course, destroy the validity of meaningfulness of provided suggestions. The opportunity to act "as if" something were real can be a gateway to deeper feelings and issues appropriate for therapeutic intervention.

LETHARGY AND RELAXATION

One can be in trance without being relaxed (refer to the earlier chapter on misconceptions), but the relaxation of mind and body is a general characteristic most people associate with trance. Most trance processes involve relaxation as a way of facilitating the dissociation of the conscious from the unconscious mind. Relaxation feels good to clients, alters their experience of themselves in a marked way, and may even convince them that they have, in fact, been hypnotized.

Self-hypnosis is an invaluable part of the treatment process, in my opinion, and clients should be given some self-hypnosis procedures to use in their own behalf. The relaxation is imperative for highly anxious clients especially, and self-hypnosis gives *all* clients the opportunity to reinforce the work you do with them. I do not recommend the purchase of pre-made hypnosis tapes for self-therapy because of their inability to meet individual needs. If a tape is desirable to the client as a self-hypnosis guide, the client can be instructed on how to make a tape for herself, or perhaps you can make one for her. Often, clients have an easier time experiencing trance with an external guide at first, such as a tape or another person, because their concentration wanders. With independent practice, this diminishes over time.

The relaxation associated with trance surfaces in a number of physical changes described in the next section, and in a voluntary passivity in which the client experiences almost anything as taking too much effort. Asking the client to talk, move, or think is often met with apparent inaction on the part of the client, simply because what has been suggested requires more energy than she cares to expend. This is another reason to take a more easygoing approach rather than a demanding one, as it can allow the client to experience trance in her own way without having to "perform."

PHYSICAL CHARACTERISTICS OF THE TRANCE STATE

How do you know your client is in hypnosis? The answer is a definite . . . you don't. At precisely what moment a person has gone from his or her usual state of awareness to a more focused trance state is unknown. Given that the trance state is a state differing from everyday mental experience only by degrees and not kind, there are no clear demarcations from the usual state to the trance state. Likewise, there are no clear dividing lines between the various degrees of trance depth. With experience, however, one notices a variety of physical characteristics associated with the trance state that may be used as general indicators of the presence of trance (Erickson, Rossi & Rossi, 1976).

Physical characteristics of trance generally are the only indicators one has available for assessing the client's experience. The exception to that is when one specifically asks for verbal or nonverbal feedback about the client's internal experience. Asking clients for feedback encourages a degree of conscious analysis of their experience, which can sometimes prove disruptive to the process. Thus, it is suggested that one practice skills in close observation of others so one may obtain feedback that is unconsciously communicated by the client. Physical indicators that may be useful to observe include:

1. Muscular relaxation—Notice the person's level of tension carried in the body and especially the facial muscles both before and during your work for comparison.

2. Muscular twitching—As the body and mind relax, often there are spasms that are wholly involuntary and are related to the neurological changes that take place with relaxation.

3. Lacrimation—As the person relaxes, occasionally the eyes may tear. Some automatically assume the person is upset and shedding a tear, but that is an unjustifiable leap to a possibly erroneous conclusion. If in doubt, ask!

4. Eye closure with fluttering eyelids—As the person begins to shift her focus and enter trance, her eyelids may flutter at a very fast rate and usually outside of her awareness. Also, rapid eye movements under the eyelid are observable throughout much of the trance process, even more so if the process involves a lot of visualization.

5. Change in breathing rate—A change, either speeding up or slowing down, of breathing is typical. Observe the client's breathing patterns before and during the process for comparison. Some people's breathing becomes shallower, some deeper, some from the chest, some from the diaphragm.

6. Change in pulse rate—A change, either speeding up but usually slowing down, of the pulse is also typical. When the client is sitting back, one can easily observe the pulsing of the carotid artery in her neck, or if one prefers (and one has the client's permission) one can hold the client's wrist "to be supportive" and take a reading of her radial pulse.

7. Jaw relaxes—Often the person's lower jaw drops and seems subjectively to weigh so much that it takes conscious effort to close it. I've known people who wouldn't participate in group hypnosis because of their embarassing tendency to drool!

8. Catalepsy—An inhibition of voluntary motion that is uniquely reflective of the absorption of trance. Unlike the sleep state in which one is in almost constant motion, the client in trance makes very few, if any, movements. It just takes too much effort, and the client typically feels dissociated from her body anyway and so forgets about it. Every once in a while, and this is especially true of children, one may experience someone who moves around a lot. In one training course, I had a student the class nicknamed "The Thrasher." When he experienced trance he liked to roll on the floor and wriggle around quite a bit. On disengaging, he described how good it felt to relax his body through movement. Even though movement seems excessive or disruptive, the client may still be in trance. One can use the other trance indicators to support an assessment of the client's degree of involvement in trance.

Each of the physical characteristics described above may be used as indicators of trance, but no one sign alone can tell the clinician what her client is actually experiencing internally. In a sense, the clinician is a visitor to someone else's world, and so should be observant, cautious, and above all respectful. Much of the assessment of when to shift from one phase of trancework to another, e.g., going from induction into utilization, will be based on how well one observes changes in the person's body and demeanor. Taking a baseline of muscular tension, breathing and pulse rates, and anything else one can find before beginning trancework gives one the opportunity to notice changes which suggest the development of a state different than the original one. One really can't always know what the content of the person's experience is, but one can observe changes that suggest an impact from the clinician's guidance. The more skilled one becomes in observing such changes, the more comfortable one can be in adapting to the ongoing experience of the client.

CONCLUSION

This chapter has attempted to give the reader some insight into the internal experience of the hypnotized person. Such a subjective experience as trance will necessarily differ in quality from person to person. Therefore, all the general characteristics of trance described in this chapter are likely to be present in most clients, but in varying degrees and, in some cases, may even be absent. Becoming effective with hypnosis presupposes a knowledge and use of these characteristics in the client's behalf.

For Discussion

1. Why are some people so intense while others are so easily distracted? What are the advantages and disadvantages of each style?

2. Based on *your* experience of trance, do you think hypnosis can be used to generate antisocial behavior in someone? Why or why not?

3. Have each person in the class describe their experience of trance. What experiences seem to be common? Which do you recognize as being unique to that person?

4. When in the course of daily living is having a parallel awareness an asset? A liability?

5. How is suggestibility different than gullibility?

Things to Do

1. Share an experience with the class of a vacation or something similar. Which details do you focus on? Why? What sort of details do class members identify as being missing or minimally present in your story? Does this indicate anything about you? What, if anything?

2. Do something, such as walk around the room and pick up objects of interest to you. While doing this, verbally describe your every movement. How does it feel to both participate and observe yourself doing something? Is it easy or hard to do? Why?

3. What commonly used phrases can you and your classmates think of that might generate unwanted responses in someone who responded to the phrase with literal interpretation?

11

Conditions
for Trancework

In this chapter, I would like to explore some of the variables beyond your communication patterns and therapeutic relationship that can affect your work. These variables are characterized as "Environmental" and "Physical."

ENVIRONMENTAL VARIABLES

There was a psychological center here in San Diego that had large egg-shaped chairs in a room with thickly carpeted walls for clients to sit in while listening to hypnosis tapes. These special chairs were equipped with numerous speakers, lights, electronic gadgetry to move the arm rests slowly downward while the client heard suggestions for arm levitation, and various other such computerized tricks. Incredible amounts of money and machinery went into this organization's impersonal electronic approach to hypnosis. If one were to ask the clinicians at this clinic about the proper environmental conditions for hypnosis, I suppose they'd say the environment they created is the ideal. I would disagree. (Apparently, their clients did also, for they are no longer in business!) From my perspective, forming an intense, warm, goal-directed alliance with the client is a necessity in making worthwhile therapeutic interventions. Everything else is secondary.

There are certain environmental conditions that I think are desirable for doing trancework, but they are not essential. First, working in a relatively quiet atmosphere is helpful. An atmosphere that is free of intruding or obnoxious noise is less distracting to the client, allowing her to focus more on her internal rather than external experiences. Realistically, however, phones ring, doors get knocked on, people converse outside your door (if you even have a door), traffic zooms by, planes pass overhead, people drop heavy objects, people sneeze, pets knock over vases, kids argue. . . . In other words, no environment is perfectly quiet and free from external noise— nor does it have to be. The key to helping the client focus herself internally without being distracted by external events lies in the clinician's ability to *tie those events into the process* (the "accept and utilize" formula again).

At the very beginning of the trance process, it may help the client diminish external awareness by offering a general suggestion to the effect that:

> Whatever sounds you may hear in the environment are routine, everyday sounds, and you can let them pass out of your awareness just as quickly as they enter . . . the sounds of the environment are so routine that you can just let them drift out of your awareness. . . .

By not specifying which sounds one is referring to, one is offering a blanket suggestion to cover all the possibilities. Also, one is avoiding the inappropriate use of negative suggestions such as "Don't notice the phone ringing," which will, of course, cause the person to notice it.

The best thing to do if an intrusion occurs is to use a "chaining" suggestion structure in which you can comment on the current reality of the intrusion, and then chain the desired response to the comment. For example, if the phone rings while the person is in trance, one might comment directly:

> . . . Isn't it nice to know the phone can ring and since you don't have to answer it you can just relax even more. . . .

Or one can comment on it indirectly:

> As you relax, your unconscious mind can *call a message* up to your conscious mind about relaxing even deeper.

Ignoring the intrusion pressures the client indirectly to pay even more attention to it, but using the "accept and utilize" structure allows one to integrate spontaneous events as mechanisms for attaining further results. Intrusions are transformed into part of the experience, altering their impact from a negative to a positive one.

Another environmental factor that may be helpful is the use of soft, soothing lighting. Lighting helps create atmosphere, and soft lighting can help facilitate comfort. I would not recommend lighting that is too dim, nor would I recommend darkness. Candlelight may be all right for some, too esoteric for others.

A third environmental factor affecting the client's ability to relax is the furniture. Beds or couches to lie prone on may be too suggestive and furthermore are likely to put the client to sleep. Furniture should be comfortable and support the client's head and body. As the client relaxes, his body tends to become heavy; neck and backaches can easily result if the ,client doesn't get adequate physical support. Recliner chairs are quite good for this reason.

Lighting, furniture and environmental sound factors are less important factors than how one uses them. The key point thus far is to *use whatever happens as part of the process,* framing the event as being perfectly all right.

PHYSICAL VARIABLES

Certain physical conditions are also worthy of consideration in doing trancework. I refer here not to physical health, but to transient physical experiences that may play a role in the hypnotic encounter. Physically, it helps if the client is comfortable; the body is adequately supported, clothing is not restrictive or binding, the temperature is comfortable, and mentally the client isn't feeling rushed or distracted by other things demanding immediate attention.

It is important that the client have nothing in her mouth (e.g., gum, candy . . .) that could choke her as she relaxes. Also, many people wear contact lenses and some contact lenses are constructed in such a way that if the client closes her eyes even briefly (a few minutes) the lenses irritate the eyes to the point of becoming painful. Ask the client if she would like to remove her glasses, contact lenses, shoes, or whatever else might inhibit her focus from going inward.

Other physical considerations include drug or alcohol influences, which are typically counterproductive to doing effective work. Prescribed medications may be excepted, but even these may potentially hinder effective trancework. Similar inhibitions can exist for the overtired or exhausted client who may be easy to put to sleep but is difficult to get to focus internally.

The less one assumes about one's client, the more objective feedback one will seek about her condition. One *cannot* assume she has normal hearing, normal physiology, no contact lenses, no gum in her mouth, no access to street drugs or alcohol, and so forth. It takes only a second to ask, and one's sensitivity can save one a lot of grief later. The key here, as in the environmental conditions, is to use the spontaneous events that arise. If a client coughs, don't fret. Use it!

As you clear your throat, your throat can relax ... and then you can relax even deeper. ...

or

It's good to clear the way in order to be able to swallow new ideas. ...

One can acknowledge that the client's trance state has lightened at that particular moment, and then one can use it to help the person go deeper into trance again. Realistically, no one ever nose-dives into deep trance anyway. *Trance is always lightening and deepening from moment to moment.* That's why saying "deeper, deeper, deeper" is a poor representation of the experience.

Following the "suggestion chaining" format of tying "what is" to "what can be" is the key to coping with environments that aren't perfect and clients who have the audacity to sneeze, cough, laugh, or cry in the middle of your trance process. It is important that you can get comfortable in tying spontaneous occurrences into your work. No environment is completely controllable—you just have to go with the flow. Ultimately, skilled communication is the principal factor in successful hypnosis—not the chair you use.

For Discussion

1. What kind of physical environment for doing trancework would you create if cost were no barrier?

2. What is your opinion of the "computerized hypnosis" approach? Why do you feel that way?

3. How might ignoring an intrusion cause a client to pay even more attention to it?

4. Can suggestions from a computer or cassette tape be as effective as those from a live person? Why or why not?

Things to Do

1. Make a list of the most common intrusions you are likely to encounter while doing trancework. Generate five direct and indirect suggestions for each intrusion that will allow it to be of positive use in the process.

2. Visit a variety of clinicians' offices who use hypnosis, noticing the type and physical arrangement of furniture. What seems most practical to you?

3. Vary the arrangement of seats from practice session to session, ranging from very close together to far apart. Do you notice any differences in people's level of responsiveness to you? How do you account for whatever differences you may observe?

SECTION II

*Practical
Framework*

12

Structuring Suggestions

If you make a recommendation to a friend about a restaurant you tried and enjoyed and then she goes to that restaurant on the basis of your recommendation, you have influenced her experience. Somewhere in that interaction was at least one element of hypnosis, for you offered a suggestion and it was accepted and later acted upon. How did you phrase your recommendation? What was your tone of voice and body posture? What is your relationship with that person? What other factors can you identify that made your recommendation the basis for a new experience for someone?

Suggesting to someone that she go to a particular restaurant or movie (or likewise, that she avoid it) is a routine, everyday type of interaction. In spite of its commonness, this kind of interaction can illustrate the nature of suggestion quite well. In making a recommendation of any sort, you are sharing information with someone about an experience you have had or a belief you hold. On the basis of your description, the other person forms an internal representation of your experience. If it is a powerful enough representation, it may motivate her to go and have a similar experience directly. In this example, information about a restaurant is transmitted from one person to another, but the information does not have to be acted upon since it is only a recommendation or suggestion. If the information is inherently appealing or is made to sound appealing in some way to the listener, then it is probably going to be accepted.

Any suggestion can be accepted or rejected, hypnotic or otherwise. The skill of a good hypnotist is in his ability to formulate suggestions in such a way as to make them acceptable. A deep trance state on the part of the client is no assurance that he will accept suggestions offered to him, even ones that are clearly in his best interest. Personal, interpersonal, and situational factors discussed in the previous chapters on suggestibility and susceptibility determine the degree of a person's responsiveness to suggestion. The focus in this chapter is on some of the interpersonal communication variables of hypnotic patterns, specifically the communication styles and structures of hypnotic suggestions.

COMMUNICATION STYLES

The power of hypnotic communication lies in its ability to act as a catalyst for organizing and using the resources of the unconscious mind. Each human being has a conscious and unconscious mind (although I have sometimes wondered whether clients I had difficulty doing trancework with had an unconscious . . .). The conscious mind is the rational, logical one for the most part, while the unconscious mind contains a person's memories, lifetime of learnings, automatic patterns, and world view. As Watzlawick (1978) pointed out, the type of communication that is most likely to be beneficial to the client is language that appeals to the unconscious. Reasoning with someone (or with yourself) about how illogical it is to feel a certain way rarely changes the feeling. I wish I had a nickel for every time I've heard someone say, "I know I shouldn't feel this way, but I can't help it."

Appreciating the differences in the information processing styles and abilities of the conscious and unconscious minds is prerequisite to the effective use of hypnosis. Formulating suggestions that are more likely to appeal to the unconscious mind's world view is one of the ways hypnosis derives its strength. Ideally, information is offered to and accepted by the client's unconscious mind. The unconscious is by no means gullible or defenseless, but it is less critical than the conscious mind. Occupying or distracting the conscious mind while engaging the resources of the unconscious mind allows a greater opportunity for generating meaningful changes. The ritualistic nature of traditional hypnotic inductions is a good example of a means for occupying a person's conscious mind, making the unconscious more accessible for therapeutic suggestions. The unconscious continuously processes information outside of one's awareness, and is capable of forming responses to that information also out of awareness. The everyday example of driving a car without paying attention to your driving is a good one to illustrate the point.

Other examples of unconscious information processing are the subliminal messages that have long been used in the field of advertising. They are imperceptible consciously, but are potentially effective at an unconscious level. I am aware of a considerable number of hypnotists who use specially made subliminal message cassette tapes that contain suggestions offered below the auditory level where such suggestions can be consciously heard (below the auditory threshold). The client listens to a tape of relaxing music or ocean waves or something similarly neutral, and embedded within the neutral stimulus are suggestions to counter whatever complaints the person has presented. The fact that the suggestions are subliminal (if they are even present, since who can know?) does not offer any greater assurance the suggestion will be accepted. The same limitations that apply to any standardized approach apply to the subliminal approach.

There are two basic styles of hypnotic communications: direct and indirect. Not only are they *not* mutually exclusive, but I doubt it is possible (or desirable) to do an effective hypnotic process exclusively in one form or the other. Realistically, both styles will be evident in a given process at various times. Furthermore, each suggestion will vary in the *degree* of directness, as if on a continuum with "direct" at one pole and "indirect" at the other. The question of which style to use at a given moment depends on

---

Table 2. Suggestion Structures and Styles

Positive Suggestions
  "You can do X"

Negative Suggestions
  "You cannot do X"

Direct Suggestions
  "You can do X"

Indirect Suggestions
  "I knew someone who enjoyed doing X"

Process Suggestions
  "You can have a special memory"

Content Suggestions
  "You can remember your third grade teacher"

Permissive Styles
  "You can allow yourself to do X"

Authoritarian Styles
  "You will do X"

Post-hypnotic Suggestions
  "Later, when you are in situation A, you can do X"

the nature of the suggestion (factors such as its potential for threatening the client) and the degree of responsiveness of the client.

DIRECT SUGGESTIONS

Direct suggestions are those that deal with the problem at hand (or the specific response desired) overtly and clearly. They are not known for their subtlety. Direct suggestions refer to the person's conscious experience a great deal, and provide specific solutions to problems with detailed instructions about how to respond.

Commonly, to begin trancework, the clinician will want the client to close her eyes. If the clinician chooses a direct approach, he might offer any of the following direct suggestions:

Close your eyes.
Please close your eyes.
You can close your eyes.
Let your eyes close.
I would like you to close your eyes.

Each of the above suggestions directly relates to obtaining eye closure as a specific response. There is no mistaking what the clinician wants the client to do. The statements are clear in their intent to get the client to close her eyes. The same direct suggestion structures might be used to obtain virtually any desired response:

Remember when you went to your first school dance? (Age regression)
Let your arm lift effortlessly and become weightless. (Arm levitation)
You can make your hand numb. (Analgesia)
Experience each minute as if it were an hour. (Time distortion)

The desired response in each of the above examples is apparent because the suggestions directly ask for it. Nothing is hidden from the client in terms of what is wanted from her. Each suggestion is intended to get a specific response. More direct suggestions may be offered to provide a concrete means for accomplishing the response:

Imagine you are in a time machine that is taking you back to your first school dance.
You can feel that your arm is tied to a large helium balloon allowing it to float.
Remember how your hand tingles when you get a shot of novocain? You can have that same sensation of numbness in your hand now.

Time passes so slowly when you are waiting for something special, and you can notice now how slowly the hands of time move.

Many hypnotists practice a direct suggestion approach exclusively. Training courses and books that offer standardized scripts for use with general problems are necessarily direct in their approach. For example, if a client presents the complaint of wanting to lose weight, a direct approach might offer suggestions such as:

You want to lose weight, and you will lose weight. You will lose weight because you will find yourself becoming choosier about what you eat and when you eat. Whenever you reach for a fattening or unnecessary food you will see the image in your mind of yourself weighing your ideal weight, and it will be very easy to choose not to overeat. You would rather lose weight than eat fattening foods. You will feel so good about yourself that losing weight becomes easier and easier, and you'll be satisfied with less and less food. You'll also want to exercise more....

This kind of direct approach may work with some people—some very obedient ones or some highly motivated ones! Of course, some people are so ready to change by the time they consult someone professionally that all you have to do is look at them sternly, shake your finger at them, and admonish them, "Don't do that anymore!" and they won't. For most people, a great deal more subtlety and complexity of suggestion are required, as well as a more highly individualized approach. Telling others bluntly what to do does not show much clinical skill, nor does it show much respect for their intelligence and creativity. People already know what to do, they just don't have access to the resources that would allow them to do it. Finally, such approaches don't involve as much of the person in the process as a more collaborative effort would. Familiarity and skill with both direct and indirect techniques are essential to the development of a broad and flexible practice of clinical hypnosis.

The advantages of direct suggestions include: 1) their direct relevance to the matters at hand (easing conscious worries in the client about your ability to deal directly with his concerns), 2) their ability to keep the client's goal well defined and in sight, 3) their direct involvement of the client in the process in an active way, and, 4) their ability to serve as a model for the resolution of any future problems that arise through the development of a conscious problem-solving strategy.

The disadvantages of direct suggestions include their overreliance on a conscious willingness to follow suggestions, making less use of the resources of the unconscious mind. Also, direct suggestions are much more likely to engender resistance in the client by dealing so directly with his problems, potentially a very threatening experience. Threatening the client increases the likelihood of defensive reactions, not the least of which is the rejection of suggestions.

Appreciating the advantages and disadvantages of the use of direct suggestions is necessary to allow you to make an informed decision as to when their use will most likely result in a successful trance experience.

INDIRECT SUGGESTIONS

Indirect suggestions are those that relate to the problem at hand (or the specific desired response) in a covert and unobtrusive way. They can be quite subtle. Such suggestions usually do not relate directly to the person's conscious experience. Rather, they are indirectly related and thus require the client to interpret them in an idiosyncratic way in order to make meaning of them. Use of indirect suggestion can have the client wondering at the conscious level what you are talking about, while at the same time his unconscious mind is connecting what you are saying to his internal experiences (underlying dynamic processes) and thus paving the way for change to take place.

Indirect suggestions can take numerous forms, including story-telling, analogies, jokes, puns, homework assignments, and disguised and embedded suggestions. Any communication device that causes or requires the client to respond without directly telling or asking him to do so involves indirect suggestion to some degree.

Indirect suggestion is a focal point of study in the utilization approach, largely due to the many creative ways they were used by Milton H. Erickson, M.D. The late Dr. Erickson was widely acknowledged for his skill and creativity in formulating successful interventions with seemingly "impossible" clients. Often, he did this in ways that seemed to have no relationship to the presenting complaint. Advanced study of clinical hypnosis is literally impossible without studying Erickson's work directly, as well as the writings about his methods by his many students and colleagues.

To contrast direct and indirect suggestions, it is suggested (after all, hypnosis is the name of the game) that you refer back to the earlier examples for obtaining eye closure through direct suggestions. If you suspect, on the basis of feedback from your client, that you would be more likely to get eye closure through indirect methods, you might offer any of the following suggestions:

A good hypnotic subject begins the trance experience by closing her eyes.
Can you allow your eyes to close?
Many of my clients like to sit there with their eyes closed.
Isn't it nice not to have to listen with your eyes open?
I wonder what you will think of that will allow you to comfortably CLOSE YOUR EYES.

Each of the above examples is seeking eye closure as a specific response, but it has never been asked for directly. The statements are general ones that the client must respond to in some way (since even no response is a response). The clinician can learn quite a bit about how the person thinks and responds from the way she relates to such suggestions.

Indirect statements may take the form of describing others' experiences, allowing the client to choose a similar response or an independent one. Another indirect pattern is to have the client become aware of routine, everyday experiences where the desired response is a natural event. As the client becomes aware of such a situation, she begins to re-experience herself as if in that suggested situation, and then the responses associated with it become a part of the current experience. For example, if you were to think of a time when you felt very romantic and loving toward someone, and really spent time recalling the details of that experience, those same feelings are likely to arise once again (ideoaffective response). Thus, instead of demanding the specific response of creating those feelings now in a direct way, I can get them indirectly by describing a context where such feelings are likely to naturally occur.

As with eye closure, indirect suggestions can be used to obtain virtually any response:

A close friend of mine has a daughter who went to her first school dance, and I don't know if you can remember yours, but it sure was an exciting time for her. *(Age regression)*

When you were in grade school you had to RAISE YOUR HAND SLOWLY when you wanted to say something important, and sometimes it would rise and you didn't even know it. *(Arm levitation)*

Can you imagine what it's like to have your first snowball fight and have so much fun you forgot to notice you weren't even wearing gloves? *(Analgesia)*

Time is so difficult to keep track of, and after all a minute can seem like 5 or 10 minutes sometimes, or even more, because you get so wrapped up in your thoughts that a minute can seem so long. *(Time distortion)*

In each of the above examples, the client's experience is seemingly less the focal point than someone else's, or else the suggestion is so general as to be impersonal. It is up to the client to adapt herself in her own unique way to the possibilities for certain responses raised by the clinician. In this way, direct commands for obedience are avoided, and the client's own ability to form an individualized response is tapped. How she finds a way to accomplish the possible response is as varied and creative as are people. My strategies for getting the response, and the inherent limitations when someone else uses them, may not be as useful to the person as the possibilities she creates for herself. Essentially, through the telling of stories or some similar indirect technique, I am suggesting to the person "how" a change can be accomplished without telling the person "what" to do.

The advantages of the indirect approaches relate primarily to their greater utilization of the unconscious mind's resources in the client's own behalf. By having suggestions presented in the form of triggers for old or new associations that may be therapeutic to experience, more of the person is involved in the therapy at multiple levels. Furthermore, by having a greater distance between the suggestion and its intended target emotion or behavior, there is less need for resistant defenses. Such distance may also create confusion in the client about how the suggestion relates to personal improvement, and thus paves the way for the client to interpret the suggestions in whatever way will be useful to her. By not forcing the client to respond to the clinician's demands, one demonstrates a greater respect for the client, a highly desirable outcome.

The disadvantages of the indirect style include the client's possible fear or anxiety that the clinician is unable or unwilling to deal directly with the problem, and "if she can't, how can I?" The clinician may then be viewed as evasive or incompetent, and the client may feel manipulated and even cheated. Another disadvantage is that the client's unconscious responses may allow for alleviation of the problem, but may leave the client consciously wondering how the change occurred. The problem may be solved but may not leave the client with access to patterns for solving future problems.

As with direct suggestions, appreciating the advantages and disadvantages of indirect suggestion usage gives one an ability to make sensitive choices about their applications. One approach is not better than another. The goal is to use either approach flexibly in order to get the desired therapeutic result.

CHOOSING A STYLE

Earlier it was stated that it is unlikely that any process can be exclusively direct or indirect, nor is it a desirable goal to try and make a process exclusively one or the other. The issue related to hypnotic styles is one of how each individual suggestion within an intervention containing perhaps hundreds of suggestions should be phrased to maximize the likelihood of it being accepted (or rejected, if that is the goal) in a meaningful way. The guidelines for choosing a style and the degree to which that style should be used are based on two major factors: the degree of insight desirable or necessary to allow the intervention to work, and the degree of responsiveness of the client.

There exists a split among psychotherapists regarding the role of insight in the treatment process. Some claim that insight is both necessary and desirable to facilitate change, while others claim insights are not required in order for meaningful changes to occur and that insight may even delay change by giving people a better cognitive understanding of the hurtful patterns with no vehicle for affectively or behaviorally changing them.

Erickson was a major proponent of the ideas that insight is not necessary to effect meaningful changes, and that insights may actually impede the therapy by fostering an overreliance on the conscious mind, the most limited part of the person. Erickson's techniques of confusing, overloading, surprising, shocking, and boring the client's conscious mind were all techniques designed to gain access to the unconscious mind, where change could occur naturally if the proper resources were tapped.

Insight-oriented approaches can have a great deal of utility for reasons I mentioned when I described the advantages of direct suggestions and also for a variety of reasons I haven't mentioned that are elaborated in other sources on the subject. A major drawback, though, is the greater length of time involved in generating conscious understandings. Another is the client's typical defense of containing the insights to the cognitive level without incorporating them into meaningful changes at an affective level ("intellectualization").

Perhaps the biggest drawback in offering insights and interpretations as the sole basis for doing therapy is in the fact that the client has made a choice, at some level, to keep certain information out of her awareness. Should a clinician take specific pieces of behavior or internal experience, attach an interpretation to them, and present them back to the client and thereby violate the client's desire to keep that information out of personal awareness? How can an interpretation of complex experience be anything but an oversimplification? Furthermore, how can an interpretation be anything but a projection on the part of the clinician? I raise these issues simply to engender the idea that there are very few, if any, absolute "right" or "wrong" ways to structure therapeutic interventions. Each client is unique as an individual, and whether insight will work for or against the therapy is a factor to weigh in formulating your interventions.

Some clients demand understanding at a conscious level, asking "Why" a lot. Others are much more interested in getting some change to occur in the problem no matter what it takes. The more a person seeks conscious understanding and tries to engage you on that level, the more an indirect approach will disrupt his normal pattern, increasing the likelihood of change. Yet, at the same time, a person who seeks conscious understanding may be put off by an indirect method, lose patience and motivation, and dismiss the experience as useless. Only experience will teach you to make assessments about which style to use with a particular client.

The second variable to consider in assessing whether to use a direct or indirect style is the degree of responsiveness of the client (or "resistance," traditionally considered a lack of responsiveness). A basic rule that you can use as a guideline for determining which style to use is this: *The degree of indirection should be directly proportional to the degree of resistance encountered or anticipated* (Zeig, 1980). In other words, the greater the degree of inability or unwillingness to follow directives on the part of the client, the more the suggestions should be offered indirectly.

If a client is compliant and highly responsive to the clinician's requests, following them in an authentic (and not in a "resistant overcooperation") and motivated way, indirection is not necessary. Conversely, if a client is resistant to directives, indirect approaches are more respectful and non-threatening because of their distance from the intended target (such as the underlying dynamics to be resolved) and thus have a greater likelihood of acceptance.

The degree of direction or indirection in offering suggestions will vary according to the unique responses of each individual you work with. As with all the hypnotic communication patterns presented in this book, what you do will rely on the feedback you get from the client. You can feel much more secure in your abilities to relate to a wider range of people if you have both direct and indirect approaches in your repertoire.

EARLIER VIEWS ON SUGGESTION STYLE

Before the recent surge of interest in the indirect methods for inducing and utilizing the trance state, the consideration of suggestion styles was limited to the demeanor of the clinician while offering direct suggestions. Styles were described on a continuum with "authoritarian" at one extreme and "permissive" at the other. These terms can still be useful in describing the relationship between clinician and client, and so are included here.

The authoritarian approach is a domineering one in which the clinician literally commands the client to respond in a particular way. Authority and power are the variables the clinician relies on, and the response from the "good" client is compliance. Stage hypnotists are necessarily authoritarian in style, requiring obedient responses from their subjects. In the authoritarian approach, a lack of obedience is evidence of "resistance," and, unfortunately, is viewed as a shortcoming of the client. Traditional literature typically suggests confronting the client about her resistance to the procedures and then attempting to resolve them by identifying them and talking them out. In the later chapter on resistance, the futility of this approach to resistance is elaborated, but the reader may anticipate how easily this approach can initiate a "power struggle."

Authoritarian approaches involve offering suggestions in the form of commands. The following suggestions are structured in an authoritarian mode:

Close your eyes when I count to three.
When I snap my fingers, you will be six years old.
When I touch your shoulder, you will go into a deep trance.
You will find it impossible to light a cigarette.
You will not remember anything from this experience.

Directing someone to respond in a way that is desirable to *you* does not show much respect for that person's needs or wants, and thus a strictly authoritarian approach should be used sparingly. At the other end of the spectrum is the "permissive" approach, one that is much more respectful of the client's ability to make choices in her own behalf about what she will and will not respond to. The permissive approach is one characterized by its emphasis on allowing the client to become aware of *possibilities* for meaningful responses, rather than making demands for such responses. The clinician offers suggestions of what the client *may* experience *if* she chooses to. The responsibility is on the client to a considerable extent to make use in her own way of information that has been provided by the clinician. Therefore, any response is deemed an adequate one by the clinician, respectful of the person's choice. In this way, "resistance" is much less debilitating a factor.

Permissive suggestions are intended to raise the possibility of a response, and the following examples may illustrate the point:

You can allow your eyes to close, if you would like.

You may choose to uncross your legs.

You can let yourself relax even more.

You can permit yourself the opportunity to experience yourself differently.

Perhaps you can let this learning guide your daily choices.

In the above examples, the client is responding to her own choices, and so what is there to resist? The clinician is simply saying, in one form or another, that the client can have an experience *if* she lets herself. The client's response in *any* direction is thus a reflection of choice and must be respected as such by the clinician. Such acceptance by the clinician adds to the rapport considerably by demonstrating a respect for the client as a person capable of making choices for herself. It may be implicit thus far but can now be stated explicitly that when the client's choices are deemed counterproductive to your treatment plan, your strategy can be revised in order to maneuver the client into a position of being more comfortable accepting your suggestions. The idea of the permissive approach is to make the suggestions you have offered the client acceptable through personal choice. The skill required in such an approach is evident.

By now you have probably noticed my pattern of pointing out strengths and weaknesses of each approach, a necessary step in evaluating when and where to use a particular suggestion style or structure. As a generalization, there are those who want to be told what to do and will follow instructions to the letter, and there are those who refuse to follow anyone's lead and will even go out of their way to reject others' input. If someone is willing to follow directives obediently, an authoritarian approach may be successfully employed. With most people, however, it will tend to set up power struggles. The permissive approach is good for creating possibilities in people who like to have a large measure of control in their lives by making their own decisions, but may frustrate the person who wants to be told in very explicit terms exactly what to do in a step-by-step fashion. Both authoritarian and permissive styles have their place in doing trancework, and as with all forms of suggestion, it is recommended that you familiarize yourself with their usage.

SUGGESTION STRUCTURES

Along with a style for offering suggestions, one must also choose a particular structure for the suggestion. Suggestion structures can take a number of different forms, described below.

POSITIVE SUGGESTIONS

Positive suggestions are by far the most common, simple, and useful type of suggestion structure. Positive suggestions are supportive and encouraging, and are phrased in such a way as to give the client the idea that he can experience or accomplish something desirable. Since words call to mind the experiences that the words (as symbols of experience) represent, positive suggestions are phrased to create desirable responses. The following suggestions are structured in a positive way (and permissively as well):

You can feel more comfortable with each breath you inhale.
You can remember a time when you felt very proud of yourself.
You are able to discover inner strengths you didn't realize you had.
You can notice how good it feels to relax.
You may notice a soothing feeling of warmth in your hands.

The positive suggestions above are examples to the client of things he can experience. Many experienced clinicians claim that suggestions should be in the positive form in order for the unconscious mind to process them, and it is further claimed that the unconscious mind does not understand negatives. My own experience is consistent with these views for reasons I will elaborate in the following discussion on negative suggestion structures.

NEGATIVE SUGGESTIONS

Negative suggestions employ a sort of "reverse psychology" approach when they are used skillfully. Negative suggestions may be used to obtain a response by suggesting the person *not* respond in the desired way. The basis for this phenomenon was described earlier when it was pointed out that words are merely symbols for experience. In order to make meaning out of the random sounds of speech, the words must be connected to the experience(s) they represent ("transderivational search").

When used deliberately and in a skilled way, negative suggestions can be most useful. The following are examples of negative suggestions. Notice what your internal experience is as you slowly read each of them.

Do not think of your favorite color.

Do not allow yourself to wonder what time it is.

I would suggest that you not notice that sensation in your leg.

You shouldn't be thinking about your high school sweetheart right now.

Please try not to notice which of your friends is the most materialistic.

Did you find yourself doing what was suggested that you *not* do? If so, why? If you were able to avoid doing what you were instructed to, how did you accomplish this? Did you have to distract yourself with some other thoughts? Would a client be able to prevent herself from following the suggestion if she didn't know about negative suggestions?

All too often, negative suggestions are employed naively and accidentally, generating an undesired response that may leave the practitioner wondering what went wrong. If a clinician says (with great sincerity and the intention of comforting the client), "Don't worry about it, just put it out of your mind," the client is most probably going to still worry and think about "it." If a lawyer says to a jury, "Don't think about the horrible crime my client committed, instead judge him as a scared, confused person," it is a safe bet the jury has just recalled all the gory details of the crime and the feelings they have about it. Accidental outcomes as a result of non-selective use of negative suggestions can undo in a sentence what might have taken considerably longer to accomplish. Use them carefully!

Mentioned earlier was the conclusion that many have reached about the unconscious being unable to respond or decipher negative suggestions in the literal way they are presented. Based on your experience of the examples of negative suggestions above, do you agree? If I ask you *not* to think of the taste of pizza, didn't you have to think of it before erasing it from your mind in whatever way you might have done that? Your unconscious mind responds to a negative with a positive. How might negative suggestions be used deliberately to facilitate the experience of trance? By suggesting to the client she not do the things you want her to (with the appropriate client and situational variables, of course), you are paving the way for her to respond in a way that can only be defined as cooperative. For example, if I say to my client, "Do not let your breathing slow down or your muscles relax," the client can now respond by either letting her breathing slow down and her muscles relax, positive signs of the beginning of trance, or she can continue in some other state, which I have paved the way for her to do. Thus, either response is a cooperative one, directly or indirectly. Other examples may include suggestions such as:

> Don't even consider the possibility that there might be a positive way to solve this problem.
>
> There's no reason why you should even think about how good it will feel to change.
>
> Don't sit in a comfortable position if you can help it. I'd prefer that you don't discover that you can relax here.

Negative suggestions are a way of short-circuiting resistances, occupying the client with negativity while asking for positive responses indirectly. The typical response of the client is to ignore the negative (since telling someone what *not* to do does not tell them what they *should* do) and respond to the implicit positive suggestion.

CONTENT SUGGESTIONS

Content suggestions are suggestions that contain very specific details describing feelings, memories, thoughts, or fantasies the client is to experience while in trance. Providing details that describe every dimension of the suggested experience can have the desired effect of assisting the client to have the experience more completely and therefore to a greater degree of satisfaction. Examples of content suggestions may include:

> Think of a red rose with soft, velvet petals and a gentle, sweet fragrance.
>
> Imagine being at the beach on a bright, clear day, feeling the sun warming your skin, smelling the salt in the ocean breeze, and hearing the pounding of the waves against the shore.
>
> Can you remember how pleasing it is to bite into a juicy orange, how your mouth waters, and the juice runs all over your fingers, and how tart it tastes?

Each of the above examples provides specific details about what you are to experience in thinking of a rose, the beach, and an orange. Perhaps those details allowed you to have the experience more fully, in which case the details were helpful. However, these examples can also illustrate a potential hazard of using content-filled suggestions, namely that the details I directed you to notice may not be the ones you would have chosen. Or, at their worst, they may have been details that ruined the experience for you. If, for example, when I said imagine the beach you recalled a negative experience at the beach or perhaps have never experienced a beach anywhere, the details will deepen a negative memory or perplex you as to what I'm getting at (since there is no personal experience to relate to my suggestions) and disrupt the experience. The potential problem with content suggestions is simply this: *The more details one provides, the greater the probability that something said will contradict a client's experience.* The end result is the client will sense that the clinician is not really "with" her and sensitive to her experience, and so is less likely to benefit from the experience.

The content-filled hypnotic process can be a most valuable one for deepening a client's involvement in the experience when it works well. One solution to the problem is to notice the many cues the client continually provides (more on that in later chapters on communication dynamics) which can give the clinician feedback on which suggestions assist in deepening the client's involvement in the experience and which seem to work against it. Another solution is to use process suggestions, discussed next.

PROCESS SUGGESTIONS

In contrast to the detailed content suggestions, process suggestions are quite sparse on detail, leaving the client free to attend to whatever details she has associated to (i.e., projected into) the suggested experience. Consequently, the clinician is in less danger of contradicting the experience of the client. If, for example, I would like the client to imagine being in a relaxing place, instead of my choosing the beach as a specific place and providing details about the beach as I might in a content-filled suggestion, I can simply suggest to my client that she imagine being somewhere relaxing. She chooses the place and which details of that place she would like to focus on.

Process instructions are so very general in nature that the client can project meaning into them and then relate to them in her own, individual way. If you are a newspaper horoscope reader, you have daily examples of process suggestions. The observations and predictions are so non-specific that they can apply to virtually anyone. The following paragraph is an example of the point:

> You are a person who likes to be with those people you care about, but sometimes you prefer to just be left alone. Sometimes you get very frustrated

with events in your life, and even lose your temper on occasion. You would like more people to appreciate you, and you think you deserve to make more money than you do.

I think the above paragraph represents most of the human beings on the planet, but did you find yourself silently agreeing and wondering, "How did he know that?" Process instructions give clients the opportunity to use their own experience and details in the process, and therefore make what seems at first glance to be too general to be effective look like a highly individualized approach. The following are examples of process instructions:

You can have a particular memory from childhood, one that you haven't thought about in a long, long time.

You will notice a certain pleasant sensation in your body as you sit there comfortably.

You may become aware of a specific sound in the room.

Can you remember that special time when you felt so good about yourself?

None of the above suggestions specifies anything—they do not say *which* memory, sensation, sound, or event. The client chooses that aspect of the experience. Notice, though, that the use of qualifiers such as "particular," "certain," "specific," and "special" can be employed to have the client sift all of her experience down to one to focus on. Which one the person chooses is a product of the interaction between conscious and unconscious choices. Typically, the client wonders how you knew what she was experiencing, not realizing how general the suggestion was because of how specific it seemed! The use of process suggestions is often harder because of the "groping-in-the-dark" aspect to them, but their ability to sidestep resistances due to contradictions between the details the clinician provides and the client's actual experience makes them imperative to master.

Process suggestions are especially valuable in doing group hypnosis processes, where the opportunity to watch each individual's responsiveness to content suggestions is virtually impossible. Using process suggestions of a general yet specific-sounding nature allows each person in the group to have an entirely different experience in response to a single set of suggestions. Thus, the diversity among people is acknowledged and encouraged. Trying to make a group of people share a common, detailed experience is a set-up for failure.

The content versus process paradigm can be viewed in another way, as dealing with the details contained in the structure of an experience, or the structure itself. Content deals with details, process the structure. For example, many people seek out a certain type of person in a romantic relationship, one who fits some measure of desirability that may or may not be conscious. If a person has a succession of intimate relationships with someone tall, dark-haired, a fashionable dresser, tight-lipped about feelings, and domineering, and each time the relationship ends in disaster, what can be concluded? I am describing the fact that people have patterns that guide their behavior. In the current example, the content is each specific person in the succession of partners. The names and faces change, but not the type of person in the pattern. The content approach might deal with the reason(s) why *this* particular relationship isn't working out, while a process approach might consider the structure of the pattern for how intimates are chosen. By altering the structure of the pattern of selection, naturally the details (content) must also change.

In terms of hypnotic suggestions, process suggestions can assist the client in bringing new learnings and new conclusions about old experiences into the picture that change the client's current experience in some useful way. Working with process or content suggestions is another choice point for the clinician in formulating an intervention. Shifting from one suggestion structure to another is an easy thing to do, so the decision about which structure to use is by no means a final one that is a "sink-or-swim" proposition. If what you are doing isn't getting the desired response, a midstream shift is a good idea.

POSTHYPNOTIC SUGGESTIONS

Posthypnotic suggestions are those given to the client while she is in a trance state about behaviors and feelings she is to have in some future context. Posthypnotic suggestions make it possible for the person to carry over into the desired context the new behaviors or understandings she has acquired during trance. Posthypnotic suggestions are a necessary part of the therapeutic process if the subject is to carry new possibilities into future experiences. *Without them, the learnings acquired during trancework will most probably be limited to the trance state itself.* If the client can have the behavior or feeling only while in a trance state, she is still restricted.

---

*The reason for this is that trance responses are "trance state-specific," meaning they are tied to one internal state. The posthypnotic suggestion permits the learning to cross internal boundaries and become available in other states of consciousness.

Posthypnotic suggestion involves suggesting to the client that when she finds herself in the particular situation she has had trouble with or when she has the hurtful feelings she doesn't want, she can take some step agreed upon during trance to remedy the problem. The following are examples of posthypnotic suggestions:

> When you come out of trance, you can have the feeling that you rested to a more satisfying degree than you have in a long, long time.
>
> When you take your examination next week, you can close your eyes and take a deep breath, and you can notice all the anxiety leaving you as you exhale.
>
> After you go home tonight, you'll have a certain memory that will make you laugh.
>
> When you find yourself in the next argument with your boss, the feeling of comfort that she cares about what you do will soothe you enough to handle the discussion calmly.

Each of the above examples is suggesting a behavior or feeling the client is to experience in some future time and place to be based on the suggestions given to her while in trance. The client may have no conscious memory for the origin of the suggestion (amnesia), but act on it unconsciously nonetheless.

Because of the potential for unconscious responses on the basis of posthypnotic suggestion, they have long been a favorite "stunt" of stage hypnotists. Stage subjects are told to respond in some entertaining way to a cue of some sort (such as a single word or gesture from the hypnotist, a song, or virtually any signal the hypnotist chooses and the subject accepts) and by accepting a suggestion of amnesia with the posthypnotic suggestions find themselves responding to the cue with the suggested behavior with no conscious awareness of why they are behaving that way. It remains a product of choice, however.

Posthypnotic suggestions are useful to assure that the desired response will become integrated into the person's everyday life, replacing dysfunctional or absent responses. Furthermore, posthypnotic suggestion can also be used to facilitate future hypnotic work by offering the suggestion that in future sessions the client can go into trance more deeply and rapidly.

SPECIALIZED SUGGESTIONS

While the suggestion structures and styles described above represent the core of the hypnotic suggestion, there are numerous other forms of suggestion that may be derived from the core components. These are described in this section.

Accessing questions

Questions that encourage the client to respond at an experiential level rather than only a verbal one are known as accessing questions. More than rhetorical questions, accessing questions focus the client on particular aspects of his experience, which are amplified through the way the question was asked: "Can you recall how very soothing and relaxing it is to lie in the warm sun and feel it warming your skin?" Accessing questions have also been called "conversational postulates."

Ambiguous suggestions

One can deliberately use ambiguity in a suggestion in order to encourage the client's projections (similar to the nonspecific "process" suggestion). The ambiguity may surround the desired action on the part of the client, or the meaning of the suggestion. For example, to suggest that, "One can be quite iron-willed and hardheaded in such matters" leaves it open to interpretation as to whether the clinician is praising perseverance or criticizing stubbornness.

Apposition of opposites

Offering suggestions that create distinct polarities of experience within the client is making use of the apposition of opposites. For example: "As your left hand becomes pleasantly cold and numb, you'll notice your right hand becoming comfortably warm and responsive."

Bind of comparable alternatives

Providing the client with a bind of comparable alternatives creates a "forced choice" situation for the client in which both choices lead to an equally desirable outcome: "Would you enjoy a deep trance experience sitting in this chair or in that chair?" For as long as the client responds within the parameters of the suggestion, the bind exists.

Confusional suggestions

Suggestions that are deliberately constructed to disorient or confuse the client in order to build responsiveness, overload an overly intellectual demeanor, and facilitate dissociation are known as confusional. For example, you can think you consciously understand the point of such suggestions, but your unconscious likes clarity, too, so if you consciously organize around conscious understandings that you unconsciously believe will consciously work for you in unconsciously structuring the conscious and unconscious patterns for knowing consciously at an unconscious level that you can overload someone's ability to comprehend, then just make sure you *use confusion when it is sensible to do so*. More is said about confusional methods in Chapter 16.

Covering all possibilities

One way to diffuse resistance and maintain responsiveness in the client is to include all her possible responses in your suggestion, thus defining any response as a useful, cooperative one: "You may think of an important memory . . . perhaps one from early in your life . . . perhaps one from very recently . . . or perhaps one from somewhere in-between. . . ." Well, what other possibilities are there? Any memory will be from her past, obviously, whether recent, immediate, or distant. Thus, any memory retrieved is in line with the suggestion, assuring a positive response.

Implied directives

An indirect way to encourage a response is through the use of implied directives. The first part of the suggestion structure is the indirect suggestion to do something from which the second half of the suggestion then directly suggests a response. For example: "When you experience your hand lifting in just a moment (indirect suggestion), you will notice that it feels very, very light (direct suggestion)."

Interspersal of suggestions

The frequent repetition of key words or phrases within an ongoing series of suggestions is making use of an interspersal approach. One can use interspersal to deepen the trance, facilitate the experience of a specific trance phenomenon, "seed" (implant) ideas for future reference, and reiterate an important point. For example: "A deep thinker, that is, one who thinks deeply, can evolve a deep understanding of the complexities of suggestions, and perhaps an even deeper understanding of herself in gaining the depth of knowledge about suggestion."

Metaphors

Metaphors have come to mean stories in the literature of clinical hypnosis. Metaphors are an indirect method to achieve a number of goals, listed in Table 17 in Chapter 19. Metaphors are considered one of the most powerful and gentle means for communicating relevant information to a client, and so are discussed in detail in several later chapters.

Paradoxical suggestions

Paradoxical suggestions contain what seem to be, at first glance, incompatible components contained within the same overall suggestion. For example: "You can take all the time in the world in the next minute to complete your inner work of integrating your new learning."

Presuppositions

A presupposition assumes the response will happen—it's simply a matter of when: "How pleasantly surprised will you be when you discover that you understand presuppositions?"

Puns

The use of humor as a reframing device can be a valuable way of engaging the client in the process while simultaneously establishing a friendly and warm emotional association to the trancework. For example: "Some people like to do hypnosis in a very predictable rhyming and rhythmic way, but you know and I know that the rhythm method is not very reliable. . . ."

Truisms

A truism is a "common sense" observation that appears to be so self-evident as to be virtually undeniable. Truisms are used to build an acceptance of the suggestion that follows it on the basis of the acceptance of the truism: "Every person is unique, we all know that (truism), which is why you can experience deep trance in your own unique way."

CONCLUSION

Words are stimuli, and they come to evoke the same or similar responses as the objects or concepts they represent. Therefore, words have to be chosen carefully, as does the manner in which the words are spoken. This chapter has detailed the different styles and structures common to diverse hypnotic communications with the hope that you may become skilled enough with each of them to use whichever will work best with your client, and not just use the ones you might happen to prefer personally.

For Discussion

1. When a friend recommends a movie or restaurant to you, what makes you decide whether or not you'd follow her recommendation?

2. Why do people reject suggestions that are clearly in their best interest?

3. What differences can you identify between people who like to be told what to do and those who don't?

4. What changes have you made on the basis of insight? What changes have you made for no apparent reason? What do you think about the role of insight in the process of change?

5. How do you feel when someone tells you how you feel? How is the feeling different when she is right than when she is wrong?

Things to Do

1. Make a list of the most common hypnotic suggestions (e.g., "Relax," "Close your eyes," "Breathe at a comfortable rate," etc.) and write 5 suggestions in each style and structure to get that idea across.

2. In class, have each student make up an imaginary product, and have each attempt to sell it to the rest of the class. Which sales pitches were best, and why? Which were least effective, and why?

3. Read the horoscopes daily. What do you discover about the generality of language?

13

Patterns of Hypnotic Communication

Described in the previous chapter were the general styles and structures for suggestion formulation. In this chapter, general guidelines for the choosing of particular words and phrases will be provided. These guidelines are intended to assist you in formulating suggestions that are likely to be accepted by the individual you are working with.

These guidelines are, for the most part, communication techniques that are based on common sense. While these guidelines generally hold true for most hypnotic processes, one should also be aware that each principle has exceptions that may be more useful to apply with a given client. Therefore, a brief discussion of each principle is provided. You are encouraged to read this section actively. By thinking of particular cases where the principle might not apply, and thinking of an alternative that would, you will be increasing your range of choices in responding to a particular person.

KEEP THE SUGGESTIONS SIMPLE AND EASY TO FOLLOW

Generally, the more complicated a set of instructions for someone to follow, the more the person must rely on the conscious mind to help sort things out. The more the person must rely on the conscious mind, the less the unconscious mind is available, defeating the purpose of doing trancework. Keeping suggestions relatively simple allows the client to flow with the process without having to critically, and therefore consciously, analyze, interpret, and judge the offered suggestions.

Keeping suggestions flowing smoothly and clearly is not as easy as one might think. I have personally seen many experienced hypnotists who have

Table 3. Hypnotic Communication Patterns

Keep suggestions easy to follow
Use the client's language
Have the client define everything experientially
Encourage and reinforce the client
Use anticipation signals
Only use touch selectively and with permission
Establish an auditory anchor
Use process suggestions to encourage projections
Selective use of sensory modalities
Encourage experimentation
Build response sets gradually
Use self as a model

engendered a lack of responsiveness in subjects by making directions too complex to follow without substantial conscious involvement. For example, in one case, a clinician did a group hypnosis process involving a great many instructions for various responses. In observing his group's responses, I noticed many of the individuals had come out of trance simply because the instructions were too complex, and the pace did not match their experience. Many of these participants complained later that the suggestions were as confusing as some game show instructions ("spin the wheel, and if an even number comes up, you'll throw the dice, but if an odd number comes up on the wheel you'll choose one of three doors and if you choose the right door you'll have your choice of four containers, one of which will have the correct combination to one of two safes . . . whew!").

The ideal hypnotic process is one that is able to elicit the desired responses in as brief yet meaningful a way as possible. The more the conscious mind is involved in trying to obtain unconscious trance behaviors, the more difficult and lengthy the trancework required. Depending on the person you are working with, too complex a process may turn her off not only to that moment's work but to future work as well.

To complicate matters, the other side of this guideline involves techniques whose power is derived from their complexity rather than from their simplicity. These techniques include confusion and overload techniques, in which confusing ideas and an overabundance of information are provided. These techniques involve placing an excessive burden on the conscious mind to the point where it can no longer keep up, ultimately becoming dissociated and thus allowing the unconscious mind to respond more independently.

Such techniques are founded on the observation that people become more responsive to others when confused (as discussed in the "Human Suggestibility" chapter). However, it is also true that some people close off and resolve the confusion within themselves, even if with misinformation. More on confusional approaches will be presented later.

How, then, do you know whether your suggestions are too complex and working against your goals? The answer is by observing your client's responses. Every moment that lightens her trance as well as every undesired response to your suggestions is indicative that she is not following you (which means you were not following her). More overt means include simply asking the client, directly or indirectly, for specific verbal and nonverbal feedback about her experience.

Keeping suggestions easy to follow is not the same as being predictable and obvious about where you are going with the trance process. If the person is able to guess where you are going and can remain a step ahead of you, there is obviously considerable conscious analysis taking place, increasing the likelihood of reduced responsiveness. If you become aware that you may have lost the client somewhere along the way, you can go back to a point where you knew she was with you (and if you are as observant as you can possibly be, you won't have to go back very far) and go from there, but obviously not in the same way.

Do not force the client to rely on conscious processes to follow you. Keep in mind that only your client can be the one to determine what can and cannot be followed. In other words, you may think your directives were explicit and easily understandable, but you are not the one following them—your client is.

USE YOUR CLIENT'S LANGUAGE

One of the ways I think hypnosis has been far ahead of most other approaches is in its promotion of the idea that using the language of the client is the best way to have an impact on him. I have described how words represent experience, and even though we use a common language, our experiences are necessarily different. Taking the client's words, attaching *your* meaning to them, translating them into the language *you* use, and communicating from *your* linguistic style are all steps that are arbitrary on your part, and are quite likely to lead to miscommunication.

In using the language of the client, you do not assume even for a moment that you mean the same thing as he does in using it. You can use the same language as your client because it is *his* world you are dealing with—not yours.

In studying numerous clinical approaches and interacting with a wide variety of clinicians representing the various approaches, I have been unfavorably impressed with how a client's communications about her experience get translated into the clinician's favorite theoretical jargon, and then get fed back to the client that way. Words are a distortion from the real-world experience anyway—why distort them even further? I have had clients that have "resolved transference issues," "built ego strength," "strength-ened their armor," and "released energy blocks." They did these and a host of other things that pleased their therapists, but left treatment not feeling much better about themselves. The main advantage of using the client's language is in your ability to *intervene in the client's problem as she experiences it, and not as you interpret it.* The client can get the sense of being understood to a greater degree, engendering greater trust in the clinician.

(continued on p. 180)

FRAME OF REFERENCE: JEFFREY K. ZEIG

Jeffrey K. Zeig, Ph.D., is the Director of the Milton H. Erickson Foundation in Phoenix, Arizona. He organized the International Congresses on Ericksonian Approaches to Hypnosis and Psychother-apy held in 1980, 1983, 1986, 1988, and the landmark Evolution of Psychotherapy Conference in 1985. In addition to maintaining a private practice, he is an adjunct Assistant Professor of Clinical Psy-chology at Arizona State University. He also conducts workshops in North America, South America, Europe, and Australia on Ericksonian approaches. Dr. Zeig, who studied with Erickson for more than six years, is the editor and author of numerous works about Erickson and about psychotherapy.

On the Value of Hypnosis: "Ericksonian hypnosis is used to elicit therapeutic *responses,* the essence of which is to get the patient to *cooperate.* Patients enter psychotherapy because they have difficulty accomplishing tasks they set for themselves. It is the job of the therapist to get the patient to follow his or her own desires to the extent possible, and to this end hypnosis can often be effective in surmounting impasses. It makes more available to patients their own potentials for self-help" (Zeig, 1985c, p. 4).

On the Utilization Approach: "*Utilization* basically says that techniques are best derived from the patient, not from the therapist. Whatever technique the patient uses to be an ineffective patient can be used by the therapist to promote effective living. For example, if the patient 'speaks schizophrenic' to distance himself, the therapist can use the same method to promote an empathic relationship. Utilization says that it is best not to bend the patient to fit a preselected technique; rather, one should tailor psychotherapy to each patient.

"Beyond utilization, Erickson's therapies were characterized not by techniques, but by some general attitudes about therapy—and for that matter, about life. One of these was flexibility in approach. Erickson would use whatever it took to promote change, be it interpretation, indirect suggestion or hypnosis. (Kristina Erickson, M.D., Erickson's youngest daughter, defined the Ericksonian approach as 'that which works.') In his later years, he even kept flexible hours. The length of the session was determined by the goal, not by the clock. He would see patients for ten minutes or four hours and then usually charge accordingly" (Zeig, 1985c, p. 37).

On First Meeting Erickson: "My initial introduction was quite unusual. At about ten-thirty at night, I arrived at Erickson's home. I was to stay in his guesthouse. I was greeted at the door by Roxanna. She introduced me to her father, gesturing to Dr. Erickson, who was seated to the immediate left of the door watching television. She stated, 'This is my father, Dr. Erickson.' Erickson slowly, mechanically moved his head upward, in small stepwise movements. When his head reached the horizontal, he slowly, mechanically, using the same stepwise movements, twisted his neck toward me. When he caught my visual attention and looked in my eyes, he again started the same mechanical, slow stepwise movements and looked down the midline of my body. To say that I was quite shocked and surprised by this 'Hello' would be an understatement. Nobody had ever said 'Hello' to me like that before. Roxanna took me into the other room and explained that her father was a practical joker.

"However, Erickson's behavior was an excellent nonverbal hypnotic induction. All the parts necessary to induce hypnosis were presented in Erickson's nonverbal behavior. He was confusing and he disrupted my conscious set. My conscious expectation was that he would shake hands and say 'Hello.' Further, Erickson modeled hypnotic phenomena. He modeled the stepwise cataleptic movement that patients show when they do an arm levitation. Moreover, his behavior focused my attention. Then, when he looked down the midline of my body, he was suggesting for me to 'go down inside.' Basically, Erickson was using nonverbal techniques to disrupt my conscious set and to pattern a new unconscious pattern set" (Zeig, 1980a, p. 20).

On His Experience of Erickson: "I vividly remember how emotionally touched I was by the experience of being with Erickson. On the second day of my visit, I watched him struggle to move himself from his wheelchair to his office chair. Then he started speaking to me through his obvious pain, intent on instructing me about how to be more effective as a person and therapist. I remember feeling powerfully moved that he would selflessly spend his limited energy to help me.

"No powerful figure I had met before had such a moving impact. There was something extraordinary about Erickson: Perhaps his profound effect was due to his acute sensitivity, respect for the individual, intensity, verve, uniqueness, and joie de vivre in the face of adversity. I saw him struggle to bring out the best in himself and it inspired me to want to do the same" (Zeig, 1985c, p. 167).

On Multiple-level Communication: "Psychotherapists learn to take a small sample of social level communication and interpret additional meaning in regard to what is 'really' happening on the patient's psychological level. It is interesting to note that, although therapists are aware of multiple-level communication and use it diagnostically, most therapists are not trained to use multiple-level communication as a therapeutic tool. It may be one of Erickson's major contributions to psychology that he demonstrates therapeutic use of multiple-level communication. Erickson demonstrates how much muscle can be packed into therapeutic communication and how much of the fat can be stripped away" (Zeig, 1980a, p. 19).

Using the language of the client is sometimes not appropriate or desirable. If the speech is too idiosyncratic, or is related to the client's particular ethnic group (or other subculture) of which you are not a member, your using the same language may be viewed as mockery and insulting. Recovery from such a mistake is difficult.

Some clinicians have a personal bias against using the client's language. I had an interaction a while ago with a very prominent sex therapist who believed that if a patient of his used layperson terminology in describing a problem, it was his duty to make a point of correcting the person with the proper scientific jargon. He gave the example that if a male patient were to present the complaint that he "couldn't get it up," his response would be to address the patient's concerns about his "erectile dysfunction and inability to perform coitus." Those seemed, to me to least, to be cold, sterile terms that really don't reflect his client's experience. When I offered my reaction for discussion, the doctor said that, "I didn't go to medical school to speak like an ignorant layman." Well, I didn't go through all that schooling for that purpose, either. I'm willing to bet, though, that he could reach a wider range of the people he works with by working with them in terms they use and can understand instead of expecting them to come to his level. It takes a lot of flexibility to want to do that, though.

The other very important aspect of noticing and using a client's language is the role of the unconscious mind in the person's language choice. More often than most clinicians consciously realize, a client's word choice reflects dimensions of the problem's dynamics at an unconscious level. This is especially true where a word or phrase is used idiosyncratically. A case description can illustrate the point.

A woman in her late forties presented the complaint that her marriage was in shambles. It being her fifth marriage, she wanted to know, "What's wrong with me that each of my husbands has been so abusive to me? I must telegraph my weakness to men." I heard the word "telegraph" in her description, and somehow it struck me as an odd word to use. There are other words or phrases that are more descriptive of the experience she was relating, but she chose the word "telegraph." What that meant to her, if anything, could not have been known to me at that exact time, and so was kept in the back of my mind as something to explore later. In the meantime, an exploration of her history of relationships with men led her to remark that she had "never had a good relationship with a man." When I hear "never" in that context, I generally like to explore the person's relationship with the opposite sex parent. In this particular case, the client related that she had not really known her father, who died in World War II when she was still quite young. Her mother dated a series of men, none for very long.

All her life, men came and went, and each time she liked one, he soon was gone. She had learned to behave in a negative and rejecting way in order to beat the man to the ending of the relationship!

In doing trancework with her—specifically, an age regression process to her earliest decisions about men—I asked her what she "telegraphed" to men. Mention of the word "telegraph" caused her to have a very strong emotional reaction, and then she had the long repressed memory of being with her father, whom she loved very much, when he received a "telegraph" to go to war—a draft notice. Seemingly all of a sudden, he was gone, never to return. In her mind she had come to the conclusion that no man was reliable—not even Dad. All of these dynamics were addressed in subsequent sessions, and she was able to learn that she didn't have to reject men first and that she could build a lasting and satisfying relationship with a man.

The point of the case is that a word the client used in an unusual way was a cue for me to use in the intervention. Noticing a client's word usage may be a significant factor in formulating an intervention based on an understanding of what the words mean to the client.

HAVE THE CLIENT DEFINE EVERYTHING

Since words are symbols of experience, using the same words does not mean you are describing the same experience. Therefore, it is imperative to have the client explain the experience as best as possible, rather than just using a word or two to represent the experience. Any words used will never completely give you an idea of what the person is subjectively experiencing, but the more definition and description of experience you have, the more opportunity you have for meaningful intervention.

Many clinicians are afraid to ask for clarification, believing it will reflect a lack of understanding. Thus, when a client says, "I have this terrible depression, ya know what I mean?" the eager-to-prove-empathy therapist is likely to say, "Yes, I know what you mean." The client's experience of depression in this example is hallucinated by the clinician. The clinician knows what depression is from previous experience (personal and professional), and now puts this client into the same category as others termed "depressed." What this particular client is experiencing is still not known. A better response might be, "Can you describe what your experience of being depressed is like for you?" Having the client describe the experience in her own way can lead to a better understanding of how and where to intervene.

This point is illustrated well in another case I worked on. A woman in her early twenties came to me for therapy for what she called "a terrific phobia of men." I thought the words "terrific" and "phobia" were odd ones to be connected, and I wanted to know what her experience of what she called a "phobia" was. Now, I assure you I didn't really have to ask what she meant by the word "phobia." After all, I went to school and know what a phobia is—an intense, irrational fear. But I wanted to know what *she* meant by it, and so I asked, "What do you mean by a phobia?" Her response was, "I have a phobia of men—you know, I just can't get enough of them, and that complicates my life." I guess a lot of people might consider that a "terrific phobia," but it was a source of distress to her.

If I had responded on the basis of *my* experience of what "phobia" means, I might have started asking her questions about fears, and perhaps caused her to believe that I really didn't understand her needs nor could I help her. By having her describe her experience, and not getting side-tracked by the label she chose to represent it, I started in a different direction, one much closer to meeting her needs.

In having clients define the meanings of the terms they use, the clinician can often help the person redefine the term and subsequently alter the experience it represents. This is the essence of a technique called "Reframing," in which an experience is changed by the use of a different term to describe the experience. Thus "cheap" can be altered to "selective," a "retreat" can be reframed as a "strategic military withdrawal," and "weird" can become "uninhibited and eccentric."

In a recent workshop I conducted, a participant said she would like to "not be so controlling." I asked her what she meant, and she responded she would like to "let others make a decision for me once in a while." Given that definition of control, i.e., who makes the decisions for her, being in control all the time can certainly be burdensome. I told her I thought her definition was an interesting one, but I defined control in another way. I define control as having choices; someone who is in control has a lot choices about what she will say or do, but someone who is not in control has no choices. "Sometimes, a person in control may not have enough control to choose to make no choices." When she deciphered what I said, her response was a look of relief and the statement "That's true. I never realized it before, but I don't need less control—I need more, so I can choose sometimes. Having more choices will change everything!" A simple redefinition of "control" that allowed for more personal freedom changed her experience of herself in a positive way. Instead of "control" being something negative, it can now be associated with a positive experience of recognizing her choices at a given time, one of which may be to let someone else be responsible for a change.

Words are the medium of exchange between the clinician and client, and the more ambiguous the words, the greater the room for miscommunication. This point emphasizes the need to be aware of both the connotative and denotative meanings of your words. If a client takes literally something you intended to be taken figuratively, the result may be an undesirable one.

USE THE PRESENT TENSE AND A POSITIVE STRUCTURE

Generally, suggestions should be phrased in the present tense and in terms of what the person is experiencing. Of course, most therapeutic suggestions are intended to influence future behavior in some way, but the hypnotic session is the bridge between what is now and what will be then. The basic structure of hypnotic suggestions is linking what is occurring now to what is desired: "As you experience this, you can start to experience that." Continuous feedback about the person's present state is necessary to make the bridge effective.

This point is especially true in the case of working with variables of time, such as in age regression. When one is working with memory, talking to the person in terms of what occurred "then" will produce a different and much less profound response than will talking to the person as if she is experiencing that situation presently. Having as much of the client in the "here-and-now" (whether the here-and-now is actually a past or future context) gives the clinician access to more of the person to work with. Current needs, motivations, feelings, values, and behaviors are available for incorporation into the process. In part, this is where hypnosis as a tool derives its power. Instead of intellectually talking about a situation one is removed from, the clinician recreates that experience *now* and deals with the resulting issues as they arise *now.*

Described earlier was the "negative suggestion." Caution was advised then about its potential inadvertent misuse. In general, suggestions should be phrased in positive ways about what the person *can* do instead of what she can't do. Remember the effect of me directing you not to think of the taste of pizza? Suggesting to someone what not do has the same effect as being told what to do simply because it does not provide an alternative focal point. An analogy about learning through reward or punishment might be useful to elaborate this point. In simply punishing someone for doing something wrong, there is nothing provided to tell the person what the right thing to do is. The person merely learns what not to do, and repeated punishment with no alternatives provided leads to frustration, anger, and finally a point where punishment is no longer effective.

Positive suggestions that assist the client in discovering what she can do are a principal goal of treatment. Negative suggestions can be effective when carefully used, but the overwhelming majority of suggestions will likely be of a positive nature.

ENCOURAGE AND COMPLIMENT THE CLIENT

Support for the client in the form of encouragement and compliments can go a long way in assisting the client to find power within himself. Accepting the client's communications, even the communications typically regarded as "resistance," is a demonstration of the positive regard that leads to what has classically been called "rapport." In my view, the process of encouraging a client is often one of guiding the client into a position where he can acknowledge personal strengths and resources previously overlooked in himself. Typically, the person seeking help feels out of control and frustrated. Empty compliments that contradict the person's low self-esteem are easily disregarded (recall the earlier discussion of cognitive dissonance). Guiding the person into a position of self-acknowledgement (contradicting his own negative self-generalizations), confirming and then complimenting that recognition has been a powerful intervention, in my experience. Having the client reach his own conclusion that he is better off than previously thought can be a more profound experience for him than simply hearing me say so.

Many clinicians I have experienced are of the belief that a client has to be "torn down" before she can be "put together." Therapy consists of attack, abuse, and negativity in the form of disrespect. I believe that a client must be approached with respect. A client's behavior is *not* the client, rather it is a reflection of what choices the person has available at a given moment. Behavior that is deemed maladaptive because of the negative conse-quences it engenders is the best or only choice the person currently has in that context. The clinician's role is to provide new alternatives that are more adaptive for the person. When the new choices fit the client well, and are provided with a recognition of the person's integrity, the process of change can be considerably smoother.

Another dimension of the suggestion to encourage and compliment the client relates to the notion of accepting the client's communications as a means for facilitating trance induction and utilization. The sophistication of the utilization approach lies in its accepting (rather than contradicting) the client's communications, and then discovering a way of utilizing them to facilitate change. If a client presents the complaint that, "I'm a no-good crazy person" and the clinician responds, "No, you're not, you're just confused," the clinician has not accepted the client's view of herself (part of forming a response is determining whether such a self-effacing statement is a genuinely felt one or just a desire to get a free compliment). A possible result is the lack of feeling understood; referring back to the principle of cognitive dissonance, a conflicting message is likely to be ignored or rationalized with no real impact on the internal belief system governing the maladaptive behavior. Accepting the client as she sees herself is the first step toward attaining a position with her from which to effect meaningful changes. Furthermore, it allows for the message "What you are doing right now is fine, because that is exactly what will allow you to accomplish the change you desire." The general structure of suggestion has previously been identified as, "As you experience this, you can start to experience that." Accepting the current state of affairs without a critical reproach is desirable in order to encourage the client to use the bridge of the intervention to reach the desired goals.

DETERMINE OWNERSHIP OF THE PROBLEM

Different therapeutic approaches have different terminology to express this concept, each one addressing the need to guide the client into accepting a measure of responsibility for what she is experiencing. If the client feels she is a "victim," or if she is a "blamer" with no responsibility at all for her experience, helping the client to change in some meaningful way is more difficult. If one believes one has no control over one's experience, attempts to demonstrate that control *is* possible will most likely be ignored or dismissed with the ever familiar "Yes, but . . . " excuses of why change is impossible (recall Seligman's model of learned helplessness [Seligman, 1975]). Helping people to discover that they have power to control the events in their lives, at the most, or their reactions to the events in their lives, at least, is a necessary component of therapeutic work.

Related to this, perhaps indirectly, is the question of whether the client is "trying" or "allowing" herself the trance experience. Trying to relax and concentrate can be a very stressful experience, just as trying to fall asleep can be stressful. Trying is not doing; in fact, the suggestibility tests of eye-closure (and eye catalepsy) and hand-clasp play on the difference between trying and doing. Trying implies effort without accomplishment, and the harder one works without attaining a result the greater the stress build-up. Clients should be encouraged to allow themselves the experience, rather than trying to have it. After all, their experience is in their control, and when one allows oneself an experience, who is there to resist? The likelihood of obtaining successful responses is thus increased.

DETERMINE THE BEST MODALITY
FOR THE TRANCE EXPERIENCE

One of the most useful concepts originating from Richard Bandler and John Grinder's Neuro-Linguistic Programming model concerns people's preferred style for gathering information, storing it, retrieving it, and communicating about it. Human experience is composed of sensory input and our world views are determined by the interpretations we derive from the various inputs. Bandler and Grinder hypothesized (1979) that most people have a preferred sense that is more well developed and more heavily relied on in processing day-to-day experience. Some people are quite visual in terms of their preferred modality, meaning they tend to think in pictures, remember or imagine images more clearly, and process the visual portion of experience more completely. Other people favor the auditory modality, thinking in terms of internal dialogue, talking to themselves about their experience, remembering or imagining sounds and conversations with great clarity, and processing the auditory portion of ongoing experience more completely. Still others favor the kinesthetic modality, thinking in terms of feelings, remembering or imagining the feelings associated with various experiences with clarity, and processing the kinesthetic portion of ongoing experience more completely.

It is important to realize that each person processes experience in all of the senses all of the time. The issue of concern here is which modality is dominant in a given context. If a clinician can identify a person's favored system of sensory experience, she can adapt communications to that favored system and increase the likelihood of meaningful influence through the attainment of greater rapport.

The language a person uses, particularly the predicates (including verbs, adverbs, and adjectives), reflects a person's favored information-processing style. Language, because it is structured for the most part at an unconscious level, reflects the unconscious patterns of thinking through the specific words chosen to reflect inner experience. Thus, if in the course of a discussion I make a point that the listener responds to by saying, "I *see* what you mean; that *looks* right to me," I can deduce a visual preference in the listener. If the listener responds to my point by saying, "I *hear* what you're saying; that *sounds* right to me," I can deduce an auditory preference. If the listener responds, "I get a *feel* for what you mean; that idea *grabs* me," I can deduce a preference for the kinesthetic modality. In each case, I can use language that will appeal to the preferred style. For example, with a visually-oriented person, using visual imagery techniques is likely to be effective, but is likely to be less effective with the person who has a strong kinesthetic orientation.

The inability to notice a client's language usage, particularly in the area of preferred sensory modalities, can be a source of resistance. Responding to a client who says, "I feel bad" with a sensorily mismatched statement like "Can you see why you feel badly?" is not likely to get a meaningful response, at least not as useful as a more matched statement might.

A study I published (1981) demonstrated the greater depth at which subjects could experience trance when the induction's predicates were matched to their preferred modality. The matching of predicates to facilitate trancework is simply another way of using the language of the client while acknowledging the uniqueness of each person. Furthermore, since all experience can ultimately be broken down into its sensory components, the use of language patterns that emphasize the sensations of an experience will have a more powerful effect than more distant, intellectual terminology. Consider the effect of the following statement:

> Think of how pleasant a walk in the woods can be . . . so enjoyable, enlightening and peaceful. . . .

Contrast that effect with a more sensory involved statement:

> Can you remember taking a walk in the woods, seeing the tall, sturdy trees against the blue sky, hearing the sounds of the birds singing and the leaves crackling under your footsteps, the feelings of peacefulness inside. . . .

The experience of hypnosis is one in which the client's emotions and sensory experiences can be amplified to higher levels, appropriate for making more use of the person's resources in facilitating change. Intellectual, conscious willpower is hardly a match for the deepseated emotions and sensory experiences of the unconscious. The evidence for this fact lies in the inability of people to overpower themselves into changing. Can you think of some aspect of yourself you have wanted to change, but been unable to thus far? Why hasn't willpower been enough? The conscious decision to start a diet, quit smoking, or begin a program of exercise is simply not enough. One has to work with the related emotions, needs, values, and belief system of the unconscious in some direct or indirect way.

The greater power is in the use of emotional, sensorily descriptive language, rather than in the use of intellectual language that appeals primarily to the conscious mind, the lesser force in guiding human behavior. The best sensory-based descriptions are those that influence the client's experience the most. Therefore, it is of great advantage to be able to listen to the client, identify her most relied on modality for the experience under consideration (since the dominant modality changes from context to context), and adapt the trance process to that modality. In this way, a greater rapport may be obtained, and the stage may be set for leading the client into a different awareness. Such a lead may be accomplished by shifting at some point into using language of the sensory system(s) outside of the person's usual awareness. Altering the person's consciousness is, of course, the essence of the trance experience, and can be accomplished by descriptively matching (what Bandler and Grinder have called "pacing") the person's favored sensory system and then gradually introducing experiences in other sensory systems ("leading"). For example, with a person whose favored modality is visual, one can pace with visual suggestions and then gradually lead into the kinesthetic area, altering the person's typical pattern of consciousness:

> As you *see* yourself sitting in that chair, you can *see* each breath you inhale soothing each muscle of your body, *visualizing* each muscle unwinding, loosening comfortably, and as you *see* each muscle relaxing you can begin to *feel* the tingle of comfort in the muscles of your arms and then *feel* the comfort growing and flowing to other parts of your body. . . .

Using sensory descriptions carefully can be a significant part of the treatment process, discussed in the utilization sections.

KEEP THE CLIENT ONLY AS INFORMED AS IS NECESSARY TO SUCCEED

While I have made it a high priority to provide relevant information to clients, it is also necessary not to provide too much information about one's interventions. Giving the client the opportunity to develop defenses by analyzing and criticizing what the clinician is doing is obviously counter-productive to the aims of therapy. Rather than tell why I am doing what I am doing, most frequently I just do it. The spontaneity from the experience of my communications is what has an impact on the person, not the explanation of what I am trying to do. If I say to a client, "I'm trying to induce confusion in you in order to disrupt your usual patterns of thinking," what is the likelihood of me getting the response I want? Answer: not much. One of the great advantages of employing hypnotic communications and strategies is their ability to make contact with the affective realm of a client's experience rather than with the cognitive realm. Dealing with one's emotions will inevitably lead to a greater impact than will dealing with one's intellect. How many times in your life have you made the statement, "I know (cognitive) I shouldn't feel this way, but I do (affective)"?

The idea of presenting and withholding information selectively can be an ethical dilemma. How can a client provide informed consent if he doesn't know what the clinician is doing? Yet, if he knows exactly what the clinician is doing, how can the intervention succeed? This is a matter that must be handled delicately on a case by case basis.

One of the most interesting dimensions of the work of the late Milton H. Erickson, M.D., was his ability to obtain compliance from his patients to demands that were sometimes nothing short of outrageous. Erickson lived in an era where a doctor's authority went virtually unchallenged, and so if he asked his patient to climb a mountain to symbolically gain a greater over-all view of things, the patient usually would. A more likely response in today's changing times is, "Why? I think I'll get two other doctors' opinions." If he explained why he wanted the patient to climb the mountain, would it have the same therapeutic impact? Yet, doesn't the patient have a right to know?

People often asked Erickson how he motivated people to do the things he wanted them do. His answer was simple: "Because they know I mean it!" Trust, rapport, and respect for the client's integrity are key ingredients in the hypnotic interaction.

GIVE YOUR CLIENTS THE TIME THEY NEED TO RESPOND

Everyone does things according to their own internal time clock, their own pace. In trance, this tendency is amplified to the point of being a critical component of the interaction. To pressure someone to respond to *your* pace of doing things just won't work in doing trancework. Instead, allow the client to form the desired response at a rate she chooses. This is more typically a beginner's mistake, caused by uncertainty and a lack of experience. Often, students in my courses first learning hypnosis ask for an arm levitation or some such response, and if the subject's arm doesn't immediately begin to lift, the student gets agitated and assumes the subject is resisting. If they start to repeat their suggestions, I will stop them and instruct them to wait. Almost invariably, after a short while, the subject's arm begins to lift and the student has now learned to be a bit more patient in letting the subject respond in her own time.

In the phase of guiding the person out of trance ("disengagement"), this is especially true. I have always disliked using a countup to guide the person out of trance (e.g., "When I count to three you will awaken, open your eyes, and be alert and refreshed") because it forces the client to adapt to your arbitrary choice of when she should come out of trance, instead of letting her choose for herself. I prefer a general closure on the order of: "When you have taken the time to complete whatever thoughts or feelings you wish to during this experience, you can bring yourself out of trance at a rate that is comfortable for you. . . ."

Let the person take the time she needs to develop the response you suggest. No need to hurry. . . .

GET PERMISSION BEFORE TOUCHING YOUR CLIENT

Can you imagine what it's like to be deeply relaxed, feeling good, absorbed in some important internal experience, and all of a sudden feeling a strange hand on your thigh? I have seen so many sessions that were going well ruined in an instant because the clinician assumed enough rapport was present (if she even thought about it, which a lot of "touchey-feeley" clinicians never do) to touch the person. It is very important to get permission to touch the person for a number of reasons.

First of all, touch is something related to intimacy—a cross into personal space. Some welcome it, while others hate to be touched and experience it as a violation of personal territory. With such persons, it can hinder rapport, not help.

Second, in the trance state the person is typically focused inwardly on some internal experience. To respond to a clinician's touch means reorienting one's focus to the external world, which is generally counterproductive to the development and maintenance of a deep trance state. If you use touch indiscriminately, you can unintentionally work against yourself.

Third, it may simply startle the person. The person may be so lost in thought, she may have forgotten that you are even there with her. To suddenly feel a hand on you can scare anybody, in *or* out of trance!

Fourth, the media have played on the misconception that hypnosis is a means for seduction. The sexual implication of touching someone unexpectedly can trigger unnecessary problems. It is always a good idea to politely ask the client for permission to touch her, for it certainly demonstrates a respect for her integrity. Whether you ask before your trancework begins or at some time during the trance process is a matter of personal preference (I prefer to do both) just so long as you secure permission before touching your client.

ESTABLISH ANTICIPATION SIGNALS

For the reasons elaborated in the previous section, it is a good idea to avoid shocking your client out of trance with an unexpected maneuver on your part. The best tool to prevent this problem from arising is the "anticipation signal." Anticipation signals are verbalizations of your intentions, effectively letting your client know what action you are going to take so as not to startle her. They also serve the function of keeping the client comfortable enough to not feel like she has to pay conscious attention to everything you say and do. Such conscious analysis is counterproductive.

Anticipation signals take the form of simple statements about what is coming next. For example, I may say, "In just a moment I am going to take your left hand by the wrist and raise it above your head." Assuming I have received permission to touch the person, I am now preparing the person for my touch rather than just taking her wrist without warning. It is a much gentler and more respectful approach, and clients appreciate that consideration. When you state, "In just a moment I'm going to . . . " and then follow through in a way that is consistent with what you stated your actions would be, a new level of trust can be reached, aiding in future work. From the client's perspective, it is very difficult to be relaxed and on guard simultaneously. Anticipation signals are a very quick, simple way to foster trust in the hypnotic relationship.

USE A VOICE AND DEMEANOR
CONSISTENT WITH YOUR INTENT

Your tools as a skilled communicator are your voice and body. If you don't have a good grasp of the dynamics of nonverbal communication, I can suggest that you read a specialized communications text that describes the incredible amount of information that is communicated nonverbally. This includes such factors as eye contact, body posture, gestures, touch, timing, use of space, tone and volume of voice, and numerous other dimensions. If you don't use those components of communication well, positive results will be slow in coming if they come at all.

It helps immeasurably to have control of your voice and body in communicating, using yourself as the mechanism to drive a suggestion home. To have tension in your voice when you suggest to your client that she relax is an avoidable incongruity. To use a normal conversional tone of voice with someone you are wanting to guide into a different state of experience is another avoidable incongruity. Using a soothing, comforting voice also serves the purpose of discouraging conscious analysis.

It is a very good idea to have a well-practiced tone of voice and relaxed body posture to model for your client what you want her to experience. To gradually shift from your usual tone of voice to one more soothing and hypnotic builds an association (what Bandler and Grinder call an "auditory anchor") in your client's mind that works in your favor each time you wish to re-induce the trance state. You don't have to formally announce, "Now let's do hypnosis." Rather you can gradually lead into using the voice your client associates to entering trance, effectively inducing trance without a formalized induction.

The nonverbal components of your communications are critical to generating successful trance experiences in your clients. It can be very helpful to make audio or videotapes of yourself to learn how you look and sound as you interact. Often, people have no idea of how they look as they interact with others, and so getting feedback from outside sources can be highly beneficial.

CHAIN SUGGESTIONS STRUCTURALLY

Like most of the other communication patterns offered as guidelines in this chapter, this particular one is pretty much a constant in doing trancework. In using the words "chaining suggestions," I am referring to the chaining of the desired response to the client's present experience. Bandler and Grinder's "pacing and leading" and Erickson's "accepting and utilizing" principles are synonymous with "chaining." The idea is to build a link (hence "chain") between what the client is currently doing and what you would like him to do. The implicit message is, "As you experience (this), you can start to experience (that)." For example, sitting there and reading these words will allow you to think of your left foot.

There are, as Bandler and Grinder (1975) have pointed out, three varieties of links between current and future experiences. They vary in strength in terms of how current behavior may be associated only to the desired behavior, or may be implied as a cause of future behavior, or will be clearly identified as *the* cause of future behavior.

The first link is the "simple conjunction." It is the weakest link and simply suggests an association between what is and what can be. It employs such connecting words as "and" and "but." For example:

> You are looking at me *and* starting to feel comfortable.
> You can see the clock *but* allow time to slow down.

As will be true with all three links, the first half of the statement matches (paces, accepts) the person's current experience while the second half suggests (leads, utilizes) a possible, but not current, experience. With the simple conjunction, there is a more distant relationship between what is and what can be.

The second link, and a stronger one, is the "implied causative," employing such connecting words as "as," "while," and "during." For example:

> *As* you notice yourself relaxing, you can let your eyes close.
> You can listen to me *while* your conscious mind drifts off.
> You can feel yourself growing more comfortable *during*
> your memory of your high school graduation.

The third, and strongest, link is the "causative predicate." It is the strongest because it claims that not only are the current and desired behaviors connected, but one actually causes the other. For example:

> Breathing deeply *will make you* relax even more.
> Shifting your body *will cause you* to want to close your eyes.

Each of these links forms a bridge to get the client to respond in a particular way on the basis of what he is doing currently. The chaining of suggestions follows the basic formula, "As you experience this, you can start to experience that." A typical trance process, therefore, may sound like this at the start:

> As you continue to look at me, you can take in a deep breath . . . and as you
> take in a deep breath, you can allow your eyes to close . . . and as your eyes

close, you can let your mind drift back to a specific memory ... and as your
mind drifts back to a specific memory you can begin to describe..........

Structurally, each suggestion is chained to the response before it, starting
with a statement feeding back to the client his current, undeniable reality.
The above example started with feeding back to the client that he was
looking at me and in so doing could take in a deep breath. Looking at
someone and taking in a deep breath are not usually connected (although
some people are breathtakingly attractive), and in the example are connected by an arbitrary link of my own creation. Each obtained response is
fed back (paced, accepted) as the basis for the desired response (the lead,
or utilization).

These links are the basis for the trance process being a flowing one and
not a choppy, disconnected one. Grammatically, of course, hypnotic phrasing is a strict grammarian's nightmare, but to the person in trance the
clinician is smooth and easy to listen to.

BE GENERAL SPECIFICALLY

If you refer back to the section on process suggestion structures, you can
review the general idea that the more details you provide for someone's
trance experience, the more opportunities there are for contradicting it.
For example, "Let your right hand feel warmer" as a suggestion for the
specific response of hand warmth is easier to resist than is a more general
process suggestion: "Let yourself notice the particular change of temperature in one of your hands." In the latter suggestion, which hand was to
change was not specified, nor was it specific whether the hand was to grow
warmer or cooler. Whatever response the person has can now be defined
as a cooperative one, and is recognized as a projection of the person's own
unconscious associations.

It is very difficult, if not impossible, to avoid the use of detail in
suggestions. Furthermore, it is not desirable to do so because often it is the
details that you provide during the trance process that make it easy to
follow. The point in this section is that the principle of "being general
specifically" can help you avoid some of the unnecessary rejections of your
suggestions. Notice as early on as possible whether you are being too
specific (or too general) on the basis of the responsiveness to you, and, if
necessary, shift.

IF DESIRABLE, SUBSTITUTE
OTHER TERMS FOR HYPNOSIS

I don't have a particular fondness for the word "hypnosis," and so whether one calls it hypnosis or one calls it something else isn't an issue of significance for me. As long as the dynamics are operant, regardless of the name, hypnosis is present. Hypnosis is a part of virtually every therapeutic modality I am aware of, but almost always under another name and woven into a different conceptual framework. The only disadvantage to that is that it might make others' work more precise if they utilized hypnotic principles without the excess baggage.

Since I have no real attachment to the word "hypnosis," if it serves my needs to use the same principles and techniques under a different, perhaps more acceptable, name, I will. If a cancer patient fears hypnosis, but really wants to experience the benefit of visualization techniques, why get into a lecture on how visualization is a specific hypnotic technique? It may create resistance needlessly.

There are many clients for whom the word "hypnosis" inspires fears and doubts, and yet these same clients are thrilled to learn "progressive relaxation," also a specific hypnotic technique. It isn't terribly important to sell your clients hypnosis; it's only important to help them. If the client reacts negatively to your query about any experience she might have had with hypnosis, you may exercise the option of using another term to label your intervention. Some specific possible alternative labels are:

Progressive muscle relaxation
Controlled relaxation
Guided relaxation
Deep relaxation
Visualization
Visual imagery
Guided imagery
Guided fantasy
Guided meditation
Mental imagery

Whatever variation you might use, as long as a focused state of attention is narrowed to suggestions offered and influence occurs, hypnosis is present. Biofeedback is self-hypnosis with electronic equipment. Meditation is self-hypnosis with a meaningless mantra as a focal point, instead of a meaningful suggestion. Visualization is hypnosis limited to the visual modality. The LaMaze method of childbirth employs breathing and relaxation exercises as the hypnotic induction. The point here is that hypnosis may be in effect without necessarily identifying it as such. If it works to the client's advantage somehow to call it by another name, it would seem wise to do so.

CONCLUSION

While this chapter covered some of the basic components of hypnotic communication, it obviously could not cover all the subtleties inherent in such patterns. You may be reminded that for each general principle discussed, there are exceptions. If you are starting to feel overwhelmed at how much there is to pay attention to in doing trancework, then I am succeeding in describing how complex an art the skilled use of hypnosis is. Let yourself feel overwhelmed *just enough* to do sensitive and effective work . . .

For Discussion

1. How do you react to being touched spontaneously? How might a spontaneous touch be viewed as an invasion of territory? Why do some people dislike to be touched?

2. What, if any, is your preferred sense for information-processing? What implications does this have for your style of intervention? What advantages and disadvantages are there in having that particular preference?

3. Is language formed at an unconscious level? How do you know?

4. What communication patterns help you experience trance more fully? Why do they have that impact?

5. What is "personal responsibility"? How far does one's responsibility for one's self go when others' behavior influences us on a continuous basis? How do you know when someone isn't accepting personal responsibility?

Things to Do

1. Analyze a hypnosis tape for its communication patterns. What patterns seem to help? Which seem to be disruptive?

2. Make a list of five therapeutic approaches and the techniques associated with them. How is hypnosis a part of each?

3. List at least one context in which each of the patterns described in this chapter would not be applicable.

14

Suggestibility Tests

You may recall the earlier discussion of the secrets of stage hypnosis in which I described the stage hypnotist's use of quick interactions in order to determine the degree of a subject's responsiveness. These interactions have traditionally been called "Suggestibility Tests." Stage hypnotists are by no means the only ones to use such tests. In fact, a large number of traditionally oriented clinicians use suggestibility tests as well.

The rationale for the use of suggestibility tests rests on all the issues presented in the chapters on "Susceptibility to Hypnosis" and "Human Suggestibility." For more traditionally oriented clinicians, use of hypnosis is predicated on the ideas that only some people are hypnotizable and people are hypnotizable to varying degrees. From their perspective, such tests are viewed as a desirable way to assess *whether* someone is hypnotizable, and, if so, to what degree. Given the perspective of trance as a natural capability and phenomenon and hypnosis as a model of communication and influence suggested throughout this book, such tests are redundant and unnecessary. I do not use formal suggestibility tests in my practice; instead, I assume the inevitable presence of suggestibility on the part of my client. Instead of attempting to discover *if* my client is suggestible I find it a much more practical use of my mental energy to discover *how* I can best structure my suggestions to increase the likelihood of their getting in. For the hypnotist who does not share this perspective, or for the hypnotist who does not yet feel experienced enough to assess a client's spontaneous communications for suggestibility dynamics, suggestibility tests may be a useful tool. That is the basis for their inclusion in this book.

Suggestibility tests are a less formal spin-off of the formalized susceptibility measures that yield quantifiable data. Suggestibility tests in clinical practice generally take the form of mini-hypnotic encounters in which a brief, ritualized set of suggestions for relaxation are offered to the subject, followed by a suggestion for a specific response. If the subject responds in the manner suggested, she has "passed" the test. More tests may follow, each one (according to traditional thought) requiring a greater degree of trance in order to provide the suggested response. If the subject does not respond in the manner suggested, she has "failed" the test. The quality of the subject's response (i.e., opposite, minimal) should be noted for informational purposes about this person's response style; thus potentially useful information can be obtained even from a poor suggestibility test performance.

FUNCTIONS OF SUGGESTIBILITY TESTS

The chief purpose of suggestibility tests is to determine degree, if any, of hypnotizability. In addition, however, suggestibility tests can serve a number of other purposes. First, by using suggestibility tests to measure responsiveness, the most valuable information obtainable concerns what approach may be best for a particular client. Specifically, should the approach be a direct or indirect one? Should suggestions be in a positive or negative form? Should the hypnotist's demeanor be a commanding, authoritarian one, or an easy-going, permissive one? Much emphasis has been placed on the relationship dynamics between clinician and client, and suggestibility tests may be a useful tool to help you assess what style you will use to approach a particular client.

A second purpose of the suggestibility test is to serve as a conditioning experience for entering a trance state. The suggestibility test is an abbreviated version of the hypnotic encounter, and by having the client focus her attention and generate a trance behavior, you provide her first "official" hypnotic experience. Use of the experience as a prototype for future experiences conditions the client to the experience of entering trance while having her experience guided by the clinician. Thus, present for the client is an opportunity to build rapport in the relationship, trust in the clinician, and confidence in her own ability to experience a trance state. Future trance experiences will involve the same dynamics to a greater degree, and so the suggestibility test may be a useful "rehearsal" for the client.

A third purpose of the suggestibility test can be its ability to accomplish what I call "pre-work work." If the suggestibility test is introduced as preliminary to the "real" therapeutic work to be done, it can be an opportunity to catch the client off guard and offer some therapeutic suggestions less subject to critical analysis by the client. The essence of hypnosis is occupying or distracting the conscious mind and its critical nature in order to gain access to the unconscious, and this is just one more technique for doing so. This can be accomplished by offering a suggestion such as, "Before we begin, would you prefer to go into a deep trance in this chair or the one there?" This particular suggestion is considered a "bind" because both of the alternatives made available to the client include going into deep trance. When we preface the bind with, "Before we begin. . . ," the client is not yet asked to actively participate and so is not consciously critical of the bind the clinician has employed. Of course, either choice the client makes presupposes the development of a deep trance, and the "pre-work work" of preparing the client for trance is accomplished.

PERFORMING SUGGESTIBILITY TESTS

Introducing and performing the suggestibility test require as much skill in communication as any other dimensions of working with hypnosis. There are the matters of timing (i.e., when in the relationship it is introduced), the explanation of its role, the style in which it is offered, the clinician's response to the client's response, and the closure and transition to the next phase of interaction.

Some clinicians use suggestibility tests right away—before the person's problem is presented, even before rapport is attained. Essentially, the implicit message given the client through such a practice is "If you're not responsive to me, then the hell with you." To my way of thinking, rapport is essential and must be earned through clinical skill. (continued on p. 203)

FRAME OF REFERENCE: ERNEST R. HILGARD

Ernest R. "Jack" Hilgard, Ph.D., retired as Emeritus Professor from Stanford University following a long and highly distinguished career. He is a past president of the American Psychological Association, and a member of the National Academy of Sciences. Together with André Weitzenhoffer, Ph.D., Hilgard established a hypnosis laboratory at Stanford in which countless valuable studies on hypnosis were conducted. Together, they co-created the Stanford Hypnotic Susceptibility Scales, and shaped the nature of hypnosis research for all the years since. Hilgard (Hilgard, 1977) is responsible for the Neo-Dissociation Theory of hypnosis, including his concept of the "hidden observer." Hilgard has been instrumental in making hypnosis a respectable and worthwhile phenomenon to study and practice.

On His Interest in Hypnosis: "I was at Yale as an instructor at the time that Clark Hull wrote his book on hypnosis and suggestibility, so I had some familiarity with it as a respectable topic for an experimenter. But, at the time I was interested in moving my career in other directions. I didn't really participate in his work, though I think it made a difference to know that it would be a reputable thing to do. So, I started rather late in my career, after I had been well established in general psychology and particularly in the psychology of learning. I had the feeling that much of psychology dealt with rather superficial aspects of mental life. I thought it would be interesting to go into something that had more psychology in it. I felt that, in some sense, hypnosis really had psychology in it. How to get the psychology *out* of it, that's our own problem!"

On the Use of the Stanford Scales in Therapy: "I think that if I take just a sociological or political point of view, a scale is really very useful, and is more useful for clinicians than they like to admit to. Whenever it's been tried on any severe thing, like severe pain, there's no question that you have greater success with a more highly hypnotizable as measured by the scale, not as measured by some external method. Not that a person without a scale couldn't arrive at it by using various kinds of tests for analgesia and that sort of thing. From my point of view, that's the same kind of item you have on the scale anyhow. But if you want to use other techniques or something of that sort or recovered memories, it's kind of nice to know how readily you can get genuine age regressions where they relive their entire childhood."

On Defining "Trance": "I never use the word 'trance,' so, in that sense it's fair to say I'm less traditional. But these things are a matter of gradation. My own position, which I have described in neo-dissociation terms, is that you could have dissociations of various degrees. . . .

"[So] when people use the word 'trance' they should really use it for a pretty massive set of dissociations so that you sense the personality change or that the whole orientation to reality is somewhat changed."

On the Need for Hypnosis Research: "It's the same problem in another sense with psychoanalysis. They never really wanted to do any real research. They thought psychoanalysis was itself a research method. You studied the individual and in a sense that's what Ericksonian treatment is—it's a research method to try and get a plan for the individual and if it works—[good!] But that isn't the way science is built. So, if there's any message I have, it is to not get scientistic, you don't have to have analysis of variance and become a slave to statistics, [but at least have] just garden variety statistics: Here's half a dozen people that have these same symptoms; they've been treated in 3 different ways. Why were the different ways chosen? Was it just arbitrary? Why were some of them started in one way and then shifted to another? Put *some* little design into it."

On the Importance of Hypnosis in His Career: "I would say that I really found the hypnosis period the most satisfactory in my career. I have this feeling that almost every time, even just in giving a simple scale of hypnosis, I learned something. It wasn't something I was necessarily ready to verbalize, but I learned about different kinds of responses to amnesia, or to age regression, or to hallucinated voices, and so on."

Source: Personal communication, 1988

The suggestibility test should *not* be introduced to the client as a "test." The word "test" has immediate implications of a "pass or fail" situation, and can raise an already uncomfortable client's anxiety level even higher. I suggest you call them "suggestibility measures" or "conditioning experiences."

The idea of a pass or fail situation is my biggest objection to the use of suggestibility tests. To demand a specific response from someone is to run the risk of not getting it. Why set a client up to fail? My emphasis is on the hypnotist's role as being one of suggesting possibilities, but respecting the client's final choice of whether the suggestion is accepted or rejected. With suggestibility tests, challenging clients to have a certain suggested experience doesn't much respect their ability to choose for themselves. A number of years ago I attended a conference put on by a local professional hypnosis group, one of whose members was demonstrating a traditional suggestibility test call the "Coué Hand Clasp." In this particular test, the subject was told his hands were stuck together and he could not pull them apart. When challenged to pull his hands apart, the subject did so without hesitation. The practitioner was so embarrassed and angry that he accused the disobedient subject of being "too resistant and negative."

The clinician's response to the subject's response is of great importance. In the above example, the practitioner's response was a poor one. If you get a response other than the one you suggested to tests or anything else, why not compliment the person's ability to choose for herself, and then chain that compliment to a suggestion for how her ability to choose can help her experience trance to a beneficial degree? This seems a much more positive response to what is classically termed "resistance," which is really just a choice not to follow a particular suggestion. Here, then, are some of the more commonly used suggestibility tests:

CHEVREUL'S PENDULUM

If you have ever played with a Ouija board, you've experienced the Chevreul's Pendulum test. A pendulum is given to the subject with the instruction to hold the chain between thumb and forefinger. The process can be made a bit more dramatic by having the subject hold the pendulum over the center of a circle containing intersecting lines drawn on a piece of paper. The circle may look like this:

The vertical axis was labeled "Y" arbitrarily to stand for our cultural head nod to respond "Yes." Likewise, I arbitrarily labeled the horizontal axis "N" to stand for our cultural head shake to respond "No."

Once the subject has the pendulum dangling over the center of the circle, a process suggestion can be given: "As you relax by breathing deeply, you can concentrate on allowing the pendulum to take on a particular motion." Notice the lack of specificity about what motion the pendulum is to take. As you observe the pendulum begin to move, you can now begin to use suggestions to amplify the movement: "That's right . . . the pendulum can begin to swing more and more along the (N, Y) axis, from (left to right or to and fro), and it can do so without you really knowing how or why . . . the pendulum can move just by your concentrating on it, and let it swing wider and wider. . . ." Then you can further suggest stopping it and switching directions to the other axis. The greater the degree of the pendulum's swing, the greater the degree of suggestibility.

As hokey as this old test may seem, it does illustrate beautifully the transderivational search and ideomotor processes first discussed in the "Conceptualizing Hypnosis" chapter. As the client processes the meaning of "left to right" or "toward you and away from you," her body responds to the mental meaning and causes small muscle movements outside of consciousness that cause the pendulum to move. Because the movement is so unconscious, the pendulum test is often a real surprise to the client and thus serves as a convincer of your hypnotic skills.

ARM LEVITATION AND CATALEPSY

The arm levitation and catalepsy technique involves offering the client suggestions that her arm begins to feel so light, so weightless, that it begins to lift off her lap effortlessly. A more concrete version might involve her visualizing a large helium balloon tied to her wrist. As the arm continues to lift higher and higher (levitation), it becomes more and more rigid (catalepsy) and unbendable. Then comes the challenge to try to bend her arm, but she will discover that the harder she tries, the more rigid it becomes. If she follows the suggestions that the harder she *tries* to bend her arm the more rigid it becomes, when she is challenged to *try*, she will be unable to bend her arm.

There is a play on words in this test (as well as in the Coué Hand Clasp and Eye Closure techniques described shortly). The play concerns the difference between "trying" and "doing." Trying implies expending energy but not "doing." The suggestions are phrased "The harder you *try* to (pull your hands apart, bend your arm, open your eyes), the more difficult it will be." The tendency for literal interpretation of the unconscious is what allows this technique to work (when it does). The next step then is providing the suggestions that "In just a moment I'll ask you to bend your arm and drop it to your lap and you'll be able to do so quite easily, quite effortlessly. Now go ahead and bend your arm and drop it slowly to your lap." Notice the difference between the "try" challenge mode versus the "do" mode.

Another variable in each of the challenge tests is the amount of time you give the person to "try." Let the person make the initial effort, find it takes more energy than expected, and then give him the suggestion to "stop trying now and continue to relax." If you give the person more than a few seconds to feel that initial effort, of course he can eventually do what you've suggested couldn't be done. Be quick to let him stop trying!

THE COUÉ HAND CLASP

Described in general above, the same "try vs. do" formula is applied in this technique to the person's hands. The subject is requested to sit comfortably, hands together and fingers interlaced. Some suggestions are offered about her hands being (tied, glued . . .) stuck together, and the harder she tries to pull them apart the more tightly stuck together they become.

EYE CLOSURE AND CATALEPSY

In this technique, the "try vs. do" formula ("The harder you try, the more difficult it will be. . . . Now try. . . . Now you can. . . . Go ahead and do. . . .") is applied to eye closure. Suggestions are given that the person's eyes are so heavy they will close, and the muscles of the eyes are so relaxed and limp that she cannot open her eyes. The harder she tries to open them, the more tightly closed they become.

THE HOT OBJECT TECHNIQUE

Like the others, this test involves translating suggestions into physical responses. In this technique, the subject is given an object to hold in her hand which she is told is going to begin to heat up. Suggestions are given that the object has been treated with a special chemical, or is plugged into an electrical outlet, and that it will begin to heat up and get hotter and hotter until it becomes too hot to hold. When it gets too hot to hold, the subject is instructed to drop it from her hand so as not to be burned. The length of time it takes to "heat up" and the degree of sensation associated with it are the measures of suggestibility in this test.

All of the five tests described above are common, traditional ones that are quite arbitrary and ritualistic in terms of the demands made on the client. There are some other, more spontaneous approaches to assessing suggestibility as well, described below.

EMBEDDED COMMANDS

Embedded commands are suggestions for specific responses that are embedded in the context of a larger communication, and therefore can escape conscious detection. For example, if I use my voice to accent slightly (e.g., through a change of voice tone or volume) the underlined words in the following sentences, I am embedding suggestions for specific responses.

"Isn't it nice to *close your eyes* at the end of the day?" I may get the eye closure response, an obvious indicator of suggestibility. Any suggestion that's embedded can get a response:

"I thought to myself I could . . . *take a deep breath* . . . and think it over."

"You can . . . *scratch the itch* . . . to succeed."

If you offer a suggestion so indirectly and the person takes a deep breath or scratches an itch, you have a positive response. More spontaneous, less imposing and arbitrary, embedded commands can be a more useful indicator of suggestibility because of their subtlety.

NONVERBAL SHIFTS

Nonverbal shifts in unconscious behavior can also be a very good indicator of suggestibility. Part of attaining rapport is the "pacing" or "mirroring" of client behaviors outside of their consciousness. By matching clients' breathing pattern, for example, you will have mirrored a part of them that is not in their awareness, and if you then shift your breathing and theirs follows, you have them responding to you unconsciously—an indicator of rapport and suggestibility.

Nonverbal shifts can take place in many behaviors: posture, gestures, scratching, eye contact, and breathing, to name a few. If you mirror a client's body posture and then shift your posture and your client shifts at that moment also, you have evidence of rapport and suggestibility at an unconscious level.

Mirroring, or pacing, is effective only to the degree that it remains out of the client's consciousness. If perceived consciously, it's no longer called pacing; rather, it's called mimicking, and rapport will be lost. Therefore, be careful in using these types of indirect techniques.

SUMMARY

Your client is giving you clues continuously through verbal and noverbal communication as to how open or receptive she will be to your suggestions. As you become more practiced in noticing client behavior on different levels (i.e., control, abstraction abilities, attentiveness), the formal suggestibility tests will probably become less important.

For Discussion

1. Have you ever played with a Ouija board? What was your reaction to it? How did you explain what happened?

2. How do you know when someone is open to your suggestions? What "body language" do you equate with open and closed mindedness? What exceptions are you aware of?

3. How responsive do you think you are to others' suggestions? What makes you think so? Do you view your level of responsiveness to others as an asset or liability? Why?

4. One person yawning reliably triggers the yawning response in others. What other suggestions are you aware of that people seem to react to automatically?

5. What does "unconscious rapport" mean?

Things to Do

1. Engage several people in a Ouija game who have no background in hypnosis and, ideally, who have no experience with the Ouija board game. What do you observe? How do they explain what happened to themselves?

2. The next time you shop, engage salespersons in a discussion about a product you intend to buy, and one you have no intention of buying. What differences are you aware of in your internal experience in the two conditions? How does your behavior differ in the two conditions?

3. Practice each of the suggestibility tests on at least 10 different people. Alter your style from authoritarian to permissive, and notice each person's response to your guidance. What do you learn about differences in response style? What explanation do you have for these differences?

15

Inducing the Formal Trance State

People routinely enter trance states spontaneously, that is, without any formal induction taking place. Theoretically, then, inducing a trance state in others should not be a particularly difficult thing to do. In fact, usually it isn't all that difficult to do, and yet it can be very, very difficult if the dynamics of communication and influence aren't skillfully applied. Having the ability to enter trance spontaneously in the course of daily living is necessary for survival, and because it is essentially a self-hypnosis of brief duration there are none of the potential interpersonal resistances present. Experiencing trance with another person who is in the role of a guide (the "hypnotist"), however, raises relationship dynamics such as issues of control, power, responsibility, etc. Consideration of such dynamics is implicit in the choosing of a style of suggestion formulation. For example, one assumes power if one chooses to offer commands to the client rather than permissive suggestions.

"Inducing a trance" implies that the clinician is doing something *to* the client. The language of hypnosis is, in many ways, limiting and misleading, for the client is not simply a passive receptacle for the clinician's suggestions. Rather, the client is an active force in the interaction to which the clinician must respond meaningfully. Guiding the person into a trance state is a more accurate representation of the clinician's role. In the capacity of guide, you can not know the exact experience the client is having, and so giving the client room to experience trance in her own way is not only desirable but necessary. The process of guiding a person into a trance state

Table 4. Stages of Hypnotic Interaction

1. Rapport building and attentional absorption
2. Trance induction and intensification
3. Trance utilization (therapy)
4. Disengagement and reorientation

is a large responsibility to assume, for the client is now focusing herself on the experience you stimulate through your communications.

Hypnotic interaction can be thought of as taking place in four stages, as Table 4 suggests.

In the first phase, rapport and attentional absorption, the client has begun to have her field of attention narrowed to the clinician and the immediate matters at hand. All of the preparations for the trance experience discussed thus far are parts of this particular phase: the discussion concerning personal motivation to change; conceptions about hypnosis; defining personal goals; identifying the specifics of the symptomatology (i.e., origin, function, secondary gains); assessing client responsiveness from the responses to your guidance in the interaction; choosing and engaging a communication style; and moving in a goal-directed fashion. Each of these components requires gradually pacing and leading the client's experience, absorbing her in the multi-dimensional experience of a therapeutic interaction.

This chapter considers the second phase of the hypnotic interaction, the trance induction and the intensifying ("deepening") of the trance state. The trance induction serves several purposes:

1. It provides a concrete stimulus for the client to focus her attention on, serving as a bridge between the "normal waking state" and the trance state.
2. It occupies the conscious mind, and in so doing dissociates it while amplifying the unconscious mind's associational abilities. This is the chief function of an induction—facilitating the dissociation of conscious and unconscious. The degree of dissociation obtained is the measure of trance depth.
3. It allows for the building of a "response set," a characteristic pattern for responding to the guidance of the clinician.

The hypnotic induction as the stimulus for the trance experience obviously plays a pivotal role in the overall quality of the interaction. There are as many inductions as there are practitioners of hypnosis, and since it is neither practical nor desirable to list them all I have included only several of the more useful and common ones. I have divided the inductions into two categories: traditional inductions and the utilization approach to trance induction. This chapter will discuss some of the traditional inductions; the utilization approaches are discussed in the next chapter.

TRADITIONAL HYPNOTIC INDUCTIONS

In using the term "traditional" to describe the trance inductions presented in this chapter, I have two meanings. The first application is for the literal translation of the word "traditional." These techniques have been effectively used for a very long time, handed down from generation to generation of hypnotists. The second is for the association to the traditional model of hypnosis described earlier in which the process of trance induction is a highly directive and ritualistic one. The traditional model presupposes the necessity of a formal ritual in order for trance to occur, which is an unnecessarily limiting perspective.

Each of these traditional inductions has key phrases and key concepts that are integral to the technique and these must necessarily be present in order for the technique to be employed. These techniques are invaluable in the practice of clinical hypnosis, and should be mastered as basic skills in hypnosis. In presenting these techniques at this point, the assumption is that there has been ample opportunity to have developed enough sensitivity to communication variables to appreciate that, as structured as these techniques are, they will need to be varied from client to client.

Experience will prove quite dramatically that you will get very different reactions to the same exact technique, such is the tremendous variation among people. Perhaps the greatest skill in doing effective trancework is in being observant enough to notice and use the responses you get in order to either amplify or shift away from what you are doing.

If what you are doing isn't working, you can have the flexibility to shift to a different technique and/or style. Stopping midway through a particular technique is a perfectly acceptable and desirable thing to do when that technique is not getting the desired response. The key to making such a midstream switch smoothly is in the transitional statement leading from where you were to where you are going. You should *never* comment, "Well, that wasn't working so let's try this." Instead, you can offer something more accepting and natural such as:

> That's right . . . you can continue to feel yourself shifting in the chair, wanting to relax . . . and you can begin to realize that paying attention to me isn't really necessary to have as soothing an experience as you'd like, and isn't it nice to know that you don't have to listen to me . . . and so why not let your mind drift off to something it finds comforting. . . .

Such a series of statements gives the client permission to have her experience of trance in her own way without confrontation of her "resistance."

Each of the techniques presented will include a discussion of some of the basic concepts involved in the technique as well as a brief sample in order to exemplify it.

BEGINNING THE TRANCE PROCESS

In beginning the trance induction, generally there are certain minimal responses you will want from the client. Suggesting, directly or indirectly, that the client assume a comfortable physical position is a good starting point. The general immobility (catalepsy) and the extra effort it takes to readjust one's position while in trance make it worthwhile to be sure the client is in a position she can effortlessly stay in over time. A second consideration may be to suggest a comfortable rate of breathing; you may notice with experience that anticipation and fascination often lead the client to breathe irregularly and even hold breaths unconsciously. A third consideration is helping the client turn her focus inward, and so suggesting that the client close her eyes at the start is generally a good idea. Eye closure blocks out external distractions and thus facilitates the trance induction. (The exception, and not a very good one in my opinion, is the "Eye Fixation" technique of induction to be described in its own section later in this chapter.)

Suggesting the client close her eyes can be done directly or indirectly. Generally, I just ask, "Can you close your eyes?" (embedded question), and if she can't (which has *never* happened) I would call for emergency medical help! Modeling eye closure is also a good technique; you can close your own eyes while suggesting to the client, "You can close your eyes . . . now . . . and allow yourself to relax comfortably." Don't keep them closed, though, because the only source of information about your client's responses is her, and she'll be much too difficult to see if your eyes are closed!

The final consideration at this beginning point is to use whatever behaviors the client offers as the basis for going into trance. This can be accomplished by commenting on them and tying them to suggestions of relaxation and entering trance. For example, each shift in the chair can make the client more comfortable. Each breath can soothe her body. . . .

With the client comfortable and responsive to the clinician, the trance induction is under way. Here, then, are specific techniques for facilitating trance.

PROGRESSIVE MUSCLE RELAXATION TECHNIQUES

The progressive muscle relaxation technique involves offering suggestions of relaxation of the various muscle groups of the body sequentially. The body is divided into as few or as many specific muscle groups as you wish, depending on how long or short you think the process need be. You can start with the client's head and work downward to her feet, or vice versa, as a matter of personal preference. (One of the questions I am asked most often is where to start. Working downward carries the implication of going "down into trance," but physical relaxation is easier to accomplish than is mental, and working upward leaves the person's mind for last. In my experience, it's six of one and half a dozen of the other in terms of which sequencing is better.)

The progressive muscle relaxation technique may sound like this:

> In just a moment I will begin to describe the various muscles of your body, and as I describe them relaxing you can notice how easily those muscles relax . . . and as you continue to breathe comfortably at a relaxing rate, you can notice how the muscles of your feet can relax now, feeling the muscles of your toes, your arches, your ankles relaxing easily, feeling the tingle of comfort soothing those muscles, relaxing you easily . . . and now you can notice how the muscles of your calves and shins relax, growing more comfortable moment by moment . . . and now the muscles around your knees can relax . . . and now the muscles of your thighs can feel more at ease and comfortable . . . and now the muscles of your hips and buttocks can relax . . . and now you can notice the muscles of your abdomen and lower back growing loose and comfortable . . . and as the muscles of your back and chest relax with each breath, you can feel more and more at ease . . . and then your arms can grow heavier and more comfortable . . . and now your neck muscles

can grow loose and limp . . . and finally the muscles of your face and head can relax and leave you feeling so comfortable, more relaxed than you've been in a long, long time. . . .

While the above example is an abbreviated version, you can be as repetitious with the suggestions of comfort at each muscle group as the client requires. The pace at which you move through the sequence has to be based on the client's reactions. You can take longer if the client is quite tense, or move along at a faster pace if the client is able to get comfortable quickly. A client who is either hurried by too rapid a pace or bored by too slow a pace is likely to be too easily distracted from the induction process. Remember, resistance arises when your suggestions don't fit well with the client's ongoing experience.

This technique takes a considerable amount of time to do, but only at first. Over time, the association of relaxation is formed to your mere mention of bodily relaxation, and after a short while of the client practicing this technique the relaxation response comes quite quickly. In other words, after a period of practice, simply going through the naming of the body parts in sequence without all the detailed suggestions of relaxation will still elicit the relaxation response from the client as a result of conditioning. This is what makes a lengthy, detailed technique in the beginning a much more practical one in later sessions; otherwise an inordinate amount of time would be spent on trance induction each session.

A second variation on the progressive muscle relaxation technique involves the same principle. By using a countdown (associating a number to each muscle group, e.g., "10 . . . relax your feet . . . 9 . . . relax your calves and shins . . . ") as part of the process, you can in later sessions simply count downward in the conditioned sequence and each number will trigger the associated relaxation response for that particular muscle group.

A third variation of this technique is called the "Deep Muscle Relaxation" technique. In this technique, the progression through the body is the same, but the client is instructed to deliberately tense the muscles of the specific group under consideration. Have the client hold the tension in the muscles for 10 seconds or so, and then release it. The relaxation of the muscles is both immediate and substantial. Try this yourself: Make a tight fist, and hold it tightly for 10 or 15 seconds. You'll notice your hand getting warmer, tingly and after a few moments it begins to shake with tension. Then let go and allow your hand to relax. Feel how relaxed the muscles are? Now imagine how you would feel if you did that with every muscle in your body! The relaxation can be quite profound. This is an especially good technique for very concrete people and for those who have great difficulty relaxing. It is physiologically true that when a muscle tenses, it *must* relax before it can tense again. The muscle enters a "refractory period," and one can even preface the "sure success" of this technique with this explanation to the client. (What you don't need to tell her is that the refractory period lasts only a fraction of a second.)

The variations of the progressive muscle relaxation are among the easiest and most effective inductions to perform. One word of caution, though. Most people I know who use hypnosis use inductions that are personally pleasing. I recommend you do inductions with the client's needs in mind, and not according to which work best on you. For example, using this body-oriented technique with someone in pain is not recommended. Can you guess why?

RELAXED SCENE EXPERIENCE

This technique involves offering suggestions to the client of experiencing herself in some special place where she can feel very relaxed, secure, and good about herself. As details of that place are described, the client can experience more and more of herself there. The client may be directly asked if she has a special place that she likes to go to think and be comfortable and then the characteristics of that place may be used in the induction. A second possibility is for the clinician to choose a place for her client that she is confident will be a relaxing place. This is a potentially dangerous choice to make blindly since one cannot know the client's experience of the place one has chosen unless one asks. If you choose the place for the client, it is important to ask "Have you ever been to _____? What was your experience like there?" Not asking for feedback creates the possibility that you may take the client to a place you enjoy but your client does not. Of course, nonverbal feedback is also valuable as you progress with your induction, but that is after the fact rather than a preventative approach. A third possibility is to avoid the mention of a specific place at all in the induction process, using contentless suggestions to facilitate the trance experience. More will be said about this alternative shortly.

In providing the details of the special place to the client, making use of predicates that match the client's primary representational system is especially important. Using the sensory terms the client uses in describing her experience of that place allows her to absorb more and more of herself in the suggested experience. Adding suggested experiences in other sensory modalities rounds out the induction and allows for a deeper involvement in her experience of being in that place for the moment. The more involvement the client has in the suggested experience, the more dissociated a state she is in, thus the framework for meaningful trancework.

The following is a brief portion of a content-filled relaxed scene experience induction. The suggestions relate to the experience of being at the beach, and begin with visually oriented suggestions which then lead into auditorily and kinesthetically oriented suggestions:

> . . . Sometime in your life you have had the experience of being very close to the ocean and seeing it in all of its beauty and vastness . . . and you can see the ocean in your mind's eye now . . . huge and mysterious, and for as far as you can see the ocean covers the earth . . . and way out on the horizon you can see the outline of ships and boats that sail the waters . . . and you can see the waves in front of you gently lap up on the beach and you can even hear them as they roll back into the ocean . . . and the thundering of the waves against the rocks is so soothing a sound and you can feel the breeze brushing across your face, relaxing you so effortlessly, so comfortably. . . .

Whatever special place you happen to use, the place is probably full of sensory delights that can ease your client into trance. It is recommended that you use as much sensorily descriptive language as you can in order to facilitate a full experience for the client.

The more detail you provide, the more the client can experience your guidance and thus provide valuable feedback to you. Unfortunately, it is also true that the more detail you provide, the more opportunity the client has to *not* experience what you suggest, since only the most responsive of clients will follow your every suggestion. Many detailed suggestions simply won't fit the client's experience at the moment, and so will be disregarded at least or disruptive at most.

The alternative is something alluded to earlier, the process (contentless) suggestions for the relaxed scene experience. When you provide no details, the client must provide her own in response to your general suggestions, and the likelihood of resistance is thus reduced. A disadvantage to the process form of this induction, however, is its briefer, more repetitious nature. Without the details of the experience, there is considerably less to talk about.

A contentless version of the relaxed scene induction might sound like this:

As you continue to sit there comfortably with your eyes closed, you can let your mind drift back to the memory of some special place, perhaps a special place that you've been to where you felt *so* good . . . so comfortable and secure and happy . . . or perhaps a place that you'd like to create and go to where you can sense how very peaceful you can feel inside when there . . . and you can allow yourself to go to that place right now, in your mind . . . you can feel yourself there, feeling the feelings you'd like to feel there . . . and you can notice the sounds of that relaxing place, soothing you . . . and you can see in your mind the images of that place, noticing how pleasing this place is to you . . . and you can feel so good there. . . .

Going on and on about the details of that place is possible without having any idea what the place is your client chose! Anywhere the client can feel comfortable is sufficient in order for this technique to be effective. Notice in the example the suggestion for "a place you'd like to create and go to." In the event that the client does not have a place in her experience where she felt good, to go to, she can then imagine a place; almost all people have some fantasy place they would like to travel to.

EYE FIXATION TECHNIQUE(S)

If not the oldest, certainly one of the oldest, techniques for inducing trance is the classic "eye fixation" method. Popularized by movies, television, Svengali, and other more reputable sources, this technique involves having the client fixate her gaze on a specific stimulus. The stimulus can be virtually anything: a spot on the ceiling or wall, the clinician's thumb, a dangling watch or crystal ball, a fireplace, a candle, a fishtank, a "hypno-disc" (a revolving disc that draws attention to its center because of its "hypnotic" design:), an hourglass, whatever. *Anything* that holds the client's attention long enough for her to respond to the simultaneous suggestions for relaxation will suffice in this technique.

As the client stares at the stimulus, suggestions are offered to notice every observable detail, and that while fixing her gaze she can experience herself growing more relaxed. There is a little bit of trickery in this technique when done properly; the client's eyes should be elevated in their sockets as she stares at the stimulus, which then allows a physiological factor to work in the clinician's favor. Eyestrain naturally occurs, and thus the client will, in fact, experience the heaviness and tiredness in her eyes that has been suggested. The client naturally attributes the sensations to the clinician's suggestions, not physiology, and the clinician's credibility can rise as a result.

Personally, I am not a fan of this technique, but it is so commonly used by so many I thought it necessary to include in this text. In that way, you can be in a position to decide for yourself what is useful and what isn't. Eye closure may take a while to get as a response with some clients, and can unnecessarily become a battleground in the "test of wills" between client and clinician. Traditional literature has often devoted a great deal of consideration to what to do when 20 minutes later the client has still not closed her eyes (recommending it be treated as resistance). I find it much easier, as I stated earlier in this chapter, to just suggest eye closure and get on with the rest of the trance process.

An eye fixation induction method might sound like this one, done permissively and contentlessly:

> As you listen to the sound of my voice, you can let your eyes search the room and find something that is of particular interest to you. . . . And when you find that particular object you can let your head begin to drop down and allow your eyes to look upward toward that object . . . . That's right. . . . And now you can continue to look at it, and you can notice every detail about the way it looks . . . and as you continue to relax and look at it, have you noticed how tired your eyes have become . . . and as they grow more tired, your eyelids can grow heavier and heavier . . . and as soon as you realize that it takes too much effort to keep your eyes open, you can let them drop down and as they drop down you can drop into a very comfortable state of physical and mental relaxation. . . .

Commenting on the client's blinking, pacing your words to the eye blinks, and even modeling eye closure can further suggest desired responses.

If after a reasonable period of time (don't hurry!) the client still has not closed her eyes, you can either switch techniques or suggest she close her eyes in a relatively direct way such as: "You can close your eyes . . . now." If you still do not get eye closure, here's where effective pacing and leading comes in: "You haven't closed your eyes yet, for some reason . . . and as you become aware of the reason . . . if you'd like you can tell me that reason. . . ." Or one can match the client by encouraging her "to keep your eyes open . . . as you learn something meaningful."

It is important to realize also that even with eyes open the client can be in a deep trance, as discussed earlier. Keen observation will tell you this and perhaps save you needless doubts and confrontations over whether the client is experiencing trance "properly."

COUNTING METHODS

Counting methods of induction generally involve counting downward (implying "going down" deeper into trance) and in between numbers offering suggestions of relaxation and comfort. At first, the slower and more detailed the process between numbers, the better. As in the progressive relaxation techniques, the client can become conditioned through experience and posthypnotic suggestions to need fewer and fewer suggestions between numbers until deep trance can be accomplished with just a simple countdown.

This technique is popular because of its simplicity, evidenced in the following transcript:

> ... In just a moment I'm going to begin counting downward from the number 10 to 1, and as I count slowly downward you can relax a little more with each number, and when I reach the number 1 you can experience yourself as very relaxed and comfortable ... and I'll begin now with the number 10 ... relaxing comfortably and breathing in ... and out ... at a rate that's comfortable for you, and 9, relaxing even more comfortably, feeling the relaxation grow a little more with each moment that passes ... and 8, feeling so much more at ease, and 7. ...

A variation involves having the client do the counting out loud downward from 100 while the clinician intersperses suggestions of relaxation. Furthermore, the clinician can intersperse suggestions that when the client discovers it takes too much effort to remember and say the next number, she can stop counting and go even deeper into trance. Rarely have I encountered someone who counted below the number 80.

A variation on the same theme is to have the client count backwards by 7 from 1000 (or some comparable numbers), requiring so much mental energy that it is a relief to be able to stop counting and just drop into trance!

THE "AS IF" METHOD

Generally a good method for more "difficult" clients, this pattern involves no direct suggestion to the client to respond in a particular way, but rather to act "as if" she were responding in the way suggested. In terms of the outcome, where the act ends and the reality of trance begins is ambiguous since the responses are identical.

A concrete example of this technique was evident in an episode of the television show M*A*S*H. Hawkeye and B.J. decided to fake a fight for Major Burns' amusement. The staged fight quickly escalated into the real thing, and two close friends were at each other's throats! Acting "as if" amplified real feelings of hostility in each of them, feelings that may have been imperceptible if not amplified in that way.

To provide an idea of how this technique might be used, here is a sample of Milton Erickson using a variation of it with Richard Bandler and John Grinder as presented by them in *Frogs Into Princes* (1979; p. 136):

> Milton said to me "You don't consider yourself a therapist, but you are a therapist." And I said "Well, not really." He said "Well, let's pretend . . . that you're a therapist who works with people. The most important thing . . . when you're pretending this . . . is to understand . . . that you are *really* not . . . You are just pretending . . . And if you pretend really well, the people that you work with will pretend to make changes. And they will forget that they are pretending . . . for the rest of their lives. But don't you be fooled by it."

Suggesting that a client act "as if" she is comfortable, relaxed, thinking about a happy moment, or whatever, paves the way for the client to really experience those suggestions without any real demands being made.

INTENSIFYING (DEEPENING) TECHNIQUES

The deepening techniques presented in this section are techniques that have been traditionally used after the formal induction in order to intensify the client's trance state. As was discussed earlier, the traditional and standardized models of hypnosis have placed a greater emphasis on trance depth than does the utilization approach. Achieving deep trance may not always be necessary, but it can allow for certain possibilities that make familiarity with trance deepening techniques a necessity.

THE STAIRS (OR ELEVATOR) GOING DOWN

In this deepening technique, the client is told to imagine (i.e., see, hear, feel) herself at the top of a flight of "special stairs" or on a "special elevator." As she experiences herself going *down* the stairs a step at a time, she can go *down* deeper into trance, or as each floor is passed in the elevator, she experiences herself going deeper into trance. A brief sample follows:

> I wonder whether you can imagine yourself standing at the top of a set of very special stairs, the stairs of relaxation . . . and as you experience yourself at the top of the stairs you can be very comfortable and you can take the first step *down,* and as you take a step down the stairs of relaxation, you can relax so very deeply. . . . And now you can take another step down, going even deeper into a very comfortable, absorbing state of mind and body, and then you can take another step down even deeper. . . .

Each step down can be emphasized as a step down deeper into trance. It is a good idea to make sure beforehand that the client doesn't have any negative associations to going downstairs (e.g., childhood spankings in the basement) or riding in an elevator.

COMPOUNDING

In the chapter on basic communication patterns of hypnosis, I discussed "verbal compounding," the tying of one suggestion to another according to the formula "As you X, you can Y." Verbal compounding serves as a deepener by continually building new responses on the framework of past responses, intensifying the trance experience.

"Manual Compounding" is the tying of verbal suggestions to physical experience. As a deepener, it can take the form of offering suggestions of going deeper into trance while experiencing physical sensations that reinforce the suggestions. For example, assuming permission has been obtained to touch the client, you can gently push downward on the client's shoulder(s) while suggesting she feel herself sinking deeper into a comfortable trance state. Or you can raise her hand, and suggest: "As I *drop* your hand back *down* to your side, you can *drop* even deeper into trance." The physical sensations of "down" can amplify the verbal suggestions of "down" and make the experience a more profound one as a result.

THE MIND'S EYE CLOSURE

I had been hypnotized a number of times, but it wasn't until I experienced this particular technique that I experienced deep trance. This technique involves offering suggestions about the presence of the "mind's eye" as the part of the mind remaining active in thinking and imaging. By being offered suggestions similar to the "Eye Fixation" suggestions of the "eyelids getting heavy" for the "mind's eyelid," the client can slowly close out stray thoughts and images and experience a deeper trance. It might sound something like this:

> ...Just as you have eyes that can see the world around you, you have an inner eye that we can call the "mind's eye"...and it can see images and process thoughts even as you relax deeply...and your mind's eye has an eyelid, and like your physical eyes the lid can grow more tired and heavy, and it can begin to drop...and as it begins to drop it slowly shuts out stray thoughts and stray images and can leave your mind perfectly free to experience whatever you'd like...and it's closing more and more...and your mind grows more quiet, more restful...and now it can close...and close out any stray thoughts or images you don't want to interfere with how relaxed you are....

This technique is an effective way of "turning off" much of the internal dialogue that goes on continuously in each of us, making deep trance easier to accomplish.

SILENCE

Silence can be a useful deepening technique if used skillfully. Following an induction, suggestions can be offered to the effect that the client can now "have some silent time to enjoy the relaxation of trance and even increase it." You may wish to preface the silence with an indicator of how long you will be silent (e.g., "You can take 60 seconds of clock time to enjoy a silent period during which you can deepen your trance state even more ... "), or you may suggest that your client signal you when she's ready to proceed. It is almost always a good idea to give some protective suggestion in the form of an "anticipation signal" so that when you begin to speak to the client again after a silent time, your voice will continue to soothe the client (*not* startle her). During the period of silence the client can be so absorbed in her trance she forgets anyone else is there!

The period of silence may sound like this:

The use of silence as a deepener can also provide an opportunity for you to compose yourself and think of what the next phase in the treatment plan is. In other words, it is a prime time in the process for the client to go deeper into trance while you figure out what you'd like to do next!

POSTHYPNOTIC SUGGESTION AND RE-INDUCTION

This deepening technique, also called "refractionation," involves giving the client already in a trance state a posthypnotic suggestion that the next time trance is reinduced she can go into trance both more deeply and more quickly. The clinician then guides the person in and out of trance several times in the same session.

Stage hypnotists gain their greatest notoriety for this same phenomenon. When a posthypnotic suggestion is given during the pre-show phase of suggestibility testing that when the hypnotist commands "Sleep!" the subject will re-enter trance, the audience is baffled and fascinated at the "power" of the hypnotist whose subjects enter trance at an unbelievably rapid rate.

Some clinicians establish what is called a "cue word" or "cue symbol" that the client is to use as a rapid means for entering trance. Building such a cue simply allows for less trance induction time and more time to *use* the trance state. Thus, the use of posthypnotic suggestion and re-induction as a deepening technique is a useful one, with the qualification that if a "cue" is used it be one that is more gentle and respectful than a harsh command to "sleep." The best cues, in my opinion, are the most subtle ones, such as a gradual change in your voice to the voice qualities associated with your "trance voice." The association to entering trance in response to the use of your voice in a particular way is one example of what is called an "auditory anchor," a conditioned pattern of response in association to an auditory stimulus.

Once the client has become experienced with entering trance, such trance experiences can serve as a basis for future experiences. In fact, making use of a client's previous trance experiences is one of the utilization approaches to induction discussed in the next chapter.

SUMMARY

Presented in this chapter were some of the most common and useful methods for inducing and deepening the trance state according to traditional, structured approaches. *Anything* that focuses the person's attention and facilitates feelings of comfort and well-being can be used as a trance induction, and those presented here are intended to provide a foundation on which to build.

Practicing these techniques will allow one to develop the ability to speak in a smooth, flowing way. Choppiness is distracting and reflects uncertainty, an unsettling experience for a client looking for guidance.

Just as there are no clear dividing lines between the different levels of trance, there are no clear dividing lines between the stages of hypnotic interaction; what has been identified as a suggestibility test in this book does not have to exclusively be a suggestibility test—it may also serve as an induction or a deepener. The inductions can be employed as suggestibility tests or deepeners, and the deepeners can be suggestibility tests or inductions. For the sake of clarity in presentation I have put the various techniques in the categories I did, but one can allow one's self the flexibility to use whatever will work when one needs it.

For Discussion

1. Should the clinician perform inductions she doesn't personally like? Why or why not?

2. How might a clinician find out whether she is moving too quickly or slowly for the client?

3. With what specific client populations should each of the inductions listed in this chapter *not* be used? Why?

4. What experiences of acting "as if" you felt a certain way have you had, and with what results?

Things to Do

1. Practice each of the techniques in this chapter on classmates, shifting your style from person to person. What feedback do you get?

2. Research other approaches to hypnotic induction, and briefly outline each.

16

Naturalistic Trance Inductions

The structured hypnotic inductions presented in the previous chapter are based on the general assumption that trance is a special, if not artificial, state. A formal procedure called an induction is employed to guide the client from a "normal, waking state" to the condition called "trance." Then, depending on the degree of susceptibility to the trance experience (i.e., the level of trance the client is capable of entering), the client can experience a variety of trance phenomena in order to build new experiences or reorganize past ones as a basis for therapeutic change. These assumptions can be useful to guide the development of skills in hypnosis; however, the utilization approach rests on different assumptions that add a different, more complex and sophisticated dimension to working with hypnotic communication patterns.

In the utilization approach, trance is not considered an extraordinary or artificially created phenomenon. Rather, trance is viewed as a natural experience occurring routinely in all persons. In adopting this perspective, one task of the skilled clinician is to recognize trance responses as they naturally occur in the course of interaction and then build on them meaningfully. In other words, the skilled clinician can create trance responses from hypnotic patterns of communication that capture the client's attention and focus him on experiences that will be therapeutically significant. The instructions to the client in this approach are typically more process-oriented than content-filled. There is often not as clear a beginning, middle or end to the induction relative to the clearer transitions of the more structured, content-oriented approaches of the previous chapter.

The spontaneity required to "accept and utilize" or "pace and lead" a client's communications makes it virtually impossible to ritualize (i.e., standardize) the practice of clinical hypnosis in this approach. For some, the lack of rigid structure is a turn-off, while for others that lack is a turn-on, for the challenge of how to develop a meaningful trance in a particular person in a specific context is a challenge, indeed. Implicit in this approach is the role of clinician as both guide and initiator of what is to happen. The clinician's responsibility is significant since the client is assumed to be capable of a meaningful trance experience, unlike the traditional and standardized model's limiting perspective that some people are not capable of meaningful trance experiences (see Appendix A).

The stimulus for the trance experience in the utilization approach lies in the unconscious associations that the clinician triggers in the client through her communications. This perspective differs considerably from the more traditional perspective that the power of the hypnotic suggestion is contained in the suggestion itself rather than in the client. Which specific associations of client experience will be triggered cannot be predicted with any certainty. Observing and using a client's responses will, of necessity, temper the approach.

Securing and maintaining the attention of the client is a beginning point for the hypnotic interaction. Talking meaningfully about the issues that brought the person into treatment, telling entertaining stories that parallel the client's experience, and behaving in unexpected ways are three common techniques for securing attention. As the client's attention is drawn to the clinician, building on the client's responses by acknowledging them and suggesting (directly or indirectly) that she can expand herself further makes use of the client's attentiveness. When the clinician notices trance responses building (absorption, changes in breathing, a fixed posture, muscular tension dissipating, etc.), he can begin to engage the person in the process of trance induction and deepening through the naturalistic techniques described in this chapter.

The transition from routine conversation to trance induction is a subtle one in this approach in comparison to the more formal, "OK, close your eyes now and let's do hypnosis," approach. Induction is not necessarily announced as a new phase the interaction is entering, but can be eased into as a natural part of the progression of treatment. Whatever the client spontaneously does during this time is accepted and utilized as part of the process, and thus the implicit message is, "What you're doing right now is what will allow you to deepen your experience further." Behaviors that seem "resistant" (e.g., fidgeting, smiling, interrupting . . .) are accepted and used as the basis for further suggestions, redefining them as acceptable and even useful responses.

The skilled manipulation of the nonverbal components of the clinician's communications is always a major factor in doing trancework, but in the utilization approach it is especially so. The changes in tone of voice, eye contact, and other analogical communications while shifting into an induction may serve as potential associations ("anchors") to entering trance in this and further experiences. For example, using your "trance voice" selectively will predictably trigger trance responses since those voice qualities are associated with the trance experience. This is but one example of how you can obtain trance responses without directly asking for them. Your body posture, gaze, and breathing patterns are further examples of potential patterns on which to build trance response associations.

The techniques for guiding a person into a trance state described in this chapter are reliable ones. Each involves narrowing the person's field of attention to her inner experiences, specifically the associations triggered by your communications. Resources long dormant can be reactivated, memories long forgotten can be rediscovered, feelings long buried can be re-experienced, and issues long troublesome can be resolved.

Table 5. Naturalistic Induction Principles

Utilization of client's reality (past or present)
Accessing questions to absorb and direct attention
Use of self as model
Notice and amplify responses
Verbal chaining: "As you X you can Y"
Presuppositions: *How* to do X, not *whether*
Interspersal of suggestions
Framing responses (incorporation)
Shift in delivery style (nonverbal)
Orient to internal experience
Elicit associations
Guide associations

NATURALISTIC INDUCTIONS

USING PAST TRANCE EXPERIENCES

The recognition of trance states arising spontaneously among people allows for a smooth transition into the induction phase of trancework. All people have at least experienced naturally occurring trance states that can be identified and made use of, while a large number of people have experienced formal trancework at one time or another. These formal experiences can be even easier to build new experiences on. The induction technique of "Using Past Trance Experiences" involves the following two general categories of previous trance experiences on which to build: 1) Informal experiences with trance, specifically the "everyday trance" experiences people have during the normal course of daily living, and 2) Formal experiences with trance, specifically the previous time(s) the client experienced trance successfully. Either approach may be offered in a process-oriented or content-filled structure, described later in this section.

In the approach building on informal experience with trance, the phase of attentional absorption typically involves some pre-induction discussion about the nature of trance states while exploring the client's associations to hypnosis. At some point, the clinician can begin to model attentiveness, immobility, slowed breathing, and can begin to hypnotically describe one or more natural situations in which trance occurs. Such situations might include long drives, absorption in a good book or movie, during a massage or jacuzzi, daydreaming, praying, and any other situation where the person has had the experience of being absorbed. The nonverbal shift from a conversational tone of voice and pace to one that is slower, quieter, and more meaningfully articulated is fundamental to guiding the person into the suggested memory of that natural trance state she has experienced. Through the absorption in that memory, trance responses (i.e., the ideo-dynamics) occur in the here-and-now, which the clinician can notice, accept, and utilize according to the "As you experience this, you can experience that" chaining formula. The client need not close her eyes in order to experience trance, but the clinician may want to suggest eye closure by offering a direct or indirect suggestion to do so. The following is an example of how this technique may sound, using a previous informal trance experience of reading, with indirect suggestions in the form of embedded commands to obtain specific responses:

You said you enjoy reading a really good book? I really enjoy reading, too, especially when I have some time all to myself ... and I know I won't be interrupted ... I can let myself *relax so deeply* ... *sitting* in a way that is *so comfortable* ... I can *sit* quietly *without moving* for what can seem like a long, long time ... and I like to read books that *let you experience yourself differently* ... ones that *allow you to change in beneficial ways* ... and *your mind can be so active in learning* while *your body gets more comfortable* with each page you turn ... and when you get too comfortable to keep reading, *you can close your eyes* and drift off ... and I'd like to tell you about a book I read that may have special meaning for you....

The above induction starts out conversationally, then turns to a sharing of personal experience the client can relate to in order to build rapport while simultaneously slowing down and building associations to entering a trance state. Then the shift takes place from "I" to "you," with an emphasis on the client's experience building into a trance state through the tonal emphasis on suggestive phrases. As the client becomes absorbed in the memory of relaxing and learning while reading, her responses build in the current context and become the basis for whatever trancework is to be done. This sample is obviously a content-filled one, providing details about the experience of reading. A process-oriented approach could also be employed, of which the following is a sample:

Can you think of a time when you were so involved in an experience that you forgot to notice things around you? Every person has had experiences where ... *you find yourself relaxing* ... remembering ... thinking ... and *you can remember* a specific experience that was pleasant ... when you could *lose track of time* ... and forget to notice outside sights and sounds ... and only your thoughts were important ... and then you could *feel so relaxed* ... and isn't it nice to know *you can be so wrapped up in your thoughts* ... that people's voices fade away ... and you're alone with your thoughts ... and feelings of comfort ... and it's at times like that that you can learn something important....

In the above sample, the process of becoming absorbed in thought is described, but no details of a specific context are provided. Rather, the client provides those details for herself when the suggestion is offered that she choose a specific experience that was pleasant.

In the approach building on formal experience with trance, the typical pre-induction phase can focus the client's attention on the range of possibilities hypnosis allows, and how previous experience with hypnosis can make future experiences more satisfying and successful. It seems worthwhile to reiterate a point made in an earlier chapter about exploring the nature and quality of the client's previous trance experience(s). If the client had a positive and meaningful experience with trance, then the clinician has a solid base on which to build. If the client had a negative experience with hypnosis, one that was unsuccessful at least or hurtful at most, then the clinician must exercise caution to refer back to the experience as little as possible in the course of doing trancework. Questioning about techniques used and identifying the situational and interpersonal variables operating at the time can save you from unwittingly duplicating a previously negative experience.

If the client has had a positive experience with hypnosis before, a content-filled approach to the use of the formal trance experience can involve engaging the client in an ever-slowing, detailed account of the experience. This approach usually involves a large degree of interaction as the induction progresses, with the clinician simultaneously questioning the client, suggesting possible responses, and building on the client's responses as they occur. The mechanism of induction is structurally the same as in using informal previous trance experiences; as the person becomes absorbed in the memory, the responses associated with that memory evolve in the here-and-now. The clinician notices, accepts, and utilizes those responses, building toward the goal of the interaction. The following is an example of this induction approach:

Clinician: You mentioned earlier that you experienced the comfort of trance before, didn't you?

Client: Yes. A while ago I saw a hypnotist for another problem I was experiencing.

Clinician: Can you recall how soothing an experience trance was?

Client: Yes, I remember feeling really relaxed. I didn't expect to be able to hear her voice, but I did. I wasn't sure I was hypnotized, but it felt really good.

Clinician: That's right. . . . Trance can be so relaxing . . . so soothing . . . and you can remember how you were sitting then, can't you?

Client: I guess so . . . (Readjusts position).

Clinician: That's right . . . and do you remember how good it felt to *breathe deeply and close your eyes?*

Client: (deep breath, eyes flutter closed) Yes.

Clinician: And you can recall what you heard then that allowed you to relax so deeply, can't you? And what did you hear?

Client: Just the hypnotist's voice . . . telling me to relax deeper and deeper . . . that it was as if I was floating. . . .

Clinician: That's right, and you can remember what it's like to *have that light, comfortable feeling everywhere in your body.* . . .

In a sense, the client is acting as her own hypnotist, giving herself the same suggestions from the past in the present, and the clinician's role is a simple one of amplification. The client knows how to experience trance, and reminds herself in detail of the nature of the trance experience and, in so doing, recreates it. By framing the interaction as a "discussion" about past experience rather than a set of current demands to respond to, the issue of resistance is largely avoided.

To use this approach in a process-oriented way, the interactional dimension of the induction can, if desired, be eliminated. The following is an example of the use of formal previous trance experiences offered in a contentless way:

You mentioned earlier that you had an experience with trance before that was a very relaxing and successful one. If you'd like, you can begin to recall what that experience was like . . . remembering how *your body can be so comfortable* . . . how *your breathing can begin to slow down* . . . and I wonder whether you'll remember how comforting it can be to simply *sit and listen* to someone describe some ways that *you can experience yourself differently* . . . and do you recall how good it felt to close your eyes . . . and the memory of *relaxing so deeply* is a part of you . . . and isn't it nice to *rediscover something familiar that can help you* . . . and you can remember the room you were in when you learned how to *feel good* . . . you can see the furniture and you can hear the sounds of that place, and as you remember you can *feel comfortable* about that experience right now. . . .

The context in which the client had her previous formal experience with hypnosis is not known to the clinician, nor does it need be as long as the clinician is certain the experience was, in fact, a good one for the client.

Making use of the client's previous experience with trance, whether formal or informal, is one of the easiest yet most effective trance induction and deepening processes. It is a spontaneous, loosely structured approach that generates little resistance because "we're not talking about *now,* we're talking about *then.*" The extra psychological distance makes a difference. In sum, the techniques involving use of past trance experiences are reliable and flexible ones, and when well practiced can comprise a significant portion of your induction repertoire.

BUILDING AN INTERNAL FOCUS

The experience of trance has been described as one of absorption, an intense concentration on some stimulus to the exclusion of others. Usually, the absorption is an internal one. In doing trancework, guiding the client into a trance state implies having the client selectively attend to the stimulus of the clinician's guidance, specifically becoming absorbed in the associations triggered by the clinician's trance process. By focusing on her internal experience, the client can suspend attentiveness to the external world and thereby subjectively experience a wider range of possibilities.

The clinician's role is to facilitate the process of building an internal focus through suggestion. In routine interaction, therapeutic or otherwise, people are expected to be more externally oriented and responsive to the other person. When one lapses into brief episodes of self-absorption, it is considered rude, inattentive, disinterested, or is even considered evidence of passive-aggressive hostility. Yet, such episodes of internal absorption are normal, natural, and to be expected. In fact, in learning and doing trancework, part of the difficulty one encounters is developing the ability to stay externally focused on the client's responses as much as is humanly possible. If you are internally absorbed while doing trancework, you are going to miss a great deal of nonverbal information communicated by your client. For example, a colleague of mine likes to close his eyes when he does trancework and immerse himself in his own trance process, along with his client, which he finds soothing and enjoyable. The problem with that is I have seen clients of his open their eyes midway and feel perplexed that their therapist is in trance and they're not! Maintaining an attentive external focus on the client is the only way for the clinician to maintain rapport through the utilization of spontaneous client responses.

The induction process of building an internal focus involves offering pacing statements of what external stimuli the client can be aware of, coupled with leading statements describing internal responses the client may experience. This can be done in any ratio of pacing to leading statements the clinician judges to be useful. In other words, how many externally oriented suggestions of experience one offers for every internally oriented suggestion of experience is dependent solely on the responsiveness of the client.

The assessment can be made very early on in the clinician-client interaction as to how internally or externally absorbed the client is in the course of routine interaction. An internal or external orientation in relating to the world is generally a fairly stable characteristic of an individual, but can vary markedly from situation to situation. Internal or external focus exists on a continuum, and no one can be exclusively one or the other in a fixed way. Probably the most internally oriented human experience is severe catatonia, and even then there is some awareness of external events. Assessing the client's general orientation and degree of focus is usually a simple process of observing how the person communicates about his experience. Does he see himself as responsible for his problem or is he a victim of evil forces beyond his control? Is he sensitive to others' feelings and perceptions or is he unaware of others' feelings and reactions to him? Is he easily distracted by external but routine things like a phone ringing or plane flying overhead? Is he or isn't he insightful about his experience? Thinking along these lines of assessment can allow you the opportunity to formulate an induction and intervention that will more likely be accepted.

Once the assessment is made of how internally or externally focused the client is at the time when you would like to begin your trance induction, you can make the judgment of what ratio of external paces to internal leads you think would be effective, modifying it as necessary according to client response. Some clients are so internally focused at the beginning point, you don't have to have much of an induction beyond "You can go into trance, now." Others may be so externally focused that they may require five or even 10 external paces before a single internal lead is offered. As the induction progresses, fewer and fewer externally-oriented statements are made while more and more internally-oriented suggestions are offered. The following is offered as an example of this induction process with someone deemed moderately externally-oriented at the start of the induction. An (e) follows each externally-oriented suggestion, and an (i) follows each internally-oriented suggestion.

You're sitting in that chair (e) and you're listening to me describe the experience of going into a trance (e) . . . and as you watch me (e) you may notice the feel of the chair underneath you, supporting your body comfortably (e) . . . and as you notice the chair you can hear the phone ringing somewhere (e) . . . and isn't it *soothing* . . . to know you don't have to answer it and so *you can let yourself relax* easily (i) . . . and you can notice the wall behind me with its interesting pictures (e) and you may notice the objects on my desk (e) . . . and as you look around the room you can hear the routine sounds of this environment (e) and you can hear the sound of the world busily going on around you (e) and *you can feel so good* in realizing that *your body can grow more at ease* (i) . . . and *your mind can begin to drift* back to a pleasant memory (i)

. . . and as your mind drifts back you can feel the texture of the chair on your fingertips (e) and as you notice how that texture feels you can also hear the things I have to say (e) . . . and as you listen *you can become aware of a certain memory* (i) . . . one that you feel is important that you'd like to re-experience and learn from (i) . . . a memory that may remind you of something you'd like to know now (i). . . .

In the above example, the induction starts with a series of statements that are pacing what the client may be aware of, matching her current experience, then offering a general statement of what she can experience. The number of paces to leads shifts as the induction progresses, leading the client into re-experiencing an important memory. You may notice the use of sensory based terms in visual, auditory, and kinesthetic modalities. A way to further tailor the process to the individual is to deliberately choose the modality of internal experience one wants the client focused on. Many of the problems clients present clinically can be described in terms of internal or external focus on a particular sensory modality. The most obvious example is pain, which can be thought of as an intense internal awareness on the kinesthetic level. Management of pain may involve shifting the focus from internal to external, or from the kinesthetic modality to another.

Most hypnotic inductions involve building an internal focus, each according to a different method. This induction provides the barest of frameworks for helping the client accomplish trance, since all that is provided here is a structured description of the process as shifting the client's focus from external to internal experience. *Which* externals and *which* internals you use in *what* combination in *which* modality and in *which* style and structure make for a huge range of possibilities. How successful your induction will be, as always, is determined primarily by how well you have assessed the client's response style and how well you can adjust your approach according to the feedback you get.

METAPHORICAL INDUCTIONS
WITH EMBEDDED SUGGESTIONS

In the earlier section on "Using Past Trance Experiences," I described how putting a little psychological distance between the desired experiences "now" through the use of experiences from "then" can make for less resistance. The use of metaphor is an even less direct induction approach, and so is even less likely to arouse resistance in the client. Rather than use the client's personal past experience as the basis for induction, metaphors may describe some other person's (or animal's, or thing's) experience at some other time in some other place. Thus, the degree of removal is even greater and the possibility for personal threat reduced even further.

In Webster's Encyclopedia of Dictionaries, a metaphor is defined as "a figure of speech which makes an *implied* comparison between things which are not *literally* alike." Metaphors in the therapeutic context may include anecdotes, jokes, analogies, or any other form of communication that conveys a meaningful message to the client on conscious and/or unconscious levels. Metaphors provide an opportunity for the client to learn from others' experience, allowing her to identify, to some degree, with the characters, issues, and resolutions of the metaphor.

Learning from the experience of others throughout recorded history has allowed human civilization to evolve. You do not have to experience something personally in order to know about it, as long as you understand and benefit from the meanings of the experience on a personal level. In growing up, you heard and read fairy tales like Snow White and Cinderella, and you learned something from them about human nature. Your parents' stories about their childhood taught you about families and growing up. In reading books of all kinds, you learned about different societies, different lifestyles, as well as different types of relationships. Even in watching television and movies, your involvement in the story allows you to experience vicariously the same feelings and events as the characters in the story, broadening your range of experience and developing resources that may be drawn upon at some future time.

The popular use of metaphorical approaches in clinical treatment is a relatively recent development, catalyzed by the work of Milton Erickson. His fascinating and often simple stories were able to capture his patients' interest on a conscious level, while his embedded suggestions allowed the patient's unconscious mind to form new associations that could serve her in therapeutic ways. More will be said about metaphorical approaches to therapy in the next chapter, while this section focuses on the use of metaphor in the induction phase.

You may recall the discussion in an earlier chapter about how a client's symptoms may be viewed as metaphors of her experience. Clinicians have historically been trained to take a client's communications and "read between the lines" to uncover their "real" meaning relative to the person's overall experience. Once the real meaning has been uncovered, the clinician's role has been to offer interpretations and, through the interpretations, generate insights that would lead to new perspectives and more adaptive behavior in the client. In other words, while a client is communicating a meaning on the conscious level, it is understood that there are deeper, unconscious meanings communicated simultaneously *if* one is perceptive enough to detect them. The multiple level communication on the part of the client has historically been responded to by the clinician in a clear, single-level interpretation.

Erickson considered interpretations as too simplistic, too reductionistic to reflect accurately the complexity of any piece of human experience. Furthermore, Erickson had greater faith in the unconscious mind than he did in the conscious mind, and thus had a greater interest in techniques that made use of the unconscious mind's resources. Erickson also thought that if the client could communicate on multiple levels, why couldn't the clinician do the same? Erickson's utilization of the unconscious in the treatment process was also out of respect for the integrity of those he worked with, for if a person's unconscious mind chose to keep some information out of her awareness (i.e., repression), was it necessary and respectful to bring the information into the person's conscious mind for her? Erickson thought not, and believed that insights may even impede the therapeutic process by keeping the person restricted to a safe, cognitive level of existence, widening the gap between intellect and emotion rather than bridging it.

The safest of alternatives to working consciously with interpretations is the therapeutic metaphor. Relating a story that can capture the client's conscious interest while at deeper levels allowing her to learn new ways of thinking, feeling, and doing is a respectful and flexible way of engaging the person in the treatment process. In the context of inducing trance, metaphors are ways to focus the client's attention on an experience that is interesting, while incorporating suggestions for desired trance responses into the story's framework.

The specific dynamics of meaningful metaphor construction could fill volumes, and so can only be superficially presented in this book. When one formulates a metaphor for the induction of trance, it is helpful to know something of the client's personal interests, values, and hobbies. Metaphors built around things that are part of the client's lifestyle are more likely to capture and maintain the person's interest. Of course, things of an intrinsically fascinating nature will also do. The broader the base of knowledge and experience the clinician has, the more sophisticated the metaphors can be. The metaphor as the induction method can introduce the client to other clients' experiences, build a rapport with the clinician, build an identification with the character(s) of the story, confuse the client as to why the story is being told and thus stimulate a search for meaning and relevance, all while building the internal focus and receptivity for the subsequent intervention.

Perhaps the easiest metaphors are those that begin with "I had another client in a similar situation to yours. . . ." When the experience of a previous client (real or otherwise) is described, the client can identify with that person, and build confidence in the clinician's experience in dealing with such problems. If, for example, a client presented the complaints of stress and a poor self-esteem, the induction might go something like this:

> You're describing to me how uncomfortably tense you feel much of the time, and I guess it isn't often that you *take the time to relax* . . . and I'd like to tell you about a client I worked with not long ago . . . a woman named Wendy who is *not unlike yourself* . . . with many responsibilities . . . and she came to me feeling so tense . . . so unsure of herself . . . and she didn't know that she didn't have to feel that way . . . and she wanted to *feel good . . . feel relaxed* . . . and when Wendy sat in that chair you happen to be sitting in . . . she actually took the time to *notice how comfortable that chair is* . . . and then she let herself *take in some deep breaths* . . . and she seemed to *just let go of the everyday concerns* . . . and she could *listen to me comfortably* . . . while her *mind could begin to wander* . . . and the memory of the last time she could *relax deeply* helped her realize she knew how to *relax so deeply* . . . and that she could take the time for herself . . . because she deserved it . . . and who doesn't. . . .

The above example is a starting point for leading into more metaphors about possible ways to build confidence and manage stress. As an induction, it begins by matching the client's concerns and then building the identification with another similar client who had a positive experience in some ways that may be of interest. There is ample room to maintain rapport by incorporating the spontaneous responses of the client into the metaphor. For an example of a metaphorical induction tailored to a specific interest of the client's, the following can illustrate a metaphor for a person who likes to watch television:

> You like to watch television when *you can take the time to unwind* . . . and watching television can certainly be an entertaining way to *spend some time relaxing* . . . and I like to watch TV whenever I can . . . but not nearly as much as my friend Richard . . . someone I really think you should know about . . . because, like you, Richard likes to watch television . . . and he can *learn a lot about life and about people* that way . . . and there was a show on once that he told me about . . . that taught him a lot about himself . . . he didn't know that

in that show there was an opportunity *to have a pleasant learning experience* ...
and he could *get very comfortable* ... and when looking at the television *the eyes
can get so tired ... they want to close ... and then listen to what's important* ... and
Richard learned something important ... because in a show he watched,
there was a man who felt very badly about himself. ...

In the above example, television as a learning device and a source of
relaxation are ideas to lead the client into a trance state. At the point where
the example stops, the clinician can go into one or more metaphors about
the client's problem and its potential resolution. In this example, the
metaphor becomes even more removed because it goes from a friend's
experience to a friend's experience of someone on television's experience.

Almost any experience can serve as a metaphorical induction to trance
when the qualities of that experience are defined as comforting and
meaningful. Engaging the person's attention on the content of the story
allows for deeper messages embedded in the story's structure to activate the
client's unconscious ability to respond in a significant way. Metaphors,
because of their indirect style, create the possibility for a response, but
whether one is obtained is dependent on the way the metaphor is introduced,
the appropriateness of the metaphor for that individual client, and the
degree of rapport maintained throughout its telling. The metaphor must
be introduced as potentially significant, either by some direct introductory
remark such as "This other client of mine I'd like to tell you about is
someone I think you could learn from ... " or indirectly through the
meaningful tone of your voice and quality of eye contact. The relevance of
the metaphor was discussed earlier, and should involve something of
interest to the client (unless you consciously choose to bore your client into
trance!). The rapport is maintained by incorporating feedback from the
client spontaneously into the metaphor.

Story telling seems to have become an art on the decline. Television has
saturated our society and placed us in the role of passive viewers of
experience to the extent that the average American television viewer
watches over six hours a day of television! Interactions between people
become fewer in frequency as more of us learn to "talk" to computers.
Developing a skill in story telling is fundamental to developing a balanced
approach to the practice of clinical hypnosis. You are encouraged to reread the classic fairy tales, fables, and old mythology, for they are excellent starting points for rediscovering the wisdom to be handed down in
story form.

INDUCTION THROUGH NEGATIVE SUGGESTION

You may recall the discussion of negative suggestion structures presented in Chapter 12. Negative suggestions, when used skillfully, can encourage positive responses in clients. They can do so in part because of the transderivational search and ideodynamic processes, and in part because of their acceptance and utilization of client resistances. Resistance as a factor in the hypnotic interaction is discussed in greater detail in a later chapter; suffice it to say here that few clients are blindly obedient to the suggestions of the clinician. Instead, each client maintains a sense of control, internal homeostasis, and autonomy through the rejection of input (evidence of "resistance" according to the clinician's way of thinking) even when the input is obviously intended to benefit the client.

In those clients where control is a critical personal issue, a tendency to respond negatively and in a contrary manner as a reliable response pattern is frequently evident. If the clinician says, "It's day," the client responding in a polar mode disagrees and says, "It's night." Such polar responsiveness is not necessarily aimed specifically at the clinician, rather it is a general response pattern that the person uses everywhere or nearly everywhere. You have undoubtedly experienced such people's ability to stir up conflict wherever they go, often puzzling over why people don't relate to them very well. The need to defend against others' input in order to maintain what must be a precarious internal balance (or else the person wouldn't be so defensive) is a basis for such response styles. Someone with a greater sense of self can maintain a strong sense of personal identity even while selectively incorporating ideas from others.

In the hypnotic interaction, the negative response style can be accepted and utilized in the service of trance induction and trance utilization. The principle underlying the use of negative suggestions is "fight fire with fire." When negative suggestions are offered to the critical, controlling client, she can naturally reject them and respond in an opposite way. Knowing the client's tendency to respond in such a manner, the clinician can use negative suggestions the client will reject in order to get the opposite response(s) that is actually desired. Beware, though, for offering such negative suggestions will seem an obvious trick unless they are offered in a very congruent and meaningful manner.

Imagine, for a moment, a client sitting opposite you who is anxious, uncertain about you and your hypnosis techniques, uncertain about herself, and who is struggling to maintain personal control. The following example of an induction through negative suggestion might be a useful one to employ.

> You've come here looking for help with your problem because you don't like the way you are feeling . . . and *you can feel differently* . . . but I don't expect you to know that yet . . . for right now . . . it's important to know . . . you can reject anything and everything I say . . . you can't be expected to *listen and learn* what you came here to . . . yet . . . and for now you can't be expected to *change in a meaningful way* . . . until you've had the opportunity to continue feeling badly a while longer . . . so don't *listen to me* . . . and don't *give yourself the chance to feel more at ease* . . . and you can continue to squirm in your chair . . . I don't want you to relax here or now . . . I don't think there's any reason for you *not to continue fidgeting* . . . so don't *sit still* and don't *let your muscles relax* . . . and don't *let your eyes close* even when *they can get so tired of staying open* . . . and some people feel good when they know they don't have to listen to me . . . talking about all the ways you don't need to *notice opportunities to change* in a comfortable way . . . and don't *allow yourself the comfort of relaxing deeply*. . . .

In the above example, suggestions for relaxing and changing were offered in the negative framework "don't do this." To the client deemed negative and resistant, on the surface no demands have been made and so there really isn't anything to resist consciously. On an unconscious level, the ideodynamics associated with the transderivational search process assure you of some degree, however small, of responsiveness to your suggestions on which to build. The key is to incorporate whatever specific spontaneous responses arise in the person into the process, redefining them as cooperative. For example, if you accept the client's fidgeting instead of labeling it a resistant behavior, it can be encouraged. By encouraging it, you define it as something useful in the interaction, even though the client's intention was to not cooperate. This technique of using negative suggestions to utilize the client's resistance is one more way of responding to resistance in addition to those described in the later chapter on resistance.

The use of negative suggestions in the induction phase of hypnotic interaction is intended to use a client's resistance to help him into a trance. At some point, the client realizes that all your suggestions about *not* relaxing, *not* letting go, *not* focusing internally, etc., have had the effect of facilitating the attainment of a trance state. This can be, and usually is, a turning point in the relationship. The client has now had his experience guided by the clinician, and not only did he survive it but actually found it pleasant and relaxing. The relief that comes from *not* having to fight to maintain control can have a profound impact on the client, who has now learned from his own experience that he can still be in control without having to fight others off negatively. This trance experience can then serve as a basis for future trance experiences in a more positive framework.

INDUCTION THROUGH CONFUSION TECHNIQUES

The process of inducing a trance state involves creating a somewhat dissociated state of experience in which the client's unconscious mind is able to function with a greater degree of autonomy from the conscious mind's influence than in the "waking" state. Confusion techniques are techniques for facilitating dissociation and, therefore, trance states. Confusion techniques are among the most complex hypnotic patterns to master because they are, well, confusing.

Human beings hate to be confused. Confusion creates an unpleasant internal state that motivates the person to resolve the conflicting input. Frequently, the person is *so* motivated to resolve the confusion she will jump to erroneous conclusions just to have a conclusion, any conclusion. Confusion techniques deliberately disrupt the client's everyday mental set in order to increase the likelihood of a suggestion getting in. Because people do not like to be confused and will hold erroneous, even self-destructive, ideas rather than allow an issue to remain unsettled, the clinician faces the task of dislodging old, hurtful thought patterns in order to build more adaptive ones. When one is certain about something, how likely is one to change one's attitude about it? Not very likely, for the more certain one is about an idea or behavior, the more stable (and thus resistant to change) one's situation.

Confusion causes uncertainty, and thus paves the way for a change in attitude and behavior. One of the most common quotes attributed to Erickson, who developed and mastered techniques of confusion, is ". . . out of confusion comes enlightenment." When people are confused, they STOP! And then they develop an internal focus (a self-induced trance state) as they quickly sort through everything they know in order to resolve the confusion. While the person's conscious mind is so preoccupied with making sense of something, the unconscious is more readily available for suggestion. In a nutshell, that's the mechanism of confusion techniques.

Confusion techniques can take a variety of forms, but generally fall into one of two categories: pattern interruption techniques and overload techniques. Pattern interruption techniques involve saying and/or doing something to interrupt the person's routine response style in a given area. One may want to interrupt a person's experience of a thought, a feeling, or behavior, or

Table 6. Assumptions Regarding Confusion Techniques

People value clarity and understanding
Confusion, or lack of clarity, creates an unpleasant internal state, i.e.,
    dissonance
Dissonance motivates attaining understanding
Wanting to attain understanding motivates a search for meaning and an
    increased receptivity to satisfactory (even if incorrect) explanations
People's behavior is patterned, and carrying out familiar patterns is most
    comfortable
Blocking the carrying out (i.e., interruption) of familiar patterns requires
    generating a novel response
The time span required to generate a new response is a period of amplified
    responsiveness to external cues

some other pattern, depending on the desired outcome. Disrupting the
pattern and shifting the person onto a "new track" can effectively break the
old pattern long enough to let the new experience have a meaningful
impact.

Interrupting a person's pattern may be accomplished through a variety
of ways (see Table 7). Changing the environmental variables surrounding
the pattern, shifting the sequence of the pattern's components, altering
others' responses to the pattern, exaggerating or emphasizing the implications of the pattern, surrounding the desired responses with confusing
irrelevancies, and building new associations to the pattern through outrageous and/or incongruent clinician responses are a few techniques to
interrupt client patterns. Furthermore, one can use gestures to interrupt a
client, one can dramatize with nonverbals the client's position (the body
postures Virginia Satir described to accompany her personality types are
useful), and one can use language patterns that are so ambiguous or are
even blatantly in violation of normal speech syntax that the client becomes
entranced through trying to figure out how a clinician can behave in such
an unpredictable, even odd, way.

The following is a transcript of Milton Erickson using a confusion
technique on a patient experiencing pain (in Haley, 1967; p. 152). Part of
Erickson's strategy involved the use of language patterns violating the
routine patterns of meaningful communication while embedding therapeutic suggestions at a deeper level. The normal flow of consciousness in
the client is interrupted in order to accommodate the unusual speech

---

Table 7. Pattern Interruption Strategies

Confusion
Surprise, shock
Humor
Reframing
Double-binds
Paradox, symptom prescriptions
Task assignments, behavioral directives
Joining the client's frame of reference (utilization)
Confrontation
Trance and trance phenomena
Ordeals
Metaphors
Amplifying polarities
Externalizations

---

patterns of Dr. Erickson, allowing the unconscious to absorb meaningful suggestions in a beneficial way.

(. . . some family member or friend) . . . *knows pain and knows no pain* and so do you wish to *know no pain* but comfort and you *do know comfort* and *no pain* and as *comfort increases* you *know* that you *cannot* say *no to ease and comfort* but you *can* say *no pain* and *know no pain* but *know comfort and ease.* . . .

While the patient's conscious mind focuses on trying to make sense at the cognitive level out of a linguistic mess, at the feeling level the associations triggered by the suggestions to feel good and feel no pain allowed the patient the desired comfort. The above transcript also demonstrates elements of the other form confusion techniques may take, namely overload. Overload as a means for creating confusion can take the forms of excessive repetition and sensory overload. In the transcript above, Erickson's repetition of the suggestions to feel comfort and feel no pain are so frequent and so excessive while embedded in other confusing statements that it would be difficult to resist each and every one on a suggestion by suggestion basis.

Repetition of suggestions is extremely tiresome (and boring) for the client's conscious mind, yet repetition is a well known enhancer of the unconscious mind's learning process. In the traditional and standardized models of hypnosis, repetition is considered necessary in order for suggestions to be accepted, but that is simply not the case. Unless used skillfully, repetition can actually alienate the client from the interaction through its simple-minded and single-minded approach. Embedded in a confusion technique, however, the suggestions that make sense can stand out as if illuminated in neon, and thus have a greater impact.

The other form of overload, sensory overload, involves so overloading the person's conscious mind with information coming in from multiple sources that it can't possibly keep up; thus the unconscious is engaged to a greater degree. An example of a sensory overload technique is the "Double Induction" technique (Gilligan, 1987). With two clinicians simultaneously doing trance inductions on a single client, the client may initially attempt to follow both clinicians' voices, but she quickly learns that she cannot consciously keep up with both for long. Whatever information is offered that escapes conscious detection and analysis can still be incorporated by the unconscious, and for the overloaded client, trance is a nice place to escape to.

The structure of the double induction is as follows: The clinicians are on opposite sides of the client, each using the language patterns that correspond to a greater degree to the brain hemisphere they have access to; the clinician talking to the client's left side (left ear) is addressing more of the right hemisphere, and thus can use more sensory-based, hypnotic communication; the clinician talking to the person's right side (right ear) is addressing more of the left hemisphere, and can thus use a more rational, sequentially ordered approach to induction.   (continued on p. 247)

FRAME OF REFERENCE: STEPHEN G. GILLIGAN

Stephen G. Gilligan, Ph.D., received his doctorate in psychology from Stanford University. He studied with Milton H. Erickson, M.D., for over four years.

Gilligan is the author of a book on Ericksonian psychotherapy, entitled *Therapeutic Trances* (1987). His other publications include articles and chapters on learning, memory, emotion and hypnotherapy.

Gilligan has been conducting training in Ericksonian psychotherapy since 1975. He is considered by many to be among the most creative and insightful practitioners of Ericksonian approaches.

On Defining "Trance": "It is an interactional sequence (usually between two or more people, but sometimes it can be internalized) that involves some experientially absorbing interactional sequence that produces an altered state of consciousness where 'automatic' responses begin to happen. That is to say, where expressions, whether they're behaviors, thoughts, images, or emotions begin to happen outside of the normal volitional or conscious control of the person. . . . That *is* a tremendously broad conceptualization and if I were an experimentalist, which I was during graduate school, I would find it completely unacceptable. I think that from a research point of view mine is a terrible definition of trance. From a clinical point of view, however, it's useful because it allows you to begin to appreciate how hypnotic inductions are used in non-formal situations, such as Hitler speaking to the German people and arousing their attention, or a family communicating to a child in a way that causes symptoms to emerge."

On Naturalistic Trances and Therapy: "I think when we consider a narrow view of hypnosis—such as in terms of 'deeper, deeper, deeper' structures or in terms of standardized hypnotizability scales—that it begins to misdirect the therapist's attention onto a certain set of incantations such as 'relax' or 'deeper, deeper' or 'your hand will lift,' rather than appreciating that there are unconscious processes already occurring in the person that the therapist's task is to elicit. . . . I make that distinction because the more the trance is a result of eliciting naturalistic patterns already in the person, the more likely the therapeutic change will be."

On Non-therapeutic Trances: "I think you have to appreciate that hypnosis is a powerful way of influencing people in relationships. It is the integrity of the practitioners, *not* how good their technique is, that really makes the ultimate difference. In a recent article, I identified seven basic differences in the contexts of the trance, including: 1) whether a person is valuing himself or not; in a therapeutic trance, a person is feeling a sense of value; in a non-therapeutic trance, he is not; 2) whether there is trust or not in the situation; 3) how the body is organizing itself—whether it's in a comfortable position, a balanced position, or a very upright position; 4) whether or not there is what I call 'content variability'—whether when the trance develops new things emerge and ideas develop naturally, or whether the person just gets stuck in the same old thing repeatedly; 5) whether or not a person can set aside a rigid perspective; in a symptomatic trance, or non-therapeutic trance, people tend to maintain the same perspective. In a therapeutic trance, they're able to change the perspective; 6) whether or not people are sensitive in an implicit or explicit way to the context that surrounds them—whether they are, as we say in California, 'connected' to something more than themselves; 7) and finally, I think there is a different relationship style in the therapeutic trance. It's cooperative, rather than competitive."

On Cooperative Therapy: " ... My interest increasingly is to really insure that there is integrity in the relationship and that there is a co-creation, a cooperation between the therapist team and the client team in terms of developing the therapeutic process.

"[I call this] the cooperative principle, because I believe that one of the ideas that has been erroneously interpreted from Erickson's work is that the therapist has sole responsibility for producing change in the client. From doing a lot of trainings and a lot of supervision ... I think the biggest pitfall I see therapists aspiring to integrate Ericksonian approaches fall into is that they feel they have to do something *to* the client. They feel that they have to put them into trance or that they have to change them. It's very difficult for them to appreciate this notion of a cooperation principle wherein there has to be an equal contribution by both therapist and client at both conscious and unconscious levels. I think that when people forget that, then it's possible for them to get into tricks. To the extent that that happens, I think they should be rightfully criticized by their colleagues."

On Milton Erickson: "My first impression of Erickson was from reading books. And what I got was an image of somebody who was incredibly clever, incredibly intelligent, very absorbing, and that he really knew how to get people's attention. That image was one in which there was a lot of manipulation involved—always thinking about how to manipulate other people. When I first met him in person, the major difference between the image I had of him before I met him and the experience of being with him was that I experienced him as being a lot more caring than the way he came across in the books. I experienced him as a lot more gentle, although I could sense his capacity to influence. It was very clear in relation to him that he had a really deep integrity about how he was using his influence. I think that he was a fantastic therapist, and I think he carved a whole new epistemology for doing therapy, and it will continue to have a very powerful influence."

Source: Personal communication, 1988

Sensory overload can involve the use of multiple (two or more) hypnotists working on a single client, or multiple stimuli (sounds, smells, sights ...) operating on different levels. If you do not have the luxury of another clinician around to try this technique, you can even make a general induction tape and play it during a session while simultaneously doing your more personalized approach "live." You can even suggest to your client that, "You can listen to me—or, you can listen to me!" Such overload techniques are especially useful in the treatment of individuals in pain (Yapko, 1988c).

Confusion techniques for the purpose of induction require a clear-headedness on the part of the clinician, demanding of her to know what she is doing at each moment. It also requires dissociation on the part of the clinician (as well as the client) in order to keep from getting caught up in the confusion she is creating! One can build confusion around virtually any dimension of experience, from the days of the week ("You can relax on Tuesday but not nearly as well as on Wednesday and if you remember on Sunday how good it felt to relax on Friday you can remember one day on a Monday to take in a deep breath and ... ") to remembering ("How can one forget how good it feels to *go deeply into a trance* when one remembers that to forget what one remembers only reminds one to forget *remembering the comfort and peace* of remembering to forget what you've forgotten to remember about forgetting tension and *remembering comfort* ... "). Confusional methods can also address specific dimensions of experience (see Table 8). By offering confusing suggestions in a manner generally regarded as meaningful, the clinician induces the client to search and find meaning at deeper levels, the best of all reasons to use confusion. Confusion tech-

Table 8. Categories of Confusion Methodologies

Cognitive
Sensory
Relational
Temporal
Role
Identity
Affective
Spatial
Behavioral

niques are especially good for clients deemed highly cognitive, for the intellect cannot keep up for very long with an abundance of irrationalities embedded with meaning that shift the intellectual client onto a more affective level of relating.

In sum, confusion techniques are among the most complex and difficult techniques to use skillfully, but be assured that when they work, they work well.

CONCLUSION

The approaches presented in this chapter are among the most spontaneous and effective means for inducing trance states in a naturalistic way. Their inability to be scripted in a word for word manner is actually their strength. Clinicians who develop skill in the use of these approaches will have done so only through multiple sessions of practicing careful observation of client responses while developing the flexibility to turn each obtained response into one that enhances the quality of the interaction.

For Discussion

1. How are transderivational search and the ideodynamic processes operating in each of the inductions described in this chapter?

2. How does one's general internal or external orientation to the world evolve? What implications for either mode of relating are there for doing trancework?

3. How does one "fight fire with fire" in everyday contexts? Give examples and describe the dynamics operating in each.

4. Should a clinician induce a trance state in a client without first announcing it? Why or why not?

5. What is the basis for Erickson's claim that "out of confusion comes enlightenment"? Is confusion useful for facilitating change? Why or why not?

Things to Do

1. List 25 common experiences where trance is evident. Outline a set of inductive suggestions for each.

2. Have two peers talk to you simultaneously on two different subjects and try to follow each. What do you experience?

3. Describe to your class hypnotically an experience in which you relaxed comfortably. What is your audience's response?

17

Trance Phenomena and Their Inductions

Voodoo, witchcraft, the supernatural, and hypnosis are frequently lumped together as "the dark side of the force" in the minds of ignorant laypeople. Along with recent trends of fundamentalist religious revival have come a number of accusations sent my way about "doing the Devil's work" because of my use of hypnosis. If you have not yet experienced such fear and ignorance, you are fortunate. I sometimes find it hard to believe, but it's true that many people have an entirely irrational fear of hypnosis. How does the typical hypnosis book still manage to work its way onto the shelf in the "Occult Books" section of many bookstores? The answer to that question lies in the many phenomena associated with a trance state that are, to the untrained observer, unusual at least and spooky at most. The various trance phenomena that will be described and defined in this chapter are the basic ingredients for the therapeutic applications of hypnosis. Furthermore, they are the basic building blocks of *all* experience; the structures of hypnosis can be brought together in ways that help or hurt, depending on their associated content. More will be said about this idea later. The various trance phenomena are the powerful subjective experiences each of us is capable of creating by virtue of our natural gifts of incredibly complex minds and bodies. They are also the "bizarre" experiences that have caused so many to fear hypnosis for so long, placing trance in the same category as unexplainable, mystical phenomena. I bear no conscious prejudices against mystical phenomena, I just don't think patterns of influential communication that can be used reliably in clinical situations should be placed in the same category as the reading of tea leaves and human palms.

The various trance phenomena are representations of specific capacities of human beings. They are experiences each person can have, limited in

250

the formal hypnosis session by the need for the right combination of personal, interpersonal, and situational factors. Each person is capable of these trance phenomena to one degree or another in the hypnotic interaction because these are everyday experiences that occur routinely in all people. (Thus, they are not evidence someone is "haunted.") In fact, they are a necessary part of experience in order to function in a normal, healthy way. To claim someone cannot be hypnotized is absurd, for if the person could not focus his attention, remember, imagine, behave in automatic ways, and demonstrate other such trance phenomena, he simply could not survive.

When I describe the various trance phenomena, I will also describe the everyday contexts in which they naturally occur. Suffice it to say here that these experiences occur routinely on a random basis. People generally do not think of these random experiences as being related to hypnosis, but they are structurally identical. Since these experiences occur routinely in people, then why learn hypnosis? The experiences are random, and when they occur people tend to dismiss them lightly with some variation of, "Gee, that's kinda strange." No further thought is given them, and they seem to "just happen." The typical person senses no control over the experience, and this is the reason for acquiring skills with hypnotic patterns. Rather than having such potentially useful experiences remain random and seemingly out of control, the person who becomes familiar with hypnosis can facilitate these experiences *at will for meaningful reasons*. A clinician who employs methods of hypnosis is providing her clients with a greater sense of control in their lives, certainly a significant contribution.

The recognition that trance phenomena occur routinely in all people is, in most ways, unique to the utilization approach. In the traditional and standardized models of hypnosis, the various trance phenomena are considered unique manifestations of the separate and distinct artificial state called "trance." The utilization approach's concept of trance as a natural experience has been described in detail earlier. The concept of trance phenomena as natural occurrences rather than artificially created manifestations of "trance" is a natural and consistent progression of theory and practice.

It is true that others in the traditional and standardized modes have claimed trance phenomena are everyday occurrences, but then the techniques used by them to obtain such responses have incongruously only been ritualistic and artificial. Such techniques, as was true for the more structured, traditional inductions, work and can work well. However, the

Table 9. Trance Phenomena*

Age Regression
Age Progression (pseudo-orientation in time)
Amnesia
Analgesia
Anesthesia
Catalepsy
Dissociation
Hallucinations (positive, negative)
Ideodynamic responses (ideoaffective, ideomotor, ideosensory)
Sensory Alterations
Time Distortion

---

*Value as Building Blocks: Neutral

arbitrary and content-filled structure is what separates them from the utilization approach which emphasizes a natural and spontaneous means for obtaining such responses. Both structured and naturalistic inductions have been presented, and in line with my desire to acquaint you with the range of possibilities, both structured and naturalistic approaches to the attainment of trance phenomena will be presented in this chapter. Applications of these trance phenomena in clinical contexts will be discussed in later chapters.

The hypnotic interaction has been described earlier as taking place in phases (i.e., attentional absorption, induction and deepening, trance utilization, and disengagement). This and later chapters will focus on the third phase, the phase of trance utilization where the trance state is used to facilitate some therapeutic intervention. Realistically, there is no clear dividing line between the different stages of trancework, and *therapy may therefore take place at any point in the process.* Usually, however, therapy is done in this utilization phase following the trance induction process. The more structured the approach, the more the attainment of trance phenomena must be limited to this particular stage. In the traditional and standardized models, the various trance phenomena could only be attempted after a formal hypnotic induction and after the client reached a certain depth. In the utilization approach, trance responses are expected to occur naturally throughout the interaction, and therefore can be accepted and utilized throughout. This approach, because of its broader framework, is more demanding of observational and clinical skill.

The trance phenomena described in the remainder of this chapter are the classic hypnotic phenomena described in the literature on hypnosis for many decades, if not centuries. A description and definition for each, examples of everyday experiences of that particular phenomenon, and approaches for obtaining that response will be presented. As you read each of the following sections, you can think of your own experience of that particular trance phenomenon, specifically what happened and what the context was. Discovering the everyday aspects of trance experience can allow you to notice more of the spontaneous trance responses arising in your clients as you interact with them, simultaneously broadening your capacity for therapeutic influence. Furthermore, the familiarity with every-day contexts where trance responses occur is the basis for the naturalistic utilization approaches. The general approach involves finding and describing a routine situation in which the desired trance response is likely to occur. The client can become absorbed in that suggested experience and can then naturally demonstrate the trance phenomenon without the clinician directly asking for it. This and related trance utilization techniques will be described in each section. Here, then, are the trance phenomena, presented in alphabetical order for easy reference.

AGE REGRESSION

DESCRIPTION

Age regression is an intense utilization of memory. Age regression techniques involve either taking the client back in time to some experience in order to re-experience it (called "revivification") as if it were happening in the here-and-now, or simply having the person remember the experience as intensely as possible (called "hypermnesia"). In revivification, the client is immersed in the experience, reliving it exactly as the memory was incorporated at the time it actually happened. In hypermnesia, the person is in the present while simultaneously recalling vividly the details of the memory.

Most people have an intuitive understanding of how profoundly our previous experiences affect our current thoughts, feelings, and behaviors. Certainly, psychology has amassed vast amounts of information to substantiate the point. Age regression as a technique provides the opportunity to go back in time, whether it be into the recent past or the distant past, in order to recover forgotten (i.e., repressed) memories of significant events or to "work through" old memories in order to reach new conclusions. It is because our previous experiences mold our current perceptions that age regression is one of the most widely used hypnotic patterns in therapeutic work. Memory is malleable and dynamic. Memories change with time, and can be therapeutically influenced because of their unstable nature.

In defining age regression as the intense utilization of memory, the everyday aspects of age regression can become apparent, for people drift into memories routinely. If a song associated with a high school sweetheart comes on the radio, the listener can become absorbed in that person's memory—things they did together and the events taking place in their lives at that time. For a period of time, the rest of the world fades from awareness while the person is internally absorbed and focused on her memories, even re-experiencing profoundly the feelings from that time in her life. Age regression is as commonplace as that kind of experience. Any cue that triggers the person to go back in time to remember or relive some event is stimulating a "spontaneous age regression," and recalling memories can have a powerful emotional impact on that person. Looking at photographs, hearing a certain song, seeing an old friend, and re-experiencing a feeling not felt in a long time are all examples of routine age regressions. The current craze of "nostalgia" in which old movie stars are resurrected, old clothing styles brought back, and old clichés and customs revitalized are all indicators of how powerfully the desire to go back to "the good old days" can influence current experience. Memories can recreate strong feelings.

FOCAL POINT: CREATING FALSE MEMORIES

The ability to unwittingly create false memories is an issue of such great importance that it is being given this special place in this book. It is a difficult issue with many different complicating variables, and it must be well considered in order to avoid the potential harm of therapy in general and hypnosis in particular.

Consider this letter advertising a workshop I received a short while ago. It is reproduced here in edited form in order to protect those responsible.

"Dr. Yapko, Director:

As bizarre as the following question seems, *please take the time to read further and give serious consideration to the subject discussed.*

During a hypnosis session, have you ever had a client that believes that he/she has had an alien (extraterrestrial) abduction or encounter? Has this person experienced missing time or repetitive dreams about unusual night visitors? In the last four years there has been a 65% increase in reported abduction cases. Many of these reports have surfaced during hypnosis sessions.

What would you do if information similar to this was revealed by one of your clients during a hypnotic session? How do you help this person?

... Some of the people have had conscious recall of the event. However, the majority of them recalled the encounter while under hypnosis—which many had sought out to help them with other problems...."

What is *your* reaction to this letter? My reaction is irritation and disbelief. Let's look at the serious implications of this letter, especially as they relate to the practice of psychotherapy.

One fact the letter doesn't mention is that a popular book called *Communion,* by Whitley Strieber, came out a few years ago. The book is an intelligent and articulate description of the author's belief he has had repeated experiences of being abducted by extraterrestrials. Prior to becoming aware of the abductions, all Strieber had were periods of time he was amnesic for, and unusual dreams of abduction in which he served as a human guinea pig for extraterrestrials' experiments. Is it a coincidence that there is a "65% increase in reported abduction cases" following the release of Strieber's book? Obviously not. If so many people can be convinced so easily of "trance channelers" (people who go into trance and become the medium through which other entities, perhaps as old as 35,000 years according to one, can share their "wisdom"), thanks to popular books like Shirley MacLaines' *Out On a Limb,* then you can convince a percentage of the population of *anything.* Hypnotic past-life regression, hypnotic ESP, hypnotic aura-reading, and countless other "applications" of hypnosis are offered to those who are open to or already have beliefs in such phenomena.

So what's the problem? The serious problem is that a clinician can suggest an experience that the individual accepts as "true." With extraterrestrial abductions, it is easy to dismiss the problem lightly.

However, consider what happens if what is suggested instead is that, "You may have been molested as a child. Let's do hypnosis to find out."

I am aware of clinicians too numerous to count who are "molestation specialists," who have a rudimentary checklist of "signs of a molest victim." These include poor self-esteem, sexual avoidance or apathy, relationship difficulties, unresolved anger toward one or both parents, and other such symptoms. Don't these same "signs" show up in almost everyone? But, *a clinician intent on finding molestation issues to resolve can plant the suggestion in the client's mind of the possibility of such an experience in her background.* Then, in hypnosis, the clinician can ask leading questions: Are you alone with your (father, uncle, family friend. . . .)? Is he touching you? Where is he touching you? Is it a touch, or does it feel like a fondle?

The client can then "discover repressed memories" that are *not* true that become the basis for a whole new identity—that of a molest victim. I am not insensitive to the fact that many *are* victims of such experiences. Rather, I am pointing out *that the use of leading questions can create a false memory* that can become a pathological frame of reference for the client that will last a lifetime. *Formal trance is not necessary for this to occur.* To then be labeled as an AMAC (Adult Molested As a Child), or an ACA (Adult Child of an Alcoholic), or any other such label is also a huge disservice to the client. It establishes an identity rooted in pathology. If we as a profession learned *anything* from David Rosenhan's ingenius experiments on normal people in psychiatric hospitals (1973), highlighting the negative and limiting nature of labeling, it is that labeling someone—especially pathologically—works against the larger goals of treatment.

It is apparent that these are extremely sensitive issues requiring substantial consideration. The primary goal in presenting them here as a "Focal Point" is to amplify in your awareness the potential for harm that exists in having an interest or framework (like molestations) that can unwittingly be too easily imposed on the client to his or her detriment.

STRATEGIES OF AGE REGRESSION

In using age regression clinically, at least two general strategies can be employed, each giving rise to a variety of techniques. The first general strategy concerns the use of age regression to go back to negative, traumatic kinds of experiences. The intention is to allow the client to release pent-up feelings while simultaneously providing new ways of looking at that situation that may help her release whatever destructive influences from that experience may still be lingering in her life. In this strategy, either revivification or hypermnesia may be employed, depending on the clinician's judgment as to how immersed in or distant from the experience the client can be in order to receive maximum benefit. For example, if a client felt rejected by her mother, the clinician may want to take the client back in time through revivification to relive one or more of the interactions critical in developing that feeling. This could be done by helping her to relive the feelings and re-experience the sights and sounds of that event while supporting her in expressing those feelings. Then, the clinician can focus her on dimensions of that experience previously not consciously attended to by her. By adding new understandings and insights to the old memory, one can help the client to feel loved and cared for by a mother who was, perhaps, guilty of nothing more than expressing her affection in a distant way because of her own limitations, rather than because of the daughter's presumed lack of worthiness. Reaching a new conclusion about an old experience can change one's feeling about one's self quite dramatically. Having the client immersed in the experience allows for the powerful emotional impact of such an experience. In contrast, if one were working with a woman who had the terrible experience of being raped, putting her back in that situation is generally an undesirable alternative, and may be approached from the more psychologically distant technique of hypermnesia. In this approach, she can safely be in the here-and-now while working through the trauma of the past.

The second general strategy of age regression is compatible with and easily integrated with the first. The strategy involves making use of a client's abilities and resources that have been demonstrated in past situations but are not currently being used by the client, unfortunately to his own detriment. Often, the client has abilities he doesn't realize he has, but because he doesn't have awareness of them and access to them they lie dormant. In using age regression, the clinician can help the client rediscover *in his own past personal experience* the very abilities that will allow him to manage his current situation in a more adaptive way. For example, if someone were complaining of difficulty in learning something new, the clinician might take the client back in time to a variety of past experiences of feeling frustrated in learning something, and then showing how each frustration eventually led to mastery of that information. Learning to get dressed, to read and write, to drive a car, and countless other experiences all started out being intimidating new experiences and later became routine, automatic abilities. Immersing the client in the experience of the satisfaction of mastering learnings that once seemed difficult can help him or her build a more positive attitude toward the present challenges.

APPROACHES

Any pattern of communication that helps the client go back in time is an approach to age regression. One set of patterns of age regression employs suggestions that involve the use of one's imagination as the trigger to recapture past experiences. Others involve more naturalistic, everyday approaches to immersion in memory. Either approach can be a good one, depending on the client.

Patterns that make use of the client's imagination include the various "special vehicle" approaches (e.g., train, plane, time machine, space ship, elevator, and the like) that can transport the client back in time to the event under consideration. The special vehicle is an artificial, concrete, and content-oriented means for structuring the experience, and thus requires a considerable amount of detail in order to facilitate the regressive process for the client. The following is an example of an age regression approach (initiated after induction and deepening) using a "special train":

> ... and now that you can experience yourself as comfortably relaxed ... you can let yourself have the experience in your mind ... of going to a special train station ... a train station unlike any you've ever experienced ... where the trains that run are so unusual in their ability to take you back in time ... and you *can* go back in time ... to experiences that you haven't thought about in a long, long time ... and you can see yourself getting onto the most interesting-looking train ... and you can find your way to a seat that is so comfortable to sit in ... so soft you can rest there ... deeply resting ... and then as you feel the train begin to move in a gentle and pleasant way ... you can experience the movement of going backwards in time ... slowly at first ... then faster ... building a powerful momentum ... and as you look out the window ... and see the events of your life moving past you like so many telephone poles you pass on the way, the memories of yesterday ... then the day before ... and the day before ... and the day before ... and all the days before ... can drift through your mind as you go further and further into the past ... when then becomes now ... and then the train begins to slow down ... and then it comes to a stop ... and now you can step off the train to find

yourself in that situation that was so important to you ... and being in that situation now, you can see the sights, hear the sounds, and feel the feelings of that time and place ... *this* time and place....

It is at this point that the opportunity for dialogue between the clinician and client may be initiated, if desired. Asking the client where in time she is, who is present, what is occurring, what she is thinking, feeling, or doing, as well as any other question(s) can lead the clinician to better understand how the experience was incorporated by the client so that a differing perspective that may be more adaptive may be offered as part of the therapy.

If the client knows when a certain significant event occurred, the clinician can regress the client back to that specific time. Often, though, the client has no idea when a certain feeling, thought, or behavior started. In such instances, the clinician can mix some process-oriented suggestions into the process, such as in the previous example in which no particular age or context for the regression were specified. In that example, it was left entirely to the client to choose an experience to focus on as representative of the problem's evolution. The clinician must ask the client to verbalize the details of her experience at some point so he can assist the client in having access to as much of the memory as possible and know where and when to intervene.

Whatever approach one chooses to employ as the facilitator for the regression experience, related details can provide the opportunity for greater involvement in the experience. To accomplish a more personally distant experience of the past event, suggestions can be provided that the client is (dissociated) present in the secure here-and-now, and it can be "as if you are watching a movie of an experience ... and as you watch comfortably ... you can learn something important from yourself over there ... "

More naturalistic approaches to age regression involve offering indirect suggestions to become engaged in memory without the formality of saying, "Now you can go back in the past." Patterns include asking experiential questions to orient the person to her own past personal history, and sharing learnings from personal or professional experiences. Asking questions to orient the person to her own past experiences as an approach involves the client in a search through her past in order to recall the appropriate events necessary to respond meaningfully. Such a search can start out as a more distant memory simply being cognitively remembered, but then skillful further questioning can begin to immerse the client in the memory in order to actually re-experience it. The following is an example of such a pattern:

Clinician: Can you remember your fourth-grade teacher? (Orienting the client to age nine or ten)

   Client: Sure, it was Miss Smith. As I recall, she was a really nice teacher. (Starting to remember that teacher and some associated childhood experiences)

Clinician: Fourth grade can certainly be an interesting time in one's life . . . many changes can take place in a person's thinking . . . I wonder if you can remember which event of that time in your life was especially important to you? . . .

   Client: Well . . . there was a time once when I got into trouble at school and my mother . . . (Relates the story's details)

Clinician: Can you . . . *see yourself clearly in that experience?* . . . as you see yourself in that experience, you can remember how you felt, can't you . . . and those feelings are feelings that are still a part of you . . . even though you haven't thought about them in a long while . . . and you can see the other people and how they look . . . how they are dressed . . . and you can hear what they say that is so important to you . . . and what do they say? . . .

As the clinician asks the client to fill in the details of the memory, the client naturally becomes more and more immersed in it to the point of re-experiencing it (notice the changing of tenses from past to present experience). This type of regression is a routine part of many psychotherapies, particularly those that focus on the past as a way of understanding and altering the present. Such gradual immersion in the memory is a smooth and natural approach for focusing on the past. The involvement becomes greater and greater as the clinician involves more and more of the person in all the sensory components of the memory to as great a degree as possible.

In order to make the experience of going back into the past less personally threatening, the clinician can indirectly facilitate regression by describing her own relevant past learnings, or the relevant past learnings of others. When the experience of others is described, the client naturally tends to project herself into the presented situation, imagining how she would feel or act in that situation. Talking about the experiences of others as children, for example, can build an identification for the client on the basis of her own experiences as a child. Thus, the regression occurs indirectly through identification and projection, and the client can go back in time to recall or re-experience the relevant memories. The following is an example of such an approach, offered to a client who felt guilty unnecessarily and unjustly about her parents having divorced when she was six years old. The regression involves taking the client back to that time in order to re-experience the feeling she had at some level that she was responsible for her parents' divorce. This metaphorical example stops before the point of making the hurtful decision, and does not go into the actual redecision therapy for such a problem.

Clinician: Children are quite remarkable, don't you think?

Client: Yes, I do.

Clinician: Sometimes kids think the whole world revolves around them ... like life is a universal game of "peek-a-boo" ... that the whole world stops for a while ... and goes away to someplace else ... who knows where ... maybe someplace really calming and beautiful ... when the child closes her eyes and the world disappears ... how well can you remember being a child ... and closing your eyes ... and wondering where everyone went? ...

Client: I used to play hide-and-seek a lot as a child, and I can remember worrying sometimes I'd be all alone, that when I closed my eyes everyone would be gone and I'd never find them again ... but, of course, that's just a child's silly fears.

Clinician: That's interesting, because a child I'm working with described that same feeling ... she's almost seven years old now, and she's feeling very proud of being in the first grade ... excited and thrilled ... the way all kids once were ... you can remember that, can't you? ... about being in school and learning to learn about how much there is to learn ... and that there is a huge and complex world out there ... a world much bigger than the world of a six-year-old ... but the six-year-old doesn't know that yet ... she still has to learn to read and write ... about science and math ... about adults and other kids ... about falling in and out of love ... and the six-year-old's world is always changing and growing ... but not so fast as she thinks ... because part of her still thinks the world revolves around her ... and that she can cause big things to happen ... and she won't learn until she's older ... that the world doesn't revolve around her at all ... that she's just six ... and afraid of being alone ...

In the above example, the clinician is matching the part of the client that is feeling overly responsible at age six with the thoughts and feelings of a six-year-old. When these are described in a way that can allow the client to recapture her similar thoughts and feelings, the client can age regress in a more spontaneous and naturalistic way. Furthermore, the seeds for the subsequent therapy are being planted simultaneously when the therapist points out in a non-threatening way the distorted perceptions of a six-year-old. This can pave the way for the client to accept that her thoughts at that time must have been distorted also, and they may therefore be more easily abandoned.

Other techniques for age regression include: 1) Affect or somatic bridging, where the client's current feeling or awareness is linked ("bridged") to the first time, or one of the first, she had that same feeling or awareness (" . . . and as you continue to be aware of that 'abandoned feeling' you've described, you can drift back in time and recall the first time you ever had that same feeling"); 2) Temporal disorientation, in which confusional suggestions are employed to disorient the client from "now" and reorient the person to "then" ("What happens now and then is that *remembering then* now reminds you now of then when then is so important and when *then becomes now* because yesterday led to today and you can *remember yesterday* as if it were now because now and then *remembering then as if it were now* can be so important . . . "); and 3) Age progression and regression, in which the client is first guided into the future at which time she can remember the things that have happened in her past ("Look forward to the times that you can look back . . . "). By orienting to the future first, even greater emotional distance is created from past experiences, making them easier to recapture and use therapeutically.

Table 10. Age Regression Strategies

Direct regression to a specific time or situation
Affect or somatic bridging
Imagery, special vehicle techniques
Indirect associational suggestions
Metaphorical approaches
Gradual regression
Temporal disorientation
Age progression and regression

Age regression is one of the most widely used and beneficial applications of clinical hypnosis. The clarity of memories that can be brought out of the unconscious is often fascinating to discover and utilize, and I don't think it is overstating the point to say that the mind's memory capacities are truly remarkable to work with.

AGE PROGRESSION

DESCRIPTION

In contrast to the utilization of the past of the various age regression approaches, age progression involves a utilization of projections of the future. Age progression involves "guiding" the client into the future, where he may have the opportunity to imagine the consequences of current changes or experiences, integrate meanings at deeper levels, and, in general, obtain more of an overview of his life than day-to-day living typically affords. You can think of it as encouraging hindsight while it is still foresight.

Projecting on the basis of current trends what things are likely to arise in the future is not just a pastime for futurists. Rather, all people have a part of them that plans for and allows for the possibilities of future experience. Common remarks like, "See you there next week," "I'll read that tomorrow and just take it easy today," "I'd like to enroll in that new program next year," and "When I retire I'd like to spend my time traveling," are all statements of intent relative to future experience. In order to make such statements, the person must project some portion of himself into that experience and imagine what it would or will be like. Any communication strategy that orients the client to future events is an age progression pattern.

Age progression patterns involve suggestions for the client to experience herself in some way at some future time. There are differing theoretical views on the dynamics of future orientation. Some hold the view that a client's future projections are purely fantasy material that have little or no relationship to the life experiences that will actually unfold over time. Such projections are considered useful in the same way as Rorschach inkblots—as interesting reflectors of unconscious dynamics only, with little bearing on the future. Others hold the view that the unconscious mind has within it a "pre-programmed destiny" (acquired early in life according to believers with a social-learning orientation, acquired genetically according to believers with a biological orientation, or acquired through the evolving soul for those with a spiritual or philosophical orientation). The destiny of the person is thought to become available to the person through hypnotic patterns of age progression, when the "all-knowing" unconscious is tapped by the clinician. My personal perspective is that age progression is an extrapolation of personal trends; motivations, feelings, behaviors, etc., of the client in trance are amplified, and the age-progressed client can become very sensitive to the implications of such personal trends. Many personal patterns, conscious or otherwise, are quite predictable. A person's unconscious can predict the future to some degree on the basis of what kind of experiences it will (and won't) allow or seek.

Age progression can be used in at least two general, complementary ways. One is as a check on one's work, and the other is as a therapeutic intervention. Both applications involve guiding the client into a future orientation, but for different purposes.

Utilizing an age progression for the purpose of checking on one's work is one way of assessing two very important dimensions of therapeutic intervention. Specifically, one can assess whether the intervention's results will be lasting ones, and what impact on the client's life system the intervention will ultimately have. These issues are discussed in detail in the later chapter "Resisting Resistance." Suffice it to say here that even though the change under consideration may seem an obviously beneficial one, there may be factors (personal, situational, or interpersonal) that can work to keep the client from fully succeeding in her endeavors. Age progression allows the client to project into the future how she looks and feels after the change, how she looks and feels handling old situations in new ways, how others react to her change, what areas continue to be difficult for her, and, in general, which areas of her life have been affected positively, which negatively. Such information can be invaluable to the clinician in formulating the intervention while simultaneously checking on the impact of his work.

If a client experiences age progression and still has the presenting complaint, the therapy isn't over. For example, if after working with a client who wants to stop smoking the clinician senses he has guided his client into accepting that she no longer needs or wants to smoke, and then the clinician does an age progression technique and the client still experiences herself a month (a day, a week, whatever) into the future as a smoker, then the therapy cannot have been successful. Questioning the age-progressed client about various dimensions of her "recent" experience can help the clinician discover what factors might play a role in the client restarting or continuing to smoke that had gone unaddressed in the intervention. If the age-progressed client claims she wasn't smoking after therapy until she got into an argument with her boyfriend, the clinician now knows he must provide some tools for effectively managing such a situation without smoking. Thus, age progression can serve result-checking as well as strategy-planning purposes.

Milton Erickson had a little sneakier, albeit sophisticated, use for age progression which he called a "pseudo-orientation in time" (Erickson, 1954). By having his patient go forward in time and relate to that time as the present, Erickson could ask his patient how she got over her problem—specifically what he said or did, or what she learned or decided that helped her overcome her problem. When the patient gave him the details of the "past" therapy that had helped her, Erickson facilitated amnesia for having done so, and thereby obtained a therapeutic strategy from the patient herself!

Posthypnotic suggestion involves age progression, and usually amnesia as well. A suggestion is given for the client to respond in a particular way in some future context, and in order for the client to accept such a suggestion, the client must experience some future orientation, however briefly. In fact, orienting the client to future possibilities is a necessary part of any psychotherapy. Even therapeutic approaches facilitating insights into the past encourage some future orientation when such insights are expected to generate new possibilities in the client's future.

APPROACHES

Patterns for facilitating age progression are numerous, ranging from structured, direct approaches to less direct communications such as presuppositions.

The direct approaches for facilitating age progression relate closely to the direct approaches described for age regression; a "special vehicle" to go into the future, a movie screen on which to watch a movie of the future, a book in which to read about the future, or a photograph collection of future events are all structured approaches to facilitate a future orientation or projection. A simple, direct approach to age progression is exemplified in the following paragraph:

> ... and now that you've had the opportunity to discover something very important about yourself, I wonder how many ways you'll find to use this new ability of yours creatively in your own behalf ... and it can be as if a long time

has passed since this session . . . a few days . . . and time passes quickly . . . then a few weeks . . . and a few months ago we spent some time together where you learned that you could feel so good . . . and you had a thought at that time that allowed you to look at yourself differently . . . and feel differently . . . and as you look back over all the time that has passed since then, how has that thought affected you? . . . How are you different? . . . What can you do now that you couldn't do back then? . . .

In the above example, the client is to integrate some new thought or learning into her life in a way that will prove beneficial. Suggesting directly to the client that it is "as if a long time has passed" orients her to the future as if it were now, a time to reflect on the recent change and its consequences. Questions such as those in the above example require increasing involvement in the "then is now" experience, and can provide concrete ideas to the clinician about other factors to include in the overall intervention.

Indirect suggestions for future orientation may include: 1) metaphorical approaches (I'd like to tell you about a client I worked with who could clearly imagine herself two months after our session doing exactly what we're talking about now and when she saw herself that way she discovered . . . "); 2) embedded commands ("I sometimes like to *look around* and *wonder* what *will happen in the future* when you can *look back at and feel good about all the changes you have made* . . . "); 3) presuppositions ("I wonder exactly where you will be and what you'll be doing when you happily realize you haven't smoked in days . . . "); and 4) indirect embedded questions ("You can tell me about how you will describe the way you solved this problem to your friends, can't you?"). Each of these approaches and examples demonstrates a capacity for guiding the client into a mental set for developing positive expectations for the future. Positive expectations about improving one's condition are fundamental to success in virtually anything, but are especially important in the healing arts. Age progression patterns are the bridge to get from here to there, from now to later. If the imagination doesn't create new directions, the will doesn't have anyplace to go but around and around.

Table 11 contains a general age progression strategy that may be adapted to individual needs in the context of psychotherapy. This strategy illustrates the idea of sequencing steps in a trance process to facilitate the greatest degree of responsiveness in the client.

The general strategy involves 11 steps, described here as follows: Step 1 involves an induction of any type. Step 2 involves offering a set of verifiable suggestions that establish a momentum for responding positively to the

Table 11. A General Age Progression Strategy

1. Induction
2. Building a response set
3. Metaphors regarding the future
4. Identifying positive resources
5. Identifying specific future contexts
6. Embedding the positive resources identified in #4
7. Rehearsal of behavioral sequence
8. Generalization of positive resources to other selected contexts
9. Post-hypnotic suggestion
10. Disengagement
11. Reorientation to waking state

clinician. Step 3 involves offering at least two metaphors regarding the future (e.g., changes will happen in science, in medicine, in society, and so forth), indirectly orienting the client to future possibilities. Step 4 involves identifying specific resources (e.g., intelligence, sensitivity, perseverance) existing in the client that are valuable. Step 5 involves identifying specific future situations the client will be facing that are a basis for concern. Step 6 involves associating the existing client resources to the likely future contexts where they would be helpful. Step 7 provides an opportunity for a "rehearsal" of the future sequence as if it were happening now. Step 8 provides a chance to identify several other contexts where that same new application of a skill would also be helpful. Step 9 involves specific suggestions to use the skill in contexts wherever it would be helpful. Step 10 brings the future-oriented work to a close and re-establishes the ties to the current context. The final step is guiding the individual out of trance.

AMNESIA

DESCRIPTION

Amnesia is a loss of memory, and can be most simply described as the experience of forgetting something. When you try to remember something, you try to bring a piece of information from your unconscious into conscious awareness. Until you read this sentence, you were very probably not thinking of your old neighborhood where you grew up. That memory, however, is in your unconscious until you gain conscious access to it. Not all memories are available to be brought into conscious awareness, though. Some experiences were too superficially attended to and were not incorporated into long-term memory, while others had no personal meaning and thus were not integrated into memory in any recoverable way. Still others were so personally threatening that they had to be defended against. The classic defense mechanism called "repression" is the primary mechanism of hypnotic or structured amnesia. Repression refers to the mind's ability to keep threatening thoughts, experiences, feelings, and impulses in the unconscious, allowing the person the opportunity to avoid having to acknowledge and deal with the threat. Some experiences are so deeply repressed as to make them irretrievable for all practical purposes.

In everyday living, examples of amnesia are abundant. How many things have you forgotten in your lifetime? Lost keys, forgotten phone numbers, missed appointments, forgotten names of people you know you know, missed assignments, showing up on the wrong day for a meeting or date, forgetting details of significant experiences, forgetting where you hid something important . . . There are countless opportunities in daily life to observe people forgetting things that may, on the surface, seem unforgettable. To the person's conscious mind, the experience of forgetting can be frustrating at least and embarrasing or even costly at most.

In the unconscious, there is frequently a detectable motivation for the act of forgetting, a reason why, even though the reason may objectively seem a poor one. Classic psychoanalysis is a long-term process of recovering repressed memories, particularly those of childhood, and bringing them into conscious awareness as "insights."

Having an insight into one's motivations and associated intrapsychic dynamics is thought to be the primary vehicle of change by a number of different schools of psychotherapy, primarily those where the conscious mind's role is considered to be the most significant in the process of change. Herein lies a fundamental difference between the utilization approach to hypnosis and those therapeutic approaches emphasizing greater conscious awareness. The utilization approach emphasizes the greater positive potentials of the unconscious mind, and thus makes considerable use of amnesia whenever possible. The unconscious is considered to be an active and capable part of each person, able to integrate memories and learnings into patterns of living that allow the person to cope. It is important to point out that a coping mechanism may allow a person to manage without it necessarily being adaptive for her (evidenced in the self-destructive coping mechanisms people commonly use such as excessive alcohol intake, overeating, and so forth).

When the unconscious is able to integrate new information that has special significance because of its point of origin and its relevance, synergistically added to the motivation to change, the client can undergo changes generated by the unconscious frequently with little or no awareness for how the change took place. Are you conscious of specific reasons why you no longer like or wear that expensive piece of clothing you bought a few years ago that you thought was so great at the time? Probably not—the change in your attitude "just happened."

Milton Erickson was a firm believer that the unconscious is more powerful in generating changes than is any other part of the person, and that if the appropriate information is provided to the client's unconscious from within her frame of reference, ideally with minimal interference from her conscious mind, the unconscious could effect rapid and lasting change. Consequently, Erickson developed a variety of ways to facilitate amnesia in order to promote change at an unconscious level. By inducing the client to consciously forget the various suggestions and experiences provided, one can enable the client's unconscious to form its own unique response, free to use the hypnotic experience as creatively and idiosyncratically as it desires. Typically, the client's solution is more creative than the clinician's.

Beyond offering therapeutic suggestions to the unconscious mind for it to do with as it sees fit, amnesia can be used more directly to repress hurtful memories. For example, if someone was the victim of a trauma, the clinician might assist the person in developing repression hypnotically if deemed appropriate to do so. Caution must be exercised in facilitating repression to assure the client that the memory is not gone forever, that it is only going to be "stored in a safe place . . . where it need not interfere with your daily living . . . " In the event that, for whatever reason, the client needs to have access to that memory, it can be available since it has only been stored, not eliminated (the mind is *not* a computer whose "tapes" can be erased). Suggestions for amnesia in such cases are likely to be accepted only when some healing (i.e., resolution, catharsis) has occurred first. Additional suggestions that dissociate the intense feelings from the memory can also be offered. (See the section on "Dissociation" later in this chapter.) Then, in the event the client does re-experience the memory, it can be without all the intense emotions previously associated with it.

Amnesia is a typical characteristic of deeper trance states. When the client emerges from deeper trance states, she may have little or no recollection for what the trance experience involved, even if no suggestion for amnesia was offered. Such amnesia is referred to as "spontaneous amnesia" for obvious reasons. If amnesia is a specific response the clinician wants, gambling on spontaneous amnesia is *not* a certain bet; rather, playing a more active role in facilitating amnesia increases the likelihood of obtaining the amnesia response in the client. Amnesia is *not* automatic with trance, as many erroneously believe. In fact, for those who rely greatly on intellectual means of self-control, paying careful attention and remembering everything that happens reduces personal insecurities. Inducing amnesia in such persons, as might be expected, is a bit more difficult. If a client is motivated to remember suggestions and experiences, she will. When spontaneous amnesia occurs, it is, in part, a reflection of the client's trust in the clinician's skills. It indicates the client didn't feel the need to scrutinize everything the clinician did.

Deciding what things a client should and shouldn't be aware of is one more area of responsibility on the part of the clinician. Ultimately, of course, the client is free to accept or reject whatever suggestions she chooses, but the clinician can influence the client in undesirable ways, as you may recall from the earlier discussion of human suggestibility. Amnesia can be a very tricky process, and its power, like that of the unconscious, is easy to underestimate.

APPROACHES

Amnesia, more so than any of the other various trance phenomena, is less likely to be obtained the more directly the clinician suggests it. Suggesting to someone that she "forget everything that took place during this time" can be very threatening on some levels, even to a responsive and obedient client. In facilitating amnesia in clients, the indirect approaches are much more palatable to people, in my experience.

If a direct approach to amnesia is employed, it is probably more likely to be accepted if offered in a more permissive manner, of which the following is an example: "You can choose to forget about that experience now, because it no longer has a place in your life . . . "

Indirect approaches may take a variety of forms, including indirect suggestions, attentional shifts, and confusion. Indirect suggestions for amnesia create the possibility of amnesia occurring without your overtly asking for it as a specific response. The following is an example of an indirect and distracting approach to amnesia:

... and as you continue to relax, each breath soothing you ... I wonder how much attention you have paid to the different thoughts floating through your mind ... your mind can be so active while it relaxes ... and then you can realize how *difficult* it is *to remember* what I was talking about exactly seven minutes ago ... and you could try to remember what I was saying nine minutes ago, or what you were thinking four minutes ago, but doesn't it seem like much too much work to try and remember ... it takes more effort than it's worth ... and so why not let yourself relax comfortably ... knowing *you don't* have to *remember* when it's too much work to. ...

The above example is indirect because it doesn't specifically suggest to the client she forget, it only describes the difficulties of remembering. Another indirect suggestion for amnesia is: "You can remember from this experience what you choose to remember ... " This suggestion carries the unspoken implication that, "You can forget what you choose to forget." I view this suggestion as a respectful way of leaving amnesia as a choice for the client to make.

Another approach to facilitating amnesia is the "attentional shift." The mechanism for this approach is easy to understand when you consider a routine interaction: You say to your friend, "I have something I have to tell you." Your friend says, "Well, I have something to tell you, too, and it's really important so let me tell you first." You agree, and so you listen and then respond to your friend's concern. Finally, when she is through, she says, "OK, now what were you going to tell me?" and you say, "Uh, well, gee, I uh ... forgot." The irritating but predictable response from the other person then is "Well, it must not have been very important!" What actually took place? Your attention was on a particular "track," a particular line of thought. But when you leave that track in order to attend to your friend's input, the flow of thought was interrupted and was difficult to retrieve, thus creating a temporary amnesia. The "tip-of-the-tongue" phenomenon is somewhat similar but reversed; a piece of information you know you have is frustratingly close to consciousness, but isn't quite there. Only when you switch tracks and think about something else does the unconscious allow the information to eventually pass into awareness.

Shifts in attention obviously have an impact on how information goes back and forth between the conscious and unconscious minds. Deliberately shifting the client's attention away from her trance experience is one way to get her to "jump tracks" and thus experience amnesia for the trance. When the client is disengaging from the trance state, the clinician can gracefully and congruently distract her by having her respond to something totally irrelevant to the trance experience. For example, the clinician can look bothered and say something like, "Oh, I just remembered I needed to ask you which tests you had done at your last physical examination. Do you recall?" By encouraging the client to shift into thinking about her last physical examination (or whatever), you give her no opportunity to consciously analyze the trance experience she just had, and it can therefore integrate at the unconscious level. Discouraging conscious analysis inhibits opportunities for the client to defend against or reject dimensions of the trance experience that such conscious analysis might deem irrational. The unconscious considers rationality less important and can respond meaningfully to things that make very little sense to the conscious mind, a point which leads me to the next approach for facilitating amnesia.

Confusion as an induction technique was discussed earlier, and so it is assumed the reader has a basic understanding of the dynamics operating in this approach. Confusion may also be used to facilitate the various trance phenomena, and can be especially useful in obtaining amnesia. In responding to confusion, the client becomes increasingly focused on trying to make sense of what's being done. As in the previous approach, the client's attention shifts from where it was to the current conflicting inputs, but the added element of the motivation to form a meaningful response makes for an even more powerful approach to attaining amnesia. The following is an example of a confusion technique for the purpose of facilitating amnesia:

> ... and now that you've had the opportunity to *discover new possibilities* ... while you can *learn from past experiences* ... your conscious mind can begin to wonder ... how it will know which things to remember ... and which things *only your unconscious need know* ... and then you can remember ... to forget ... or *you may choose to forget* to remember ... but when you *remember to forget* what you've forgotten to remember ... your memory of forgetting forgets what it has forgotten ... but *you can only forget what you've forgotten* when you realize *it's too difficult to remember* anyway ... and then *you can forget* all the confusion and relax even more deeply. ...

As more of the client's attention attempts to sort out the confusion, the unconscious can respond to all, or most, of the suggestions for forgetting. Whereas the attentional shift is typically used at the close of the trance experience (although not necessarily so), the confusion approach is one more easily integrated at any point in the trance process.

Other approaches to facilitating amnesia include: 1) Metaphors, in which stories are told with embedded suggestions for forgetting (" ... and

Table 12. Techniques of Hypnotic Amnesia

Indirect Suggestion
Distraction
Structured/Direct
Confusion
Metaphor
Seeding
Dissociation

when she opened her eyes it was as if from a deep sleep, barely able to remember anything but the good feelings of a restful night. ... "); 2) Seeding, in which advance hints are provided of the amnesia suggestions to come later ("Some people experience such deep or meaningful trance states that when they reorient later it's surprising how little there is to remember ... and then they change for the better anyway ... "); and 3) Dissociation, in which suggestions can be offered about remembering and forgetting as separate mechanisms that can function independently ("Your ability to remember is complemented by your ability to forget ... and when your thoughts remember that situation, your feelings can forget to be there because they are remembering someplace else to be of greater importance. ... ")

Observation of one's self and others can teach one a lot about the routine nature of amnesia. Further study of the nature of human memory is also recommended to guide one's developing skills in the use of amnesia.

ANALGESIA AND ANESTHESIA

DESCRIPTION

Hypnotically induced analgesia and anesthesia are on a continuum of diminishing bodily sensation. Analgesia refers to a reduction in the sensation of pain, allowing associated sensations (e.g., pressure, temperature, position) that orient the client to her body to remain. Anesthesia refers to a complete or near complete elimination of sensation in all or part of the body. Applications and approaches for analgesia and anesthesia overlap to a great extent, and so for the sake of simplicity only the term "analgesia" will be used in this discussion of these trance phenomena.

Hypnotically induced analgesia is truly one of the most remarkable capacities human beings have. The potential to reduce pain to a manageable level is a genuine tribute to the capabilities of the human mind, and constitutes one of the most meaningful applications of therapeutic hypnosis.

Working with clients in pain requires a very broad base of understanding of hypnotic principles, human physiology, psychological motivations, human information processing, and interpersonal dynamics. Clients in pain are in some ways easy to work with because of their (usually) high level of motivation, and yet in other ways such clients are exceptionally difficult to work with because of the impact of the pain on all levels of their lives. Therefore, approaching the person in pain must be done sensitively, with an appreciation that the pain is more than pain: It is a source of anxiety, feelings of helplessness and depression, increased dependency, and restricted social contact. Even pain emanating from clearly organic causes has psychological components to it, particularly how the suffering person experiences the pain and its consequences. It is the psychological dimension of the pain that is most overtly affected by hypnosis for a variety of reasons that all seem to stem from the greater self-mastery hypnosis affords. Fear and anxiety, feelings of helplessness, and negative expectations can all be reduced with the use of hypnosis. The physical components of the pain are also addressed by the use of hypnosis, evidenced in the various healing strategies employing hypnotic patterns.

To date, no specific mechanism has been identified that can adequately account for the physical effect of hypnosis on the person in pain. Theories about increased endorphins and the fortified immunological system have been proposed to explain the pain reduction and accelerated healing hypnosis facilitates, but none clearly explains the nuts-and-bolts of how it works. Understanding and explaining how hypnosis physiologically reduces pain is beyond the scope of this text; the reader can simply be aware that this area is one of the most fascinating and highly researched in the field of psychophysiology. Fortunately, effective use of hypnotic analgesia is not contingent on having its physiological mechanism(s) defined. The person in pain is capable of using her mind to change her perception of the pain in ways that will be described shortly, and this ability is amplified with hypnosis.

Hypnotic analgesia is typically one of the trance phenomena that people react to with the most skepticism, asking, "If a person is in pain from cancer or some other physical cause, how can something psychological make a difference?" Most people even go a step further and hold the misconception that if the person's pain *is* reduced through hypnosis "then it must have been all in her head in the first place." Nothing is farther from the truth. First, trance and the various trance phenomena (including analgesia and anesthesia) are everyday experiences. Second, as was pointed out earlier, physical pain has very real psychological components. The relationship between pain and anxiety is an intense, circular one. Pain causes anxiety, which intensifies the pain, which intensifies the anxiety, and on and on . . . By merely facilitating the relaxation hypnosis affords, one can interrupt the cycle.

Consider routine experiences that closely approximate the experience of hypnotic analgesia. You can probably recall a time when you were very involved in an activity (perhaps while playing a sport, fixing a car, moving furniture, or the like), and only after the activity's completion did you notice you had cut or bruised yourself—and only then did it begin to hurt! Your awareness was distracted from genuine physical damage—the essence of hypnotic analgesia. Employing hypnosis to facilitate analgesia can give one control over the experience of pain, rather than such useful distraction being only a random event. The fact that pain is modifiable through hypnosis is *not* indicative that the person's pain is psychogenic.

Using hypnosis in the management of pain is advantageous for some very important reasons. First, and foremost in my opinion, is the opportunity for greater self control and, therefore, greater personal responsibility for one's level of well being. Feeling victimized, whether by pain or by other people, puts one in a helpless position from which it is difficult to do any real healing. Having self control is extremely important to the person in pain, and hypnosis facilitates its acquisition. Second, because the ability to experience trance is a natural one existing within the person, pain medications may be reduced or even eliminated. Hypnosis has no side effects, nor is it addictive. The pain is reduced in differing degrees in different people, but whatever the result, it is obtained safely and naturally. Third, hypnosis permits a higher level of functioning and enhances the healing process in persons who utilize hypnotic patterns. Remaining as active as one's condition allows is important at all levels, and can make a significant difference in the problem's progression. The expectation of wellness, the experience of comfort, and the diminished anxiety and fear can all be important factors in facilitating recovery, at most, or retarding decline, at least.

Developing the ability to assist those you work with by offering approaches to pain management can be invaluable, but a few words of caution are in order. First, pain is a warning sign that something is wrong. The various hypnotic approaches are essentially "band-aids," for while they may assist the client in being more comfortable, their healing abilities remain uncertain. A person's pain must be viewed as a danger sign, and appropriate medical evaluation and treatment are not only encouraged, they are *demanded*. Harm can easily be done if the pain is inhibited with little or no knowledge of its cause. Delaying or discouraging appropriate medical care is tantamount to malpractice. Second, if one is not medically licensed or medically supervised, one should not be working with pain at all. Period. Practicing outside the realm of one's qualifications is also tantamount to malpractice. Third, simply working with a person in pain without a recognition for the meaning of the pain in the person's life is a potentially dangerous oversimplification of the problem. Each person's life can be thought of in terms of its many components. The underlying needs (i.e., motivations, dynamics) as well as the pain's impact on a variety of levels (personal, familial, professional, etc.) must be acknowledged and considered in the formulation of each person's treatment plan.

In sum, hypnosis can offer physical relief and an emotional wellspring of positive possibilities to the person in pain. Over time and with practice, such persons can benefit from the increased self control and self-reliance hypnosis may afford.

APPROACHES

Analgesia often arises spontaneously during trance for the client who is sufficiently absorbed in the experience. Associated with the inhibition of voluntary movement (catalepsy) evident in the hypnotized person is a diminished awareness for one's body, hence the analgesia. Therefore, any approach that successfully shifts the person's awareness away from the bodily sensation(s) under consideration can have an indirect analgesic effect. With training and reinforcing practice sessions, the client in pain can learn to distract herself, and then refocus on positive ideas, feelings, memories, or whatever she chooses as a focal point. The teaching of self-hypnosis is essential in order for this approach to the management of pain to work.

A considerable number of direct and indirect strategies can be employed to facilitate analgesia (see Table 13). The few presented here in detail include direct suggestion of analgesia, glove anesthesia, pain displacement, and physical dissociation. The rest are mentioned at the end of this section.

Table 13. Approaches to Pain Management
With Hypnosis

1. Direct suggestion
2. Indirect suggestion
   interspersal
   metaphor
3. Amnesia
4. Sensory alteration
   analgesia
   anesthesia
   shifting PRS
5. Symptom substitution
6. Symptom displacement
7. Dissociation
   generalized
   localized
8. Reinterpretation/reframing
9. Confusion
   overload
   interruption
10. Gradual diminution
11. Regression to pre-pain period
12. Pseudo-orientation in time
13. Time distortion

Direct suggestion of analgesia as an approach involves offering suggestions for the lack of sensation in the specific part of the client that is painful to her. If, for example, a client is experiencing pain in her abdomen arising from an organic source, a direct analgesia approach might be structured as follows:

> ... and as you feel your arms and legs getting heavier ... you can see the muscles in your abdomen loosening ... relaxing ... as if they were guitar strings you were unwinding ... and as you see those muscles in your abdomen relax, you can feel a pleasant tingle ... the tingle of comfort ... and whenever you have had a part of you become numb, like an arm or leg that fell asleep ... you could feel that same tingle ... like the pleasing tingle in your abdomen now ... tingling more ... and isn't it both interesting and soothing to discover the sensation of no sensation there? That's right ... the sensation of no sensation ... a tingling, pleasing comfortable feeling of numbness there. ...

When you build the "sensation of no sensation" directly in the client's abdomen, she can experience direct relief in the troublesome area. As discussed in greater detail in the later chapter "Resisting Resistance," however, there is also likely to be greater resistance attached to the troubled area. Therefore, going after the analgesia response directly in the afflicted area is less likely to be effective. Directly suggesting numbness or the feeling of just having received an injection of Novocaine will likely be effective only with the most responsive of clients.

Another direct approach, though slightly less so, is the "glove anesthesia." In this sensory alteration process, the client is given suggestions to experience anesthesia in either or both of her hands. When the anesthesia has been accomplished, further suggestions may be given that the anesthesia can be effectively transferred to whatever part of her body she chooses. Glove anesthesia permits a mobility for the anesthesia when the clinician suggests that a touch of the anesthetized hand to any part of the body will transfer the numbness to that spot. Direct suggestion for analgesia does not have such mobility, since it is localized to a specific, fixed spot. Suggestions for glove anesthesia might take the following form:

> . . . and in a moment when I take your hand, I'm going to place it in a position it can stay in easily and comfortably (clinician takes the client's hand and props it up on her elbow) . . . and you can easily hold your hand in this position . . . and as you do so you can notice how . . . this hand begins to feel different from your other one . . . more removed from you . . . more distant . . . and while the rest of you remains very warm and comfortable . . . this hand can begin to experience coolness . . . as if a cold wind were floating over your hand . . . cooling it, chilling it . . . and as it gets colder . . . and colder . . . while the rest of you remains comfortably warm . . . the pleasantly cool feelings in your hand get stronger . . . cooler . . . colder . . . and as your hand gets comfortably colder . . . it can tingle with a cool numbness . . . and when I touch your hand . . . you can realize that the only sensation you feel is a cool numbness and you can place your hand anywhere you'd like to feel that cool numbness. . . .

In the above example of glove anesthesia, the sensation of numbness is built around a change in perception of temperature, i.e., the coolness of the hand. Suggesting descriptively the experience of making snowballs bare-handed or the experience of reaching into the freezer for a tray of ice cubes can facilitate the experience of coolness and numbness.

Another approach to facilitate analgesia involves the displacement of the pain. This might mean "moving the pain" (shifting the perception of pain from one area to another), or it might mean restricting the perception of the pain to a smaller and less inconvenient area. For example, a client experiencing pain in her arm might be given the following suggestions for displacement:

> . . . as you continue to recall how you learned long ago about your body . . . as all people must . . . you might begin to remember learning how delicately balanced the body is . . . a muscle that allows you to bend your leg has a counterpart that allows you to straighten your leg again . . . and while there are muscles that let your head lift . . . there are also muscles that . . . *let your head drop down . . . deeply relaxed . . .* and there is a part of *you* that *can feel comfort* where there was once discomfort . . . and as the comfort flows into the area where you'd most like it . . . and dislodges the discomfort, letting it flow down . . . and as you feel it flowing down your arm you can feel it collecting in your baby finger . . . so small and so easy to forget about. . . .

Transferring the pain of an arm to a finger can allow for a higher level of functioning and less preoccupation with discomfort since it can be confined to such a small part of the body. Essentially, this is a strategy of "symptom substitution," the deliberate creation of a new "outlet," one that is now within the control of the clinician and client.

The next approach to analgesia involves a variable that is operating in each of the other analgesia approaches as well as in hypnotic patterns in general. That variable is "dissociation," and it involves the capacity to divide one's attentional and behavioral abilities. Physical dissociation causes the subjective experience of feeling separated from all or part of one's body, and thus the pain. Have you ever felt, however briefly, as if your body was going through something you really weren't a part of? Even though intellectually you knew you were "all together" at the time, you may have felt distant and removed from the experience. That kind of experience is representative of dissociation. After receiving chemical anesthesia, for example, one can watch one's self get stitches; one knows the doctor is sewing one's own skin together, but since there is no feeling present, the experience can be just a curious procedure one feels removed from.

Physical dissociation as an approach to facilitating analgesia can involve guiding the client into the subjective experience that her mind and body are existing on two different levels of experience. There can be sufficient distance between them for the client not to notice what her body is experiencing. The following sample may illustrate the point:

> . . . and when your thoughts begin to travel faster than your body can keep up with . . . you can rediscover how the mind can travel so far and so fast . . . and

you can wonder about things that exist in the universe . . . the size of the mighty ocean . . . the age of huge trees that fill the sky . . . and the number of stars in the sky . . . things you have wondered about from time to time . . . and you can let your mind float freely to the place you find yourself drawn to . . . while your body stays here . . . comfortably here . . . no need to move it . . . no need to let it hold you back . . . you can just enjoy the freedom of letting your mind float freely . . . to the places you most enjoy . . . and while your mind is there . . . and your body is here . . . and it can be so comforting to know that your body is here . . . waiting . . . comfortably . . . patiently for as long as you'd like to float freely . . . without having to notice it . . . because your mind can go anywhere it wants to go. . . .

Suggesting that the mind "go somewhere" creates a dissociation when the body isn't invited to go along. Such separation can be maintained beyond the formal trance state when posthypnotic suggestions are offered that tie the capacity for dissociation to events in everyday living.

As a final approach to the hypnotic management of pain, one can refer back to the transcript of the confusion technique by Milton Erickson in the earlier chapter on hypnotic inductions. In that transcript, Erickson used a verbal confusion between "know pain" and "no pain" in order to facilitate the experience of comfort in his patient. Confusion captures the client's attention, leaving little awareness for discomfort.

Other approaches to analgesia include: 1) *Amnesia,* in which the client is offered suggestions to forget having had pain. This interrupts the experience of the pain being continuous, and thus paves the way for intermittent and increasing periods of comfort as far as the client can remember; 2) *Gradual diminution,* in which suggestions are offered that the discomfort decreases slowly over some specific span of time; 3) *Pseudo-orientation in time,* in which the client is age progressed to a period post-recovery; 4) *Time distortion,* in which moments of comfort can be expanded in subjective perception (see the later section in this chapter on time distortion); and 5) *Regression,* in which the person is age regressed back to a period that is prior to the pain's onset.

As a final note on the hypnotic management of pain, one's wording is very important. The word "pain" has a strong emotional attachment to it, for it represents an emotionally charged experience that is most unpleasant. Use of the word "pain," therefore, should be avoided whenever possible. One can substitute reframing or reinterpreting words like "pressure," "discomfort," or "uncomfortable sensation" in the place of the word "pain."

Integrating hypnosis with other therapeutic modalities can make for a well balanced intervention for the client in pain. I have been encouraged in recent years by the number of medical practitioners discovering the viability of hypnosis as a tool in the overall treatment of the pain patient. Working hypnotically with patients in pain can be a specialty in itself, and is a most humane means for helping such patients cope with one of the most distressing and devastating human conditions. Chapter 20 contains a session transcript that reflects the value of trancework for pain patients.

CATALEPSY

DESCRIPTION

The degree of catalepsy evident in a trance subject has historically been considered to be directly related to the degree of trance depth or experiential involvement. Catalepsy is defined as the inhibition of voluntary movement associated with the intense focusing on a specific stimulus. The degree to which the client is focused on the associations triggered by the clinician is the degree to which the client can demonstrate cataleptic responses. Such responses may include a fixed gaze, general immobility, the "waxy flexibility" usually associated with the catatonic patient who maintains her limbs in whatever position the clinician places them, muscular rigidity, unconscious movements, and the slowing of basic physical processes such as breathing, blinking, and swallowing. Signs of catalepsy can be relied on to a large extent as indicators of trance (both formally induced and spontaneous trances) or they may be suggested for specific therapeutic reasons to be described shortly. Catalepsy must be considered one of the most basic features of trance, for it is associated directly or indirectly with virtually every other trance phenomenon. Catalepsy is the result of focusing on a new and different reality, whatever it may be, and thus paves the way to let go of the "old" reality long enough to create a therapeutic experience of age regression, analgesia, sensory distortions, or whatever.

As Ernest Rossi pointed out in his discussion of catalepsy (Erickson & Rossi, 1981), the "everyday trance" is truly a period of catalepsy where the person is daydreaming, self-absorbed, enthralled, captivated, but always preoccupied to the point of temporary immobilization by the intensity of the focus. Routinely over dinner, for example, people stop mid-reach for the pepper (or whatever) when the conversation turns intense for the moment. People stand rigidly fixed in one spot, one position when more and more of the mind is called on to make sense out of a situation that seems to require a meaningful response.

Stage hypnotists typically demonstrate catalepsy by suggesting extreme stiffness of the subject's entire body and then suspending the subject's body between two chairs. Some add a little more dramatic flair to the demonstration by standing on the subject while she is suspended in that way. Suggesting and obtaining rigidity of the body in this way is called a "full-body catalepsy." Suggestions to the client that her arm is so stiff and rigid that she will find herself unable to bend it is a demonstration of "arm catalepsy" if these suggestions are accepted. Suggestions to the client that the eyelids or eye muscles of her closed eyes are so rigid or relaxed as to prevent the eyes from opening may be accepted by the client, resulting in "eye catalepsy." Such suggestions of catalepsy are frequently used to assess a client's responsiveness to suggestion, as you may recall from the discussion of suggestibility tests. Responses to arm levitation procedures and the special "Handshake Technique" that Milton Erickson developed (Gilligan, 1987), as well as to the various pattern-interruption approaches are overt demonstrations of catalepsy. Arm levitation as a response shows a catalepsy of the arm suspended in mid-air. The "Handshake Technique" involves initiating a routine handshake, and interrupting the usual sequence by doing something else at the moment just before hands would have touched. The other person's hand is left suspended in air, and the individual is now highly responsive as she tries to make sense out of an unusual situation.

For a long, long time catalepsy was considered to be a very passive response on the part of the client, but then again so was trance in general. In order for someone to focus so intently on the suggestions of the clinician, the demonstration of catalepsy must be viewed in the same way as the trance response in general—as an active and dynamic process requiring the active formulation of meaningful responses. Catalepsy implies an intense engagement on one or more levels that indicates a high degree of activity and receptiveness to the guidance of the clinician on other levels. This is why a client focused on one level may have her arm placed in a position and leave it there, literally too preoccupied with other things to think to move it.

Therapeutic purposes for obtaining catalepsy as a response are numerous, but can be described in two general ways. Catalepsy can either serve to facilitate further trance involvement through the client's recognition of her own unconscious mind's ability to respond in automatic ways, or as a target response in itself. Catalepsy as a target response may be used, for example, to assist any patient whose movements must be minimal in order to recover more quickly and comfortably. As a facilitator of further trance experience, catalepsy can be a basis for securing and maintaining attention (thus an inducer), facilitating greater independent activity of the unconscious mind and increasing the degree of involvement or focus of the client (thus a deepener).

APPROACHES

Anything that captures the intense interest of the client can facilitate cataleptic responses, including interesting stories, surprises or shocks, and confusion. Obtaining catalepsy as a response from the client can be accomplished directly or indirectly, verbally and nonverbally, as desired. Direct suggestions for arm catalepsy are evident in the following suggestions for arm levitation:

> . . . as you continue to breathe in . . . and out . . . at a rate that's comfortable for you . . . you can notice which of your arms is beginning to feel lighter than the other . . . light, almost weightless . . . and your hand can begin to float easily and effortlessly . . . rising . . . that's right . . . as it floats in the air as if attached to a large balloon, you can be surprised to discover how pleasurable it is to experience your arm floating straight out before you . . . as if it were completely weightless . . . and it can stay there while you begin to notice another sensation that can be of interest to you. . . .

An indirect way to encourage catalepsy is to offer general suggestions for relaxation and immobility, such as in the following:

> . . . it can feel so good to know your body knows how to take care of itself . . . it knows how to breathe comfortably . . . in, and slowly out . . . effortlessly . . . and it will keep on breathing effortlessly as your mind drifts off to some special memory you haven't thought about in a long, long time . . . and it also knows how to *sit quietly still* while you enjoy that memory . . . and isn't it comforting . . . and soothing . . . to know *your arms can rest* heavily on the chair with *no need to move* them? . . . and *it takes more effort than it's worth to move* when you are so comfortable. . . .

Both of the above examples are obviously examples of the use of verbal approaches for attaining catalepsy. The use of gestures and touch can facilitate catalepsy on a nonverbal level. Many of the beginning students of hypnosis feel anxious and pressured to "make something happen." This may show up in the clinician as trying too hard, showing exaggerated animation, i.e., gestures, fast and expressive verbalizations, and the like.

In facilitating catalepsy, the best thing the clinician has going for her is herself. Probably the best and most practical example of facilitating trance or catalepsy through nonverbal means of suggestion is the indirect technique of modeling. Using your body as a model, you can deliberately shift from the animated patterns of routine conversation to a demonstration to your client of the potential immobility of the trance state. By gradually focusing yourself intently on your client, suspending bodily movement, and verbalizing your suggestions in an increasingly "hypnotic" way (employing the communication patterns described throughout), you are modeling to your client the possibility for catalepsy. If the rapport is adequate, the client can follow the clinician's leads. Often, the only barrier to effective trance induction and utilization is the clinician's distracting demeanor! It is difficult to get into a relaxed, focused state when one's guide is shifting positions continually, flailing her arms, reaching, note-taking, and so forth. Using yourself as a model for catalepsy can be a powerful means for facilitating the trance experience for the client. You can even go a step further in modeling by gesturing slowly and deliberately stopping mid-gesture at well chosen times as if preoccupied, thereby demonstrating the possibility of being so absorbed in thought as to lose track of voluntary motions.

Catalepsy takes a variety of forms, and as a constant feature of the trance experience is a necessary trance phenomenon to understand. Many advanced techniques build on the unconscious responses associated with catalepsy. While general immobility is the typical application or sign of catalepsy, one may be reminded that catalepsy has been defined as the inhibition of voluntary movement, which leaves ample room for unconscious movement. The client in trance may move in unconscious ways that are considered cataleptic, discussed later in the section on ideodynamic responses.

DISSOCIATION

DESCRIPTION

Dissociation has been described earlier as related to the more autonomous functioning of the conscious and unconscious minds in contrast to their normal, more integrated functioning. Dissociation is defined as the ability to break a global experience into its component parts, amplifying awareness for one part while diminishing awareness for the others. Dissociation as a trance phenomenon allows for all the intriguing possibilities hypnosis as a tool affords. Dissociation is a natural experience, for all persons are capable of processing and responding to information in ways they are not even aware of. Each person has had the experience of feeling divided within himself, as if both participant and observer simultaneously in some experience. Even common clichés reflect dissociated states: "*I'm beside myself with joy . . . ,*" "Part of me wants to go, but *another part of me* doesn't . . . ," "*I'm out of my head* to do this . . . "

Through dissociation, people do not have to be attached to their immediate experience, involved and "present." They can "go through the motions," but not really be "there." The conscious mind can drift off somewhere, preoccupied with whatever else has its attention, and therefore the unconscious is free to respond in whatever way it chooses. Thus, the deeper the trance state, the greater the degree of dissociation and the greater the opportunity for unconscious responses.

Dissociation may be used in a wide variety of ways. Splitting an integrated experience into parts can make for some very interesting possibilities. For example, one might split the intellectual component of an experience from the emotional component. This particular dissociative phenomenon is demonstrated routinely in many stage hypnosis shows. The stage hypnotist suggests to his subject that she imagine (positively hallucinate) she is watching the funniest movie she has ever seen. The subject complies and begins to laugh uproariously. Then the stage hypnotist has the subject hallucinate seeing the saddest movie she has ever seen, and the subject begins to cry, often with real tears. Many stage hypnotists then ask the subject, "What is so funny or sad about the movie?" and the average subject responds by saying, "I don't know." The subject isn't merely reluctant to describe what events transpired in the movie to generate such apparently intense emotions. Rather, the subject simply doesn't know, as she truthfully stated. Experiencing the emotion has been suggested by the stage hypnotist, but it is not associated with a particular memory; it is a feeling dissociated from a particular context. How might such dissociated affect be clinically useful?

On a daily basis, people talk to disembodied voices through an instrument called the "telephone." Physical processes go on routinely (e.g., blinking, swallowing, adjusting the body, breathing, etc.) without any conscious involvement whatsoever. Dissociation can be a useful mechanism to enhance or diminish the quality of each life experience, or it can be a maladaptive coping mechanism with destructive consequences, as seen in the various psychiatric disorders directly involving dissociation, such as multiple personalities, fugue states, functional amnesia, and psychosis.

Trancework necessarily involves dissociation, which is the reason dissociation was also discussed earlier as a basic trance characteristic. Dissociation allows for the automatic, or spontaneous, responses of the client to occur; the repressed memory can be remembered, the hand can lift unconsciously, the body can forget to move or notice sensation, and so forth. Facilitating the expression of a specific part of a person can have profound therapeutic impact. Finding and treating the part of the client that has felt weak and powerless, for example, when other parts of the person feel strong and able enough to take meaningful risks can give the clinician an opportunity to help the client resolve a troublesome procrastination problem that has existed "for no apparent reason." As another example, addressing the unconscious part of the man who is feeling weak, powerless, and angry in the context of an intimate relationship can allow him to fortify that part in a way that is adaptive. Giving that part the opportunity to express itself more directly can help rid him of that part's previous symptomatic mode of expression. Another example of the use of dissociation is as a means of pain management. As described in the earlier section on hypnotic analgesia, the area of the body afflicted with pain may be dissociated from the rest of the body as one possible pain management strategy. Another might be to dissociate mind from body. (See the case transcripts in Chapters 19 and 20 which contain numerous dissociative suggestions).

Countless other examples of dissociation can be found in the literature on hypnosis, but the best examples are those of daily living. What situations do you observe people responding to in an automatic way? When are people least integrated in terms of mind and body? Intellect and emotion? Past and present? Optimism and pessimism? Masculine and feminine? The more polarities you generate on a variety of levels (i.e., physical, mental, emotional, and spiritual) to describe the range of experiences people are capable of, the more you can appreciate how many different interrelated parts there are of human beings; each is capable of being dissociated and amplified for clinical use.

Dissociation as a trance phenomenon should be used in as supportive a manner as possible. One of the assumptions Milton Erickson held in his work was the idea that people already had within them the resources they needed to make meaningful changes. The problem is that they don't have access to them because they are dissociated. The clinician's role is to build new associations (i.e., cues, triggers, bridges) that will give the client access to more of her own abilities in the desired context.

APPROACHES

Suggestions that facilitate divisions of experience are suggestions for dissociation. For example, each of the trance inductions described earlier will generate a conscious-unconscious dissociation through their emphasis on the client's ability to experience things and learn things effortlessly and automatically. The conscious mind is given ideas and experiences to focus on while the unconscious is encouraged to respond in other ways and learn at levels beyond awareness. In addition to the hypnotic induction processes, dissociation can be facilitated through a variety of approaches, including direct suggestions of division, Erickson's "middle of nowhere" technique, and indirect suggestion of division.

Direct suggestions for division let the client discover (or rediscover, as the case may be) that it is possible to have experiences on different levels, and that these experiences can occur spontaneously, automatically and with no planning. Suggestions for hand levitation exemplify such a dissociation, as do the other cataleptic movements. Suggesting analgesia by "feeling your body resting comfortably here while you see that small part of your body that *was* uncomfortable over there" is another direct suggestion for division. Suggesting age regression by saying, "Your feelings can go back to age six while the rest of you remains an adult with me in the here-and-now" is yet another example of direct suggestion of dissociation. Anything suggested that fits the pattern of the general formula statement that "part of you is experiencing this while another part of you is experiencing that" is a direct suggestion for dissociation. Further examples are evident in a variety of models of psychotherapy that make abundant use of dissociation without ever really identifying it as such, including Gestalt (which emphasizes the integration of parts) and Transactional Analysis (which dissociates each person into a "Parent-Adult-Child").

A technique of dissociation that Milton Erickson often used is called the "middle of nowhere." Since one is guided to someplace called "nowhere," the paradox has the effect of dividing the person between the experience of being someplace but no place. An example of this approach might sound like this:

> . . . and when you sit that way it can become so easy to recognize that a part of you is here . . . but when the rest of you drifts away . . . and it can drift away . . . and you really don't know where it goes, do you? . . . to the middle of nowhere . . . where there is no time . . . and there is no place . . . in the middle of nowhere . . . there can just be my voice . . . and your thoughts . . . and nowhere is such a fine place to be . . . because nowhere else can one be so free to be nowhere . . . after all, you always have to be somewhere, sometime . . . but not now . . . nowhere is fine . . . and the middle of nowhere is a very pleasant place to be, isn't it? . . .

In this example, the client is encouraged to let herself go to nowhere in particular, with no need to have any ties to anyone, any place, or any thing. As the client experiences herself splitting her awareness between "here" and "there," the dissociation is intensifying.

Dissociation is indirectly suggested whenever suggestions for a particular trance phenomenon are offered. Use of metaphors, confusion, and other forms of indirect suggestion all may facilitate dissociation. Confusion as a facilitator for dissociation is an indirect technique in which the conscious mind attempts to make sense of communication that seems nonsensical. Confusion preoccupies the conscious mind to the point of leaving the unconscious open for suggestion. Overloading and pattern interruption are basic approaches of confusion and were described in detail earlier.

Indirect suggestions for dissociation are contained in the following metaphorical example:

> . . . and I thought it might interest you to learn that I had a similar experience to the one you described . . . an experience that taught me a lot about myself and others . . . and isn't it amazing how one can learn important things from experiences that seem so routine? . . . as if a part of us is experiencing it, and another part is watching us go through the experience . . . wondering what will happen . . . and how we'll feel when it's over . . . and then the things that were so confusing at one level are made clear by the parts of us that understand . . . at a much deeper level . . . how to think creatively . . . and there's a creative part in everyone, I'm sure you'd agree . . . and in the experience I had, I. . . .

In this example, dissociation is suggested on a number of different occasions. A part is created that "experiences," another part that "observes," another that will "wonder," another that can "feel," another that can "clarify," and still another that can be "creative." Each of these parts can now be isolated, addressed, and utilized to accomplish some therapeutic goal. Each of these parts can be identified by the client as present in herself, even though the suggestions are offered indirectly as comments by the clinician about himself or as comments about people in general.

In facilitating dissociation, the final consideration for the clinician is related to the process of reintegration. Should the dissociated part(s) be reintegrated fully? Partially? Or not at all? Certainly an area of pain is best left dissociated, at least in part. Positive parts, such as the creative or adaptive parts, would probably need to be fully reintegrated. The task here for the clinician is to have some insight into the needs and motivations of her client to know what beneficial or harmful consequences are associated with dissociating or reintegrating parts of the person. You may recall that age progression as an approach can be useful to help in this process.

Given the numerous daily experiences each of us has with trance and dissociation, it should be apparent that all trancework involves making use of the processes that people use routinely to create their subjective ideas of reality. Developing insight into the multifaceted nature of dissociation can have an enormous impact on the future of clinical interventions, for in every psychological disorder known to me, an element of dissociation is present.

HALLUCINATIONS AND SENSORY ALTERATIONS

DESCRIPTION

Residents of state psychiatric hospitals will, given the chance, patiently explain to you the cultural biases against hallucinating. Generally, people find it a bit unnerving in daily life to encounter someone who is experiencing things that no one else is. Comedian Lily Tomlin asks the question, "Why is it that when I talk to God I'm praying, but when God talks to me I'm schizophrenic?" Hallucinations that are involuntary or are utilized as a coping mechanism (albeit a highly dysfunctional one) are projections from the psychotic patient's unconscious. Hallucinations created hypnotically are suggested experiences the client can have that are removed from current, more objective realities. For example, one therapeutic application might be to have a client go back in time (age regression) and have a meaningful conversation with a parent now deceased in order to settle some lingering personal issues.

A hallucination is, by definition, a sensory experience that does *not* arise from external stimulation. Simplistically, there are five senses in the normal human being; hallucinations may therefore exist in any or all of the sensory systems. For the sake of simplicity, the kinesthetic sense in this discussion will include separate but related sensory systems capable of detecting pressure, temperature, muscle feedback that orients one to one's body and position in space, and changes in motion. It is possible to hypnotically facilitate visual, auditory, kinesthetic (tactile), gustatory, and olfactory hallucinations. Hallucinations can be further characterized as being either "positive" or "negative." These terms do *not* refer to the emotional impact of the hallucination(s) on the person experiencing it. Rather, these terms refer to the structure of the hallucinations.

A positive hallucination is defined as having the (visual, auditory, kinesthetic, olfactory, gustatory) experience of something that is not objectively present. You can take a slow, pleasing breath and as you inhale you can smell the fragrance of baby powder . . . and as you smell the fragrance of baby powder, you can realize that you have just had a positive olfactory hallucination. That didn't hurt a bit, did it? A negative hallucination is *not* experiencing something sensorily that *is* objectively present (the flip-side of the positive hallucination). As you read this sentence, your awareness can drift to a sound in your environment that you didn't notice until just now . . . and as you become aware of that sound and the feeling of surprise that you didn't notice it earlier, you can realize that you have just had a negative auditory hallucination.

In facilitating hallucinations, the clinician is altering awareness for sensory input. Many hallucinations associated with hypnosis arise spontaneously. For example, hypnotic analgesia can be thought of as a diminished awareness for the kinesthetic level of sensory experience that may arise spontaneously because of the catalepsy associated with trance. Another way to describe the same phenomenon is to say that as one becomes increasingly absorbed on other sensory levels, one negatively hallucinates kinesthetic experience. As a second example, hypnotic amnesia can be described as the conscious forgetting of experience, but another way of describing the same phenomenon is to say the client negatively hallucinates the components of the experience. Specifically, a client might not remember what was said to her during the trance experience because she was so involved on another level that she negatively hallucinated the voice and suggestions of the clinician.

Positive and negative hallucinations occur routinely in the course of everyday living. Everyday examples of positive hallucinations include having a taste for food you crave, feeling itchy all over when you find an insect on your body, thinking you see someone you're trying to avoid wherever you turn, hearing someone call your name when no one is around, and thinking you smell something burning when nothing is. Everyday examples of negative hallucinations include not hearing the doorbell ring because you're engrossed in something, not noticing something on your way to work and then seeing it one day and exclaiming, "Wow! Where did that come from?", and not noticing that the milk you're drinking has gone sour until someone else tastes it and goes, "Yecch!"

Sensory alterations and hallucinations are essentially interchangeable terms. In order to facilitate hallucinations, the clinician must alter the client's sensory awareness. In altering the client's sensory awareness, sensory hallucinations must be created. The client will have one or more of her senses made more or less sensitive, depending on the desired outcome.

Hallucinations may be used therapeutically to immerse the client in a situation that can't be reproduced in the "real" world. Guiding the client into a situation where she can experience herself or the world differently obviously increases the range of her experience and can thus instill a valuable new resource in her. When one hallucinates the details of the experience vividly, the suggested reality can become every bit as real and powerful as "real" life. The client can then have the experience of hearing words she longed to hear, experiencing feelings she missed feeling, seeing places and people she needed to see, etc. Through suggested hallucinations, the client can (or can't) have experiences that will facilitate her personal growth and development.

APPROACHES

Hallucinations can and often do arise spontaneously. Negatively hallucinating one's body or the voice of the clinician are common experiences for the client in trance. Also common are experiences of seeing and hearing faces and voices of the past during the trance state, even smelling the remembered person's cologne.

To deliberately facilitate the experience of hallucinations, both direct and indirect approaches can work well. Stage hypnotists demonstrate a direct approach to positive hallucinations when they suggest to their subjects that they can laugh uproariously when they "see the audience nude." A direct suggestion to experience something is often sufficient; probably by the time the clinician attempts facilitating hallucinations, the rapport and responsiveness are already accomplished. Also, transderivational search and ideosensory responses play a significant role in the experience of hallucinations.

Suggestions for hallucinations, whether positive or negative, should generally be offered in a positive suggestion structure so the client knows what she *should* experience, not what she shouldn't. For example, you can refer back to the early part of this section in which I offered a direct suggestion for the experience of smelling baby powder. I let you know in a very direct and specific way what kind of experience you could have. In working with a client, the more details the clinician provides, the more sensory experiences the client can have. Thus, if one wants the client to see her deceased mother in the chair opposite her in order to have the meaningful conversation that never took place, the positive hallucination will be enhanced by having the client see her mother's clothing, smelling her perfume, touching her shoulder, seeing her position and hearing her voice. All of these suggestions can be directly offered, immersing the client in the experience more and more intensely with each suggestion. In general, positive hallucinations are fairly easily accomplished through direct suggestions, of which the following are some examples:

> . . . You can look over there and see someone you've wanted to see whom you haven't seen in a long, long time . . . and how does she look? . . .

> . . . You can hear a voice telling you something you really shouldn't not know . . . and whose voice is it? . . . and what does it say? . . .

> . . . You can smell the aroma of the coffee perking . . . and that smell brings you back to a situation you haven't remembered in a long, long time . . . and where are you? . . .

In the above examples, while the sensory modality the positive hallucination is to occur in is specified, the content of the hallucination is not. The person, the voice, and the situation to be experienced by the client in the above suggestions are left to the client's projections. If the clinician wanted to, it would be just as easy to specify that the client see a specified person, hear a specified voice, or experience a particular situation, providing all the appropriate sensory details.

Indirect suggestions may also be used to facilitate hallucinations. Suggesting that the client be aware of her arm is an indirect suggestion to not notice her leg. Referring back to the earlier discussion on negative suggestions, it should be apparent why the negative suggestion, "Don't notice the pain in your neck," for a negative kinesthetic hallucination won't work. Thus, indirect suggestions for hallucinations usually take the form of positive suggestions for experiences that would preclude the unwanted experience. For example, rather than directly suggest, "You won't know anyone else is present," in order for the client to negatively hallucinate other people in the vicinity, such a negative hallucination is indirectly accomplished by directly suggesting, "You can be alone" or by the indirect suggestion, "Where did everyone else go?"

The following suggestions exemplify indirect suggestions for hallucinations:

. . . and how does it feel to see yourself standing over there as a child? . . .

. . . and whose voice is that that you're hearing? . . .

. . . and why didn't you notice earlier that your hands were floating effortlessly? . . .

. . . and when I went to the woods to *hear the silence* and *smell the fragrance of pine needles*, and I'm sure you know those sensations, too. . . .

In the above examples, suggestions in the form of presuppositions are used to facilitate seeing one's self, hearing a voice, and feeling floating hands. By asking the client how it feels to see the child, whose voice it is she hears, or when she noticed her hands floating, the clinician presupposes the client is having these experiences, an indirect suggestion to do so. The last example is a metaphor with embedded commands to indirectly suggest certain sensory experiences. "Hearing the silence" is also an indirect suggestion to negatively hallucinate ongoing auditory stimuli.

Since the client suspends reality-testing during the trance state, much of the normal external stimuli usually present are reduced or eliminated. The brain's need for stimulation in order to function normally (as evidenced in extreme sensory isolation studies) is a basis for hallucinations—the mind's self-stimulation in the absence of sufficient external stimulation. When one works with hypnotically induced hallucinations, the potential may exist for developing a greater insight into the origin of psychosis, and therefore into the "normal" mind as well. This is but one area where research employing hypnotic patterns may eventually make meaningful contributions to the advancement of clinical treatment.

IDEODYNAMIC RESPONSES

DESCRIPTION

In an earlier chapter I discussed the perspective of hypnosis arising as a result of triggering the associations between words and experience. You may recall that in that section I briefly described the intense mind-body relationship, which was exemplified in a later discussion of the physical reactions associated with mental experiences when describing the Chevreul's Pendulum suggestibility test. The powerful effects of conditioning can be observed in a lot of different ways in daily life (there's no need to think about what would happen if you yelled "Fire!" in an auditorium ... is there?), since so much of our daily functioning is done on an automatic, unconscious level. If you had to pay attention to every single thing you did each day, by the time you got showered and dressed it would be time to call it a day! Our automatic functioning frees the conscious mind to involve itself in higher-order activity. The automatic functions that humans are capable of exist on three different levels: motoric, sensory, and affective. Collectively, these are the "ideodynamic responses"; individually, the responses are the "ideomotor response," the "ideosensory response," and the "ideoaffective response." Each is an automatic response generated at an unconscious level in response to a stimulus, either external or internal.

The ideomotor response is the physical manifestation of mental experience, or, in other words, the body's unconscious reactions to one's thoughts. The Chevreul's Pendulum is a hokey but useful demonstration of this relationship. Being a passenger in a car and moving to hit the brake is also an example. So-called "body language" is an entire category filled with thousands of examples (the body moves unconsciously as an analogue to what is verbalized) of ideomotor responses.

The body's movements are usually slight—so slight that they remain out of awareness (hence, unconscious), but they can usually be observed by the naked eye. Certainly they are most easily measured with devices such as the polygraph which can measure variables such as heart rate, galvanic skin response, and level of muscular tension. The polygraph is an obvious example of the ability to detect measurable changes in the body that the test subject is unaware of as he responds to questions from the examiner.

Ideomotor responses may be facilitated for diagnostic and/or therapeutic purposes. Diagnostically, the clinician may suggest to the client an automatic physical response to questions. For example, one might suggest that if the response to the question is "Yes," the client's head will slowly nod automatically and effortlessly, and if the answer is "No," the client's head can shake from side to side. It is not uncommon for a client to verbalize the "Yes" response while simultaneously indicating the "No" response with her head. Which would you believe? If you would be prone to believe the verbal response, I have some real estate I'd like to talk to you about purchasing . . . nothing wrong with it, it's just under a few feet of water . . . While the ideomotor response is certainly not a lie-detector, it can provide evidence of the existence of multiple cognitive controls and conflicting feelings within the client.

Therapeutically, the ideomotor response can be used to facilitate dissociation, to deepen the trance state, as an indicator of responsiveness, and even as a means for exchange between clinician and client when such techniques as "automatic writing" or "automatic talking" are employed. Automatic writing refers to the ability of the client to write (or draw) without conscious involvement in doing so. Signing your name and doodling are examples of automatic writing and drawing. Automatic talking involves having the client speak without a conscious involvement in doing so. Talking to one's self, reading aloud, and absentmindedly carrying on a conversation are examples of automatic talking. Direct but permissive suggestions are given to the client, for example, that he "can write and wait with eagerness to see what was written by your hand." The cataleptic client can move in automatic, usually jerky, movements as he carries out ideomotor responses like hand levitation, finger signals (suggested to the client in order for him to provide information or to indicate when he has finished a thought, recovered a memory, is ready to go on, or whatever), and head nods.

Ideosensory responses are automatic experiences of sensation associated with the processing of suggestions. Having the normal range of sensation and a kinesthetic memory for what the experience of the sensation was is the basis of the ideosensory response. When someone suggests that you recall the experience of having peanut butter stuck to the roof of your mouth, the sensation can come back to you quite automatically as you make sense of what was asked of you. The taste and feel of peanut butter in your mouth is immediately available to you only because of your past experience with it. The suggestion would have no effect if you had never tasted peanut butter or if you do not have a mouth. Describing in elaborate detail the various sensory components associated with an experience allows the client to re-experience those sensations to a degree determined by the amount and type of past personal experience with it, and the degree of kinesthetic awareness the person generally has.

Ideoaffective responses are the automatic emotional responses attached to the various experiences each person has. People have a diverse range of emotional responses to life's events, each differing in the types as well as degrees of intensity of response. It is difficult, if not impossible, to feel entirely neutral about something. Therefore, as the client experiences the suggestions of the clinician, different feelings associated with the ideas contained in the suggestions come to the surface. Buried negative feelings of hurt and despair can arise in a flash, as can positive feelings of joy and pleasure.

The ideodynamics are simply components of a total experience. Every experience one has occurs on a variety of levels, each adding to the overall experience in a different and complementary way. In doing trancework, the ideodynamics are important variables for two important reasons. First, they reflect the inner experience of the client at the levels where change is sought. Second, they are a part of the current therapeutic experience, and will be the action, feeling, and sensory-based components of the therapy that the person will rely on as the basis for change in the future.

APPROACHES

Unlike many of the other trance phenomena, the ideodynamics will occur no matter what you do. There is virtually no way the client can prevent unconscious body movements, or keep from re-experiencing feelings and sensations. In facilitating the ideodynamic responses hypnotically, the issue becomes one of whether the client responds well to suggestions for specific automatic responses or not. The feelings, sensations, and movements that the clinician suggests will be responded to more easily the greater the degree of dissociation present, since the ideodynamics are defined as unconscious responses. Therefore, facilitating dissociation is a necessary first step before attempting procedures like automatic writing or finger signaling.

Direct suggestions offered permissively are useful for facilitating ideo-dynamic responses. The following suggestions are examples of this type:

> ... as you let your body relax ... your head begins to slowly drop downward ... and let it do as it wishes. ... *(ideomotor response)*

> ... and as your muscles continue to relax ... you can feel the tingle in that spot. ... *(ideosensory)*

> ... while you remember that picture of yourself as a child ... you can notice the feeling that the picture recreates within you. ... *(ideoaffective)*

Each of the above suggestions directly suggests an automatic experience not consciously created. They "just happen" as the client follows the suggestion, and the client doesn't have to will them at all.

Indirect suggestions for ideodynamic responses are also very useful, as long as the clinician chooses words carefully since the words used will engender the specific response obtained. Examples of indirect suggestions for ideodynamics include:

> ... I don't think your conscious mind will know your unconscious knows about that event until your finger has lifted. ... *(ideomotor response)*

> ... I wonder whether you can recall how good it feels to cool off by jumping into a cool swimming pool after feeling hot and dried out from the heat of the sun. ... *(ideosensory response)*

> ... It can be a great relief to find out that what you thought would be a major car repair is only a minor one. ... *(ideoaffective response)*

Preoccupying the client with the content of the suggestion facilitates the ideodynamic response, for while the client projects herself into the described situation and attempts to make meaning of it, her unconscious is already responding. Discovering the idiosyncratic patterns of nonverbal communication each person demonstrates can be a rich source of information about that person. Noticing such patterns and interpreting them are two different things, however, and while I encourage noticing patterns, I am not as quick to encourage their interpretation. Saying a gesture "means" this or a posture "means" that is a gross oversimplification and is more likely to be only a projection of the observer's unconscious than anything else.

Ideodynamic responses are responsible for the most direct contact the clinician will have with her client's unconscious. Doesn't that *automatically* entitle them to careful consideration?

TIME DISTORTION

DESCRIPTION

The experience of time is a purely subjective one, meaning one experiences the passing of time in one's own way at any given moment. Everyone has had the experience of doing something pleasurable and fun, and discovering that what seemed like a short period of time was actually a relatively long one: "Time flies when you're having fun." Likewise, you have probably had the experience of being in a situation that was difficult or boring, and after checking your watch and waiting . . . for what seems like three days . . . you then check your watch again and find, much to your distress, that only five minutes have gone by. The passing of time can seem much longer or much shorter than is objectively true, depending on one's focus of attention. Such distortions of time take place in the "everyday trances" all people experience, and like all experiences that are subjective, the experience of time can be significantly altered in deliberate ways hypnotically.

Facilitating the distortion of time in a client's perception can make for a very useful therapeutic experience. When a client is in pain, for example, condensing a long period of painful existence into what seems like a very short period of time can be a most humane intervention. Expanding the perception of time of comfort in between the contractions of a woman in labor can make the birthing experience a much more comfortable one. Having a long work day seem shorter can make a difficult job a little easier to take. Having only a short period of clock time in which to take an examination and yet experiencing plenty of time subjectively can allow for better performance. These are but a few potential examples of useful applications of the trance phenomenon of time distortion.

APPROACHES

Approaches for facilitating time distortion can range from "simply getting out of the way" and letting time distortion arise spontaneously to the offering of direct and indirect suggestions for its evolution. Time distortion tends to arise with no suggestions for it at all, for once someone closes her eyes and becomes absorbed in internal experience (e.g., thoughts, memories, sensations, etc.), the outside world is in the background and the chance to make a realistic assessment of how much clock time has elapsed is more difficult. Try this yourself: Check the time, let your eyes close, and then let your mind drift to wherever it happens to go. Open your eyes again after what you feel is five minutes of clock time. How far off are you? Did you under- or overestimate? Most people in this brief exercise would think more time had elapsed than actually did. If you ever had to be silent for an entire minute as a child in school, you know how only a minute of forced silence can seem like an hour! For the client in trance, the involvement necessary to maintain the trance state usually precludes maintaining any objective sense for the passing of time.

Direct suggestion for time distortion, especially offered permissively, can facilitate the experience well. The following are examples of direct suggestions for time distortion:

> ... and it can seem to you as if a long period of time has gone by ... and that you have had many hours of rest....

> ... an hour can seem like a minute ... and time can pass so quickly ... when each thought passes through your mind at a rate so fast that it's easier to just let your thoughts pass quickly by than try to catch one....

> ... your mind and body have been so busy here ... and it takes so much time to do everything you've done ... hours seem to have passed while you have been so preoccupied....

Indirect suggestions for time distortion gently plant the notion that the experience of time can be altered. Indirect suggestions, stories containing examples of experiences where time was distorted, conversational postulates, and double-binds are all capable of facilitating time distortion. The following suggestions provide an example of each:

> ... keeping track of time is so difficult sometimes ... and right now it's hard to know whether five minutes or six minutes have gone by, and how can anyone really know whether only five-and-one-quarter minutes have gone by or five-and-one-half ... or five-and-six-eighths or five-and-seven-eighths minutes have gone by.... *(indirect suggestion for an expanded experience of time)*

> ... I worked with a client not long ago who felt so uncomfortable when she first came in ... her problem bothered her a lot ... but when she closed her eyes and let herself listen to me ... deeply ... she forgot to notice how much time went by ... and she let herself relax so deeply ... it seemed like hours of comfort ... soothed her mind and body ... and she felt so good ... for a long time afterwards.... *(metaphor regarding an experience of time distortion)*

... and you've been so comfortable sitting and listening to me, haven't you? ... That's right ... and it isn't easy to know how long ... very long ... a period of time has passed, is it? ... *(conversational postulate)*

... and now I wonder whether you realize how fast and short this period of time has gone by ... and you can guess if you'd like ... would you say it's been only five minutes or would you say it's been only ten? ... *(forced choice orienting the person to a specific time span)*

In the first example above, by getting so specific about how much time has elapsed and framing all the choices within a short period of time, one can help the client become oriented to that time frame and thus feel as if a lengthy process actually took only five to six minutes. If the clinician wants to expand time, the frame used can be an exaggerated one (e.g., for a ten-minute trance session, the clinician can suggest how difficult it is to know if twenty or twenty-and-one-half minutes went by ...). In the second example, a metaphor is offered that lets the client know she can be comfortable for what feels like a long time by being in trance through the building of an identification between her and the person in the story. In the third example, the conversational postulate is employed; by asking the client to realize how difficult it is to assess the length of elapsed time, the presupposition is that a long time has passed. In the last example, the client is forced to choose between two times that are both much shorter than the actual time elapsed. Time can be expanded by making the (double-bind) choices much longer than the actual time elapsed.

Time distortion can have the effect of convincing the client that she has, in fact, been in a trance state. When she disengages from the trance state and discovers how distorted her perception of time has been, she knows she has experienced something out of the ordinary. The result can be a new respect for the complexity and sophistication of her own inner world. A boost in self-esteem accomplished so easily is one of the most positive dimensions of doing trancework.

ENDING THE TRANCE STATE (DISENGAGEMENT)

As good as it feels to be in trance, eventually one has to disengage from the trance state. Disengagement is the final stage of hypnotic interaction. The client may indicate a readiness to disengage through a diminished focus of her attention and by beginning to move and stretch. The clinician has to make a decision at the moment of observing such signs as to whether the work is done for that session or whether the client's initiation of disengagement is some form of avoidance that can be addressed therapeutically. The clinician is directing the therapy session, and should generally be the one to decide when initiating disengagement is appropriate, just as he decides when trance induction is appropriate. In deciding when disengagement is appropriate, the clinician can also decide on what the manner of disengagement will be. When and how to disengage is a matter of individual clinical judgment, based on the overall treatment plan and the accomplishments of that specific session. The clinician has, by this time, employed a suggestion style and structure in his approach to the client, and the disengagement can be consistent with these. If the clinician has been relatively direct throughout, he can offer such suggestions as the following for disengagement:

> . . . You can bring yourself out of trance at a rate that is comfortable for you . . . taking as much time as you'd like to in order to complete this experience for yourself. . . .

> . . . When you're ready, you can open your eyes and reorient yourself to the here-and-now, feeling relaxed and refreshed. . . .

> . . . When you open your eyes in a few minutes and rediscover the outside world . . . you'll be able to notice how good it feels to have been in trance. . . .

Most direct approaches to disengagement (traditionally called "awakening") have employed a counting method: "I'm going to count to three and snap my fingers and you will then be wide awake . . . " Such an approach is not particularly respectful of the client's need to disengage from the trance state at his *own* rate. Expecting a client to respond to an arbitrary count and come out of trance simply because the clinician wants him to does not allow him whatever time he may want to complete the experience for himself. Furthermore, expecting *any* human being to respond to a finger-snap is simply degrading and undesirable.

If the trance state has been an informal, spontaneous one, the clinician can choose to be consistent in her approach by offering indirect suggestions for disengagement. The following are exemplary of such an approach:

> . . . and I wonder whether you've realized how comfortable it has been to let your mind consider that possibility . . . and that can certainly be an *eye-opening experience*. . . .

> . . . and after a nice rest such as the one you've just had you can certainly *alert yourself* to the joys of living. . . .

... did I tell you how I learned about that? ... I was so preoccupied with myself that I didn't notice things around me much ... but one can *become less self-absorbed* and *move around* in the world and *notice things outside yourself* ... *opening your eyes* to new possibilities. ...

In deciding on the when and how of disengagement, the clinician can consider such factors as whether amnesia is desirable to suggest and what type(s), if any, of posthypnotic suggestions might be offered. How the trance experience is concluded will have a significant impact on the client, since human memory is generally stronger for the most recent events (the "recency effect"). In other words, the feeling the client has as she disengages from trance are the feelings she is most likely to associate with the trance experience. This is another reason why it is usually the best option to allow her the time she wants or needs to complete her processing of the events of the trance experience. Letting the client disengage at her own chosen rate allows her the opportunity to feel relaxed and unhurried under the clinician's care.

CONCLUSION

This chapter has described the most basic building blocks for the therapeutic applications of hypnosis. Clinical interventions will always involve some or all of the trance phenomena, and it is therefore imperative that one be clear about what each of these subjective experiences each human being is capable of really is. Before one can apply them in the meaningful ways described, it is most helpful to observe these experiences as they arise in daily living, attempting to uncover what stimulus in the observed event acted as the trigger for the phenomenon. Such careful observation of the range of human experiences occurring routinely can make their amplification in the trance state significantly easier to accomplish. As building blocks, the various trance phenomena can be arranged and rearranged in an unlimited number of configurations. The process of planning a specific intervention for a particular client can involve the development of a strategy. The clinician can decide which trance phenomena would be useful experiences for the client to have. More specifically, the clinician can decide the type(s) of orienting ideas to be presented, the type and style of induction to be used, which trance utilizations to use with special consideration for content, style, and degree of involvement.

With the various trance phenomena serving as the foundation on which to build the intervention, the task of the clinician to organize such experiences in a meaningful way is a great one. This task is considered in greater detail in the next chapter.

For Discussion

1. What is your reaction to discovering the routine nature of trance phenomena?

2. What is your opinion about past-life regression (regressing someone hypnotically to a previous incarnation), hypnotic ESP (amplifying extrasensory perception hypnotically), and other paranormal applications of hypnosis?

3. How can each of the trance phenomena be seen in the various mental disorders? (For example, a multiple personality disorder involves dissociation of personality parts, and amnesia for the existence of each part.)

4. In what instances, if any, might facilitating any of the various trance phenomena be contraindicated?

5. How might you use age progression to assist your learning of hypnosis?

Things to Do

1. List 10 routine contexts in which each of the trance phenomena arise. What factors seem to precipitate the phenomena arising?

2. During an age regression process, have your subject write her name while at different ages. Do you observe differences in writing style that are age-appropriate?

3. Make a list of the 20 most significant events in your development. Which ones would you characterize as being positive; which negative? Which ones seem to have the most emotion attached to them? Why?

4. Check with local hospitals to find out what their policies are regarding the use of hypnotic anesthesia in their operating rooms. What do you find out?

18

Therapeutic Utilization of the Trance State

Throughout this book there have been numerous descriptions of ways to apply hypnosis in clinical contexts. Utilizing the capacity for each person to experience himself differently in deliberate ways in order for the client to reach a personal goal is the essence of clinical hypnosis. In the first section of this chapter, some of the most basic patterns of hypnotic intervention are described in general terms. In this chapter's latter section, some of the most common problems a clinician is likely to encounter are briefly described, with emphasis on how hypnosis may be employed in the treatment process.

The assumptions associated with the use of hypnosis in psychotherapy are presented in Table 14.

Table 14. Assumptions Inherent in Hypnotic Psychotherapy

Influence is inevitable; all therapy is directive to some degree
The clinician is an agent of change
The client wants change to occur
The problem is in the client's map, not the client
The client has utilizable resources for change
No one is completely helpless
Each person is making the best choice available
Choice is better than no perceived choice

SYMPTOM STRUCTURES AND TRANCE PHENOMENA

I have previously described the trance phenomena as the building blocks of experience. In varying combinations and degrees of purity, the various trance phenomena comprise ongoing experience, whether good or bad. Developing the ability to view everyday experiences in terms of the associated trance phenomena can give you the ability to identify the structures of experiences, not just the content.

In the context of conducting therapy, having the ability to identify the trance phenomena associated with a client's symptoms permits you a more rapid and comprehensive understanding of her problem. Knowing the steps involved in the creation of the symptom permits you the opportunity to choose at what point in the sequence you may introduce an interruption that alters the sequence in some beneficial way.

Consider the example of someone with a fear of flying. If this person cannot get on an airplane because she is visualizing the plane taking off, the engines flaming out, the plane going down, and then she sees twisted metal and body parts scattered all over, then it is easy to appreciate how a fear of flying is generated. In this case, the woman is using visual imagery to create terrifying images that produce very high levels of anxiety. Even the most superficial hypnosis approach would at least offer suggestions to think about flying comfortably, seeing images of the wonderful things to be experienced at the destination. In essence, the clinician is saying, "Here. Visualize these relaxing images instead of those terrible images." While the content of the visual imagery changes, both the solution and the problem are comprised of images of the future (age progression) that feel real in the present.

In the same way that age progression is evident in some anxiety disorders, it is possible to similarly characterize other problems according to associated trance phenomena. Table 15 provides some relevant principles and examples.

The dissociative aspect of symptoms is an especially noteworthy point to appreciate. Clients routinely describe how the symptom "just happens," meaning it is not a voluntary response on the part of the individual. In defining therapy as involving pattern interruption and pattern building, as virtually all therapies must do, it is clear that the role of the clinician is to establish new associations to the client's dysfunctional or self-limiting behaviors, thoughts, and feelings. Such associations can best be built through direct experience, such as hypnotic processes or

Table 15. Symptom Phenomena as Trance Phenomena

1. Identify trance phenomena evident in symptomatic
   pattern, for example:
   Overweight
   physical dissociation
   sensory alteration
   Smoking
   physical dissociation
   sensory alteration
   Depression
   age regression
   catalepsy
   sensory alteration
   Multiple Personality Disorder
   dissociation
   amnesia
2. Use complementary trance phenomena in interventions
3. Contextualize responses

through experiential approaches, such as task assignments and behavioral prescriptions.

Consider the average smoker from this vantage point. She is entirely unaware of the damage to her body with each puff of the cigarette. She does not feel her heart rate and blood pressure increase, nor does she feel the hundreds of toxins circulating through her body. She does not smell her clothes, hair, breath, or surroundings (car, home, office), and, generally speaking, is oblivious to the effects of smoking. Do you know when many people decide to quit smoking? When the elevator at work breaks! Taking the stairs highlights very quickly their degree of physical (un)fitness.

Clearly, a smoker is in a physically dissociated state. How else could one be oblivious to the physical damage associated with breathing toxic fumes?

The main idea in identifying trance phenomena underlying symptom phenomena is that *therapy takes the form of the complementary experience.* In smoking, for example, dissociation is a large part of the problem. Thus, *association* is going to be a large part of the solution. Building associational cues (triggers) to increased body and sensory awareness is the likely path to the successful treatment of smokers. Tying these cues to the specific contexts through the use of posthypnotic suggestions is the final step of the treatment.

Notice how the intervention described for smokers is not one based on an interpretation of the "meaning" of the smoking. Such an interpretation could only be my projection. Thus, interpreting smoking as a suicidal wish, a socially defiant behavior, an oral gratification representing a fixation at the oral stage of psychosexual development, or any other such assignment of meaning is arbitrary and unprovable. What is clear, however, is that the smoker is dissociated, for *whatever* reason, and requires that new healthy associations to her body be established.

The key points, then, of this section are twofold. First, utilizing trance phenomena as a reference point can be a useful means for understanding symptom structures. Second, when such trance phenomena are evident in the problem structure, a solution can take the form of building new associations through the use of complementary trance phenomena.

As was done for several disorders in Table 15, it may be useful for you to identify which trance phenomena are evident in the type(s) of disorders you tend to treat most frequently.

PATTERNS OF INTERVENTION

Applications of hypnosis are as diverse and creative as the number of clinicians who work with it. There is no human problem that can be solved in all people through a "one size fits all" formula. Simple and direct suggestions for a problem's resolution are considered a possible treatment intervention since they can work with a certain relatively small percentage of the population, but the patterns described here are offered in response to the recognition that most people need something a little more multi-dimensional. Individualizing treatment is a necessity, and typically that means tailoring general patterns of intervention to the specific needs of the client. This process is akin to learning the rules and vocabulary of a language, but still expressing one's self in one's own way. There are, therefore, patterns that range from relatively simple to very complex and subtle. The following are some of the simpler and more common hypnotic patterns for intervening in client problems. More complex and subtle techniques are available in the literature for the clinician interested in advancing her skills beyond the level of this text. The patterns described here are listed in alphabetical order for easy reference.

CHANGING PERSONAL HISTORY

The pattern of intervention called "Changing Personal History" (Bandler & Grinder, 1979) has been one used routinely in clinical intervention over the years, with a variety of forms and names. Probably the simplest yet most effective description of this pattern was offered in their book *Frogs Into Princes*. Changing personal history as a therapeutic intervention can involve age regression, age progression, catalepsy, dissociation, hallucinations, and time distortion. The strategy is appropriate to use when a client is presenting a problem that has its origins in an ongoing life decision that is proving maladaptive. One decision sets up a lifetime of experiences that support it, even if hurtful. For example, if a client had the experience of being abused as a child and made the decision (i.e., formed the generalization) that the world is an abusive place and people are not to be trusted or related to in a positive way, the clinician might take the client back in time to her earliest memories and facilitate the (imaginary) experience for her of feeling loved, cared for, and protected by others. When the resources of affection and caring are provided and she is then guided forward through time while having those missing resources subjectively present through all her life experiences, her feelings about herself and others can change in a healthier direction.

In the case of a client I worked with whose mother had died when he was a boy of seven, he had "decided" (not consciously) that "women were not to be trusted and gotten close to because they leave you." The strategy of changing personal history was used in his case. When he was taken back to his fondest memories of his mother (times when he felt her closeness and love), it was possible to make those good feelings of having her around available to him when he wanted them. This was done through the building of an "anchor" or association to those good feelings; specifically, he could see her and hear her voice respond to him whenever I touched his arm.

The next step was to establish amnesia for his mother's death. Once this was established, we could go through his life's experiences, both good and bad, and have him able to share them with his mother. She could grow older with him and be there for him in the way he needed her. The experience of having his mother "with him" through his developing years allowed him to later alter his feeling toward women, especially when he had the insight that "dying probably wasn't her idea, anyway."

In helping "change" his personal history, I provided access to a resource that allowed him to experience each of his life's experiences with the "missing piece," allowing him to feel, hear, and see life from a different perspective. Some people integrate the new experiences and treat it as if it were their real history out of some need or desire. Others are just grateful to have had the experience and accompanying internal changes while recognizing that it was all part of the trance. In working with this pattern, one rapidly develops an appreciation for how subjective "reality" really is. That's my reality anyway.

CRITICAL (TRAUMATIC) INCIDENT PROCESS

To go through life without experiencing trauma is an idea for futuristic science fiction, because it just doesn't happen in real life. No one escapes hurtful experiences, and no one is going to get out of this life alive. Cars crash, people die, wars are fought, and even despite these harsh realities it is the "everyday" traumas that can have the most serious impact. The mean kid who made fun of your freckles, the hole in your pants at the most embarrassing moment possible, and the stupid comment that should never have been said are all examples of the "everyday trauma" that can have incredible impact on one's life. Years later such traumas often seem silly and irrational, yet can still carry a big emotional wallop. In persons who have suffered a trauma of some sort (even if the trauma may seem trivial to the clinician, it is the client's feeling that is the determinant of what is traumatic), the traumatic event may be a turning point in the person's life. If it is a turning point for the worse, which not all traumas are, then the critical incident process may be an appropriate treatment strategy.

The critical incident process involves revivification, catalepsy, dissociation, age progression, and hallucinations. This is an emotionally powerful process, intending to release pent-up emotions associated with a traumatic event ("catharsis"). If the client has conscious memory for the content of the critical incident, you may simply proceed in a relatively straightforward way. If the traumatic incident has been repressed, the process is a bit tricky, since the client's unconscious has protectively chosen to keep the information out of her awareness. In such an instance, you can still do a critical incident process, but you must be careful to let the client work at her own rate and to never push the client to deal with something directly she

---

Table 16. General Structure of a
Critical Incident Process

Induction, establish anchor to comfort
Age regression to context
Exploration of context
Elicit affective associations
Identify central distortion(s)
Catharsis
Dissociation of affect
Dimensional shifting of representation/reframing
Restructuring of focus and memory content
Amplification of alternate representation(s)
Age progression with new resource
Post-hypnotic suggestion for future accessing
Reorientation

---

chooses not to, except as an absolute last resort. Ideomotor questioning can be enormously useful here to help assess whether the client's unconscious is ready, willing, and able to deal with the traumatic experience and/or the consequences in the client's life.

The critical incident process as a treatment strategy takes the form of a revivification in which the client is regressed back to the time of the traumatic experience. Generally, it is a good idea to first do a regression to a positive experience, demonstrating to the client that she can trust the clinician's guidance, find happiness (or *something* positive) within herself, and control the trance experience.

Once the client has become immersed in the experience, the clinician's primary role is to offer support and secondarily to amplify a part of the experience the client had previously not attended to—how insecure (angry, hurt, panicked . . .) the other person might have been, how well she coped in the face of adversity, or some such thing. One might change the history of the situation by adding something new to the interaction to make it easier to bear. By supporting the client's expression of pain, the clinician can usually guide her to a point where she can feel differently about the situation. Frequently, just releasing all the pent-up emotion in a supportive atmosphere has ample therapeutic value. Guiding the client into a new awareness is an added bonus. To complete the experience, the client can age progress, integrating the changes in feeling associated with the release of the hurt, bringing with her new conclusions about the old experience and herself.

One can use the critical incident process to revivify an experience that was critical in the client's life in a positive way, should one desire. Typically, though, the experiences that wreak the biggest emotional havoc are traumatic ones, requiring a great deal of sensitivity on the part of the clinician. Many clinicians I am aware of are "emotional voyeurs" who want or need to help their clients "get in touch with the pain." A lot of people have suffered enough by the time they consult the clinician; guiding the client through the traumatic incident process with no precise goal in mind is capable of amplifying hurt needlessly. Caution is advised.

HOMEWORK ASSIGNMENTS

Many therapeutic approaches make use of "homework," tasks the client is given to carry out in between therapy sessions. These are intended to amplify thoughts, feelings, and behaviors that the clinician judges important in the therapy. The homework assignment operates on the level of experience, a more powerful level than the typical verbal therapy addresses. The homework assignment is hypnotic in the sense that it can be thought of as an experiential metaphor in the treatment process. In other words, if properly given, it will address the unconscious dynamics of the presenting problem. When the client engages in an activity that will cause her to see herself differently while confronting her limiting thoughts, feelings, and behaviors, the desired change may be accomplished.

For example, working with one depressed client, I instructed her to hike a local mountain trail called the Azalea Glen Springs Trail. Sounds beautiful, doesn't it? Can you imagine the mountain springs rushing over the rocky terrain? Well, don't. The "spring" is little more than a metal pipe dripping water out of the side of a hill. This particular client, as part of her depressed mental set, imagines everyone is better than she is, everyone is more important, and so on. She tended to build things up beyond what they were in a way that always put her at the bottom. In instructing her to hike the trail, I knew she'd imagine the springs as beautiful and flowing water. I also knew she'd be in for a surprise when she got there (after several miles of moderately difficult hiking) and found such a disappointing sight. When I saw her the day after her hike, she was the most animated she'd been since I'd met her. She found it very, very funny that after all that hiking all she found was a pipe in the ground. During her descent she thought very hard about why I would ask her to hike such a disappointing trail, and had the realization that she had set herself up for disappointment by building the springs up into something special in her mind when it turned out the springs weren't really the way she imagined them. She broadened her thinking, and had the "big aha!"—that she is almost always building things up to be better than they really are. She then decided to make greater effort to find out the value of things from experience, rather than from assumptions rooted in her insecurity.

This homework assignment provided her a much more intense experience of herself than would my saying to her (in or out of trance), "You build things up in your mind to be better than they really are and you shouldn't." The hike served a number of therapeutic purposes: It matched her "going uphill against the world" feelings, it got her physically active (a great tool in dissipating depression), it caused her to confront her unconscious pattern of maximizing everything and everyone else while minimizing herself, and it boosted her self-esteem by giving her a greater feeling of being in control of herself, for she had accomplished something meaningful all by herself.

Assigning tasks that will address the client's concerns can take a variety of forms. In addition to the symbolic task described above, another type of assignment can involve "making the symptom inconvenient" for the person. Typically, a symptom is coddled and catered to, for the client adapts his life to its presence. Having the client do something that will make the symptom inconvenient can effect a surprisingly rapid and lasting change. For example, one client I worked with indirectly using this approach was a girl age nine who refused to go to bed because she wanted to be with her parents in their room at night as they watched television. Consequently, she was up late, couldn't get up on time to go to school, and was tired and inattentive much of the time.

The girl's parents fought with her to go to bed, but to no avail. When they consulted me as to what they should do with her, I told them that I did not need to see her if they would follow my instructions. I told them to kindly and affectionately send her on frequent errands: "Mommy wants a glass of water, will you please go downstairs and get me one?" or "Daddy forgot to check the front door, will you go downstairs and make sure it's locked?" and so forth. Each time she came back and got comfortable, they sent her somewhere. It took only three nights for her to come to the conclusion that being with mom and dad wasn't so much fun after all, and that she could be a lot more comfortable in her own room.

Homework assignments involve more of the person in therapy than does verbal dialogue alone. It also allows the treatment to generalize to times and places outside the clinician's office, allowing changes to be more easily integrated into the client's life. In the example of the nine-year-old girl above, a more traditional intervention might have overtly focused on separation anxiety, individuation, family issues, parental encouragement of the symptomatic behavior, and so forth; these issues were addressed indirectly in the girl with greater speed and less trauma to her integrity. The greater the degree of removal from the client's conscious mind from which the assignment is able to address the problem's dynamics, the greater the opportunity for success. Homework assignments can make a point on a variety of levels simultaneously, and when used skillfully are an art form in their own right.

Milton Erickson used homework assignments routinely in his work, designing assignments that might, on the surface, seem to make no sense whatsoever. Underneath, however, they made a lot of sense in their ability to address his patient's unconscious needs. Erickson was a master at motivating his patients to follow his "crazy" assignments, and in his later years he was often asked how he was able to do so. His response was, typically, "They follow my instructions because ... they know I mean it." Translation: If you have rapport and your client's trust, you can have a very powerful effect on her.

REFRAMING

The meaning of a communication is determined to a large extent by the context in which it appears. A single word such as "no" can actually mean a wide variety of things ranging from a firm "no" to "I don't know" to "I guess so," depending on the tone of voice, body posture dynamics, and context. Changing the context of a communication changes its meaning. A behavior may be perfectly acceptable in one situation, but not in another. Consider the act of stealing as an example. Stealing money from a blind beggar is an act no one would condone. Stealing a serum that will cure your mother's terminal cancer from a greedy neighbor who wants a million dollars you don't have for the cure is the same act of stealing—yet it stimulates empathy in most people, not anger and a desire to punish the offender. Lying by the government to the public is considered a betrayal—unless it's for "national security." A man who acts strangely is "crazy" if he's poor—but "eccentric" if he's wealthy.

The various euphemisms that abound in the English language are all simple and effective "reframings." Reframing is changing the meaning by changing the way an event is perceived. Psychotherapy in whatever form it happens to take at a given moment necessarily involves reframing. Liabilities are turned into assets, traumatic events are converted into learning experiences, and so forth. Reframing can be used to deliberately disrupt a client's usual mental set, inducing a spontaneous trance (giving rise to catalepsy, ideodynamic responses, time distortion, and dissociative responses). Reframing can be accomplished with a single remark, or can involve a lengthier, more absorbing experience. Any approach that allows the client to have a different perspective on the problem involves a reframe.

There is a highly gifted speaker on the subject of "Love," Dr. Leo Buscaglia (1982), whose numerous books all manage to find their way onto the bestseller list. Dr. Buscaglia does a great reframe when he somberly observes that each of us human beings has experienced hurt, sadness, and loneliness, and then asks, "Isn't that wonderful?" When he describes negative feelings as "wonderful," certainly that causes us to look at those feelings differently and challenges us to find a sensible basis for his describing them so peculiarly. When we realize, as he intends us to, that it is those negative feelings, as well as positive ones, that unite us as human beings by allowing us to share common emotions, such feelings *are* truly wonderful. I doubt, though, that anyone in Dr. Buscaglia's audience thought of sadness as wonderful before his reframe.

Humor involves reframing as the vehicle for the joke. The punch line inevitably causes us to look at the incident(s) in the story differently. Consider this joke told to me by one of my clients: A police officer spots an old, deteriorated van driving down the street and notices it doesn't have license plates. Upon pulling the driver over, and walking up to him to ask him where his license plates are, the officer notices fifty penguins standing in the back of the van. The officer, not expecting to see penguins in a van, yells at the driver: "I pulled you over because you don't have any license plates, but now I want to know what the hell you're doing with these penguins in your van. No, actually I don't want to know, just take them to the zoo. You got it mister? Just take these penguins to the zoo!" As the van driver pulls away, the police officer shakes his head and mutters to himself "Well, now I've seen it all." The very next day while on patrol, the officer sees the same van and decides to pull it over again, this time to address the license plate problem. When he steps up to the driver's window, he sees the fifty penguins still in the van—only this time they are all wearing sunglasses!

Furious, the officer says, "Mister, I thought I told you to take those penguins to the zoo." The driver's response was, "Well, I did. And, today, I'm taking them to the beach!"

The clinical skill involved in reframing is to suspend the client's belief system long enough to consider an alternate viewpoint. Turning the "half empty" glass into a "half full" one is an obvious example of how a negative viewpoint can be transformed into a positive one. Reframing can work in the other direction, too. An action a client engaged in that she felt fine about until the clinician said "How could you let yourself do that?" could rapidly turn her comfort into pain. The "psychological voyeurs" I described earlier usually have a knack for finding and amplifying pain (reframing *all* coping mechanisms as barriers to effective living) that might better have been dealt with in other ways.

Most interventions, though, are intended to transform pain into comfort. The underlying assumption in doing reframing as an intervention strategy is that every experience (i.e., thought, feeling, behavior) has some positive value *somewhere*. By taking an experience that the client views as a negative one and commenting on how and why that same experience can be an asset to her *somewhere*, one can change the client's attitude about that experience—the negativity can be discharged.

As another example, a woman complained that her husband's habit of snoring was disturbing her sleep. She was told an emotionally charged story by a widow friend she happened to complain to. The widow described how much she longed to hear her deceased husband's snoring, something she hated about him when he was alive. The impact on the woman complaining was to immediately develop an appreciation for her husband's snoring, because it was clear evidence he was still alive and well. The snoring behavior was the same, only the woman's attitude was changed—a successful reframe.

Finding a way to turn a minus into a plus (or vice versa) is a basic part of clinical work. Using the techniques of reframing can make the transformation of a client's personal reality a more efficient and deliberate process.

SYMPTOM PRESCRIPTION

Symptom prescription as a therapeutic strategy involves the direct or indirect encouragement of the client's symptom(s). When the client is encouraged to do what he is already doing, but in a way slightly different through some adjustment requested by the clinician, the symptom is experienced differently. It is no longer a puzzling thing that "just happens," but rather something arising in response to the clinician's direction. Consequently, it loses its original meaning and associations.

Symptom prescription, in a sense, is a sort of "reverse psychology" approach. For example, in the case of a woman I treated for depression, I prescribed that this woman lie in bed for four hours a day. Lying in bed was something she was already doing as part of her depression, but it was at *her* leisure. I adjusted her behavior by instructing her to get up early in the morning, shower, dress, have breakfast, do a few chores, and then go back to bed for the prescribed four-hour period. After following my instructions for several days, she found the bed that was once a haven was now a prison. She "had to" be there, by "doctor's order." She reacted very emotionally to her bed, and later pleaded with me to not have to lie in bed anymore. As a final prescription, I instructed her to have a "leaving bed" party, complete with hats, balloons, cake, and the presence of her family. It symbolized for her a genuine transition, especially when her party "guests" sat on her bed to be with her. Bed just wasn't the desirable place to be that it once was. As a result, this particular client has been able to get on with other dimensions of her life in a very positive way.

Encouraging someone to do what she is already doing robs her action of spontaneity and personal ownership (i.e., it's not "hers" anymore). When the pattern loses spontaneity and personal ownership, it provides no gratification for continuing to engage in that behavior. As another example, I may prescribe that an overweight client who is "always thinking about food" carry around at all times food and an alarm clock. I then instruct the client to set the alarm to go off every 15 minutes and, when it does, to go ahead and eat. The client who is "always eating" and "always thinking about food" now must do so at my directive. The typical result is an overweight client who gets sick of eating and thinking about food, and rebels by asserting, "I won't do that anymore." Which is, of course, fine with me.

A key to having symptom prescription work lies in the rationale provided with the prescription. If the rationale doesn't meet the client in his frame of reference, he will not be likely to follow the prescription. Furthermore, there are multiple dimensions of a presenting problem (its associated feelings, thoughts, behaviors, relational components, symbolic components, etc.) and the symptom prescription must be offered carefully in order to address the appropriate dimension(s). Finally, the modification on the symptomatic behavior the clinician introduces in her prescription is a key element, since it is this modification that will, when used successfully, alter the entire pattern.

The applications of the symptom prescription paradigm are broad in scope. Encouraging a "resistant" person to "be resistant" then redefines that resistance as cooperation. Encouraging a client to have a relapse redefines a relapse (unless the client resists and refuses to have one, which is better yet) as an acceptable and required part of the treatment process. Encouraging clients to do what they are already doing can give what seems like an uncontrolled symptom some concrete defining limits that make it a little easier for them to deal with effectively. The symptom that was out of the client's control now comes under yours—and you can feel free to alter it in a beneficial way.

THERAPEUTIC METAPHORS

The changes and learnings that can take place through listening to stories is one of the most interesting aspects of communications with the unconscious. How metaphors may be used to induce trance and embed suggestions has been described and exemplified in detail earlier. Metaphors can be effectively used in the therapeutic phase of the clinicial interaction as well; the building and telling of metaphors is a complex and powerful therapeutic skill to acquire. Therapeutic metaphors are stories that can be created in such a way as to parallel the client's problems, and may be told in such a way as to absorb the client in the metaphor. Often, the client may project meanings into the story that the clinician didn't even intend to communicate and that have greater impact than the intended meanings!

The best metaphors are usually those available in the client's own personal experience. If you take the time to review incidents in the client's life that had special meaning for them from their having taught something valuable about life, you can have access to a wealth of potentially meaningful metaphors. Likewise, your own background and personal history reflect important learning experiences. The more one participates in life, the more experiences one has to draw on. Cases you have worked on or read about that illustrate worthwhile points are also a good source of metaphors. Other sources include storybooks, movies, jokes, anecdotes that illustrate points about human nature, newspaper stories, and virtually anywhere else you have the opportunity to learn important lessons from others' experience.

Learning to tell stories in a hypnotic manner (i.e., meaningfully, utilizing the client's responses, embedding suggestions, etc.) is a skill that is invaluable. The necessity of inducing a formal trance diminishes as more and more trance responses are obtained as the story is first introduced and then told. The natural ability of the client to drift in and out of trance as she listens to the clinician is able to be tapped and amplified by the clinician wanting to use a metaphorical approach. An implication of this approach is that change can, at times, be relatively effortless, a possibility that the clinician can allow for. After all, some changes *do* take place rather "spontaneously," with no real internal tug-of-war apparent. For example, the foods you hated as a child that you enjoy now are probably not foods you forced yourself to learn to like. Your taste changed, that's all—and it changed effortlessly. Obviously, not all or even most changes take place so effortlessly, but the therapeutic metaphor stands a good chance of facilitating such a change, and can thus be a very, very useful approach.

SUMMARY

Each of the half-dozen patterns of intervention described above have been presented in a general way in order to acquaint the reader with some of the possibilities inherent in the pattern. These patterns are evident in the hypnotic transcripts in Chapter 19. There are numerous components of each pattern that must be considered and properly integrated in order for the pattern to be effective. Each pattern has been described in greater detail elsewhere in the literature, and for a more complete understanding of the concepts and techniques of each, other writings in these areas are invaluable. Many of these are contained in the bibliography at the end of the book. Furthermore, while the patterns included here are representative of some of the best (i.e., most effective and reliable) hypnotic interventions, they are only the tip of the iceberg in terms of available therapeutic patterns involving hypnosis.

COMMON CLINICAL COMPLAINTS

In clinical practice one encounters a wide range of presenting complaints. Some problems are rare, others quite common. In this section is a brief and superficial consideration of six of the most common clinical complaints and how hypnosis might be used directly or indirectly in their treatment.

The next chapter contains transcripts of hypnosis sessions performed with actual clients.

ANXIETY, STRESS

Some have called this the "Age of Anxiety," and there is some justification for doing so. The demands that exist on each person today in order to live effectively are higher than at any other time in the past. Just as soon as we get used to one technological advance, it becomes obsolete. Traditional values holding society together are rapidly deteriorating. Gender roles are much less specific, confounding many people. Employment is a more demanding and complex arena. The sources of stress are numerous and inevitable; stress cannot be prevented, only managed.

Hypnosis as a management tool can help build relaxation skills and a sense of self control. I believe teaching clients the skill of self-hypnosis (trance inductions and utilizations they can perform on themselves whenever they'd like to) is a necessary part of using hypnosis in clinicial contexts. Simply knowing one has the ability to relax deeply and reorganize one's thoughts, feelings, and behaviors can have a powerful effect in helping one manage one's stress and anxiety. After all, the stress is often in the client's interpretation of events, not just in the events themselves. Managing anxiety effectively allows for better concentration and study, better self-esteem, better time management, better job performance, greater receptivity to new ideas, and better just about everything. Hypnosis can facilitate alternate perspectives and thus alternate responses. Many strategies utilizing hypnosis for treating anxiety are contained in *Brief Therapy Approaches to Treating Anxiety and Depression* (Yapko, 1989).

DEPRESSION

Depression is a very complex, multidimensional problem that virtually all people experience from time to time in varying degrees. It is estimated that 30–40 million people in the United States suffer depression severe enough to require treatment. There are numerous theories or models describing why people get depressed, ranging from biological to psychological. Psychotherapy for depression seems an essential mode of treatment, particularly in light of recent data that indicate the prevalence of depression has increased as much as tenfold in the so-called "baby-boomer" generation

(Seligman, 1988). Such a large increase can best be accounted for in terms of social and environmental factors, not biological ones. Addressing the depressed person's relationship problems, cognitive distortions, faulty attributions, and other depressogenic patterns with hypnotically based methods can be a well-considered approach. In another volume, *When Living Hurts: Directives for Treating Depression* (1988a), I described nearly 100 hypnotically based strategies for intervening therapeutically in depression.

Hypnosis may be used superficially to soothe anxiety, interrupt negative rumination, increase responsiveness, and establish positive expectancy. It may be used more intensively to facilitate flexibility in rigid, distorted patterns of thinking or interpreting events, reframe meanings attached to experience rooted in faulty belief systems, and build positive frames of reference for responding to life from a more effective framework.

The ability to intervene on multiple dimensions simultaneously—some in awareness, others not—is a great advantage to working hypnotically with depressed clients. It means the unconscious can be engaged in the therapy process more immediately, which is less limiting than the treatment being restricted to conscious, insight-oriented approaches exclusively. Furthermore, recognizing the role of dissociation in depression allows risk factors in the client's experience to be identified and treated, a preventative opportunity that can reduce the likelihood of future depressive episodes.

RELATIONSHIP PROBLEMS

Considering the fact that the majority of marriages in this country end in divorce, as well as the fact that more people today live alone than ever before, the indication is quite clear that people are having a harder time building and maintaining healthy relationships with others than ever before. Why? The changing roles of men and women, the de-emphasis of the family structure, the increasing technological advances that keep diminishing our need for contact with others, the ease of divorce, and the casual attitudes about sex (though herpes and AIDS are certainly having a negative impact on such attitudes) are just some of the factors affecting each person's ability to relate to another in a positive and balanced way. In intervening in relationship problems, one must consider each person's expectations, communication skills, and subjective views on issues like "power" and "intimacy." Often, the partners in a relationship have inadequate communication skills, ill-defined or inappropriate expectations, poor self-esteem, fears of intimacy or a commitment, and other such barriers to an effective relationship.

Hypnotic strategies may be employed to clarify expectations, increase the level of motivation to resolve differences within the relationship, enhance communication skills, and resolve unconscious conflicts about intimacy and commitment. Metaphorical approaches, symptom prescription, and reframing are effective patterns to use in relationship counseling. Changing personal history is a good strategy to use in working individually with someone who experiences relationship problems, building in the resources necessary to effectively relate to another person. Helping the person to clarify what she really wants for herself and what she values is a good starting point for any clinical problem, but is especially necessary in the context of relationship counseling.

SELF-ESTEEM PROBLEMS

One's self-esteem is the subjective assessment of one's value as a human being. It is formed in part by the feedback one gets from others, but it is formed to a large extent by one's belief system. You may refer back to the earlier discussion of cognitive dissonance and its implication for what experiences a person will and will not permit herself. A person's poor self-esteem comes from an underlying belief that she is inadequate on levels deemed important, or central, to her personality. The person may conclude she is "a failure" because she only came in second in a world competition, or she may feel angry and disappointed with herself for not expressing how she really felt in a situation.

When one works with self-esteem problems hypnotically, the client can be encouraged to take control of situations by planning and executing a course of action very efficiently. One can engage the client's attention intensely as she learns about another person's experience: how the person in the metaphor experienced the same or structurally similar problem, how she handled it, and what the consequences were. Through the therapeutic metaphor the client can acquire learnings that have a greater impact than does simply stating the story's point. The metaphor can match (to whatever degree the clinician desires) the client's frame of reference, feelings, level of experience, expectations, and unconscious dynamics. Once an identification is built through such matching, the therapeutic metaphor can go on to suggest solutions, encourage actions, and embed suggestions.

The utilization of therapeutic metaphors is, because of their indirect nature, an approach that generally engenders much less resistance than do direct approaches. When the client feels "safe" that the clinician is simply telling an interesting story, she doesn't have to be consciously critical, and the unconscious is therefore more readily available to respond. The clinician can vary the metaphor's degree of removal from the problem at hand, for the more removed the stories are the less threatening they are. Likewise, the more removed they are the more confusing they are, sending the client into a search, at some level, for the "real" meaning. Therefore, the therapeutic metaphor doesn't have to be a perfect match to the client's experience in order to be therapeutically effective.

Hypnosis can help the client learn to generalize control to other areas of her life. Discovering one is more capable and effective than one thought (in business, social situations, self-management) is the means for improving self-esteem. Often, like the depressed client who necessarily has poor self-esteem as a feature of the depression, the person with self-esteem problems has poorly defined goals, and a strong need for approval by others to the point of compromising her own values in order to get it. Consequently, the bind arises of doing more and more to get approval while liking one's self less and less in the process because of the "selling out" it takes to get such approval. Helping the client build a recognition of and tolerance for the idea that she will not be liked by everyone is a necessary first step in encouraging her to do things for herself that *she* will respect. Prescribing that she placate everyone possible but not necessarily *everyone*, reframing self-sacrifice as "wimpy" rather than noble, and changing personal history to include acceptance she enjoyed and rejection she survived easily are some potential hypnotic interventions.

SUBSTANCE ABUSE

Some of the most serious and pervasive problems in our society today fall under the general heading of substance abuse. Excessive use of alcohol and other drugs, cigarette smoking, and overeating are all examples of substance abuse. In each case, the person is experiencing feelings, consciously or otherwise, that are uncomfortable. The substance is turned to as a way of altering one's feelings. It can have a soothing, calming effect, or it can stimulate guilt and anxiety—but at least then the person has a concrete reason for feeling bad and whatever was originally bothering her has been successfully avoided.

In all cases of substance abuse I have worked with, the client was in a dissociated state to some degree, with diminished awareness of the effects of the substance on his body. Substance abusers gradually build their lives around the substance: Cigarette smokers don't take the stairs, and obese people don't look at their bodies in the mirror. Each wants to avoid situations that will force them to confront the physical effects of their habit, and so dissociation from the body becomes a means to do so.

Hypnosis can be used to recultivate body awareness, build self-esteem and a sense of independence that whatever situations are encountered can be dealt with *without* self-abuse, make the experience of engaging in substance abuse inconvenient, resolve the underlying depression so common yet so infrequently diagnosed among substance abusers (frequently the substance abuse is self-medication for the anxiety associated with depression), and even to hypnotically recreate the good feelings of the substance without its ingestion.

Resolving substance abuse problems can be a process of reintegrating the dissociated elements and reframing both the meaning of the self-destructive behavior and the implications of the client's belief system. Obesity in particular is the most difficult to treat, in my experience. One can successfully live life without tobacco, alcohol and other drugs. However, one cannot live without eating; it is typically easier to eliminate a substance from one's life than it is to modify its intake. Building a positive body image and body awareness, visualizing one's self at the target weight, implementing behavioral changes in food intake, and using self-hypnosis to manage the anxiety of change effectively are all means for assisting clients in the weight loss endeavor in particular and in substance abuse in general.

SEXUAL DYSFUNCTIONS

Engaging in sexual relations can be one of the nicest of all trance states to be in, wouldn't you agree? Not for many people, though. For them, sexual activity is inhibited or eliminated because of sexual problems. The various sexual problems (e.g., erectile dysfunctions, premature ejaculation, disorders of sexual desire, etc.) can occur for a wide variety of reasons, including: 1) misinformation about human anatomy or sexual functioning in general; 2) negative feelings about sex because of negative experiences with it, such as guilt from a conservative religious upbringing; 3) poor self-esteem and body concept; 4) poor quality relationships based, in part, on inappropriate expectations; 5) organic problems resulting in impaired functioning, as well as other less common reasons.

Once the organic reasons for impaired or absent sexual functioning are ruled out, the clinician's task is to assess what factors are causing and/or contributing to the sexual problem. Metaphors of other clients' problems can be useful in helping diagnose the client's problem (the observant clinician can observe the ideodynamic changes in response to different parts of the story), as well as in offering suggestions and directives.

Persons with sexual problems are generally in a dissociated state relative to their sexual functioning. There is a part of them attempting to engage in sexual activity, and another part that is observing and criticizing perform- ance. The result is diffuse concentration that dissipates the trance state necessary to function well sexually. Hypnosis may be employed to facilitate the process of reintegration so that *all* of the person may be in the "here- and-now," experiencing and enjoying the sexual activity. One intervention involves altering sensory awareness by heightening kinesthetic sensitivity hypnotically. This is essentially an amplified sensate-focus technique that more traditional sex therapists employ in the treatment of sexual dysfunction.

Anxiety about sexual performance is a primary target for hypnotic interventions in cases of sexual dysfunction. Anxiety causes poor per- formance, which causes more anxiety, which then escalates the probability of poor performance, and so on in a vicious circle. Using the comfort of trance to allow the client to "let go" is a good model for "letting go" during sexual activity—fundamental to sexual enjoyment. Teaching self-hypnosis to help the client master the anxiety allows the relaxation to generalize to the context where she'd like to have it.

Reframing sex as a natural, healthy function is one more use for hyp- notic patterns in sexual therapy. Giving the directive to "avoid sex at all costs this week" can facilitate the "I'll show you by doing it" attitude in the client. Changing personal history to reteach a positive attitude toward sex is also a viable treatment strategy. Age progressing the client to see himself sexually active and satisfied is yet another potential application of hypnosis. Hypno- sis and sex therapy are two highly compatible and easily integrated approaches to the treatment of sexual dysfunction.

CONCLUSION

Learning how, when, and where to apply the many different potentially therapeutic experiences that are available through hypnosis requires years and years of practice and study. This chapter aimed to expose the student of clinical hypnosis to a few of the many ways hypnosis may be creatively and meaningfully applied. The deeper one's understanding of the numerous components that are a part of each and every symptom, the greater the respect one can have for the overall integrity of the finely balanced system called "the client."

For Discussion

1. What are the advantages and disadvantages of individualizing treatment? Do they offset each other? Why or why not?

2. Can you identify a belief you hold to be true about yourself that has prevented you from having certain experiences? How did it do that? With what effect?

3. What evidence do you have that reality is subjective? Is there an objective reality? How do you know?

4. When, if ever, should a client be forced to deal with something directly that is intensely painful? Why do you say so?

5. Discuss what you think these statements mean:
   a) Personal problems are a result of negative self-hypnosis.
   b) All change involves trance. Do you agree? Why or why not?

Things to Do

1. Research a wide variety of therapeutic interventions in your field. How is hypnosis directly or indirectly a part of those interventions?

2. Have each member of the class identify as many euphemisms as she or he can. How is "reframing" evident in each? What euphemisms exist in your field?

3. Have each member of the class tell a personally meaningful story of an experience in which a significant lesson was learned. What is your internal experience as you listen? How does it compare to simply hearing the story's point stated outright?

19

Hypnotic
Trance-Scripts

THEMES OF THERAPY

A distinction has clearly been made between the content and the structure of a suggestion. Similarly, such a distinction can be made between the structure and content of a client's problem. For example, someone may have a series of unsuccessful relationships and report continually getting involved with the same type of "wrong" person (each was alcoholic, or abusive, or emotionally distant, or problematic in some other way). Even though the names and faces are different (content) from relationship to relationship, the way (the structure) the person chooses someone to get involved with remains hurtfully the same.

Should the clinician focus on why each individual relationship ended in failure? Or, should the therapist focus on the poor system the person has for choosing relationship partners? I choose the latter approach. From this perspective, there are greater opportunities to facilitate deeper and more meaningful therapeutic changes in the client. Spending an inordinate amount of time sifting through all the content-related details of each relationship's problems is simply not necessary. If you introduce new and better ways to make competent relationship decisions on a structural level, the content *must* also change as a direct and predictable consequence.

When one thinks along these lines, it becomes possible to identify the common structures, or themes, that repeatedly surface in the problems clinicians are asked to treat. Consider, for example, the range of problems that individuals can experience when the problem theme is "letting go." Learning to "let go" is a necessity of life. Knowing when and how to "let go" as a life skill permits you to end one involvement in order to begin another. For those individuals who show an impairment of this ability, the symptoms can be quite diverse: staying in a relationship that is pathological or abusive, staying in a job that is unchallenging and unrewarding, smothering a child with overprotection to the point of blocking her ability to achieve a healthy independence, compulsively accumulating unnecessary or even trivial things, an inability to get over a death or relationship breakup, and many other such common problems. Thus, while the content of these examples of problems that clients present may differ markedly, each shares a common theme of the afflicted individual having a problem in "letting go." It is a sensible goal of treatment, then, to want to teach the client not only to "let go" in the immediate problem situation at hand, but also to extend the learning to the many other life situations where the individual will need that same ability. By extending the learning into other contexts that are not (yet) problematic, there is a preventative element to the therapeutic intervention.

It is a point of choice in the therapy process, then, as to whether you would like to intervene on the level of content, of structure, or on both. In general, interventions addressing only the content level tend to produce the most transient results. Focusing on content can be useful, but only to the extent that it helps identify associated problem structures and facilitate rapport.

THERAPEUTIC METAPHORS

There are many, many themes common to human experience that surface in the therapy context. This chapter will provide you with a few of them as they relate to particular clients with whom I did trancework. These trance processes reflect a balance of direct and indirect suggestions, as well as the other suggestion styles and structures identified earlier. You will be exposed to therapeutic metaphors in each of the transcripts—stories or analogies that are meant to elicit and guide the client's internal associations. Metaphors are one form of indirect suggestion that can have multiple functions (see Table 17), and are especially useful to address a problem theme the metaphor can parallel.

Metaphors are both engaging and nonthreatening to the client because they are only indirectly related to her sensitive issues; this makes it easier for the client to learn the relevant therapeutic principle(s) in a less emotionally charged atmosphere (see Table 18). Metaphors can be created quite readily when the underlying theme of the presenting problem has been identified. Table 19 provides some guidelines for the creation of therapeutic metaphors.

Table 17. Functions of Anecdotes
in Psychotherapy*

Diagnosis
Establishing Rapport
Treatment

- To make or illustrate a point
- To suggest solutions
- To get people to recognize themselves
- To seed ideas and increase motivation
- To embed directives
- To decrease resistance
- To reframe and redefine a problem

*Based on Zeig, 1980a

Table 18. Principles of Metaphorical Communication

Keypoint: The greater the perceived resistance, the greater the
need for indirection.

Symptoms may be viewed as metaphorical communications

Metaphors may be therapeutic in their ability to match
the client's indirect communication style

Metaphors contextualize learnings

Metaphors allow for accessing of resources

Metaphors encourage a search for relevance, projection

In general, the best metaphors are those that come directly out of the client's own experience. For example, teaching skills in "letting go" as a goal of treatment can be made easier by referencing the fact that the client has previously experienced making a move in her life. As she is oriented to "moving" through a metaphor, she can be reminded of how moving involves giving up the known for the unknown, leaving the past for the

---

Table 19. Structuring Therapeutic Metaphors

1. Gather information including:

   • significant persons involved
   • characteristics of the problem, situation
   • the desired outcome
   • available resources to be accessed
   • dimension(s) to be addressed

2. Pace previous attempts, frustrations

3. Build Metaphor of task analogous to problem

   • select a context based on client interest
   • isomorphic characters, plots
   • reframing of problem
   • direct or indirect resolution suggestions
   • discovery of alternate responses

4. Mapping Metaphors

   • number and sequence of metaphors on a theme

---

future, how the process involves getting rid of burdensome accumulations no longer necessary or meaningful, and so forth. Tying those associations to the current problem situation establishes a new framework for moving and "letting go."

Perhaps the easiest metaphors begin with "Once I had a client, not unlike you, who . . ." Such metaphors are encouraging to most clients, who appreciate knowing they are not alone in their problems and that you have successfully treated similar problems. If the client identifies with the person in the story, the positive associations to therapeutic solutions can be more easily established.

It is important to keep in mind that the use of metaphors is not a "given" in doing trancework. All the previous guidelines provided about suggestion formulation must be taken into account. If you launch into a story with a client without evaluating her style and demeanor, you could create a problem for yourself when she confronts you about wasting time talking about other people's problems instead of about hers! The subsequent loss of rapport can hinder further treatment results.

SESSION TRANSCRIPTS

While it has been repeatedly emphasized throughout this book that the effective use of clinical hypnosis involves tailoring approaches to the unique characteristics of each client, some samples of trancework may help you integrate all the information contained in this book about hypnosis more easily. The following trance session transcripts were derived from actual sessions with clients seeking help for a variety of problems. I hope you will study them with a deep consideration of the personal, interpersonal, and contextual variables that led to the creation of that particular piece of trancework. You will be given background on each of the clients, an explanation as to the goal(s) for that particular session, and how they relate to the larger goal(s) for the client's therapy.

As a final point regarding these transcripts, I want to point out that what I have chosen to present in this chapter are only those things that I said to the client in order to illustrate the various forms trancework may take. The next chapter contains a different and complete session transcript with commentary, providing a fuller representation of how trancework is a cooperative and individualized process. In reading the following transcripts, your learning of hypnotic patterns can be enhanced by actively considering the offered suggestions and reasoning out the rationale for their inclusion.

CASE 1: SELF-DEFINITION AND TAKING CARE OF SELF

The client is a woman in her early sixties who initially sought treatment for nightmares, recurring traumatic images associated with childhood episodes of molestation, poor self-esteem, and an inability to effectively set limits on others. Supporting her working through the feelings associated with her traumas was one obvious and necessary part of her treatment plan. Another part of her therapy focused on her lack of sense of self—what many call a lack of "ego boundaries." Assertiveness and limit-setting capabilities are only possible to achieve later—after there is first a sense of a self worth protecting. The following transcipt represents part of one trance session conducted early in her therapy addressing the theme of building boundaries and a definition of self.

All right, Molly, you can begin by taking in a few deep ... relaxing breaths ... getting yourself comfortable ... getting yourself oriented now ... to enter into internal experience for a while ... so that you can really enjoy the balance between conscious awareness and unconscious awareness ... let each breath relax you . . . let your thoughts run loose for a while . . . until they tire themselves out . . . and then little by little, they can slow . . . becoming very slow . . . so that more and more of your mental energy can be spent on learning . . . at the deepest levels within yourself . . . of the experience of comfort . . . about the experience of being so distant . . . from all the usual focal points of your awareness . . . so that you really can know deeply . . . that all the inner terrain . . . your inner landscape . . . can be traveled comfortably . . . looking at this natural formation . . . and that natural formation . . . the feelings and thoughts . . . the historical markers . . . your curiosity . . . and a very deep recognition . . . of inner capabilities . . . and it's interesting to observe the evolution . . . what the experience of development is like . . . to see a newly born baby . . . and no one really knows *whether* the baby thinks or *what* the baby thinks . . . and to watch an infant discover its own fingers, its own toes . . . to see the amused look on an infant's face . . . when it discovers that it can make a finger wiggle . . . at will . . . and little by little . . . that infant learns . . . this is *my* body . . . and it is separate and distinct from any other part of the world . . . from all other people and places and things . . . and each square inch of your skin . . . is a boundary . . . between your inner world . . . and the outer world . . . and it really isn't possible for you to jump out of your skin . . . you are *self-contained* . . . and it's interesting . . . that there are some people who don't have a home in which to live . . . who believe that the sky is their roof . . . that the earth is their home . . . and then there are others who mark off huge territories, acres of land . . . they clearly mark that it is theirs . . . and each wall . . . keeps something in and keeps something out . . . and there are walls of stone . . . walls of wood . . . steel reinforced walls . . . and there are the walls . . . that you can build for yourself . . . deliberately and happily . . . that are permeable walls . . . the kind that can selectively let things in and let things out . . . and it's that kind of a wall . . . that allows just enough distance from discomfort . . . to be able to drive down a freeway . . . comfortably . . . it is the kind of permeable wall . . . that when someone makes a comment during a conversation . . . that perhaps you can relate to . . . that permits a comfortable distance . . . a protective . . . distance from which to consider each bit of input . . . and you can feel secure that each person's feedback to you will have to check in at your front gate . . . before you decide to let it in or not . . . before you decide whether to react or not . . . and *if* you react . . . to decide *how* you'll react . . . based on what works . . . and feels good at the deepest levels within yourself . . . so, why not have a construction party? . . . and build a pretty wall . . . and a creative wall . . . and I wonder what colors you'll use . . . what materials you'll use . . . and what does the check-in gate look like? . . . and how very much room is there . . . for lots and lots of growth . . . and the walls . . . can always be moved when you so desire . . . they can be built up or built down . . . you can put in peep holes and panoramic windows . . . after all, the walls are yours . . . and all I know is that the ability . . . to walk into an open space . . . has at one level . . . unlimited freedom . . . but at another level . . . where's the structure to guide experience meaningfully? . . . and when I moved into this particular office that I'm in now ... it was a huge space ... I had to draft a plan ... detailing how many walls I wanted ... and where I wanted them ... how many outlets ... and how many doors ... and did I want the doors opening in or opening out ... how many "on" switches and how many "off" switches ... and there's a part of you that knows very well ... that designing uses for space ... is a real art ... and you discovered over time ... that each part of you ... *all* the parts of you ... have some space ... and how you want to use that space ... is certainly a matter of individual design ... and the aesthetics ... of a high wall here, or a low wall there ... more space for this part and less space for that part ... and you can really enjoy ... the incredible clarity ... that comes along ... with increasingly sophisticated designs ... movable and removable walls ... and what a relief to know ... that nothing that you experience need necessarily flow right through all of you ... that you have lots of inner protection ... walls of inner strength ... and you've seen pictures of the Great *Wall* of China ... and you've heard of the Wailing *Wall* ... and you've read about the Berlin *Wall* ... and you know about *Wall* Street ... and maybe you've even heard about *Wall* Drug, South Dakota ... and the natural *wall* of the Rocky Mountains ... the sheer cliff *walls* of La Jolla ... and with all the different possibilities ... your unconscious mind can ... without any real effort on your part ... it can plan ... and build ... and if you were to work for the Border Patrol ... you'd really know about the importance of enforcing and protecting the walls that separate inner from outer ... twenty-four hours a day ... seven days a week ... one really must protect one's borders ... and there are alot of deeper meanings ... that I really know ... you can absorb and use ... a day at a time ... and so take your time ... to process ... to architect ... and then ... when you feel like you want to ... and when you're ready to ... that's when you can re-orient ... and open your eyes when you are ready ....

Multiple sessions were conducted with Molly emphasizing inner awareness, the recognition and acceptance of her own uniqueness, the ability to make choices in her own behalf, and the ability to deal with past traumas so as to permit future growth.

CASE 2: PAIN MANAGEMENT

The client is a woman in her late thirties who suffers chronic pain in her neck and shoulders, a consequence of a car accident in which she was rear-ended while stopped at a red light. She had several neurological evaluations prior to consulting me, and was told that the pain would most likely eventually diminish, though not in the near future. The client is a professional woman who, as a result of her injuries and residual pain, is currently unable to work. She is married, and in all other respects is a high functioning, competent woman. She did not evidence depression or anxiety beyond what would be considered normal for her circumstances. Thus, other than instructing her in the use of dissociative techniques of hypnotic pain management over the course of a few sessions, further therapy was deemed unnecessary. The following transcript was from the fourth of five sessions.

... Okay, Madeline ... Are you comfortable? ... *(Nods)* ... Good ... you can begin by taking in a few deep, relaxing breaths ... and then whenever you're ready ... you can just allow your eyes to close ... so that you can begin now ... to go inside ... to be able to explore within yourself ... find those most comfortable ... thoughts ... and feelings ... that can allow you that very, very relaxed state ... of mind and body ... and you might remember ... that you've experienced trance with me before ... and so I know from at least those experiences ... as well as other trance experiences you've had ... both on your own and with others ... that you know from your own direct experience ... what it's like to breathe comfortably ... and to sit comfortably ... what it's like to get so absorbed in your own thoughts ... that for a little while you forget ... that the rest of the world is going about ... its usual business ... and one of the most soothing, relaxing recognitions ... is that you really don't have to pay attention ... to anything other than what pleases you for the moment ... and the nature of the conscious mind is such ... that it will naturally drift ... from here to there ... and to nowhere in particular ... and wherever your conscious mind drifts to at any moment ... is just fine ... whether you notice the routine sounds of the environment ... or your own thoughts ... or your own reactions to the different things that I say ... or the *changes that take place in your body* ... as your mind drifts ... to the different awarenesses ... and it can be very comforting to know ... that that is the nature of the conscious mind ... it can drift in ... and out ... it can notice and not notice ... it can think and enjoy not having to think ... or having to analyze critically ... and so it can accept easily ... the different possibilities ... and while your conscious mind is certainly capable of processing ... whatever it happens to notice ... the part of you that is infinitely ... more interesting and powerful is your unconscious ... the part of you that can listen ... and respond ... even when your conscious mind drifts elsewhere ... and your own unconscious mind ... has abilities that your conscious mind sometimes forgets about ... and when you're conscious of your unconscious mind's abilities ... and can consciously analyze and access ... the unconscious awareness ... of what your conscious mind knows and doesn't know ... and what's easier to understand consciously than unconsciously ... that's when you can appreciate the comfort of recognizing ... how the mind and the body ... can work so closely together sometimes ... when that's important ... and how other times ... the conscious mind and the unconscious mind ... can drift off elsewhere ... and the mind's greatest ability is the freedom ... to go wherever imagination wills it ... and some people like the freedom of having their minds float through space and through time . . . others like to drift back in time to the comfort . . . of a very special soothing place . . . that's prominent in their memory . . . and is vivid in their senses . . . and the fact that *your mind can drift* off . . . way over there . . . *while your body rests* . . . over here . . . is certainly an interesting experience . . . and sometimes people forget . . . how when their mind is drifting there . . . and their body is resting here . . . that their body can continue . . . to take care of itself . . . the automatic, unconscious . . . self-preserving . . . nature of your body over here . . . can give your mind the comfort over there . . . that allows a comfortable distance . . . that gives you the freedom to simply know how differently . . . you can feel . . . and when your mind drifts . . . that's when it's easy to not notice things that change . . . and I don't know whether you know that your breathing has changed . . . that your pulse rate has changed . . . and what it feels like to have . . . your body somewhere . . . close enough . . . to use if you want it or need it . . . but without impinging on the freedom . . . to float freely and comfortably . . . that light . . . airy feeling . . . and as you experience that interesting sensation . . . it can be *very* interesting to discover . . . how easy it is to forget . . . to notice where your left foot is relative to your right . . . until I draw your attention to it . . . what it feels like to wear a wristwatch on your left wrist . . . it's easy to forget . . . what it feels like . . . to have earrings in your ears . . . or to have the chair supporting your body comfortably . . . and you know and I know . . . that the mind and body . . . are closely related . . . and so are thoughts and feelings . . . and so is past and present . . . but you're also very aware that things change . . . and that awareness offers . . . a buffer . . . a comfort zone . . . that leaves just enough room between the present and the past . . . to make the present of comfort a gift that you can enjoy for months to come . . . and the comfort zone . . . between the present and the future . . . where the present can be just comfortable enough . . . to allow a future of feeling better . . . a day at a time . . . and you know that sometimes . . . people don't understand the relationship between past and present . . . anymore than they understand the relationship . . . between thoughts and feelings . . . but you have a feeling that your thoughts matter . . . and your thoughts about your feelings can allow your feelings some distance . . . a safe, comfortable distance . . . between what you experience now and what you felt then . . . and what you're going to think tomorrow . . . but you'll have to wait until tomorrow . . . for your conscious mind to know . . . what your unconscious has already discovered . . . that it takes far more effort than it's worth . . . to move your hand . . . when it's so much easier . . . you can be so much more comfortable sitting beside yourself so much more comfortably . . . when your mind is there . . . and your body is here . . . and it's just enough distance to be so much more comfortable than you thought you *could* be . . . and you can be very aware . . . of that interesting sensation . . . of being separate from your body . . . and having all of yourself . . . in the experience of deep trance . . . and you know and I know that as distant as your body feels on one level . . . it also feels close enough on another level . . . to be aware of its need to continue to breathe ... in ... and slowly out ... so effortlessly ... and so comfortably ... and as your mind continues to float there ... and your body continues to rest comfortably over here ... your conscious mind can certainly be curious ... about the comfortable sensations of feeling the separation existing ... and you don't really have to analyze too carefully which part of you is the most comfortable at the moment ... you can simply allow yourself instead ... to enjoy the comfort that goes along ... without really being sure ... exactly ... where your fingers are ... or where your hair is ... it can be very soothing to know that you can drift back ... into an awareness of your body when you choose to ... and that for the moment ... you can simply enjoy the choice ... of letting your mind be there ... while *your body rests comfortably* over here ... and I know that doesn't make much sense to your conscious mind ... but fortunately ... even though your conscious mind is very smart ... your unconscious mind is a lot smarter than you are ... and all the learnings of your lifetime ... allow you the *comfortable position now* of being able to drift freely ... far enough away ... yet close enough to your body ... to *be so comfortable* ... in ways your conscious mind is only beginning to discover ... and each time that you listen to this tape or each time that you sit quietly with your eyes closed ... your unconscious mind can add a new and interesting dimension to the experience ... your overall awareness ... of your ability to be as close to or as far away from ... your body as you'd like to be ... and when you recognize ... powerfully within yourself ... how much more control you have than you ever thought possible ... then you can enjoy the feeling of comfort ... that you really can rest comfortably ... and that you really can heal surprisingly quickly ... now that more parts of you have begun some work on the job ... and so, Madeline ... I'd like you to take your time ... and reorient yourself to whatever degree that you wish to ... in order to bring ... yourself out of trance to whatever degree you wish ... and by that, I mean that if you choose to keep your body in trance while you bring your mind out of trance ... I can certainly understand that choice ... or if you choose to bring your body out of trance ... but leave the comfort intact to enjoy the rest of the day ... I can certainly understand that choice ... and whatever choice you make ... I'll certainly be aware ... that when you allow your eyes to open ... you'll be ready to get on with the rest of today in a much more comfortable state of mind and body ... and that will certainly be an eye-opening experience. ...

The suggestion of being able to keep her body comfortably in trance while in a "waking" state was one that Madeline found especially useful. The many suggestions throughout for disorientation and dissociation (mind and body, conscious and unconscious, past and present, and body parts) facilitated a very deep experience of trance that permitted substantial relief from pain during her lengthy recovery.

CASE 3: GOAL (FUTURE) ORIENTATION

The client is a man in his late fifties who has presented the problems of "being stuck" in an unstable "on-again, off-again" relationship that he finds distressing, having high blood pressure, and procrastinating around issues of his career. He presented as "wanting to achieve enough personal growth to be able to move forward with my life." He did not have any specific goals in mind as to what would represent "moving forward." Thus, one goal of treatment was to evolve a sense of direction in his life. During the course of treatment, a trance session was utilized to encourage the development of enough of a sense of the future to compel him to take some decisive courses of action in the present. The client is an educator who claimed to be well acquainted with clinical hypnosis in general and the work of Milton Erickson in particular. This transcript is from the third of a dozen sessions.

> ... Okay, Jerry, you can begin by taking in a few deep, relaxing breaths ...
> and little by little ... you can let the various recollections ... drift through
> your awareness ... of what it's like to be in deep trance ... in a way that's
> pleasing and comfortable ... and it's been quite a while ... since you last
> experienced ... a formal trance process ... with me as guide ... but there was
> a time ... not all that long ago ... when you first became accustomed ... to
> hearing my voice ... get quieter ... to hearing me ... speak in a very slow ...
> deliberate way ... and it was during that initial experience ... when you were
> first beginning to learn something about trance ... and were open to much
> deeper possibilities ... that you allowed yourself to experience ... some of
> the most interesting dimensions ... of doing trancework ... and since quite
> some time from our first trance has elapsed ... and since you've grown in so
> many ways since ... it can certainly be much easier ... to drift into a deeper
> trance ... and a much more comfortable state of mind and body ... moment
> by moment ... and this is one ... very worthwhile opportunity ... to
> rediscover ... your ability ... to drift ... in a way that's useful ... in a way that's
> meaningful ... and I know ... that the various possibilities ... as you explore
> your experiences ... can certainly be most intriguing ... as the various
> possibilities ... allow you to rediscover ... old awarenesses ... that pave the
> way for new awarenesses ... and as the new awarenesses drift ... into your
> consciousness ... that's when it's so easy ... to discover how little attention ...
> is necessary ... to allow all kinds of comfort ... that we can build upon ... in a
> future experience ... of each day ... and I'm aware that your mind is drifting
> ... to nowhere in particular ... that the things that you think about at this
> moment ... are tied ... to past experiences ... and future expectations ...
> and you know and I know ... that so often ... if the seed ... can get planted
> today ... it generates the greatest amount ... of worthwhile ... future
> possibilities ... and as Erickson correctly pointed out ... you can't change the

patient's past . . . you can only change his perspective of it . . . and how much the past relates to your future . . . you'll presently come to know . . . because it's the present that is connected to your past . . . and leads to your future possibilities . . . that you're willing to explore . . . and your presence here . . . confirms that . . . as you make yourself the present . . . of a positive future . . . that wisely incorporates learnings of the past . . . of things that you experience presently . . . and all that talk about past and present and future . . . isn't really meant to disorient you in any way . . . that might be worthwhile . . . but it certainly can help you . . . in seeing the perspective . . . that the impulses of the moment . . . can be looked at differently . . . as you discover . . . that the most worthwhile things to be made . . . you can make on the inside . . . from within . . . in your deep self . . . your deep self . . . and if you think back . . . through the worthwhile things that you've already experienced . . . few of them came easily . . . for the simple reason . . . that whatever you've obtained . . . you've worked for . . . and there were so many times . . . on your way to becoming a teacher . . . that it would have been so much easier . . . to skip class . . . and go play . . . to go to the beach . . . or to go for a run . . . and you certainly would have been justified in doing so . . . but you felt deeply . . . there was something more important to be gained . . . in the name of sacrifice . . . and every self-sacrifice for self-improvement really isn't much of a self-sacrifice . . . because when you think about the relationship between sacrifices and improvements . . . and you improve the sacrifice . . . and you sacrifice more than you improve . . . you really haven't sacrificed . . . you've just improved . . . and gone a step further . . . and the questions from within . . . that generate the momentum to grow . . . and experience . . . is a *dwindling internal pressure* . . . that each experience can comfort . . . each new opportunity . . . for growth . . . can be recognized for what is . . . and there's been so much that you've learned over time . . . so many ways that you've changed . . . and as each change equalizes the pressures outside . . . by responding deeply to the appropriate demands from inside . . . you've become so skilled . . . and the results have shown . . . and you can have a very powerful impact . . . when you allow yourself . . . to release . . . maybe to teach . . . in a sharing way . . . what you already know . . . and going to school is only one way . . . to evolve . . . and change . . . in a self-sacrificing way . . . that leads to a greater sense of self . . . than anything you've experienced before . . . and all through your past . . . there was self-sacrificing . . . that had an aura . . . of taking care of yourself . . . beneath them . . . and when one becomes a parent . . . it's apparent . . . that the selflessness of parenthood . . . is the shiny surface . . . of a selfish decision . . . to have children . . . that one hopes will reflect one's self . . . with pride . . . and accomplishment . . . and the debate about the selfish nature of the selfish decision to have children . . . continues . . . and the sacrifice . . . of a loving relationship . . . that gives you what you want . . . and you know what it means to give . . . in order to get . . . and whatever you may have to openly give . . . grows . . . easily . . . and as you understand more and more deeply within . . . that giving to get . . . is the greatest way . . . to *build a solid relationship* . . . especially with yourself . . . especially . . . with yourself . . . and so . . . why not . . . selfishly and selflessly . . . sacrifice a little bit of time each day . . . to give to yourself . . . in order to get from yourself . . . a much more comfortable . . . and *much less pressured* . . . way of doing things . . . a much less pressured . . . way of circulating blood . . . in a body that's so healthy . . . with comfort . . . and the ability to relax deeply . . . and you know from the people that you work with . . . that you can pretend that they're not listening . . . but you know that their unconscious mind is . . . and they can pretend they're not listening . . . but don't you be fooled by it . . . because there's a part of each person . . . no matter how educated or otherwise . . . that has the ability to learn . . . and to grow . . . and to change . . . and someone can work hard at staying the same . . . but you know and I know that change is inevitable . . . and so don't you be fooled by it . . . and I'm going to be silent for a minute . . . as you explore within yourself . . . the thoughts and feelings . . . that pass through your awareness . . . that become significant for you in ways that your conscious mind has yet to discover . . . and when I again speak to you in a minute . . . my voice can just relax you even more deeply . . . and the minute of silence begins . . . now . . . (one minute of silence) . . . that's right . . . you can just continue to relax . . . to continue to be at ease and resting comfortably . . . and you've allowed me to be aware . . . of the multiple purposes of our session . . . learning opportunities and personal growth opportunities . . . professional growth . . . and meaningful experiences . . . and I wonder how much you'll be able to discover . . . from these trance experiences . . . as you notice the different ideas and the different perspectives . . . and you can enjoy knowing . . . that each trance process . . . will have a different effect . . . and generate a different pattern . . . in ways that your unconscious mind . . . can allow . . . while your conscious mind looks forward . . . to discovering . . . the range of possibilities . . . a day at a time . . . and so, take what ever time you'd like to . . . to process your thoughts . . . the different dimensions of your experience . . . and to think about your expectations . . . and which learnings will be most appropriate to utilize . . . this week . . . and which learnings can wait until next week . . . and then, whenever you're ready . . . you can begin to re-orient yourself to here and now . . . this room and this place . . . and whenever you'd like to . . . you can slowly move to re-orient yourself . . . and then you can allow your eyes to open . . .

The client reflected on the basic truth that anything he had of value, he worked hard for. He was easily able to recall what seemed like a sacrifice at the time when he was in school taking classes while others were out enjoying recreational activities. The session motivated him to confront the aimlessness in each of the areas of his life, and led to later sessions addressing issues of goal-setting, setting aside immediate gratification while striving for worthwhile future possibilities, and being more responsive ("giving to get") in his relationship.

CASE 4: ADAPTABILITY

The following transcript represents a trance session that was conducted with a psychologist in his mid-fifties attending one of my hypnosis training courses. While he found the concepts and techniques of hypnosis highly illuminating as a model for better understanding subjective experience relative to psychotherapy, he was having difficulty shifting his perspectives from his previous psychodynamic methods. He asked to have a trance session to help him better assimilate the new learnings and to evolve greater flexibility in his treatment approaches. This session was done before the other class members in a context defined more as educational than clinical. It was the first and only time I worked individually with this man.

... Ben, you can arrange yourself in the most comfortable of positions ... and then a little at a time ... you can orient yourself to the possibility ... of being very relaxed ... very comfortable ... very much at ease within yourself ... and I know that it was Ernest Hilgard ... who formulated the idea ... that a person's ability to be hypnotized ... to go into deep trance ... was a fixed characteristic ... one that really wouldn't change much over time ... and I wonder whether you're discovering ... a good and satisfying basis for disagreeing with Hilgard ... perhaps discovering that people *can* go into deeper trances ... reaching deeper levels more quickly ... through practice ... through experience ... and you may be interested in knowing ... just how *deeply into trance* you can go ... or just how quickly you can reach ... a very comfortable level ... within yourself ... it really doesn't matter much ... whether you focus on depth ... or speed ... or Hilgard ... or yourself ... all that really matters ... is the enjoyment that goes along ... with discovering that at all levels within yourself ... that you really can *be comfortable* ... and I know that it's important to you to have your mind be active ... to think and to analyze ... and to always be oriented ... to as much as what's going on around you as you can ... that's the pattern ... that you've evolved through a lifetime of learning ... and you know and I know ... as mental health professionals ... that sometimes people are the masters of what they learn ... and other times ... people are the victims of what they learn ... and each time that you take time to learn something new ... you have a chance ... to integrate it with what you already know ... deeply ... and I don't know how much you know ... about what you know ... about what Milton Erickson knew ... about what he knows ... and how people know what they know ... and don't know about what they don't know ... and a famous humorist once said ... it's not what you don't know ... that's the problem ... it's what you know that ain't so ... and Milton Erickson ... a gentlemen that you're by now familiar with ... didn't really believe in formal theories of personality ... Milton wouldn't be the one to describe your patterns as ... obsessive or compulsive ... he wouldn't be the one to label a person with a particular

name ... and yet ... some people insist on doing exactly that ... and I
worked in a hospital long enough ... to know ... that doctors will say ...
how's the broken leg in room 210? ... how's the manic in room 325? ...
where's the depressive in room 104? ... and if no one has a name anymore ...
no one is a person ... just a label ... and it was Erickson's belief system ... and
I wonder just what you think ... deeply ... in reaction to Erickson's observation ... that while your unconscious mind has ... ample resources that can
be used to help facilitate changes ... in yourself and in others ... it's the
learned limitations ... the learned limitations ... that reinforce what Erickson referred to as rigidity ... of patterned behavior ... that a person learns a
certain sequence ... a certain style ... a certain response pattern ... and then
that's what he does over and over again ... in a very rigid sort of way ... and
when you suggest a deviation from that pattern ... you may get resistance ...
and when you suggest that someone step outside ... the boundaries of his
patterns ... you may get resistance ... and it isn't until someone breaks his
own pattern ... by responding to the same old situation ... in a new way ...
that the most meaningful changes occur ... and there are rigid thought
patterns ... rigid emotional patterns ... rigid behavioral patterns ... rigid
social patterns ... rigid therapy patterns ... dynamically speaking ... stereotyped responses in specific situations ... and why not step outside ... the
usual boundaries ... why not demand a new response from yourself in an
old situation ... why not do something differently ... and enjoy the new
results ... and enjoy discovering ... that you really can *be flexible* enough ...
to *respond differently* ... in ways that are only first being discovered ... by your
conscious mind ... and I wonder how many new things you can do today ...
and how many out of character responses you can generate today ... and can
you be flexible enough ... to respond differently ... and when your usual
level of tension gives way to the deep relaxation you have now ... that's a
change in pattern ... and when discomfort becomes comfort ... that's a
change, also ... and little by little ... you're beginning to discover ... new
possibilities in old situations ... in ways that can feel so good ... on all levels
... and why not ... allow yourself ... a different response ... in that situation
where it would be most helpful ... and least restrictive ... opening the door
to new possibilities ... and closing the door ... on outdated learnings ... a
day at a time ... and so take your time ... process the part of my message that
your conscious mind can understand ... safely ... and pretend that there
aren't any deeper meanings ... for your unconscious to learn ... and then
when you feel like you're ready to ... and want to re-orient to here and now
... you can begin that process ... of bringing yourself ... to a different level
of responses ... and when you're ready to ... you can just allow your eyes to
open. ...

After the trance process, the demonstration subject reported being
aware of an important reframing that had taken place for him during the
session. He claimed he had not thought of his therapy approaches as

rigid—he had simply thought of them as "proper procedure." In hearing his patterns described as "stereotyped responses" and the idea that growth comes from "stepping outside the usual boundaries," he reported feeling a freedom to experiment he had not previously felt. Over the course of the remaining days in the course, he commented several times on the "liberating effect of having more ways to conduct therapy."

CASE 5: WEIGHT MANAGEMENT

The client is a woman in her early forties, employed as a computer programmer, who presented the concern of wanting to maintain the weight loss she had succeeded in obtaining through a program she participated in. She had been able to gain control over all of her dysfunctional eating habits, with the exception of snacking on bread, particularly French sourdough baguettes. She wanted to be able to develop moderation in her bread intake, much as she had with the other foods in her diet. She is a woman who values logic, and has a long history of being fairly dissociated from her feelings. This transcript represents the second of three sessions.

> . . . All right Gerda, . . . you can take in a few deep, relaxing breaths . . . and orient yourself now to inner experience for a while . . . somewhere . . . a little deeper than rationality . . . somewhere beneath . . . logic . . . somewhere to the right of your left brain . . . somewhere above . . . everyday living . . . and when you're above and below . . . the right of things that are left . . . then every direction provides a new opportunity or deeper sense . . . of comfort . . . and for a very long time . . . you've had many experiences of being able to think rationally . . . to relate at a deeper level . . . to the logic of computers . . . the sequencing of programs . . . all exercises . . . for the intellect . . . but you know and I know . . . that the true balance of things . . . rests . . . on continuous movements . . . continuous minor adjustments . . . in daily experiences . . . that move us from balance to imbalance . . . back to balance . . . hoping and adjusting . . . and all of that . . . about *imbalance is very heavy* . . . and *balance is light* . . . red light . . . blue light . . . white light . . . light feelings . . . light beer . . . light air . . . light thoughts . . . and what makes something that's heavier than air . . . float . . . . and which part of your body is lighter? . . . left side . . . or right side . . . top half . . . or bottom half . . . the front of your back . . . the back of your front . . . you really don't know . . . but when you experience . . . the kind of uplifting experience . . . that really raises your awareness . . . for how distant one part of you can seem . . . while another part seems to float . . . right in front of you . . . and if thoughts are over here . . . and feelings are over there . . . then you might . . . be oriented to a disorienting experience . . . and whether it's temporal disorientation or physical disorientation . . . being

oriented to how disoriented your body can be ... then you're oriented to thought ... and have you noticed how disoriented your thoughts can be when *you're so oriented to your body* ... and it can seem so close and yet so far ... and you can think you understand and that you know what you hear ... but if you don't know what you hear when you're here then maybe you know what is there ... and when you play ... that light ... carefree feeling returns ... and your thoughts can smile ... and what a sensation when your body giggles ... and which part ... experiences humor? and what about ... being disoriented to the usual cues ... the usual patterns ... that you'd really like to *scale down* ... and *lightening up* allows for that possibility ... and remember once I described that the ocean has the ability to maintain itself ... and at a much deeper level ... your unconscious is learning nature's way of maintaining a body ... of water ... and how much of the body is water? ... and you know when there's chemistry ... which molecule ... and which atoms ... have a natural attraction ... and what is the chemical makeup ... of sourdough bread in comparison to rye? ... and when they bag it (baguette) ... to take it home ... any change in your deeper structure provides an interesting opportunity for growth ... and that's an awful lot to digest ... in one sitting ... but when the conscious mind is overloaded ... that's when the unconscious gets to enjoy the spotlight for a while ... and that's when it can really shine ... and I don't know if anybody really knows why that's true ... all I know is ... you have a conscious mind ... that's very smart ... and an unconscious mind ... that's even smarter ... and I remember ... a colleague of mine named Jeff Zeig telling me once ... that Erickson told him once ... that variety ... is the spice ... of life ... but he said it a little differently ... he sat Jeff down ... and he said that each person enjoys meals differently ... some really enjoy seven course dinners ... and which course is the right first course? ... some enjoy soup ... followed by salad ... some prefer it the other way around ... and one might enjoy ... something to cleanse their palate with ... and which side dish goes with which main dish? ... and I knew one individual who enjoyed dessert first ... which I thought was a very heavy decision to make ... but with each person there are differences ... and Erickson droned on and on describing ... how many different ways there are to *eat in a way that's healthy and satisfying* ... he finally led to the conclusion that if man cannot live by bread alone ... then a woman probably shouldn't either ... and when Jeff was working too hard ... Erickson reminded him ... there's more to life than protein ... and how does an unconscious mind understand deeper messages? ... and translate them into *subtle changes that really feel good* ... well, let your conscious mind chew on that for a while ... and if you ever have the experience of being crusty and discovering yourself taking it too seriously ... there will come an opportunity to remind yourself ... that when you don't understand why you do what you do ... that's the time for the services of a good trance-later ... or perhaps a trance now ... I don't know which ... but I do know ... that it could be the feeling ... of amusement guiding you ... it doesn't detract from the significance of what you've learned ... it can be the lingering feeling ... long after ... of feeling good about what you've done ...

and whether you'll remember that ... consciously or unconsciously ... or both ... you really won't know ... until you re-orient in a moment ... and find your eyes opening ... to discover what you know ... that's different ... take your time ... before you have that eye-opening experience....

The client's response to the confusional suggestions was an amused detachment that highlighted to her how impactful things on a nonrational level could be. Given her usual emphasis on logic, a pattern which did not assist her in losing weight or keeping it off, she found it meaningful to discover how subjective and malleable her experiences really are. She made frequent use of the tape of this session that was given to her, and found the phrase that woman "cannot live by bread alone" coming back to her in a lighthearted way when passing by the bakery where she normally stopped and bought bread. The use of humor in the session associated a positive emotional tone to the content of the session. As with all patterns, humor must be used selectively.

CASE 6: STRESS MANAGEMENT

The client is a man in his mid-thirties who presented the problem of "too many things raining down on me to cope with." His job as an administrator in a construction company was undergoing a major shift in responsibilities, his first child (age four) was suffering health problems, and his wife was pregnant with their third child. He felt as though every domain of his life was unsettled and a source of stress, and wanted to learn to manage stress more effectively in order to prevent any debilitating effects. He shared his fantasy of escaping to a Caribbean island, and wished there was a way to prevent stressful events from happening in his life. The following transcript represents a trance process done in the first of seven sessions.

... Alright Ken, you can begin by taking in a few, deep relaxing breaths ... and you can begin now to orient yourself ... to the possibility of feeling ... very comfortable ... and very relaxed ... and little by little as the world goes on around you ... why not make yourself really comfortable ... of course the more absorbed you get ... in your own inner experience ... the less it really matters what's going on in the world around you ... everybody needs a little bit of time away ... a little bit of a break ... to turn their attention in a different direction ... and one of my favorite television shows is M*A*S*H ... and I don't know if you're a fan of that show or not ... but it will happen from time to time ... that the M*A*S*H hospital ... will be shelled by the enemy ... and numerous explosions take place ... as the shells rain down ...

and everyone runs around scared and overwhelmed . . . unsure if they'll be able to survive . . . and you can imagine . . . how fighting for your life . . . can be a very serious battle . . . and then what always happens at some point along the way . . . is that the shelling stops . . . and someone will offer the comment . . . to *listen to the silence* . . . (pause) . . . and in living life each day . . . the shelling takes a lot of different forms . . . the shelling can be hassles with other people . . . concerns about the environment . . . doubts with one's self about what one should do . . . the battles can be inside . . . they can be outside . . . they can be brief . . . they can be tolerable . . . they can be inspirational . . . they can cause growth . . . they can foster creativity in finding ways to see beyond the moment . . . but there come quiet times . . . times when all the hoopla is over . . . when the noise stops . . . when your thoughts slow down . . . and when nothing really seems to matter very much . . . and it's those quiet times that prepare you so well . . . for the times that aren't so quiet . . . the few seconds that can feel like a lot longer period of quiet . . . they restore comfort . . . and balance . . . that strengthen you . . . for any . . . and all future occasions . . . where patience and understanding . . . might work quite well . . . and right now you're in one of those periods of silence . . . and the world is so unpredictable . . . it's hard to know . . . whether things will still be quiet . . . next week . . . next month . . . next year . . . and it really doesn't matter . . . all that really matters . . . is how you use your quiet period now . . . whether you use the time to strengthen yourself . . . and pamper yourself . . . to congratulate yourself . . . and to appreciate your ability to grow and do much more than just survive . . . and for a while when I was much younger . . . I had the experience of living on the island of Jamaica . . . I lived in a very small village . . . on the west end of the island . . . where very few Americans actually go . . . and nobody there knew how to read . . . nobody knew how to write . . . nobody was informed about world events . . . the Jamaicans were shocked and disbelieving . . . when I described to them how Americans had put men on the moon . . . and brought them back safely again . . . and despite their ignorance . . . there was a certain satisfaction . . . in understanding the island on which they lived . . . where most of the time the sky is so clear and blue . . . but as is typical of the tropics . . . every once in a while . . . huge clouds would roll in . . . and there would be heavy rain and thunder and lightning . . . and then the clouds would roll out again . . . and at first I found it very unsettling . . . that unexpectedly . . . my enjoyment of the sunshine . . . could be interrupted at any moment . . . and obviously, I had no control . . . over thunder . . . and rain . . . and you learn very quickly . . . that the loudness . . . can be so well appreciated by the counter balance of quiet . . . and that it's the loudness . . . that makes the rain forest come alive . . . and allows the growth to take place . . . and sometimes it's inconvenient . . . sometimes it seems unnecessary . . . but the fact of the matter . . . is that the darkness of rain . . . leads to the lush vegetation's growth . . . that permits the pleasure . . . and all things are balanced . . . and how good it feels for you to be settled comfortably . . . and how well it prepares you for periods of being unsettled . . . just as periods of being unsettled . . . allow you to really appreciate . . . settled, comfortable times ... like now ... and why not enjoy ... quiet times ... and appreciate what they have to offer ... and why not accept the inevitable ... that rain falls ... and people change ... and things get better ... a day at a time ... as you grow more tolerant ... and enjoy greater periods of comfort and stability ... it can grow easier and easier ... to move flexibly and fluidly ... through the rain and through the shine ... whether you're in Jamaica or San Diego ... Europe or Africa ... the sunshine on the inside ... makes it easy to deal with the rain on the outside ... and someone once said ... no news is good news ... but you'll have to make your mind up about that for yourself ... and taking the time to enjoy feelings of comfort ... to enjoy the quiet inside ... how good it feels ... to know ... that the shelling has stopped ... and experiencing the comfort ... is certainly a privilege ... and so why not carry it with you everywhere ... everywhere that comfort is permitted ... and share some of it and keep some of it ... let some go ... hold on to some ... and as you begin the process of reorienting yourself ... bring just enough back with you ... to enjoy the quiet ... and then when you feel like you're ready to ... you can quietly open your eyes. ...

The client found the trance process "a good break" from the routine pressures he faced, and found it interesting that I would reference M*A*S*H, which is one of his favorite programs. He thought of Hawkeye in particular, and how he uses humor to stay sane in an insane situation. He decided that he would act similarly, and gave himself the assignment of making a point of telling jokes to people as a way of easing tense situations. He thought that approach to be a positive stress management tool in addition to the self-hypnosis he was taught, and related it further to things he had read about humor and healing. Subsequent sessions involved addressing specific problems needing his attention.

CONCLUSION

Each of the six trance-scripts included in this chapter was provided for the general purpose of illustrating what forms a trance process might take. You may have noticed how each session was constructed according to characteristics of the individual client being treated. It is precisely for this reason that these transcripts are not likely to be useful to anyone else, even with a similar problem, without considerable retailoring. Thus, the inability to standardize utilization approach interventions should be more readily apparent to you. Hopefully, though, your creativity is stimulated by thinking about what you might have said and done differently in working with such clients. There are lots of right ways to do trancework, and it's the result you get that lets you know whether you were on the right track or not. An interesting or elaborate trance process does not mean much if it doesn't facilitate the desired responses.

For Discussion

1. Do you think it would be useful to have a book of prepared scripts to use for specific client problems? Why or why not?

2. What do you think about the idea of common themes of human experience relative to therapy interventions?

3. Do you like learning from others' experiences? What limits, if any, are you aware of in employing metaphors as a teaching tool?

Things to Do

1. For each trance-script, identify the stages of induction, deepening, utilization, and disengagement. Do you see clear dividing lines between stages?

2. Identify the suggestion structures and styles in each of the trance processes.

3. Find the places where metaphors, confusion, ambiguity, puns, and other such mechanisms are employed. How are they introduced and utilized?

4. Identify and list the most common (repetitive) themes you encounter in the client problems you encounter. What themes of therapy can you identify as relevant to treatment?

20

The Case of Vicki: Hypnosis for Coping with Terminal Cancer

This chapter* presents the verbatim transcript of a single-session intervention with a 42-year-old woman named Vicki. Analysis and commentary are provided in order to show more clearly how deliberate a "spontaneous" treatment can be.

BACKGROUND OF THE SESSION

Vicki was referred to me for a single hypnosis session by her co-therapists, Lillian and Harold. She had been in treatment with them over the course of several years and, as you will see, benefited greatly from her work with them. She had gone from apparent emotional instability with no real focus in life to becoming a highly successful graduate student pursuing an eventual career in counseling. Her new life plan came to a screeching halt, however, when she was formally diagnosed as having advanced-stage cancer throughout her body, with a very short time to live.

Lillian and Harold, associates from a mutual university affiliation, referred Vicki to me for a hypnosis session with the hope that hypnosis might be useful in helping her manage the emotional shock and the physical discomfort associated with her terminal condition. Lillian was the one who contacted me and asked if I could see Vicki. As it so happened, I was unable to see her in the immediate future because of having overscheduled

*A two-hour videotape of this session, entitled *The Case of Vicki: Patterns of Trancework,* is available through Brunner/Mazel Publishers, 19 Union Square West, New York, NY 10003, (212) 924-3344.

myself. I volunteered, however, that I would be able to do a session with her if she was willing to do it in the context of an advanced hypnosis course I was teaching. Lillian's immediate reaction was a positive one; she believed that the opportunity for Vicki to work some things out in a group context would be of great benefit to her.

As is typical for me when I am referred a new client, I prefer not to hear the diagnostic impression of the person making the referral. I much prefer to arrive at my own diagnostic impressions without the influence of someone else's judgment. Thus, when Lillian began to describe Vicki, I asked her to share only minimal information about her, specifically the goals associated with the referral. When I see someone more than once, I am then likely to call the referring clinician after the first session and ask for whatever data she may have on the client.

So, at the outset of the session, I knew only Vicki's name, her general goal of wanting to cope as well as possible with truly tragic circumstances, and the fact that she was held in high regard by Lillian and Harold. When I called Vicki to suggest a time and describe the context in which we could meet, she unhesitatingly agreed. No further discussion took place during that phone contact.

CONTEXT OF THE SESSION

The session was held in my group training room the day after I called Vicki to set up the appointment. She had been expecting my call and was highly responsive to my invitation to conduct the session before a group of psychotherapists learning to utilize hypnosis. In fact, there were 10 individuals who observed the session, all of whom were instructed to be silent observers so as to not interrupt the natural flow of the session.

Vicki arrived on time (after lunch) for the session and was seated in a chair opposite me. I had asked Lillian and Harold not to say much about what she could expect in working with me, but as it turns out, she had already heard of me from other sources. Her expectations for the session were clearly positive, and it evidently helped her when I defined the context as more of an educational one than a clinical one.

The transcript of this session, both the interview and the intervention, is unedited, preserving its integrity. You may wish to read the verbatim transcript in entirety first, and then read it a second time with reference to the analysis and commentary. Some final comments are provided immediately following the session transcript.

THE CASE OF VICKI:
TRANSCRIPT, COMMENTARY, AND ANALYSIS

Verbatim Transcript   **Commentary and Analysis**

The Interview

V: My greatest concern at the moment is, because I know that I have a very short time to live that I don't want to spend it being zonked out on drugs. And, so I would like to have some way of coping with the pain without being... I'm not afraid of becoming an addict. I can live being an addict, I suppose, but I don't want to miss the time that I have left. I would like to have ... my interest is in being able to alleviate pain without drugs.

M: I really know very little about what's going on with you and in your life right now. Can you give me a little bit of background?

V: I have cancer that is, they don't even know where the primary is, but it's throughout my body. I have it in the brain, in the bone, in the lung, in the adrenal glands, in the lymph system—everywhere. And they say —my doctor says "I'll be surprised if you don't live a month. I'll be astounded if you live a year and we think we're talking 3 to 4 months." And I'm okay with that... I'm not— the death part is not the hard part. The hard part is being able to get done all that I want to get done in the time that I have left, and make

Vicki's beginning remarks orient me to her goal of managing her condition naturalistically. Notice her immediate emphasis on the issue of "time," a dominant theme which becomes a core dimension of the trance session.

Vicki's time frame has been established by the physician giving her the prognosis. She speaks in terms of "parts," distinguishing one part of her experience from another. This is a clue that she will be able to benefit from an approach that emphasizes dissociation, since she is sure that everybody's dealing with it which is the second hardest part. My family wants to stick their head in the sand and they don't want to deal with it and I keep saying "You have to because you don't—I don't have time to wait for you and do it your own way. You have to do it my way now, you know." So time is the thing and being drugged and they want right away to put you on very heavy drugs and I'm very sensitive to drugs and it just makes me sleep which I don't want to sleep my time away, you know. I have a lot of things to say and a lot of things to do and I want to be able to do those things in the time that I have.

already used to thinking in terms of "part of me is experiencing this while part of me is experiencing that." Further interviewing will permit me the opportunity to determine just how adept at dissociation she really is. The issue of "time" is reiterated as she introduces the "power struggle" she experiences with her family.

M: How long ago were you diagnosed, Vicki?

V: Three weeks ago.

M: Okay.

Vicki lets me know she wants to be active during this time, saying and doing the things she feels are necessary.

V: Anger's another thing that I wish I had time to deal with because I have a lot of anger because I've been going to doctors for 4 years, saying I'm sick, I'm very sick, I'm sick, and they say "No, you're a hypochondriac. You just think you're sick. You're making yourself—" all these things and even doctors that refused to examine me. And I have a lot of anger at doctors because if I had been diagnosed, if they would have listened to me as I was listening to my body tell me that I was sick it would have been a different trip. So I have

Vicki acknowledges she has angry feelings, but indicates she does not have the time to deal with her feelings—a realistic choice to make given the shortage of time.

a lot of anger at doctors that, but I finally decided that I just don't have time to deal with that so I'm going to skip that part.

M: You're saying that you presented physical complaints to doctors, and basically they ignored it?

V: Yeah, I could tell you a lot of horror stories about that but, you know, even doctors that just refused to examine me, which at that point, my idea was even hypochondriacs get sick! I at least deserve an examination and was told "No." I mean a lot of really bad ... Even 7 months ago, I went so far as to have a biopsy done and the doctor missed it, because he was going on vacation that day and he was in a hurry and he was ... You know all these just really coincidental things kind of things that—you can't really put—I mean everything has its explanation but the whole thing makes a real ugly package, you know. So a lot of anger there that I'm just kind of trying not to—I'm just saying that I don't have time. You have to prioritize and you have to say what's really important and getting my family okay with this and getting my affairs in order and dealing with it spiritually and physically is more important than kicking butts.

M: Can you tell me a little bit about your family and what the family situation is right now?

Vicki states clearly that she is able to dissociate from her angry feelings out of necessity. This needs to be acknowledged, but it is not yet known whether she is truly able to dissociate her feelings to the extent she claims.

Further acknowledgement of angry feelings she attempts to dissociate from. She also shows an ability to prioritize and sequence her involvements, evidence of a more concrete and linear style of thinking—important diagnostic information for the construction of an appropriate trance session.

Information is sought regarding her support network and associated relationship issues.

V: I'm in the process of divorce which is being a real complication for me because my husband has decided that, well he's figured out that—we were very close to making a financial agreement—we haven't lived together for 5 years and he has another family—and we were very close to coming to a financial agreement which was substantial but he's figured out now that if he prolongs, he gets it all. So he's decided that he's not going to participate in any way financially and that he's just going to drag it off and ... That was a real shock, that was a real shock for me because I think if he would have called me and had been—this is the hard part *(becomes tearful)*—I would have helped him and he won't help me but that's only financial consideration, puts me in a financial bind because I'm not eligible for aid because I'm married and his income is considered, but he won't give me any of it, so I'm stuck. He thinks I should go to Balboa Hospital and the one thing I don't want is to spend the rest of my life sitting in a waiting room at Balboa Hospital, that's the one thing I don't want to do. So that part of my family is not, the rest of my family is very supportive. I have a lot of very supportive friends and I have a daughter that's 23 and she wants to run and hide and I'm not letting her and it's being difficult for her and that, she's probably my num-

Vicki identifies her husband as a source of distress.

ber 1 concern. Just a lot of friends that are being real supportive and that helps a lot. I'm amazed at how many people are—I think that is a really amazing thing to learn how many people go away and how many —the ones who go away and the ones that stay. A lot of people that I grew up with, I grew up with kind of a large gang of people; we all ran around together for years in San Diego and I was the youngest of the group and it's being real hard for them because it's, all of a sudden their own vulnerabilities are coming through and they're having to deal with feelings of their own that are making it difficult for them. There's a lot to deal with.

M: Are they talking with you about those things?

V: The hardest thing—everybody reacts different and—a few years ago I lived in Colorado and my family called me and said my uncle who I was very close to was dying of cancer and if I wanted to see him I should come and I did. And when I got here they said "Now, we don't talk about it to him." And I went along with that because it was my family's wish and all the while that he died, he never mentioned to them that he was dying and they never mentioned to him and everybody, I mean it was so stupid and when I got back to Colorado I thought the worst thing

Vicki identifies her daughter as a source of distress.

that I did was not to sit down with him and say "You want to talk about it?" So I did a lot of thinking at that time about it and now, to me, I have to talk about it and some people find that really difficult to deal with. It's just the way that I have to do it. I have to. And the more that I do it, the more okay I feel and not only that but the more I do it, the more I know that other people are okay and if other people are okay, I feel better. So it has kind of a circular benefit for me. It's scary to some people, like my daughter is not a very verbal person and she wants to stick her head in the sand and it's real hard for me to get through to her. We're managing to do it, but it's hard.

M: What would you want her to know? What would you want her to understand?

V: Something really—like a miracle happened the other day because when she first found out, she took off and went to Mexico and really running. I keep sitting her down saying "This is serious. You can't run away. We don't have time to play games. You have to, we have to deal with it." "Well, what do you want me to do, what do you want from me?" She's really confused about it and, for some reason I'm able to get across to other people what my needs are, but I can't to her because she's so afraid. And the other day she got back from Mexico and she was at my

Vicki makes it perfectly clear that she wants to and *needs* to talk about her situation. Thus, the pace of the interaction will be tailored to her need, respecting its value to her.

house and she was sitting on the bed and she was giving me this "what do you want from me?" and "I don't know what you want from me" and I just, I didn't know what to say and in popped one of her friends that she'd had ever since she was real little, popped in the door and ran in the bedroom and plopped down on the bed and said "My God. Tell me what it's like to know you're going to die." You know , my daughter's sitting there and this is her friend and ... So Linne and I started to talk and I started to tell her, and then she'd say "And then what does it feel like? Does it hurt?" Just asking this whole, the kind of questions that you don't know how to ask and here's this kid sitting there asking and my daughter kind of curled up on the pillows and was a little mouse and said ... We asked, we went on for about 2 hours, and we asked her, no participation at all, she was like the mouse in the room. We talked about her like she wasn't there and Linne said "What's your greatest fear?" and I said that my greatest fear is that I won't be able to sit and talk to her the way, or talk to Carrie the way I can talk to you. Still there was nothing required of her at all. But things changed after that, things changed. You know, it was like all of a sudden she had at least some understanding of what my needs were and how communication can work beneficially and openness is necessary as I don't

A good example from her life of the value of indirect communication. As in couples or family therapy, talking to person A in the presence of person B influences B despite the lack of direct interaction.

have time to play games. Everybody keeps saying to me "You have to let her accept it in her own way, in her own time." And I was saying "That's fine. I've known that for years." And everything we come across, in your own time and in your own way you will accept. Right now, I don't have time so I have to push and maybe I'll push too hard and it'll hurt her more than help her but I have to take that chance because I don't have the time. So it's . . .

M: Do you have the sense that there are things that you want to say to her and she to you?

V: My biggest fear is that 5 years down the road she's not going to be able to deal with it because she's going to say "I stuck my head in the sand and I should have sat down and talked." It's more urgent for her than for me. I don't have trouble verbalizing; I say what I feel and what I think and I don't feel . . . There's a lot of things I feel like I want to say, you know, "Put your seat belt on" and stuff, but things that I would like to share, family things, but the urgency in my mind is in her ability to deal with it herself after it's over; that she can say we spent quality time, that we did the best we could do for each other in whatever time we had, that she doesn't feel guilty, and that she doesn't have this after thing that's going to make it harder for her to facilitate the rest of her life.

Time is reiterated as a vital issue.

Vicki shows an ability to have foresight that is of an immediate and realistic quality.

M: So when you were talking earlier about family members sticking their head in the sand, were you referring specifically to her or others as well?

V: Her father—my first—my husband that I'm trying to get a divorce from, I've been married 15 years— her father I was married to years ago and we've been really close friends all these years and he was at the hospital when they did the diagnosis and he took off and hasn't been seen since. I mean, he's the one that taught her how to do this. And he's not dealing with it, and that's okay. I'm not really too concerned with him. Another one that I'm really concerned with is my mother. My mother's 69 and, but really she's 99. I take care of her totally and so, and I think in my mind the hardest thing in the world to do would be to lose a child. I've never been close to my mother, my mother and I have never been close. And we're becoming that now. She's trying very hard to understand my philosophies which—she's never listened to me and now she's listening and she'll get my philosophy books and she'll bring them and want me to read to her and she asks me questions and she talks to me. I think that's a neat thing that's happening. I feel much closer to her. I have a son, this is another sad part, I have a son that is in trouble and my husband has turned him against me and he hates me. That

Vicki identifies her mother as a source of distress.

Vicki emphasizes how she values being listened to, a dominant theme throughout her presentation.

Vicki identifies her estranged son as a source of distress.

hurts me a lot. I expect probably not to see him again and if I did see him again I think it would be a difficult time. He's a strange boy and he would come to me and he would say "I love you," and a lot of things that he doesn't feel. He's not bonded to me very much and he, you know, I do better, I do better with people that put it out just the way it is: "I don't feel very close to you but I wish I'd had a chance to get to know you," or something like that, rather than "I love you and I can't stand losing you" and all the stuff that's just crap, you know. I don't want any crap. If I do get a chance to see him again I think that that's going to be very difficult to deal with. He doesn't have the emotional—he's a very immature, emotionally immature person who just needs a lot of, lot of time to get it together. So I don't, I really—that's a hard one and I don't know what's going to happen with that. I have an aunt that doesn't speak to me, that ... My family were taught, my mother and all of my family were taught when they were very young that when you got angry at someone you quit talking to them. I don't know who ever thought that one up but I guess years ago that was the way that you dealt with a lot of things.

M: Instead of talking it out and working it through.

V: You don't talk at all. I mean if you, if I don't like the way, something you

Vicki has an aunt who is a source of distress, who embodies the "if you're angry, clam up" approach that Vicki feels is a waste of valuable communication time. By now, it is clear that Vicki has few, if any, conflict-free relationships; thus, relationships as a focal point for hypnotically building comfort would seem an unlikely path.

said to me today, just something you said to me, I might stop talking to you for 5 years. I mean that's the way they do it. And my aunt hasn't spoken to me for about 9 months because of one day I said something that she didn't like. It's so ridiculous I can't believe it. Now, she's frantic, she's panicky. She won't come to me and talk to me; she won't make an overt gesture to me. But she like sends me cookies under the counter. I send them back and my mother says that I'm being really ugly and not understanding and I am, I suppose, but I think that if I accept the cookies under the table, that's all I'll ever get. I think for both of us it's important that she comes. I think she has something to learn if she would come and talk to me and so I won't take the cookies. She's really panicky. I've decided that I'm not going to die and leave her with her guilt but I'm not going to just take the cookies either. I'm going to play it out a little bit. There's a streak in me.

M: What do you expect to happen? That she will come see you?

V: I don't know. Either she'll go farther away or she'll come and talk to me. I think that she's a very controlling person; she always wants to have control of everything and if she was in my life right now she'd say "Now what are we going to do with this? and, who's going to take care of this?" and all these things— she'd want to

Vicki sees herself as competent in dealing with things directly, a relevant piece of information for later formulating suggestions.

Vicki's sense of urgency about resolving things is not evident here, further evidence of an ability to compartmentalize experience.

take over and control everything. I won't let people control me and so we conflict there. See, she wants to run the show, she wants to, so that's where the conflict is. So if she was in my life right now, she would be causing conflict in my life right now, there's no doubt about that. She's going to have to come to a place where she can say, she's got to let me make my own decisions about my own life and my own way that I want to die and not tell me, try to tell me how to do it. I don't let people do that, and that's why we don't get along. I think that that'll work out eventually. I'm not too concerned about that.

Acknowledges tendencies to engage in power struggles, letting me know that if I want to succeed, it will be by treating her as an equal, not as someone to direct.

M: So you really have your own mind and it's just trying to get these people to understand that . . .

Rapport-building confirmation that I've heard the message about respecting her need to maintain control.

V: Yeah, I know what I want. No doubt about it.

M: How have you dealt these last three weeks with getting the prognosis?

V: That was really the easy part because I knew I was sick. I knew I was dying. I knew it a long time ago. I just couldn't get any doctor to confirm that. So it's something that I've been dealing with a long time and . . .

Another reference to a "part" (either easy or hard, in this case "easy").

M: Are you saying that it was almost a bit of relief to have some confirmation?

V: Well, it certainly wasn't what I wanted to hear.

M: I wouldn't think so.

V: I wanted to hear that I had something curable. But it was a relief to have some kind of diagnosis. It's an awful thing to know that you're awfully sick and have people tell you that you're not. To be in the kind of double bind or that kind of conflict is really an awful place to be, and I've been there for four years. Pretty soon you start to believe that you're crazy. Then you start to act crazy, and then you become crazy and then you fall into all the patterns; people categorize you and you're labelled and then you have no hope of getting out. That's an awful place to be. There's no way to dig out of that kind of a hole, until it's too late like it has . . . I think that's one of—the medical profession, even the psychological profession, we tend very much to categorize people and label them and expect them to behave and do according to what their labels are and that's so wrong because there's so much more. Everybody's different, everybody's an individual. We get going so fast and we never stop to listen and really look at people the way, for who they are and their differences, people don't fit into little boxes.

Vicki introduces her very, very strong opinions about being labelled, clearly a reflection of the emotional intensity that could only be a direct by-product of having been hurt by such a process.

She started to say that it was too late for her, but blocked it; acceptance is not fully achieved, which is probably to her advantage.

Vicki warning me of what *not* to do in treating her, as well as what *to* do.

M: What do you think somebody who would have been a little bit smarter, a little bit more perceptive, a little bit more sensitive would have

Asking for clarification of exactly what position she would like me to take in dealing with her.

done? What do you think the best way would have been to have responded to you?

V: Just listen to me. I got a diagnosis only because of my own tantrum. One day I threw a tantrum. You see, I knew that there was something in my lung and, like I said, 6 or 7 months ago I had a lung biopsy, and then I kept going back to doctors and going back and they kept saying "It's not your lung. We did the lung, right? We had a biopsy on your lung, we checked your lung. It's not your . . . " I said "But it *is* my lung. I lived in this body 42 years. I kind of got to know it a little bit. Something is wrong in my lung." "No, it's not your lung because we've done all the tests on your lung." So we go off, we go off, and I went through the 7 months and then one day I just had a tantrum. I said "Can't somebody at least do a chest x-ray? What the hell is it going to hurt to do a chest x-ray?" "All right, if you'll just shut up we'll do it." And then it was a tumor about this size (the size of a golfball) that shows up in my lung. And if I hadn't had that tantrum that day they would've never even at this time had a diagnosis. So I think that people, doctors don't listen and we tend to let them not listen which is a big mistake because they're gods and they know what they're talking about and they went to school and they know all this stuff and they don't. If you

Vicki letting me know not to hurry her, not to label her, and to treat her respectfully as an individual who needs to be listened to.

Vicki has moved into "preacher" mode to make sure that all present are mandated with the task of listening to their patients.

have a doctor that's not listening, you should find another one because they may know scientifically but they don't live it. If you know your body, you live in your body, you have more, you know more about your body than they're ever going to know because they don't live there. They think that most people aren't smart enough to know that, I guess. I don't know.

M: What is the medical intervention at this point? What has been pre-scribed for you? What are you sup-posed to be doing?

I want to know what her treatment plan is and whether she knows what to expect.

V: At the moment, I'm doing a lot of radiation therapy. I'm not into heavy therapies and I'm more the kind of person who would rather die with dignity. I'm not going to, I don't want to spend the rest of my life being sick to death. I'd rather have a shorter life and not be sick than a long life, but I did consent to the radiation therapy which is about the only thing they had to offer me anyway. We're way beyond surgery; we're way beyond chemotherapy. Radiation therapy can, they tell me that it's not going to increase the length of my life but maybe the quality of my life. And I've had a few days where I doubted that, because it did make me sick. Now, I'm beginning to believe it. I had a very large tumor in my shoul-der and I lost all the use of my right arm and it was very painful and they said that if I didn't do something

She asserts the value of quality of life rather than quantity.

about it, it was going to explode my shoulder. It was a real toss up. They did the radiation therapy and it was a real toss up whether there was going to get to be enough radiation, if the radiation was going to be beneficial before it exploded. It came, I mean I could tell, it came right to the very line and then the tumor did start to decrease and the pain decreased so I know that by doing that I saved my shoulder and now I'm even gaining some use of that. The tumors in my brain which they said radiation therapy is going to probably decrease the amount of seizures and so forth that I will have, so it seemed reasonable to me to try that. Also in the lung, the tumor presses on the vena cava which is where all the blood drains from the, and that's the real dangerous part of that, so if it can decrease it somewhat, to cause that—it's not going to extend my life, it's just going to make it more comfortable probably, for a longer time.

M: Are you currently taking any drugs?

V: I'm real selective about that. They want to always keep putting me on more and more drugs and I, like I say, I don't want to miss anything.

Vicki reasserts her desire to minimize the influence of drugs on her functioning.

M: Some of the drugs seem to have a mental effect?

V: I tell you. When you get to this place you, this is a drug addict's dream. You just tell them what you want, anything you want, they ...—morphine, the whole shmear. I just, I did Tylenol III for a while, and then when the shoulder got real bad I went to Percocet, and now I'm cutting back because it's not as painful and so I'm back to Tylenol III now, and I'm trying to maintain on that. But I haven't closed my mind, I don't want to be, you know I'm not a martyr; I don't want to be, I can't enjoy and do the things that I want to do if I'm in terrible pain so it's a real balance for me and I'm hoping that this is going to make it easier to stay awake and still not be in pain. I don't like pain, so I'm not into pain, but I'm not into being drugged up either. It's a balance that I have to maintain and just decide as I go. I have this whole dresser full of pills; some make you not throw up, and I'm also doing some mega-vitamin kind of stuff so—the radiation, in the next week all of my hair is going to fall out and I'm going not to be able to eat solid food for about a week because the irritation to the esophagus, so I figure that next week is going to be a real tough one to get through and then I'll be okay. So you have to kind of see as you go along, what you need to do as far as medicine is concerned. But as long as I'm making the decisions, I feel okay about it. I've been looking into hospice care because I have this really strong thing about I don't want to die in a hospital and I don't want to be hooked

Drugs are an acceptable last resort, but the first choice is self-management.

This mention of difficulty eating is noted as something to address in the trance session.

Her need for control is reiterated.

up to machines and I want, I'm looking into hospice kind of situations and I like a lot of what they have to say and then they get to the bottom and they said "Who's your doctor?" and I told them and they said "He won't cooperate with us." I said then we have to find a new doctor because I'm not going to die in a hospital and I'm not going to die hooked up to a machine, with a doctor that's going to keep me alive that way. I don't want that. And the legal situation being what it is, that's— you really need to know that before, because it depends on the doctor. So I'm working on those kinds of things.

M: Are you currently experiencing any discomfort in your body?

The first reframe—pain as "discomfort," a less charged term.

V: At this moment? My shoulder I suppose. It's a lot better than it has been but it's uncomfortable. I can't raise my arm.

M: On a day-to-day basis, over the last few days, has the discomfort been limited to your shoulder or do you experience it in other places as well?

I am asking how localized or generalized her experience of pain is.

V: My chest. I'm getting more and more uncomfortable in my chest. The more and more pain in my, the more radiation they do to my chest, the more irritated the esophagus becomes, and like I said, for a week I won't be able to eat solid foods, so it becomes quite irritated.

M: Can you describe what that means —irritated?

I want a sensory description of what she expects in order to address it

V: They call it, they say it's like esophagitis. You get a real bad sore throat and you can't swallow things. I've been having difficulty swallowing for some time, but I do anyway because I'm a little pig. Not much makes me stop eating so, but just like having a bad ulcer is what it's going to be like. It just kind of hurts. But it's temporary. That part is temporary. It'll go away when the treatments end. Like hair grows back.

M: Can you describe a little bit what the sensation in your shoulder is like?

V: My shoulder is so much better but it's like it's just a lot of pain. There was a lot of pain in my shoulder and it does, it feels just like there's something huge inside the joint which is exactly what it was, and it's pressing, pressing, pressing, pressing so hard that the bone was getting ready to explode, and it's just growing, growing, and there's no room for it to grow so it just, and that's the kind of pain it is. Not only that but it makes me unable to move my arm in certain ways. I can't lift my arm. I can't go up. I can use my fingers, and I can do—it's funny the things that, you know, because I'm right handed, so it's been really kind of a hard thing to deal with and there's, it feels like somebody hit me in the shoulder with a baseball bat and it's just this horrible bruise. There's no bruise, but it feels like, if you looked there'd be black and blue everywhere. It's

in the trance session, since eating and maintaining body weight are important.

Vicki's ability to recognize the situation as changeable is a powerful deterrent to her giving up.

More sensory descriptions to use in the trance.

getting a lot better. I suppose there's a considerable amount of chest pain, but I've been dealing with that for a long time so it's kind of ... See, I learned, it's kind of a strange thing because for four years I've had a lot of pain. It started in my joints and my muscles, all over my body. Like terrible arthritis, and I kept going to doctors and they'd say there's no arthritis here. Of course it wasn't, it was cancer but they didn't look past and they kept telling me that there wasn't anything that could be causing that pain and so I finally got to the point where I said "Okay. I'm a full time student; I'm a very active person; I can't get slowed down by pain and so there just won't be pain." So I spent a lot of time teaching myself how not to perceive the pain or how to let my brain override the pain to some degree. And now that I have a diagnosis I find myself feeling the pain, allowing myself to feel the pain. So it's a real different kind of thing for me to do and now that I've allowed myself to feel the pain I'm trying to find this place in between where I, because I know that the mind controls so much of what you feel, there must be a place where I can, I don't want to be totally unaware of it, but I want to be able to deal with it because I got so confused in this period where you feel pain and people are telling you there's no pain. It gets you real confused. I don't know exactly what

Vicki describes an ability to use mental mechanisms to overcome pain, a potentially meaningful indicator of what ability or abilities to amplify hypnotically.

Vicki's references to confusion reflect the antitherapeutic aspects of confusion. Since certainty and clarity at all times is not possible, given the advanced state of her illness, it seemed important to be able to establish a new association to the ex-

I'm feeling is what I'm feeling. Know what I mean? Well, my level of feeling is, may not be, what's real. I don't know where "real" is anymore.

M: That must be pretty confusing.

V: That part is. Yeah, I think that I got to the point where I'd say "No it doesn't hurt," when it really did hurt. Because doctors convinced me that there wasn't anything there and I didn't want to be crazy so I went along with it. It does strange things to your head.

M: All that time that you said that basically, you didn't let yourself experience the pain—how did you do that?

V: I just didn't focus on it mostly. I learned not to focus on it. I had a lot of things going on in my life. I had a lot of important things to do and I would just focus on other things.

M: Being in school?

V: Being in school.

M: Family relationships? Other kinds of things? Were you working?

V: No. Well, I was for a while. That was too hard. I did get to the point where I knew that I wasn't able to do all that I used to be able to do and I did cut back. I was working full time and going to school full time and that became way, way too much for me. So I stopped. I worked and saved as much money as I could and then

perience of confusion that would make it tolerable. Thus, confusional suggestions were planned into the session.

The previous experience of confusion has a negative association to being out of touch with reality to her own detriment.

I am wanting to identify what method —the sequence of steps she took— to psychologically manage her pain.

She lets me know it was through distraction.

I dropped out of work and went to school full time and that was just really exciting for me. But I spent a lot of time resting. I did meditation things, I did a lot of relaxation—I learned to do a lot of relaxation things that helped me not focus on it.

Vicki lets me know she has previous trance experiences to access in the form of meditation and relaxation procedures, and that these were helpful. Thus, they can safely be referenced in the trance session.

M: I'd like to hear a little bit more about that—the relaxation, the meditation, some of the things that are probably going to parallel a little bit what we're going to be doing. Can you tell me a little bit about those things that you've already learned?

I want the specifics of what she has experienced in order to know which parts to amplify and which to gloss over.

V: One thing that I'm doing right now that's really exciting to me is guided imagery. I think that's really exciting.

M: You're working with someone, doing that?

V: Lillian and Harold. And I think that's really exciting. I'm really into the—all my whole life has kind of centered around how much control the mind has over your body. I kind of always believed that you could make yourself sick and you could make yourself not sick. I don't think I believe it so much anymore. I've always kind of thought along those lines. I know that you can control an awful lot with your mind and so I've always been interested in learning how to do that.

Vicki professes to have held an attitude of "mind over matter" that is now untenable.

M: And so Lillian and Harold are doing formal guided imagery sessions with you? What kinds of things and how are you responding to it?

V: I guess you don't ever know really how you could respond to it but it's a kind of white light kind of melting away the tumors. I have tornadoes that come down—white tornadoes that come down and get rid of—and I can get into it. I really get into it. I see it. I try to do it quite a bit every day and I spend time on that radiation—getting radiation therapy is like going and putting yourself in a giant microwave and turning it on is how I visualize it. I try to do it while I'm there but it's such an awesome place to be it's kind of hard to do there. Sometimes I can do it, sometimes I can't. There's a big switch on the wall that says "Emergency Shut Off" and I look at it and I just want to get up and shut it off. I suspect very strongly that radiation is the cause of my problems. I was radiated as a child in an experimental kind of thing and most of the people that had this radiation as children are coming up with this kind of . . . It's hard to imagine that radiation is the cause and radiation is how we diagnose and how we treat. Those things are hard to put together. To put yourself in a microwave is kind of a difficult thing to do. But other places it works a lot better. It feels good to me. I don't know if it's

More specifics are needed if I am to make meaningful references to their work.

Vicki is being taught methods of visualization that she claims to benefit from.

working or not but it feels good to me and so I do it.

M: So you're able to relax and you're able to get into it? Great.

I am wanting to amplify her capability.

V: Sometimes. Depending where I'm at. Sometimes it's easier than other times. Sometimes it's just really fantastic. I also do meditation which I've done for a long time and that's always helped me and so I hang on to that. I haven't really done too much other kind of relaxation. For a while, I was doing it but now that they've got me on—Tylenol III puts me in a place that's never-never land. I don't really need to relax for that reason. I think that I'm really probably much more relaxed than most people. My doctor says that he never has anybody fall asleep on the radiation table before and every once in a while I fall asleep, and my arm will fall off in all positions. I've always been the kind of person that you give an aspirin to and I go to sleep, so I react very strongly to these drugs.

M: What is your experience with the Tylenol III in terms of what it does to you mentally? You're saying that's one of the drugs that you want to get away from or at least reduce.

I want specifics of the mental effects she is wanting to minimize or eliminate, since these are instrumental in her seeking my help in the first place.

V: Well, it has codeine and I'd like to not have to take drugs that dull my—they're doing radiation to my brain. Radiation destroys good cells as well as bad cells. My area of study is physiological psychology so I know a little bit of physiology and I know that the brain cells don't regenerate. Now, they radiate my shoulder and I know that they destroy the good cells as well as the bad cells and that they can regenerate to some degree. But I know my brain cells can't so I'm very much afraid of losing my brain cells and I find myself not thinking good, not remembering things, talking to someone on the phone one day and the next day not remembering. A lot of memory stuff leaving and it makes me feel a bit panicky. I don't know if it's the radiation or if it's just that I have so many things on my mind and my mind is so totally occupied with all that's going on. I have this really silly thing ever since I can't remember how old—I've never been able to throw anything away. A little piece of string—somebody in the world needs this little piece of string and I'm not going to take it to the dump, I'm going to save it for this person who might need it and maybe I'll have a garage sale some day and sell it for a penny.

So all my life I've saved all these things and I know if I die everybody's going to take all my junk and put it in the garbage can and that just kills me. One of my real goals is I have to have, I finally have to have my yard sale. I also have to look at each and everything that I have that I love and care about—I have these little stickers that I'm sticking on the

Vicki shares that a lack of clarity and an impairment of memory are the things she fears.

Vicki introduces an ongoing issue in her life of "letting go." She will burden herself on the chance that someone may want the item, defining herself as a provider to others. This issue is an important one, since making plans surrounding death—the ultimate "letting go"—is a necessary task. Thus, "letting go" is a theme to be integrated into the trance session.

She wants people to value what she does.

Vicki introduces the solution of a "yard sale" as a means to "let go"; this solution is noted, and is later referenced during the trance process.

backs of—I have to figure out who's going to love this thing the most. So I have all these things to do, so I have a lot of things on my mind. It could be that just the mind is so full that it doesn't have time to remember who I talked to on the phone yesterday. Maybe the radiation isn't the only thing that's killing my mind. Maybe it's just too full.

M: The burden of thinking about everything, and everybody.

V: But I do worry about that. I don't want to destroy my brain. I want my brain to survive.

M: How long will the radiation continue?

V: One more week at this point, and then, of course, they have to keep watching because what they expect is—they expect that it's in a lot of places in my body that they haven't been able to detect yet and so it's just a matter of keeping up with that. I'm only doing it—they're not going to even touch my adrenal glands, they're so far gone. It's not a vital organ or—you can have it real bad in your adrenal glands before it's going to kill you. That's not what's going to kill me. So that each time that it shows up somewhere else then it has to be re-evaluated to see what— and I have to learn enough to be able to evaluate myself and decide whether I want to go through the therapy—sometimes the cure is worse

Reinforcing a nonpathological basis for her memory lapse in order to minimize counterproductive anxiety.

than the disease. I'm afraid of that, so each thing has to be evaluated on its individual kind of basis.

M: You said that you had been working and then you stopped working and went back to school. That's a pretty major change. How did that come about?

Moving away from pathology, I am interested in identifying and accessing specific resources she has that have been employed in previous transitions.

V: I've wanted to go to school all my life and I put my husband through school and I raised a family and it always got put off.

M: Sort of time to do something for yourself.

Validating the worth of the investment in herself.

V: I got to a point where I figured out that I had some value and I had some worth. I lived 15 years in a violent marriage. My husband was a very violent person and I spent most of my life thinking that I wasn't very deserving and wasn't very—that I was worthless, very low self-esteem. It's taken the last 5 years, I've really gotten that turned around and figured out that I had a lot of value and a lot of worth and knew where I wanted to go and what I wanted to do, exactly what I wanted. A lot of very definite goals and even have it all figured out how I'm going to get there. I'd been carrying a 4.0 average at school and so I've been feeling very good about myself. At first I thought I feel real sad that I'm not going to reach my goals but then I decided that maybe the important thing was to figure out that I could and that I had the

Being goal-directed is only a recent development, but she shows an ability to effectively operate in that way.

An interpretation of the "meaning" of her disease.

worth and the value and maybe that's the lesson I had to learn.

M: That's a pretty amazing discovery.

By accepting her interpretation, she is permitted to focus on her progress rather than the frustration of never reaching her goal.

V: To get there wasn't the main thing. To just discover was the main thing.

She accepts that ratification.

M: How did you find that after all those years of being in such a difficult relationship?

I am asking her to identify her method—the sequence of steps used —to effect a significant transition. She may identify a usable resource for the later trance session.

V: Well, it's a long story. Twenty years ago I had, my husband put me in a psychiatric hospital and I was diagnosed catatonic-schizophrenia, a back ward patient that would never be out of the hospital again and that's an awfully hard label to overcome. Two months ago I went out into the community and I wanted to get into a women's group, a women's support group, I guess about 4 months ago, and I started interviewing clinicians because I learned to do that. So if they interviewed me, I interviewed them. And this woman I hit with some of my background because I've been in and out of hospitals a good part of my life and she told me that I was too sick to be in her group. After one hour of talking to me, and then charging me for the session which I thought was kind of crummy. There's so much of that that goes on that I use it as kind of a tester now. If you see my labels faster than you see

Here are some of the specifics that led to the earlier sermon about labelling.

Another personal rejection on the basis of an impersonal label.

me then I can just get up and walk away. I don't need you in my life anymore. That's a real dangerous thing that happens. I progressed, I fought and I never gave up and I overcame all those things, mostly . . . Another thing that I think was important in my history is that they, of course at that time, drugs were coming in, psychotropic drugs and they gave me so many psychotropic drugs and I had such horrible side effects from them. I would try to tell people I'm . . . and nobody would listen to me and they would say "You need more Thorazine." The more they gave me, the sicker I got. I kept trying to tell people, nobody listened. That's when I first learned that people don't listen. My husband kept me in this kind of mind set. I guess it's pretty awful but I overcame it, that's the thing.

M: I'm amazed. It's obviously against all the odds . . .

V: That's why my interest is in physiological psychology because I had just had a complete hysterectomy. There was a lot of physiological things going on in my life at the time that this happened and I really truly believe that there's so much to the chemical brain structure. I really do. I think it was my biggest problem beside the fact that my husband stole away my person or I let my husband steal my person. And that I had such low self-esteem. I think the chemical

She identifies "fighting and never giving up" as the relevant resources for her changes.

She is attributing her emotional difficulties to a chemical imbalance.

What she learned in therapy—to accept responsibility—is given lip service, but she clearly has not yet make up of my body at the time was a real key factor and so that's why my interest of study was in that area. I thought that I wanted to make some discoveries that—I knew what it felt like to be on the inside. I knew what it felt like to be in a psychiatric hospital where nobody listened. Have you ever read that study, I forget who did it, where the psychologists all admitted themselves and they . . . Well, that was my life. People don't hear you. You're a non-entity and that's such a horrible thing to be.

M: Did you have the idea that you could be a 4.0 student? Go back to school and accomplish these things all that time?

V: Not all that time. No.

M: You got in touch with that much later?

V: There came a point where I—one day I was living with my husband on the East coast and my husband's a commander in the Navy. He was stationed in the East. And the anger grew and grew with him and I found myself standing over him one night with a fireplace poker and I knew that I was going to kill him if I didn't get away from him. The next day I found myself standing on a bridge, the Brooklyn Bridge or one of those bridges, and I was going to jump and I said "What is it that I'm sorry I didn't do?" Is there any thing that I'm sorry . . . I just couldn't take it

internalized the lesson. In her situation, that is actually an advantage since a more internal attribution would likely lead to depression.

I am wanting to amplify her ability to pleasantly surprise herself with abilities she did not know she had.

anymore, and I said, you know, I always wanted to go to Colorado and I never did. Then I thought, what the hell. Why don't I go to Colorado and if I can't—if it doesn't work out then I'll jump off a mountain. So I went home and I packed myself a backpack and I got in my husband's wallet and I got about $400 out and I took off and I went to Colorado and that's when things turned around for me, because—it was the middle of winter, I slept—I lived on the street. I had a hard time but I began to realize that there was a "me" and I could function totally without him, that I didn't need someone to tell me that I was okay or I wasn't okay. It also goes back to childhood. My father was killed when I was a year old, in the War. My mother was an alcoholic and a drug addict. I had no siblings. I never lived with any one family more than just a few months. I mean I was never—I didn't have a family life so I didn't know how to do that. I never had any . . . So I was used to people who didn't love me and it was like this super goal to find people who don't know how to love and make them love me. My husband never knew how to love; he was incapable of loving. He isn't capable of loving and yet, just somebody who could easily love me wasn't what I needed. I needed the mother who couldn't, the husband that couldn't, I needed all the couldn'ts to do it. That became my whole life's

The benefits of her therapy are showing in these insights about her life patterns.

goal. Well, that's a stupid goal. I mean I wasted my whole life trying to do that and it doesn't work. So I learned that. That was one thing that I learned. That if you want somebody to love you, you have to find—first of all it has to come from within. You're your own best parent, that you have to love yourself, which is such a cliché that unless you really get inside yourself and learn that it sounds so stupid. For years I thought "love yourself," people keep saying that but how stupid, what a stupid thing to say. But it's real and I got to the place where I did. And then . . .

Vicki is letting me know that individuation and self-validation were the keys to her reaching for and achieving more substantial goals.

M: You really feel that now?

Testing the strength of her convictions.

V: Yes. Oh, yes, absolutely. But it's a—it sounds so stupid when you're telling someone who doesn't know what you mean.

M: Almost any feeling sounds a little trite when you say it but if you really feel it and it's strong, that's what matters.

Joining her viewpoint, and validating her right to feel as she does.

V: Yeah, so I learned that probably just by being with myself and I started getting it together in Colorado and I became sick in Colorado, that's where I was. I loved Colorado. It was like my world. I made this world. I lived 12,000 feet high, in the country, way out in the woods and it was like the happiest time of my life. But I started getting sick and I had to get out of the altitude so I came back here.

Also to take care of my mother. But also because I wanted to go back to school. And I thought that I couldn't. I was afraid to try. I'd been told for so many years that I was stupid and that I couldn't do anything right. It's awfully hard—you know, just one day believe it and then the next day not believe that this whole long process that goes on . . . But I knew that if I didn't try I was never going to find out so I signed up for 6 units. I took two classes just to see that if maybe, maybe I could and I did.

M: Must have been a thrill to find out you could.

V: Yeah, it was. And it got, and then each time I started adding more units until I was up to 16 and still carrying a 4.0 and that felt good. I mean it was like super high then. I was just—but it was also, it made me understand that if I would have tried to do it when I was 17 or 18 when I got out of high school, I would not have done it. That there's something that drives you when you want the information. You have to want that information or it doesn't work. I go to school and I compete with these 18-19-year-olds and I thought "Oh, they're so used to studying, it's going to be so hard." They don't want to be there and so it's really easy competition, but you have to want to and you have to be studying something that you're interested in and

Amplifying the feeling of accomplishment following the uncertainty of taking a risk.

want the information and it's not any work at all. You just soak it in, just love to . . .

M: Have you been seeing Lillian and Harold all this time or how has that been working?

How much of your gains have been made all on your own, how much with the support of your therapists?

V: Lillian came into my life through my son who doesn't do very well. I finally got my son away from my husband, got him out here with me and got him into seeing Lillian but he's really kind of too far gone to do anything and then Lillian just became a very close friend. I have a close, close relationship with Lillian and Harold both, mostly through some therapy, just friendship and they're just very special people in my life.

M: She said the same about you. She said "Michael, this lady's a knockout. You'll love her" and I can see why she said that. So you've known her for a while?

Sharing my positive regard for her.

V: Four years.

M: Well, the guided imagery things that you've been doing with them— Lillian told me very little—she just said that the guided imagery was something that you had been working with a little bit. She told me basically what you told me, that part of what you were looking for was some more naturalistic way of keeping yourself clear, keeping yourself as comfortable as you can be and I understand that, I wonder now if

Sharing what was told to me about her, and confirming to her that I have heard what she wants.

you think there's anything else I might need to know?

V: I don't know. What do you need to know?

M: It was interesting to me to hear you say that you could keep yourself comfortable by focusing on other things even though there was pain at different times, doctors weren't picking anything up, but that you were uncomfortable and that you found ways to deal with it. It wasn't anything formal that you were doing; it was just part of your lifestyle to get yourself to work on other things and not really pay that much attention to it. Have you ever had any formal experience in learning specific techniques for managing discomfort?

Amplifying the resource within her of being able to benefit from distraction; amplifying also that she could experience pain reduction naturalistically despite the apparent absence of a formal strategy for doing so.

Asking whether she has had any previous formal experience with pain reduction methods.

V: No. Well, that's not true. I did, for a while, biofeedback. I even tried some hypnosis with someone that . . . and it didn't work, which I probably should have told you before I came here. I think it had a lot to do with . . . I wasn't very trusting of the person. Again, he did his thing and his thing was his thing and he wasn't listening to what my needs were and that's such an important thing for me. I didn't trust because I kept— I have a lot of—it goes back to psychologists—and I had some experiences where psychiatrists mostly have made big blackouts in my life. I'm afraid of that and I think I got afraid of that in the hypnosis because

She reports previous trance experience that was unsuccessful. Details are needed in order to avoid accessing any part of that experience.

She lets me know that a lack of trust was the divisive factor, fueled by his lack of listening to her.

She associates a lack of memory with negative experience; thus, amnesia during or after the trance is contraindicated.

I wanted to record the sessions and he wouldn't let me. I was afraid of that blackout and I think I was fighting it. They've done a lot of sodium amytol kinds of things with me and wouldn't ever tell me what happened during those periods of blackout and I don't like that. I don't like people stealing part of my life away from me and not sharing it with me.

The fact that our session was being conducted before a group was no doubt of comfort to her. As is typical of my sessions, the session was also being recorded on both video and audio tape with the promise having been made that she would receive a copy of the tape.

M: A little bit scary to lose pieces of what's going on.

Joining her perception.

V: Right. And I was afraid this guy was doing that and so I wasn't very successful because I think that I was fighting.

M: Was that here in San Diego?

V: Yes.

M: Recently?

V: About a year ago, year and a half ago.

M: Do you remember specifically what it was he was saying or what it was he was doing that you were finding difficult to relate to?

Here I am asking for the details of what went on so that I could be sure to do things differently.

V: I think that it was just the general . . .

M: The atmosphere of what was happening?

V: It was something general about him that didn't listen. There was something general about not letting me record, like what are you hiding? I wasn't trusting that. Not explaining

Again, the emphasis is made on needing to be heard.

things to me. I have to be super explained to and if you explain something to me 14 times and I don't understand it, then I'll ask you again and if you don't explain it to me 16 times then, I mean sometimes it takes a while to soak in but I've got to have that information in order to process whatever I process. And he was getting annoyed with me that I was asking the same kind of questions over and over and I don't know, I went for a long time. I went for five-six months before I finally said "This is a waste of my money and your time and I don't think we're getting anywhere." It was also interlinked with the biofeedback and he was putting these things on my forehead and I was having so much pain in other places in my body, I didn't understand why it was on my forehead. Sure, there was a good reason for that but I didn't understand it. He wouldn't explain it to me. Also he was into—he got off the track and he was into a lot of regression. Now, I'm into regression and once he found out that I was into that, then that was his focus and it wasn't my focus. I would like to have done that as a side line, kind of an interest area of my very own, but not for the therapeutic thing that I was trying to get at at the moment. Once he found out that I had that interest, then the whole thing switched to that area and I couldn't get him back over here to

Vicki lets me know that she values understanding and participation. To not utilize these values—that is, to expect her to just follow directions blindly—would undoubtedly meet with her resistance. As is generally true, much of the "resistance" of therapy arises from the clinician's inability to recognize and utilize the client's values and capabilities. Thus, resistance can be defined as interpersonal as well as intrapersonal.

Whether these aspects of her treatment are "true" is less relevant than the fact that this is how she incorporated the experiences into her memory. If true, here is another example of a clinician not listening to his or her client, fueling Vicki's obviously strong need to be heard. The client is *the* source of information. She knows her internal world better than anyone else ever will.

the therapeutic kind of thing. So I thought that he was using me, that he was doing it for his own little bag because he found somebody that would allow him to do regressive therapy. My spiritual interests—a lot of my spiritual interests are in reincarnation and he was doing some previous lifetime kind of regression with me which is very fascinating and very interesting and I'm into it, totally into it, but at that moment in time it wasn't what I wanted to pay him to do. And he got stuck there so . . . It may have been my fault.

Her belief in reincarnation is noted as a possible association to use later.

M: I think it's a valid concern to want the work to be along the lines of what your needs are instead of what his interests are.

Vicki acknowledges she may not have been entirely a helpless victim.

Validating she is entitled to get what she wants, providing assurance of that in her interaction with me.

V: At the time my financial situation is kind of balancing and I felt like I had to spend my money where the most benefit was to be had. You can spend so much money on fun and games . . .

M: But the work's got to be done sooner or later. Have you talked with Lillian at all about what I do? What you could expect here? What the possibilities were?

Attempting to have Vicki define her expectations of me, first by asking about the information accompanying the referral by Lillian.

V: Uh- uh.

She asserts that Lillian said little to her about me.

M: Lillian and I work together at the university. That's how we know each other.

Helping her understand my connection to Lillian, referencing her positive association to Lillian and

V: Yeah, she told me that.

M: And I work a lot with hypnosis and . . .

V: The reason I was interested is that I've been asking around about hypnosis and everybody that it seemed like I talked to said they had studied under you and she came up with you and I thought that was just a greater idea than coming to somebody that studied under you. Go right to the source. I haven't got time to fool around.

M: Makes sense to me. Well, certainly one of the things that's so fascinating about the mind is its ability to control what goes on in the body the way that you were describing earlier. The ability to focus on discomfort or focus on other things and lose track of discomfort is one of the capabilities and it seems to me that part of what you're asking for, at least, is to be able to develop a way to be able to experience yourself more comfortably, more naturally.

We can do that. The kinds of guided imagery things that you've been doing with Lillian are hypnotic procedures. I don't know if she's ever described them that way before but it's a form of hypnosis.

Visual imagery is one form of hypnosis and it involves, obviously, images and so it's very much a visual kind of process. Some people are real visual. They can form . . .

the university—both positive forces in her life.

Vicki shares with me that she has had exposure to my reputation from multiple sources.

The issue of "time" is reiterated.

Amplifying her awareness for her beliefs about the mind-body relationship, and referencing the previous discussion of absorption and distraction as a natural means of pain reduction within the scope of her experience.

As a preliminary to formal induction, I am feeding back to Vicki what she has expressed an ability to do, a desire to do, and identifying a mechanism to do it.
Positive expectancy.

Reframing her previous successes as based in hypnosis, directly relating them to our work, thus amplifying the expectation of being able to succeed with me.
Reframing her known methods of comfort as hypnotic, and assessing her true ability to visualize, since so much of her spontaneous speech would indicate a kinesthetic primary representational system.

V: I don't consider myself a real visual person.

M: Would you consider yourself more
of a feeling kind of person?

V: Feelings? Yes. And even a little
more auditory than visual. I get into
the imagery. I think it's because I
want to so much but I do find that
feelings are the number one and
maybe auditory number two.

M: And so even though visual imagery is not first on the list you've
still been able to make use of it.

V: Oh, I want to so much. Normally,
visual things haven't worked for me
too much in the past, so I was surprised that this is, I'm getting into
this so much but it's not my best
mode I don't think.

M: Are there times during the day
that you are comfortable?

V: They vary a lot. You know, some
days I do okay—the radiation therapy makes you very, very, very exhausted. It takes, drains all your
energy. So I've gotten to the point
now where I say "Okay, I can do my
treatments and one other thing."
Then I spend the rest of the time
resting. My doctor said next week
therapy, no more. Just go home and
go to bed. I try to keep my mind
okay, that's not the way I want to do
it. I've got to be able to function and
do things, but it's only going to be
another week. Sometimes that's hard
to remember.

She validates my doubt that her visual ability is her most well developed one.

Amplifying for her that her motivation really does enhance her ability.

I am looking for the exceptions to
her painful times in order to amplify
them.

Vicki's hope rests on having one difficult week followed by periods of
normal activity.

Sometimes, for a while it was like I was being very sick in the morning and then in the evening I was feeling better, and then it got where I felt great in the morning and then I felt sick. So it kind of starting to switch around a lot.

M: There's no set pattern to it?

V: Right. So I'm kind of just going with it. Just kind of going with it. I have one more week—it's hard for me to remember that the sickness, the really—the day before yesterday morning my daughter stayed all night with me. I'm not allowed to stay alone any more, at night. And now they've decided even in the day I'm not supposed to be alone because of the threat of seizures. But most of the time I feel good. Well, the morning before yesterday, my daughter got up and went to work and I thought I'd be fine until my aunt came to help me take a shower and take me to my treatment, and I could get my bowl of cereal which I was going to have and everything went to hell. I got up, I didn't make it to the bathroom in time. I messed myself and I started throwing up and I threw up all over the house and I got the bowl of cereal and I dumped it on the floor and pretty soon I just found myself sitting in the middle of the floor, saying "I'd rather be dead." And when you get that kind of moment, when things come just *(raspberry)*, it's so hard to grab hold of that

She does not have awareness for any predictable pattern of good or bad times. Given her desire for control, the unpredictable nature of time relative to her illness sensitizes her even more to time-related suggestions.

Double-checking for the possibility of relevant patterns.

string that says "It's the treatments. In a week it's going to get better; you're going to feel better. It's not going to go like this for the rest of the time." There are going to be good days and there's going to be productive days, so you really have to grab hold of that and sometimes it's hard to hold on to but it doesn't usually go away for too awfully long. I have a pretty good grip on it.

M: It sure sounds that way to me. Well, I've been asking you all kinds of questions. I wonder if you have any for me.

V: I don't know. I can't think right now.

Her ability to see the situation as unstable (changeable) is obviously vital to her ability to maintain.

Validating her positive view of her ability to manage.

The basic framing of our work has already been established, rapport is excellent, and she has been sufficiently heard.

The Trance Session

M: Well, then let me describe a little bit of what I'd like to be able to do. Having worked with imagery before, and having worked with meditation and the different kinds of relaxation processes, you know what it's like to be able to close your eyes, go inside, have different kinds of experiences internally. Basically I'm going to talk about different ideas, different possibilities. There isn't really anything that you have to do, Vicki. All I really want you to do is give yourself the opportunity to experience whatever it occurs to you to

---

Assuming a more active position to begin directing the course of the remainder of the session. Referencing the methods she knows and likes and utilizing parts of them to begin building the response set necessary for trance induction and utilization.

Defining my role as someone simply offering possibilities, emphasizing her control in being able to choose what she does and does not take in. Giving her the freedom to experience herself in whatever way occurs

experience. I'm going to be talking about different possibilities, different potentials, and it's really going to be for you to take what makes sense to you, leave behind what doesn't make sense to you, and that's about it. Different ideas. But you'll hear everything, know everything, everything will be real clear for you, because that's what you're looking for, that kind of clarity in your thinking, that kind of clarity in your perception. But certainly one of the things that will become real clear to you is how you can use your own thoughts to creates sensations in yourself that you find real comfortable, other kinds of sensations that you feel real interesting, and it will be for you to pick and choose what you want to experience.

If you feel like you're ready to, arrange yourself in a position that's comfortable.

V: I have a hard time to sit up straight and put both feet on the floor. Harold says everything works better that way. So I've been trying it that way.

M: You can sit any way you want to. In all my years of study I have yet to find the one right way to sit, so just whatever is most comfortable for you.

V: I've been having, I think the next place that's going to show up is in my feet and legs because I've been having a lot of pain in my feet and

to her, rather than imposing any specific demand on her.

Reassuring her she will not be unaware of what transpires, given her negative associations to amnesia.

Reassuring her that she will have the mental clarity she defined as a primary goal of treatment.

Reaffirming her ability to maintain control of the interaction.

Vicki presents a previous learning that is rigid, unnecessary, and worst of all, inhibits her ability to respond well.

Again she is given permission to be in control and choose what is best for her. If I give her that control, then who is in control?

She informs me that her legs are currently in pain and that she has negative expectations for them.

legs. I'm kind of suspicious of that area.

M: (Shifting positions) Are you comfortable?

Indirect suggestion to get comfortable.

V: Except that I just had this huge big Mexican dinner and I think the beans are going to get me. My digestive—I have a little bit of heartburn.

Another somatic sensation to take into account.

M: Let's make that one of the sensations that we work with.

Begin by taking in a few relaxing breaths . . . and when you feel like you're ready to, Vicki, you can just . . . let your eyes close . . . so that you can go inside for a little while . . . That's right. And certainly you know from previous experience how you can relax . . . what kinds of things that you like to experience that you find the most soothing . . . what kinds of experience make the most sense to you . . . and as you pointed out, there isn't anyone who knows you the way that you do . . . so is there anybody that's in a more comfortable position to know what's right for you, to know what's good for you? . . . If you want to . . . you can . . . *listen very carefully to the things that I talk about,* but you really don't need to, Vicki . . . You can allow yourself . . . that's right . . . the exquisite luxury of letting your mind travel or relax . . . It can do a lot or it can do nothing . . . It can listen and it can not listen . . . But you can certainly allow yourself the experience of being very

Permissive suggestion for eye closure.

Building an internal focus.

Accessing previous trance experiences.

Accepting her need to be the authority over herself.

Utilizing her desire to be the authority on her own experience.
Embedded command for attentiveness.

Permissive suggestion for dissociation.

Covering all possibilities.

comfortable within yourself . . . and certainly you know from previous experiences . . . that sometimes *you can get so absorbed* in interesting possibilities . . . it doesn't really matter whether it's white lights or deep breathing . . . or an interesting voice, or soothing sensation . . . because as someone who's been studying psychology . . . you certainly know enough about the complexity of the mind, the complexity of physiology . . . to know that there is an automatic sort of pattern . . . that allows for the rhythmic rise and fall of breathing . . . the kind of balance of each breath in and each breath out . . . and because the mind is so complex, it's really convenient, really a *comfort* to know that while the conscious mind tends to notice whatever captures its attention for the moment . . . that there's a *deeper* part of you that can really *experience a surprising level of relaxation and comfort* . . . It's really not unlike having the rest of the world drift for a while . . . It's there but it's not there . . . It's here but it's there . . . It's right here, close by, and it's so far off in the distance . . . and to be able to *get absorbed in the interesting sensations* of what it feels like to have a watch on your wrist . . . or a necklace around your neck . . . or the feel of the chair . . . each an interesting sensation in its own right . . . Close . . . Distant . . . And how far away is far enough? And I really don't know which sen-

Permissive suggestion for comfort. Accessing previous trance experiences.
Embedded suggestion for absorption.

Encouraging flexibility in that there are a variety of ways to experience trance meaningfully.

Utilizing her interest in psychology and her newly enhanced self-image derived from her education.

Suggesting an amplification for an appreciation of unconscious control mechanisms.

Marking the word "comfort."

Marking the word "deeper."

Embedded commands.

Introducing spatial dissociation— separating specific locations in space.

Embedded command while reframing sensations as "interesting."
External kinesthetic focal points to shift away from internal kinesthetic focal points to begin facilitating pain relief.
Dissociation of sensation suggestions.

sations are the most soothing ... because that varies so much from individual to individual ...

Some people really enjoy the sensation of looking at an unusual cloud that can seem so out of place against a blue sky ... Some really enjoy the sensation of a very well-written piece of music that has just the right rhythm, just the right blend of instruments ... And if you've ever had the experience of a particularly enjoyable melody ... that sort of floats through your mind ... and you catch yourself humming that song ... or all of a sudden realizing that you're singing that song and you really don't know why that song seems so important ... Sometimes it's a corny song; sometimes it's a real favorite ... And it's interesting how some lyrics remain unforgettable ... and I bet you know what the eighth word in the national anthem is ... But when you take time to ... *sit quietly* ... and you experience the sensation of a particularly enjoyable and soothing voice that might be your own as you talk to yourself ... It might be mine as you listen ... I really don't know ... All I know is you have a conscious mind that can be very aware of the things that seem the most important ... Isn't it interesting how something can seem so important at one time and seem so unimportant at another time? ... And time ... how a minute can seem like an hour ... how a day

Encouraging redefining sensations in her awareness as "soothing" while utilizing her belief in the uniqueness of each person.

Visual suggestion, distracting from kinesthetic awareness.

Auditory suggestion, distracting from kinesthetic awareness.

Amplifying auditory absorption.

Unconscious involvement.

Memory can remain intact.

Preoccupying her on an auditory level with a distracting reference. Auditory focus.

Auditory focus, soothing internal and external dialogue.

Reassuring her that she can be as aware as she needs or wants to be.

A truism regarding the inevitability of change.

Time distortion, expansion.

can be an interesting one to experience ... When you think about all
the things you've accumulated, it
really reminded me of what base-
ments are for and what attics are for
... Old issues of *National Geographic,*
out-dated *Time* magazines, and a
string here, marble there, and isn't it
interesting ... because I was working with a young boy not long ago
who taught me a very important lesson as sometimes only kids can ...

Referencing her issue of "letting go"
by addressing the subject of accumulating things.

A "time" reference of outdated, no
longer relevant things.

Introducing a metaphor on the general theme of "letting go."

And it was a lesson that I really think
has a wider spread value than what I
might even understand now ... because it's a little boy who's lived here
in San Diego all of his life, all 8 years
of it ... And kids being what kids
are, he really has a very difficult
time understanding that there are
other places to live ... But when he
was told that he was going to be
moving soon he really didn't understand that things were going to be
a little different ... He wanted to
take his entire house and he wanted
to take his school and all of his friends
and teachers and that part was the
easy part ... The hard part came
when his mother told him "You're
really going to have to clean out
your drawers and closet.

Referencing children as a source of
learning, perhaps establishing a new
association to her own children.
Learnings can increase in value over
time.

The egocentricity of a child's thinking is amplified to encourage sensitive handling of her children.

The absurdity of "wanting to take it
all with you," reframing "holding on"
as undesirable.

Easy and hard parts, feeding back
her framing of experience in those
terms.

You're not going to want to take all
that junk with you." And how do
you decide which baseball cards to
throw away or give away? That's really
interesting because what he discovered was that all these things that

Indirect suggestion to "let go."

On re-evaluation, "letting go" was
easy because what mattered once
didn't matter anymore.

seemed so important, weren't important anymore ... The favorite toy
that he had when he was 3 wasn't
much fun when he was 8 ... There
aren't a lot of 8 year olds I know that
enjoy little pegboards and rattles ...
And it gave him an incredible sense   Amplifying a positive feeling for "let-
of accomplishment, a powerful rec-   ting go," reframing it as clear evi-
ognition of how much he had grown,   dence of growth.
that he had outgrown all these things,
and it was an *uplifting* experience   Incorporating Vicki's head lifting.
for him to discover that being a little
older and a little wiser allowed for
different possibilities now ... And I   Reinforcing that change in the
really don't know how, I really don't   absence of insight is possible.
know why, but then again, 8-year-old
boys really have mysterious ways ...
But going through the drawers and
closets showed him how much he'd
grown and changed without even
trying ... and what it really meant to
him was that he could move on   Marking.
comfortably, comfortably, and there   Marking.
might be a ... *deeper* ... meaning.
Sometimes it's hard to know; sometimes it really pays to listen at a deeper
level ... And you know that ...   Validating her knowledge.

And I wonder whether you've noticed   Ratifying trance through evidence
that your breathing has changed ...   of a visible physical change.
how much effort it takes to move ...   Indirect suggestion for catalepsy.
how absorbed all of you can be in
the comfortable experience of right
now ... And now becomes later, and   Time distortion, extending comfort
later you really can be comfortable   into the future.
... And one of the most interesting
dimensions of experiencing deep
comfort ... is that sensations seem
different because there is a disori-   Physical disorientation, preliminary

enting effect when you get so comfortable . . . it becomes hard to know
which side is more relaxed . . . Is it
your left side or is it your right side?
. . . and if your left side drifts off
comfortably . . . then which side is
left? And if it's your front, then do
we really know if it's the front of
your back that's comfortable or the
back of your front? . . . And it's very
difficult to know whether it's your
top half or the bottom half, or the
middle half of the back or the front
half that's the most comfortable . . .
That's right. And I knew one person
who was exceptionally skilled at being
able to *experience this part of the body as
very comfortably distinct* from that part
of their body which seemed disconnected over there, even though they
had the peculiar feeling that there
was something here that they just
weren't really in touch with . . . But I
know this much . . . that when you
take in a breath . . . and when your
mind is curious . . . and you're really
not sure which part's here and which
part's there . . . and which part's left
or right, and you have the right to
know what's left . . . it can take a
different turn for the better . . . and
that's something that *you really can be
clear* about . . . But there's something
that you might really want to know
about the sensation of comfort that
grows more profound moment by
moment . . . And what's so interesting is that your legs haven't moved
and your arms haven't moved and

to a confusion technique. Associating comfort to disorientation.

Left/right disorientation, dissociation.

Front/back disorientation, dissociation.

Top/bottom disorientation, dissociation.

Metaphor for physical dissociation.

Embedded command for dissociation and comfort.

Diminished kinesthetic awareness.

Uncertainty and dissociation.

Uncertain perceptions about her
body but mentally clear there is an
improvement.

Increased comfort.

Catalepsy is evident and is fed back
to her, amplifying it.

you know and I know that you could move them if you could think of a good reason to ... but how much more enjoyable to experience the luxury of a very relaxed body ... a very comfortable experience of being here, being fully here mentally, of being over there physically ... That's right ... And without disturbing your relaxation ... you might find it a particularly interesting experience to *have your throat and voice so comfortable* and relaxed that you could describe to me what you're experiencing, and why not verbalize what you're aware of right now, Vicki?

Reaffirming she is in control of the experience.

Suggestions for mental and physical dissociation.

Protective suggestions to remain comfortable preceding the suggestion to speak.
Throat comfort, later extended to next week (when she anticipated it being painful).

V: Heartburn is gone.

Suggestion to verbalize while remaining in trance.

M: You can say that again.

V: My heartburn is gone.

I didn't hear what she'd said, and so I suggested she repeat it.

M: Good. Your body's comfortable.

V: It feels soft.

Reinforcing her experience of comfort.

M: Is it a good experience?

V: Yes.

Amplifying its positive value.

M: Good. It's an interesting experience, isn't it? To have your body in trance ... To have your mind comfortable ... And how far away is your body from where you are?

Reinforcing the dissociation of mind and body.

Presupposition of having accomplished the dissociation.

V: Not far.

M: Just close enough for when you need it ... That's right. And just far enough to *really be comfortable* ... And what an interesting experience to know that *you can be so comfortable* ...

Framing her responses as a good one.

Reframing comfort as "interesting," associating comfort to even mild men-

Can you describe what it feels like to be just far enough away from your body to really be comfortable?

V: Nice. Safe.

M: Good ... That's right ... That's right ... It's that nice, safe, comfortable feeling that you really can memorize in very intense, vivid detail ... Very comfortable ... And what your unconscious mind might really want to know is that *you can be so comfortable whenever you want to be* ... And it's interesting, very interesting ... how the most everyday experiences can be the most profound reminders of what it's like to have a mind here and a body there ...

tal experiences.
Questioning to deepen the experience of dissociation.

Feeding back her terms for the experience.
Amplifying a clear memory of the experience of comfort to use as a later reference point.
Affirming the ability is hers and that it can be applied at later times of her choosing.
Associating the experience of comfort to everyday experiences ("anchoring").
Dissociation of the mind and body as a vehicle for everyday comfort.

what it's like to notice a cloud ... or a moving van ... or an 8-year-old boy ... or hands that rest comfortably in a lap of luxury ... and you really never know ...

Everyday cues referencing the trance process and recreating comfort.
Reinforcing that just sitting as she is, with her hands in her lap, she can be comfortable.

because sometimes it's looking at your watch that reminds you that

Associating time—and the everyday experience of looking at her watch —to comfort.

it's time to be comfortable ... Sometimes it's kicking off your shoes to remember that you're 2 feet ahead of yourself when you're here and there comfortably ... Sometimes it's giving yourself a hand, in the most simple and elegant of ways ... I really don't know ... I know one individual who tends to ... *eat with a real gusto* ... because she really likes the

Embedded suggestion.
Associating taking off her shoes to the experience of dissociation.

Self-help as a means of obtaining comfort.

Metaphor for appetite enhancement.
Embedded command.

strong sensations of being well-fed ... and somehow she has it in her mind that every time she opens the refrigerator door, she has that cool comfort ...

Positive association to eating.

Associating comfort and appetite to opening the refrigerator.

and the little light goes on ... and I don't know what it is about white lights ... and I really don't know what it is about food ... but the interesting thing is that *it really works* for her ... And she really can *be comfortable standing up in a kitchen,* and sitting down in a ... *living* ... room, and napping and talking seem to really regenerate the feelings of comfort ... but I don't think that I need to remind you that *you can relax* ... that *you can be safe and comfortable anywhere.* After all ... you're here with me and you can hear with me ... and you can hear with you ... and you can hear you talking to yourself ... in the strangest of places you can hear you, soothing, comforting, distancing ... keeping close the feelings of comfort ... and everything else can fade into the distance ... into the distance, like baseball cards and string ... And there really is no reason that I'm aware of to limit one's thinking to believe that a yard sale has to be in a yard, when you can have one inside, as many times a day as you'd like to ... And you can

Utilizing her "white light" association for comfort.

Embedded command, association of comfort to specific places.

Marking.

Extending comfort through all routine activities.
Extending comfort to *any* context.

Internal dialogue can be comforting and meaningful, regardless of where she finds herself.

Amplifying comfort, distancing anything else.

Referencing and amplifying "letting go" what is no longer necessary.

Referencing her idea of a yard sale as a vehicle for getting rid of what she no longer needs, including internal feelings or thoughts she finds distressing.

be a yard which is 3 feet away from yourself ... being here but three

Dissociation.

feet over there . . . experiencing comfort now and later . . . front and back . . . top and bottom . . . left and right . . . and the right to comfort is what's left . . . And that's what I'd really like you to know . . . and why not look ahead to a little bit later . . . or a lot later . . . or something in between a little and a lot . . . and as you look forward, can you see how comfortable you are? . . . (Nods) . . . Good . . . And you know that a week passes quickly . . . and you know that a week passes slowly . . . depending on point of view . . . and since it's you and your point of view . . . you might as well know that it's fully up to you . . . to have a fast day and a slow day depending on *your* choice . . . because 24 hours, 7 days in a row, or 16 hours 10 days in a row, or 13 hours 13 days in a row, really don't matter, but when it's two weeks of . . . *feeling so strongly* . . . about how time has been well-used, . . . you really can look back when you're looking ahead at yourself looking back . . . feeling good . . . and safe . . . and comfortable . . . And that's a *strong feeling* to hold on to, isn't it? (Nods) . . . Good . . . And since you can look forward to that experience of comfort, why not have that be the feeling that you hold on to tightly? . . . When I ask you to reorient in just a moment . . . the one thing that I really want you to know is that *you have done marvelously* . . . and why not enjoy the sense of pride in discovering that *you can use*

Associating comfort to the previous disorientation and dissociation suggestions.

Future orientation (posthypnotic suggestions) to include comfort.

Time distortion, either expansion or contraction as she wishes.

Time expansion through confusion.

Embedded suggestion.

Time disorientation; comfort embedded throughout.

A suggestion for strength.

Posthypnotic suggestion for later comfort, extending the current experience into later contexts.
Anticipation signal regarding disengagement.
Reinforcing her having succeeded in this context.

your head to be comfortable, and you can use your body to *alter sensation comfortably* . . . in the way that you'd like to . . . and let that be the guiding memory and experience for *this experience of comfort that you really can hold on to—here, there and everywhere that you go* . . . and when you know that you can do that . . . and when you feel the strength and comfort that you can do that . . . that's when you can begin to slowly reorient yourself mentally . . . but you may want to keep the physical disorientation of being here and being there . . . using your body but letting it come close and drift away as you see fit . . . So take whatever time you'd like to, Vicki, to process your experience and feelings, and then when you feel like you're ready to and when you want to . . . that's when you can bring back every comfortable sensation . . . for today, and tomorrow, and all your tomorrows that become todays. And when you're ready to, you can let your eyes open. (Pause). You did great!

Reinforcing that she has successfully done what she set out to do.
Redefining her relationship to her body.

Establishing success as the memorable association to this experience.
Maintaining comfort and generalizing it to the rest of her life.
Integrating the learnings and new associations.

Suggesting the possibility of maintaining the dissociation as a means for remaining comfortable.

Suggesting obtaining closure on the experience before disengaging.

Maintaining comfort post-trance.
Future comfort.

Permissive disengagement.

V: (Difficulty opening her eyes). It's bright. (*Closes her eyes again.*)

M: Take a moment. No need to reorient fully . . . just yet. That's right . . . Discover each comfortable sensation.

V: (Long pause before opening her eyes and moving). I like that.

M: Good. You sat just right!

Validating her responses and posture humorously.

V: I didn't even know I was sitting.

Confirmation of the extent of her physical dissociation.

M: It's nice not to know, isn't it?

Reframing uncertainty as pleasant.

V: Um-hum. The part that I—something that I liked very much that I never thought of before was "time." Some days *do* go fast, and some days go slow. It never entered my mind that I could have some control over that, so that's something new to think about. I liked that part.

The issue of "time" was so central to her, it's little surprise that she latched onto a mechanism to control her perception of it.

M: How are you feeling?

V: I liked that a lot. I got very much in touch with being over there and being over here. I hope I don't forget.

Confirmation of her positive regard for the session, and her experience of physical dissociation. She expresses concern for her memory of the session.

M: You're going to have a tape of this that I'm going to give you right now and then as you requested I'll be happy to make a copy of the video and then if you'd like I could either mail it to you or maybe we'll get together again sometime and give it to you then. But you'll have an audio tape right now and a video tape a little bit later, so that way . . . *you'll always have a reminder.*

Immediate reassurance that she has full and ready access to the experience via her memory as well as the tape of the session.

V: It was a very nice experience.

Embedded suggestion, referencing all the posthypnotic suggestions given throughout the session.

M: Good. Would you be willing to . . .

V: Yes!!

She cut me off to quickly agree to *whatever* I would ask of her! I think that is fairly good evidence for a high level of rapport!

M: . . . answer some questions? *Turning to class)* Are there any questions?

(*To class*) You can come out of trance now!

V: (Surprise) Does it really affect everybody, really?

M: (Laughs) They pretend that it doesn't, but I know better!   Playful closure to the session.

V: I don't know how it could not.   Orienting to the others and beginning to engage with them.

The session concludes with Vicki responding to specific questions about her experience during the trance session as well as her remarkable personal history. After about 15 minutes of questions, she left. We parted most amiably.

FINAL COMMENTS

Vicki passed away less than eight weeks later. I received a thank-you note from her a few days after our session, and spoke to her once on the phone soon after. She was able to make use of the physical dissociation and time distortion techniques for a short while after our meeting, but her illness soon became too severe to self-manage.

I cannot imagine a more dramatic way to get across the message to helping professionals to "listen to your client" than to be exposed to Vicki. Clearly, though, the right to be heard is one requiring expression, a point which did not catch up with Vicki until it was already too late. Therapy must truly be a cooperative process.

21

Resisting Resistance

The literature pertaining to clinical hypnosis has generally had quite a bit to say about the issue of client resistance. Overwhelmingly, resistance was considered to be a manifestation of the client's defenses for coping with sensitive intrapsychic conflicts. "Proper" treatment was a confrontive inquiry about the resistance, first acknowledging it, next attempting to uncover its origin and function, and then collaborating on its resolution. From this perspective, resistance was always the client's problem by serving as an intrapsychic coping device requiring analysis and interpretation. When it interfered with the progress of therapy, as it inevitably did, the client was blamed as the saboteur. Accusations and interpretations were thrust at the client who obviously "really didn't want to change," or perhaps was "too resistant to succeed."

Resistance is, for all intents and purposes, a force that works against the aims of therapy. Resistance has long been recognized as an integral and unavoidable component of the therapeutic process, and virtually every therapeutic approach I am aware of has roughly equivalent recognitions of its existence. Only the rationale for its existence and techniques for its acknowledgment and treatment differ from approach to approach.

Defining resistance as a force that works against the aims of therapy does not place blame on either the clinician or client. Rather than view people coming in voluntarily (dealing with persons in treatment involuntarily differs in some ways) for help as not really wanting help, it seems much more practical to view resistance as a communication from the client about his limitations in relating to the world (of which the clinician is a part). In other words, resistance isn't a fixed property of the client, but rather can be viewed as a communication indicating the limits of what the client can and cannot do. Rather than blame the client, the communication can be accepted as a valid indication of the person's experience of himself.

Placing this general perspective in the context of doing trancework, resistance is not necessarily an indication of unconscious sabotage on the part of the client. It is frequently the case that the client is simply making a choice not to respond in the desired way to suggestions for any of a variety of other reasons, each of which has a common denominator: The suggestion simply does not fit with the person's experience, and, in fact, may even contradict it. Resistance may be viewed as an interpersonal statement that says that whatever therapeutic strategies and maneuvers are being performed are not acceptable at some level(s) to the client.

Resistance is a very real force, and can be tied to one or both of the two main areas of treatment: resistance to formal trancework, and/or resistance to therapeutic progress.

RESISTANCE TO HYPNOSIS

Undesirable responses to trancework are manifested in a variety of ways. The client may actively or passively refuse to go into trance, or may enter trance but refuse to follow the guidance of the clinician. Examples of such nonconforming behavior include, but are not limited to: fidgeting, smiling, laughing, crying, interrupting, spontaneous disengagements, polar (opposite) responses, overcooperation, coughing, and direct or passive-aggressive hostility aimed at the clinician. Such responses as these are *not* to be assumed resistant. They may be idiosyncratic responses that occur without interfering with the course of treatment.

Origins of the resistance to hypnosis can be numerous. One of the most common is the fear of what will happen during the trance process. If the client is misinformed about the nature of the trance experience, he may fear it. All the misconceptions discussed in detail earlier may be all someone knows about hypnosis. If you thought you might divulge sensitive information, be coerced into doing things against your will, or be controlled by someone you really don't know much about, would *you* want to be hypnotized?

Resistance to hypnosis may also arise because of past failures associated with it, either from personal experience or the experience of credible others. Resistance may also arise from negative feelings toward the clinician (thus highlighting the value of rapport). Resistance may also arise from contextual variables such as the immediate environment, the client's mood, health, and even the weather.

Much resistance to hypnosis, however, is attributable to the quality of the suggestions, specifically how well they match the client's experience. If I give a client a suggestion to feel her muscles relaxing, and she isn't experiencing that sensation, my suggestion does not fit her experience and is easily rejected. Does that make her a poor subject, me a poor hypnotist, or both? My belief is that the outcome is a shared responsibility. The basis of the "pacing and leading" or "accepting and utilizing" suggestion formula is to match the client's experience through careful feedback to him as a way of demonstrating that you understand his experience. The result is rapport, and by linking what is to what can be one can increase the likelihood of a suggestion being accepted. To impose arbitrary suggestions on a client that he experience something *you* want him to experience (e.g., arm levitation) that has little relationship to what he is experiencing or wants to experience is a basis for choosing not to follow your suggestion. Furthermore, your client may be in so comfortable a state of mind and body that your demands, simple as they may seem, are too much a strain for him. Even beyond that, your client may be giving himself suggestions that are more meaningful than yours! Why shouldn't he be free to have that experience without being harassed as too "resistant"?

Hypnosis increases the range of a person's control, not decreases it. Suggestions that don't fit well, by mismatching experience or by placing too much demand on the person, can be and usually are rejected. To expect blind obedience on the part of the client is necessary for the stage hypnotist, but is wholly inappropriate in the clinical context.

RESISTANCE TO THERAPEUTIC PROGRESS

Resistance to the aims of therapy has an extensive overlap with the dynamics of resistance to hypnosis. Such resistance is manifested by such examples as appointments being missed, cancelled, or tardily arrived at. Assigned tasks ("homework") not being carried out, the setting up of a "power struggle" with the therapist for control of the relationship, clock-watching, interrupting, terminating treatment prematurely, overcooperation, inappropriate gift-giving, and requests for special favors are further evidence of treatment blocks.

Origins of the resistance to the aims of treatment can be numerous. Blocks may arise, because of the client's intrapsychic conflicts, i.e., ambivalences, that have been described in detail in analytic writings. They may arise because of the fear of change, since for many change is a risky process because of the giving up of the known for the uncertainty of the unknown. Small changes can give rise to big changes in one's life, and for many that is a frightening prospect. Even when the client hates herself for her symptoms, a life without them is a vague, scary obscurity. The reluctance to let go of the old, albeit dysfunctional, and familiar is the classic sign of resistance. It is for this reason that the clinician, in order to intervene successfully, must understand the impact of the client's symptom(s) on her world. Symptoms can be viewed as a metaphor, or symbol, of the person's experience. They reflect limitations the person is experiencing in relating flexibly to the world around her. Perhaps most importantly, symptoms have a consequence. Symptoms affect the client's self-image, social network, behavioral possibilities, affective realm, physiology, and spiritual makeup. To attempt removal of a symptom without appreciating its role in the person's universe is nothing short of irresponsible. The client's unconscious may prevent symptom removal to protect her, and the resistance to the clinician's efforts is incidental.

This point is further elaborated in the later chapter on the potential hazards of doing trancework. Suffice it to say here that what seems like resistance to the clinician may simply be a self-preserving maneuver by the client. In order to facilitate therapeutic progress, you must understand a symptom's function(s) and provide alternatives that satisfy the symptom's underlying need without having to have the destructive symptom present.

Resistance to therapeutic progress may also be attributed to the type of intervention employed if it involves strategies and maneuvers that are unacceptable to the client. Furthermore, if the clinician is working at a rate faster or slower than her client, resistance surfaces. Resistance may also arise from negative feelings toward the clinician, or their opposite—idealized, romantic feelings that place a clinician on a pedestal she must inevitably fall from. Finally, contextual variables play a role as well, including such factors as environmental conditions, client disposition and health, and the like. It should be apparent that all the sensitivity that goes into effective trancework is just a part of the larger therapeutic picture, for all the same guidelines apply.

RESPONDING TO RESISTANCE

How to deal with communication deemed "resistant" is, of course, a function of how one conceptualizes it. How resistance is defined and whose responsibility it is thought to be will determine whether one views resistance as a property of the client, a property of the clinician (Bandler and Grinder [1979] have flatly stated that there is no such thing as resistance, there are only poor therapists), or an interactional outcome of the two.

Blaming the client by figuratively shaking her and kicking her in the shins while interrogating "Why are you so resistant?" is a poor alternative. The client needs and wants professional help, not a hard time. On the other hand, no therapist can succeed with 100% of his clients. While it is important to keep expanding one's range of skills, the clinician can't be given *all* the responsibility for treatment outcomes. After all, the relationship involves at least two....

Accepting the resistance as a valid communication from the client prevents having to ascribe blame to one or the other person in the relationship. More importantly, it paves the way to elevate the relationship to a new level of collaboration through what Milton Erickson called the "utilization of resistance."

Erickson's perspective on resistance was a unique one that makes a great deal of sense; better yet, *it works!* The basic utilization formula of "accept and utilize" applies here. In practice it takes the form of being able to skillfully accept the client's response as a valid one while developing a way to utilize the response in service of further suggestions. For example, if Erickson was performing an arm levitation and offering suggestions of the subject's arm becoming lighter and lighter and the subject reports experiencing her arm as getting heavier and heavier, Erickson would say something like "That's right, that's fine, and your arm can get heavier still." By accepting the client's response as a valid one, the response can be built upon. This redefines the resistant behavior as cooperative behavior. If the clinician defines everything the client does as cooperative, where is the resistance? Finding a way to make the nonconforming behavior an asset to the person can change the feeling attached to it substantially.

Another technique for managing resistance is more of a preventative one employing process suggestions. By not asking for a specific response and covering all the possible responses, whatever the client does is cooperative. For example:

> You can notice the temperature in one of your hands, and as you continue to breathe in and out at your own comfortable rate, you may notice how your hand becomes warmer, or perhaps cooler, or you may notice how the temperature remains the same....

Her hand is going to get warmer, cooler, or stay the same. What other possibilities are there? Therefore, any response she generates is a cooperative one.

Erickson was of the belief that clients need to be able to resist directives (to maintain a sense of autonomy), and one of the strategies he employed was offering the client two or more directives simultaneously so that the client could resist one and accept the other(s). For example, I may direct a client to "Sit down, close your eyes, take a deep breath, and remember an experience from childhood you can talk about." By offering so many directives, the probability is I will get most or all of the desired responses. Even if the client resists one, I will have gotten the others and can resuggest the other in a different form later if I care to. Notice also in the above suggestion the phrase " ... an experience ... you can talk about." The implication to the client is that she can refuse to talk about some experiences, allowing her to resist telling me something while simultaneously following my guidelines.

Another technique for managing resistance is the strategy Haley (1973) described as "encouraging resistance." When you encourage resistance, usually with intentional use of negative suggestions, in order for the client to resist resisting, she must cooperate (sort of a "reverse psychology"). For example, if I want the client to sit down, but anticipate that a directive to do so will be met with resistance, I can instead suggest:

> You don't have to sit down. I don't expect you can *make yourself comfortable* (embedded command) here. It will be much better for you to stand just as you are.

By my encouraging her to resist and remain standing, her resistance to me can now allow her to be seated. Either way, sitting or standing, her behavior is defined as cooperative (sitting is what I want her to do, standing is what I've directed her to do).

Responding to a client's resistances in a way that is accepting and non-confrontational requires a great deal of flexibility and respect for the integrity of the client. Flexibility refers to the ability to have a variety of ways to get a point across without having to beat the client over the head with it. Flexibility means being willing to go the extra distance to operate on the client's level, joining her reality instead of expecting or demanding her to come to yours. It also means not having so rigid a set of expectations and procedures that would not allow for unique, individual responses.

(continued on p. 413)

FRAME OF REFERENCE: JAY HALEY

Jay Haley, M.A., is one of the most influential figures in the field of psychotherapy, and is recognized as such by all those who have ever even glanced at works dealing with hypnosis, systems theory, and family therapy. He is Director of the Haley-Madanes Institute of Washington, D.C., a leading training center for those interested in the strategic and interpersonal approaches to family therapy. Haley has authored seven books, co-authored two, and edited five more. He was the first recipient of the Lifetime Achievement Award of the Milton H. Erickson Foundation. His analysis and presentation of Erickson's work almost singlehandedly made the work available to the mental health profession, for which we are all greatly indebted. His dry wit and ability to sense and articulate the ironies of the therapy business are simply unparalleled by anyone.

On Starting to See Families: "We realized that what Bateson hypothesized as happening in the childhood of the schizophrenic was happening *currently*—if you look at the way they were communicating. So, we made a tremendous shift from etiology and childhood experiences as causal to current social situations as causal. There was a family whose supposed 'psychotic' son sent his mother a Mother's Day card which said 'You've always been like a mother to me.' The mother brought it with her to a session and said 'There's something wrong with this.' But it was *that* level of communication that interested us. So, I started seeing that family regularly for a long time, and then we all started seeing families."

On Hypnosis and Double-binds: "In hypnosis we found the first double-bind. Bateson had this idea of the double-bind, but we couldn't find one. And I remember when I realized that a hypnotist was directing a person to behave spontaneously—that was the double-bind, a classical paradoxical conflict."

On Treating Schizophrenia: "The most successful therapy for schizophrenia is that which assumes they're normal and they should go back to work or school. If you assume they're handicapped by something physiological, and therefore need medication, you lose on the therapy, because the family doesn't push them, the doctors don't push them. They think there's something really wrong with themselves. Everybody organizes around the handicapped person, and the therapy fails!"

On Meeting Erickson: "Everyone was scared of Erickson, because they never knew what he was doing to influence you. He was so agile of mind that he got bored doing any one thing, so he was always doing two or three things at once. So, as you're chatting about a case, he was trying to get you to put a hand on a table or turn the other way or cross your legs the other way."

On Types of Hypnosis: "I tend to think of three different hypnoses: 1) the personal hypnosis, where you go through a yoga experience or meditation experience, or whatever; 2) research hypnosis, where you're trying to find the limits of influence of hypnosis in various ways—in terms of deafness, color-blindness, or whatever; and then 3) there's clinical hypnosis, where you're trying to change someone— and I don't think that has anything to do with the other two hypnoses."

On Teaching Hypnosis: "To teach hypnosis clinically, you have to show someone how to do it with a patient and then watch them do it with a patient while you guide them in doing it. That's how it was taught at the turn of the century—live supervision. And to just teach them how to hypnotize is not a solution. It's so different *changing* someone; the person's motivation is different, the responses are different. I can remember when I went into practice and had some nice formal ways of inducing trance. I would get clients who came to be hypno- tized and they'd sit down in the chair and go into trance when I said 'Hello.' Then I would wake them up to put them through the 'proper' ritual! Then I realized that the setting determined how they were going to be and it really wasn't necessary to hypnotize them. But you wouldn't realize that if you were teaching hypnosis in a class."

On Erickson: "The contemporaries of Erickson thought of him as the best among equals. There were a number of therapists who thought they were just about as good as he was. The younger generation of therapists think of him as 'The Guru,' and think of him as magical or whatever. I'm of the older generation who just thought of him as a man who knew his business as a therapist. He worked at it, he practiced with it, he experimented with it, and he innovated remark- able procedures."

Source: Personal Communication, 1988

One of my favorite quotes is one attributed to Abraham Maslow: "When the only tool you have is a hammer, everything around you begins to look like a nail." It is important not to build resistance in your client by doing things the way you think they should be done with no regard for your client's expectations, beliefs, and values. If you attempt a maneuver that fails or a communication that is responded to unfavorably, don't get a bigger hammer, i.e., don't do the same thing over again just a little harder! *Shift* your approach smoothly, even compliment the person's resistance if you care to comment on her ability to make choices in her own behalf. Then, do something else.

A general guideline for managing resistance describes the relationship between directiveness and resistance. Not many people like to be told exactly what to do, and ordering someone to respond obediently as in direct authoritarian suggestions encourages resistance. The guideline is this: The greater the resistance (anticipated or derived), the greater the need for indirection. In other words, the degree the client resists direction is the degree to which an indirect style is recommended. The indirect techniques (such as homework assignments and metaphors) are valuable tools in getting points across in a gentler and more subtle manner. As Zeig (1980a) pointed out, if a client is going to be obedient and highly responsive, the use of indirect techniques isn't really necessary. Having proficient skills

---

Table 20. Potential
Responses To Resistance

1. Ignore
2. Examine
3. Encourage
4. Prescribe
5. Confuse
6. Dissociate
7. Associate
8. Intersperse
9. Deflect
10. Diffuse
11. Confront
12. Redefine
13. Interpret

in the use of direct and indirect techniques allows for a much wider range of influence than does the use of direct suggestions alone.

CONCLUSION

Resistance to change is a basic feature of humankind. We spend so much of our lives trying to build a ritualized pattern of behavior so as to expend the least amount of physical and mental energy, and after developing such a pattern we complain of "being stuck in a rut."

Resistance doesn't always show up in detectable ways (some are so unconscious and subtle), and resistance can't always be used in the service of change. Some clients simply will not change, others only slightly. The discussion of resistance in this chapter is intended to present the idea that much of resistance is interpersonal, arising from a demanding, insensitive approach. Furthermore, other resistances relate to a lack of appreciation for the role of the symptom in the person's life. A greater number of interventions will succeed when the clinician is able to get a single point across in a large number of ways, using the feedback from each unique individual as his guide for knowing what to do as well as what not to.

For Discussion

1. What change(s) would you like to make that you have had difficulty changing thus far? How would you react to someone who suggested you must not really want to change it? What resistances to change can you identify as underlying your inability to change thus far?

2. What reasons can you suggest for why people both seek change and avoid it?

3. Can all people change whatever trait they wish to? Why or why not? How does your belief in response to this question influence your work?

4. How is resistance a reflection of one's limitations?

5. What examples can you cite for how people work to get into a predictable pattern and then complain about its routineness? When is a predictable pattern an asset? A liability?

Things to Do

1. In a "Hand Dance" exercise with your study partner, sit opposite each other, eyes closed, and hands held up to each other as if to play "Pattycake." Silently, one will begin to move her hands in all directions with the other person following, keeping your hands together. When a minute or so has gone by, switch so the other person leads. What feelings come up? Did you experience resistance? Why?

2. Research ways resistance has been considered over the years. Who gets blamed for it? How is it treated?

22

Hypnotic Hazards and Ethical Guidelines

In the earlier chapter addressing misconceptions about hypnosis, one of the misconceptions discussed briefly concerned the potential harm to a client undergoing treatment through trancework. In that discussion, I made the point that hypnosis is a tool, not a therapy, and that it could be applied skillfully or it could be misused and potentially harm the client. This places full responsibility on the clinician to exercise caution and sensitivity in the use of hypnotic techniques.

By dealing more directly with the client's unconscious mind and intrapsychic dynamics, the clinician has the opportunity to gain access to an internal world that is delicately balanced. To be insensitive to the powerful emotions that may be triggered, traditionally called an "abreaction," can place the client in jeopardy emotionally, not to mention wasting an opportunity to do some real healing. If a clinician is uncomfortable in dealing with strong emotional associations that may be triggered by what was originally intended to be the most soothing of trance experiences, the choice exists to either *get* comfortable or avoid doing any work of real emotional impact (i.e., doing therapy in an entirely intellectual style).

In this chapter I would like to discuss some of the potential unexpected reactions to trancework that necessitate a healthy respect for the power of the tool. Before you begin to fantasize unspeakably horrible possibilities, let me assure you of a couple of things: First, if you are respectful of the innate integrity of your client, you will avoid virtually all of the potential pitfalls. Second, if you can appreciate that an abreaction has great potential therapeutic value through the release of insight and emotion if guided skillfully, abreactions won't have to be feared. That doesn't mean they have to be encouraged either, but they can be viewed as an open door to a powerful therapeutic experience.

There are no dangers attributable to the trance state in and of itself. Whatever difficulties may arise as a result of trance experiences have to do with the associations triggered by all the communication elements present in the interaction. These include the relationship between clinician and client, the communication style employed, the specific suggestion content, the contextual variables, and, most importantly, the client's intrapersonal communications.

The "dangers" associated with the use of hypnosis have been grossly exaggerated in traditional literature on hypnosis. Scares of hypnosis inevitably precipitating psychosis, neurosis, hysteria, and suicide have appeared in older literature. Such ideas are still being taught in some places where they should know better. The following story is all too true an example of what I mean. A friend of mine completed training in osteopathic medicine at a conservative eastern university. During a six-week rotation in psychiatry, he "learned" that hypnosis precipitates psychosis. He asked me quite somberly, "Michael, are you sure you know what you're doing?" My first impulse as a response was to cause physical harm, I confess, but being a pacifist I decided to explain the basis for the medical and psychoanalytic perspectives on hypnosis ("After all, Freud abandoned it ... "). I think I helped him to understand why problems may arise in the indiscriminate use of hypnosis because of some of the very reasons I will describe now in identifying potential difficulties and their resolution.

SYMPTOM SUBSTITUTION

The most common argument against the use of hypnosis I experience personally concerns the potential for "symptom substitution." Symptom substitution refers to the onset of a new symptom, perhaps but not necessarily a worse one, in the place of the old symptom removed during treatment. In order for one to charge hypnosis with this potential liability, hypnosis must be viewed as a symptomatic treatment as opposed to a more dynamic approach addressing underlying root causes. The dynamic theory is that there is a psychic energy associated with internal conflicts that is relieved by the development of a symptom—an outlet for the energy. By removing the outlet, the energy must be redirected elsewhere and a new outlet developed. Other "symptomatic" approaches, most notably behaviorism, have faced this same charge.

In the case of hypnosis, there is a twist that makes the response to the criticism somewhat complex. Hypnosis *can* be used symptomatically (standardization of approach is an example), and, in my opinion, *is* used this way all too often, partially because of the lack of laws regulating formal training and the competent practice of hypnosis. Simple, direct suggestion aimed at a target symptom can be used by untrained laypeople with no real understanding of the issues presented throughout this chapter in particular and this book in general. Without an understanding of the role of a symptom in a person's life and the related dynamics, symptom substitution can be (but isn't necessarily) an unwanted, unexpected outcome.

The twist is that while hypnosis can be used symptomatically, its greatest strength is derived from its ability to be used in a more substantive way, such as in addressing a symptom's underlying dynamics and consequences. It is this type of practice I wanted to promote throughout this book through my consideration of so many issues and concepts associated with the responsible practice of clinical hypnosis.

The primary issues associated with the potential for unwanted symptom substitution are first, a symptom's function (when it has one), and second, the associated secondary gains. *If these two issues are not adequately addressed,* directly or indirectly, *success in treatment is virtually impossible.*

The idea of a symptom frequently, but not always, serving a useful purpose even though it may be uncomfortable to a person is probably not a difficult idea to grasp. To view it as a way of coping, a way of controlling others, a way of getting what one wants, a way of avoiding responsibility, and a way of maintaining a stable position in an erratic world are all ways of giving the symptom a special respect for its value instead of derogating it as stupid and meaningless. If the function or value of a symptom is not considered, how is that same need in the person to be managed more constructively through the therapeutic alternatives you provide?

In the psychiatric hospitals I have worked in, the staffs did something I considered to be a bit odd. It is a purely subjective estimate on my part that 98.36% of psychiatric patients are cigarette smokers, most of whom are chain-smokers. Cigarettes entertain them in what can often be a boring environment, they are a medium of exchange in the patient barter system, they are a status symbol, but mostly they just help the patients manage their anxiety by giving them a series of temporary focal points. Staff members, noticing the value of cigarettes, use them for leverage to get the patients to do whatever staff wants them to. "Difficult" patients lose their smoking privilege and must earn the right to smoke. This ploy works enough times to keep it going, but some patients don't react well to it. Within a short time after the cigarettes are taken, the patient ends up in seclusion for "acting out." This is a prime example of what I mean when I talk about the value of a symptom. In this example, cigarette smoking is not just a bad habit—it's the glue holding the fragile patient together. Removing an outlet and providing no better alternative can lead to rapid deterioration. Of course, the patient teaches the staff not to do *that* again . . . In emotionally healthier people, this process is not nearly as extreme, but a similar potential exists. The idea of responsible treatment is to acknowledge the function of the symptom and to develop alternatives that will satisfy the underlying dynamics in a more constructive way.

Closely related is the issue of "secondary gain." Secondary gain refers to the "payoff" for a symptom—the advantages the symptom allows the person. The payoff is rarely, if ever, a conscious one. Rather, it is an unconscious system which supports the symptom's existence. Realistically, the symptom has an impact on the person's personal and interpersonal worlds: her family, friends, spouse, therapist, and whoever else might be in the sphere of the symptom's influence. If the impact is one that encourages the symptom, the symptom is easy to maintain. In fact, one of the better techniques, in my opinion, that was a part of Erickson's approach and is a part of mine as well is a technique I call "Making the Symptom Inconvenient." Haley (1984) described the same approach as "Ordeal Therapy." This intervention involves somehow making engaging in the symptomatic behavior so inconvenient that the symptom is abandoned in favor of behaving in a more positive mode.

Supporting the symptom, or providing a secondary gain, is easy to illustrate. Suppose you broke your leg in a skiing accident and your family and friends rallied to your side to take care of your every need with the motto: "Rest up, don't aggravate your leg, we'll take care of everything!" Well, when you are served your meals in bed, get to watch TV all day, catch up on your reading, and get more attention than from anything else you've done, is it hard to understand how you might learn to "tolerate" your predicament? Is it any wonder that six months later your doctor is asking why you haven't gotten up and about when you should have months ago? Can you see why you might respond, "But, Doc, it hurts so badly!"

Every symptom has a consequence which must be addressed somewhere in the treatment process. Removing the payoffs can often change the symptom with nothing else imposed on the client. In any event, symptom substitution need not occur if the symptom's purpose(s) and secondary gain(s) are identified and resolved within the treatment process. Whether these issues should be presented to the client as "insights" or not (perhaps choosing to address them indirectly) is a matter of professional orientation and clinical judgment.

Ideally, resolution of the problem of symptom substitution occurs preventatively by addressing the issues above. If symptom substitution should arise for some reason, the new symptom can be addressed more directly in terms of its origin, purpose, secondary gains, and meaning to the client. It can be removed through suggestion, through techniques like age progression, or Bandler and Grinder's "ecology check" (1979), described in the next paragraph.

Age progression was discussed in detail in the chapter describing trance phenomena. Suffice it to say here that taking the client forward in time (through fantasy projection) allows the person to assess realistically the impact of the proposed changes. Such assessment consists of evaluating whether alleviation of the symptom has been helpful or hurtful, and in what ways. The "ecology check" is a more sophisticated technique based on the recognition that the person is composed of multiple interrelated parts. A change in one part of the person is necessarily going to have an impact on the other parts, hopefully, positively, but perhaps not. The "ecology check" is a way to have access to the unconscious mind's perspective on the impact of the symptom's removal. The check essentially involves establishing direct communication, verbal or otherwise, with the unconscious mind, having it implement the change under consideration, and noticing the change in the internal environment of the person. Specifically, the person is to notice whether the change is an acceptable one at all levels. If so, the unconscious is asked whether the part of the person formerly responsible for the old symptom can now be responsible for integrating the new alternative(s) provided in treatment into the desired context. This technique is a useful way of addressing both a symptom's functions and secondary gains. In my experience, it is inadequate resolution of the issues of symptom function and secondary gain that cause failures in treatment, as well as successes that are only temporary where the person accomplishes what they came for but later reverts back to the old, dysfunctional pattern.

As a final point, there are occasions where symptom substitution may be a desirable alternative as a part of treatment. In other words, intentionally creating an "acceptable" symptom may be a choice a clinician and client make together. Channeling a client's physical pain from one part of her body and concentrating it in her little finger, for example, may be a desirable alternative for the patient.

Developing an appreciation for the complexity of these issues will facilitate not only trancework, but therapeutic intervention in general. Ideally, the issue of symptom substitution associated with the use of hypnosis can become a dead issue at last.

FAILURE TO REMOVE SUGGESTIONS

A common fear expressed to me by my students concerns the failure to remove suggestions. With all the things there are to occupy the clinician's mind in doing trancework (formulating meaningful suggestions while closely observing and utilizing client responses), what happens if she forgets to remove a suggestion?

The response to this seemingly hazardous condition is a relatively simple one. The suggestions for particular responses of the person in trance are trance-state specific. In other words, they are operative only as long as the person is in the trance state. There is no carryover of the trance-obtained responses into the client's "waking" state unless there has been a suggestion to do so. You may remember that is the purpose of the posthypnotic suggestion—to allow the responses obtained in trance to generalize to other contexts. Without the posthypnotic suggestion (from the client to herself or from the clinician) to carry the response over to some other context, the response is just an interesting one observable during hypnosis. Thus, if the clinician forgets to remove suggestions given during trance at the end of the trance process, the suggestion is highly likely to dissipate automatically upon disengagement. If the exception occurs (see the Frame of Reference comments by André Weitzenhoffer on this subject in Chapter 4) and the client continues to experience a suggestion that was not intended post-hypnotically, it is a safe bet the client has given himself the posthypnotic suggestion to do so. Trance may be reinduced and the suggestion removed if desired.

Another alternative is to appreciate that the suggestion must have some special significance to the client or he would not have maintained it. Trance may be reinduced in order to discover its significance. Suggestions are followed only as long as they are appropriate, i.e., beneficial. The point to remember is that any suggestion can be accepted or rejected, and the maintenance of a suggestion unintended to exist outside of the trance state is a choice by the client.

Failing to remove a suggestion is generally not a source of overwhelming concern because of the trance-specific responsiveness of clients. The same happens to be true of therapy in general—often the client feels better-than-usual (e.g., more self-confident, appreciated) while in the therapist's office, but these feelings are tied to that specific place. The therapist tries to generalize the feelings and abilities from his office and relationship to the client to the real world of the client, but getting the client to carry the skills from the office to the real world is usually not all that easy to do.

In sum, the suggestions will most probably dissipate on disengaging from the trance state, but in the exception where this does not occur, the client may be rehypnotized and the suggestion removed in whatever manner is deemed appropriate.

SPONTANEOUS REGRESSION AND ABREACTION

The terms "spontaneous regression" and "abreaction" are *not* synonymous terms, but rather are so closely related in their association that I have chosen to discuss them together in this section. A spontaneous regression is the experience of repressed past experiences coming into awareness. Abreaction has been defined earlier in this chapter as the expression of pent-up emotions. Together, these two account for the often unexpected emotionalism that makes hypnosis such a powerful tool. When you are doing something seemingly as simple as a general relaxation procedure, a client may flash on some word or image that you use which is associated to an emotionally charged memory, bringing up feelings of hurt, pain, anger, or the like.

The spontaneous regression back to some unpleasant memory is an indicator of what is commonly called "unfinished business," experiences requiring further resolution of feelings. Sometimes the repression is so great that the material remains out of consciousness even during trance, and the person complains of a headache or some such discomfort after the trance experience.

Even the most skilled clinician cannot know what land mines are in the client's unconscious waiting be be tripped in doing therapy or trancework. Each human being has his or her own unique personal history and idiosyncratic associations to words and experiences. What seems like a neutral term to one person may be the trigger to some intense personal experience to another. Therefore, the possibility of doing extensive trancework without ever experiencing an abreaction is highly unlikely. Some people, on the other hand, instigate abreactions by a sort of "psychological voyeurism," assuming that intense emotionality is therapeutically necessary as well as fascinating to observe.

Abreactions can manifest themselves in a variety of ways, including crying, hyperventilation, trembling of the body (or specific body parts), hysterical conversions, premature disengagement from trance, hallucinations, delusions, and autistic-like rocking motions. Each of the above behaviors is not automatically indicative of an abreaction, but should be responded to cautiously and sensitively. The first and foremost thing to remember is this: *You can feel comfortable asking your client to describe her experience.* Give protective suggestions, and be supportive of her experience, using the general "accept and utilize" formula. The person has opened up with some sensitive information, and it is an unnecessary waste to let the moment pass and do nothing. Allow the abreaction, but be helpful to the client in helping her reach a new perspective on the experience—after all, that's what therapy is for, isn't it? One can't change the past, only attitudes toward it.

Use calming suggestions, and even if the reaction is wholly unexpected you are learning here and now to expect the unexpected. Make sure your voice is soothing and confident, and move in a casual way as opposed to short, rapid movements. In general, the best thing you can do is use hypnosis to resolve the situation and attain some closure. Even if your client's hour is up, your responsibility to that person isn't over. Make certain she can leave in a collected manner.

If a client opens up with some sensitive information that you are simply not equipped to handle for whatever reason, I suggest that you make sure the client is immediately referred to an appropriate helping professional (thus the value of a good referral list). A suggestion such as the following may be employed in such instances:

> ... And you've become aware now of some feelings that are very strong and some memories that are needing some attention ... and you can know comfortably that as these images and feelings drift into your awareness that they can be handled skillfully and that you can help yourself by keeping this information in a safe place within you until they can be brought out with the person best able to help you with them, and so you can let these images and feelings drift to the safe place within you until you are ready to share them when the time is right. ...

Essentially, the suggestions above are telling the client that she can put the information away safely for now and deal with them later in a context that is more appropriate. Such protective suggestions can have a very soothing effect on the person, and can build even greater trust for your open acknowledgment of your limits in intervening.

ETHICAL GUIDELINES

The above descriptions of potential difficulties that may arise in the use of trancework indirectly comment on the need for formal education in the dynamics of human behavior, the need to be respectful of the integrity of each human being, and the need to know one's own limits in providing therapeutic interventions.

As a helping professional, it is assumed that you have only the best of intentions for your clients, and that the understandings of human nature and the capacity for interpersonal influence you learn here will be used in a constructive way. Therefore, there is only a superficial coverage of ethical guidelines provided here.

1. The number one priority is to help, not hurt. If you feel that, for *any* reason, you are unable to work well with either the person or problem presented to you, then evaluate honestly whether it would be best to refer that person elsewhere—and do so when appropriate.

2. A professional's responsibility is to educate, not show off. Hypnosis lends itself to both, and it is my sincere hope that the trance phenomena you are learning to induce are used and/or demonstrated only in appropriate clinical or educational settings.

3. Have your relationship with your client(s) as clearly defined as possible, including the nature of the intervention, the duration, the cost, the expectations, evaluation points, etc. Involving and educating your client will almost certainly make for a better, more productive relationship.

4. Do not go beyond your range of expertise, or misrepresent yourself. Human problems are very complex and can't be reduced to a paragraph of dynamics. If you feel you are out of your league when presented with a problem, refer the person to someone better able to meet her needs.

5. Presenting misinformation and/or the use of indirect techniques will sometimes be judged to be the best approach. Be careful—such approaches can help a client, but they can also backfire. Have alternatives prepared every step of the way by thinking your intervention strategy through. In other words, be prepared!

6. Always involve, when appropriate, the proper qualified health professionals. When working on a physical symptom, unless you are a physician you should have a medical referral and medical clearance to work with the problem. Practicing medicine (psychology, nutrition, etc.) without a license or without adequate knowledge and backup is nothing short of irresponsible.

More importantly, I repeat my urge to never go beyond your range of expertise. Using hypnotic techniques without adequate knowledge is potentially dangerous, and damaging someone through ignorance is unforgivable.

CONCLUSION

The concepts and techniques presented in this chapter are ones that rank as some of the most important in this book. It is my hope that this chapter served the purpose of sensitizing you to the issues associated with the responsible practice of hypnosis.

Hypnosis as a tool is of potentially great value, and its use can grow at a faster rate in the professional community when each practitioner who uses hypnosis does so in a sensitive way. As its professional use grows, clients can get better, and that's what we're all striving for, isn't it?

For Discussion

1. Have you ever experienced an abreaction? In what context? What factors allowed the abreaction to occur? What effect did it have?

2. Have you ever experienced symptom substitution? If so, why? Have you been cured of symptoms that did not resurface in other forms? How?

3. When the secondary gain of a symptom doesn't seem adequate to cover the "cost" of the symptom in terms of pain or inconvenience, what else do you think maintains the symptom's presence?

4. What steps can you take to "expect the unexpected?"

5. What differences are you aware of between something being "legal" and "ethical"? How and where is the dividing line drawn for you as an individual?

Things to Do

1. Interview some traditionally oriented psychologists and psychiatrists, and ask them what dangers they associate with the use of hypnosis. Do you feel their responses reflect current knowledge? Why or why not?

2. Develop a strong referral list of a number of competent professionals in as many areas of health care as you can. Contact these professionals directly in order to be certain you know when a referral to them is appropriate and what their system for providing care is.

3. As an individual, but preferably as a class, create a list of ethical guidelines specifically for the practice of clinical hypnosis based on case examples contributed by each class member.

23

Going Deeper Into Trance

I don't know who it was that originally made the observation, "The more you know, the more you know how little you know." Whoever it was, I wonder if he or she was talking about hypnosis when making that comment. Well, probably not. But it holds true for the study of hypnosis nonetheless. I hope that by the time you have reached this concluding chapter you will have discovered the richness and complexity that hypnosis as a communication tool affords.

One of the most frustrating things to people in the field of clinical hypnosis is the fact that people with far less education in hypnosis than this introductory level book provides are engaged in providing services to the public that they are not qualified to provide. A second source of frustration to those in the field of clinical hypnosis lies in the observation that many people take courses in hypnosis and then, when the course is over, the acquired skills are not utilized and soon fade into the past. My belief is that when the practice of hypnosis was limited to the ritualistic and time-consuming techniques of the past, hypnosis as a tool was limited in its effectiveness and applicability. I further believe that when hypnosis is broadened from "hocus-pocus" to a model of deliberate and effective communication, increasing numbers of professionals can integrate hypnotic patterns into their work. My goal was not and is not to transform readers of this text into "official hypnotists." Rather, my goal has been to provide you with an introduction to a field that can significantly expand the range of your communication skills. Even if you never formally induce another trance again in your life, my guess is that you'll reflexively think twice before saying something like, "Don't think about what's bothering you." From this introduction to the field, I hope that you can be sufficiently intrigued by the range of possibilities hypnosis as a tool has to offer that you will be encouraged to continue developing skills with it. There are a variety of ways to do so.

There are numerous books and publications that deal with the subject of clinical hypnosis. The sources listed in this book's bibliography can provide a starting point for meaningful reading and, of course, the bibliography in each listed source can provide further sources for learning. The scientific journals dedicated to the field of hypnosis are invaluable sources from which to acquire the most recent concepts and approaches in the professional practice of hypnosis. Two major hypnosis organizations publish scientific journals. The information on where to write in order to attain membership in these organizations and in order to subscribe to the journals is listed below:

The American Journal of Clinical Hypnosis
published by the American Society of Clinical Hypnosis

For membership (includes journal) write to:
2250 East Devon Avenue
Suite 336
Des Plaines, Illinois 60018
address subscriptions to "Business Manager"

The International Journal of Clinical and Experimental Hypnosis
published by The Society for Clinical & Experimental Hypnosis, Inc.

For journal subscriptions only write to:
The International Journal of Clinical and Experimental Hypnosis
111 North 49th Street
Philadelphia, PA. 19139

For membership (includes journal) write to:
The Society for Clinical and Experimental Hypnosis, Inc.
129-A Kings Park Drive
Liverpool, New York 13088

While the importance of reading cannot be overstated, neither can the value of further experiential training. Beyond the training many universities now provide, and the private training programs offered by many professionals, the hypnosis organizations listed above provide training programs to qualified professionals both on national and local levels. The

American Society of Clinical Hypnosis (ASCH) has branches in major cities, with training programs held routinely. The Milton H. Erickson Foundation, in Phoenix, Arizona, is dedicated to the advancement of Ericksonian hypnosis, and presents the national and international Erickson Congresses—major events at which scholarly papers, demonstrations, workshops, and discussions are held over several days solely on the topic of hypnosis. In addition to sponsoring the Congresses, the Foundation publishes an interesting newsletter which includes a guide to when and where training programs will be offered. To get on the Foundation's mailing list, write to the following address:

> The Milton H. Erickson Foundation, Inc.
> 3606 N. 24th Street
> Phoenix, Arizona 85016

In addition to the organizations mentioned above, there are smaller, often more specialized groups that are too numerous to mention here. The quality of training, the eligibility for membership, and the goals and functions of the various groups differ greatly. Affiliation with an organization should ultimately be a synergistic relationship, not a one-sided one, and selectivity is therefore encouraged.

At the close, it is difficult for me to assess whether or not I have been able to transmit my respect and appreciation for hypnosis effectively. I frequently found myself wanting to say more about each of the topics presented, but felt obligated to preserve this text's integrity as an introductory one. There is much, much more to be said about the human mind, personality, communication, and trance states. Our current understandings are ever-expanding, and there appears to be no upper limit to how much can be known. Knowledge and personality are the deepest trance states of all.

Appendix A

**GENERAL PRINCIPLES CONTRASTING THE VIEWS
OF THE MAJOR MODELS OF HYPNOSIS**

Variable	Traditional	Standardized	Ericksonian (Utilization)
Individualized approach?	No	No	Yes
Naturalistic concept of trance?	No	No	Yes
Naturalistic techniques?	No	No	Yes
Hypnotist's demeanor?	Authoritarian	Authoritarian or permissive	Authoritarian or permissive
Suggestion style used?	Direct	Direct	Direct or indirect
Degree of compliance demanded?	High	High	Low
How is power in the relationship distributed?	Unequally in favor of the hypnotist	Unequally in favor of the client	Equally
Content or process oriented?	Content	Content	Either or both
Who can experience trance meaningfully?	Some	Some	All
Source of resistance?	Intrapersonal	Intrapersonal	Intra- or interpersonal
Reaction to resistance?	Confrontation or interpretation	Confrontation or interpretation	Utilization
Emphasizes trance depth?	Yes	Yes	No
Makes use of formal suggestibility tests?	Yes	Yes	No
Structure of process?	Linear	Linear	Mosaic
Relative value of insights?	Low	Low	Low
View of the symptoms' intentions?	Negative	Negative	Positive
Etiology of symptoms?	Intrapersonal	Intrapersonal	Inter- or intrapersonal

(continued)

431

APPENDIX A *(continued)*

Variable	Traditional	Standardized	Ericksonian (Utilization)
Symptomatic vs. dynamic approach?	Either or both	Symptomatic	Either or both
Recognition of secondary gains?	No	No	Yes
Characterization of the unconscious?	Negative	Negative	Neutral
Role of the unconscious?	Reactive	Reactive	Active

Reprinted with permission from Yapko (1986) in Zilbergeld et al. (Eds.), *Hypnosis: Questions and Answers.* New York: Norton.

Glossary

Abreaction: Unexpected and intense negative emotional reaction to the content or structure of an intervention triggered by negative associations. (p. 416)

Accessing questions: Questions that encourage an experiential rather than verbal response. (p. 170)

Affect bridge: A technique to regress an individual to the first time a particular emotion was experienced. (p. 262)

Age progression: The intensified utilization of projections regarding the future. (p. 263)

Age regression: The intensified utilization of memory. (p. 253)

Ambiguous suggestion: A suggestion deliberately structured to allow for multiple interpretations. (p. 170)

Amnesia: The experience of being unable to remember some experience or piece of information. (p. 267)

Analgesia: A reduction in sensation. (p. 273)

Anchor: An association (trigger for experience) in any of the sensory modalities. (p. 193)

Anesthesia: A full elimination of sensation. (p. 273)

Anticipation signal: A statement of intention offered to the client in order to prevent him or her from being startled or having to analyze the experience. (p. 192)

Apposition of opposites: Suggestions creating simultaneous polarities of experience. (p. 170)

Bind of comparable alternatives: A suggestion creating the illusion of a forced choice. (p. 170)

Catalepsy: The inhibition of voluntary movement. (p. 281)

Changing personal history: A therapy technique involving the reliving of a negative past experience with a new resource to use in order to facilitate a new, positive outcome. (p. 308)

Confusion techniques: Techniques designed to interrupt the rigid mind-set of an individual on some specific dimension of experience. (p. 171)

Covering all possibilities: Suggestions allowing for all possible responses to be defined as cooperative. (p. 171)

Critical incident process: A regression to a significant experience primarily in order to experience a cathartic release of emotions. (p. 309)

Cue: An agreed upon association to signal the start of a trance process. (p. 223)

Direct suggestion: A suggestion that deals directly with the presented problem and/or with a desired response. (p. 154)

Dissociation: The ability to break a global experience into its component parts, amplifying awareness for one part while diminishing awareness for the others. (pp. 284–285)

Ecology check: A technique for experientially assessing the consequences of a change. (p. 420)

Embedded commands: Suggestions for specific responses embedded in the context of a larger communication. (p. 206)

Formal hypnosis: Clearly and overtly identified use of structured hypnotic approaches. (p. 13)

Framing responses: Suggesting a meaning be associated to a specific response. (p. 146)

Hallucinations: A "positive hallucination" involves sensory experiences that do not arise from external stimulation. A "negative hallucination" involves no sensory experience of perceptible external stimuli. (p. 290)

Hemispheric asymmetry theory: The theory emphasizes the differences between the two brain hemispheres, speculating that the normally non-dominant right hemisphere with its unique holistic and intuitive characteristics becomes dominant in hypnosis. (p. 65)

Hidden observer: The name Ernest Higard gave to the part of the person in trance that remains objective about ongoing experience. (p. 137)

Homework assignments: Tasks to be conducted by the client between therapy sessions to amplify relevant learnings. (p. 311)

Hypermnesia: A form of age regression in which details of a memory are enhanced. (p. 253)

Implied directives: A suggestion that presupposes a response on which a second direct suggestion can be based. (p. 171)

Indirect suggestion: A suggestion that relates to the presented problem or desired response in an indirect, even covert, way. (p. 156)

Induction: Any attention-focusing method intended to facilitate the dissociative and responsive dimensions of the trance state. (p. 209)

Interspersal of suggestions: The use of repetition of key suggestive words or phrases to amplify their value. (p. 171)

Lacrimation: A tearing of the eyes associated with relaxing that may be misinterpreted as evidence of the client being upset. (p. 141)

Learned helplessness: A model of depression developed by Martin Seligman that describes the tendency to generalize helplessness from even just one experience of being exposed to aversive, uncontrollable stimuli. (p. 93)

Literal interpretation: The tendency for many hypnotized persons to respond to the literal rather than figurative meaning of words or phrases. (p. 138)

Metaphors: Stories that may be utilized diagnostically or therapeutically to elicit and guide the client's associations. (p. 327)

Neo-Dissociation Theory: A view proposed by Ernest Hilgard where the trance state is seen as a dissociative state in which the unconscious is capable of functioning more autonomously yet parallel to the conscious mind. (p. 65)

Paradoxical suggestions: Seemingly internally incompatible suggestions contained within the same phrase. (p. 172)

Presuppositions: The use of an assumption that the client will respond cooperatively. (p. 172)

Puns: The use of a humorous reframing. (p. 172)

Rapport: The positive and mutually responsive relationship between client and therapist that develops in direct proportion to the therapist's ability to join the client's frame of reference. (p. 64)

Refractionation: Guiding the client in and out of trance multiple times in a single session for deepening purposes. (p. 223)

Reframing: Changing the emotional association to an experience by reinterpreting its meaning, as in redefining a liability as an asset. (p. 314)

Resistance: A force potentially arising from personal, interpersonal, or situational factors that works against the aims of treatment. (p. 405)

Revivification: A form of age regression in which the memory is *relived* as if it were occurring for the first time in the "here-and-now." (p. 253)

Seeding: A foreshadowing of suggestions and experiences yet to come in order to build receptivity and familiarity with them. (p. 273)

Selective attention: The perceptual process of focusing on a specific stimulus to the exclusion of other co-existing stimuli. (p. 106)

Somatic bridge: A technique to regress an individual to the first time a particular sensation was experienced. (p. 262)

Spontaneous regression: A focus on and absorption in a memory without a formal suggestion to do so. (p. 422)

Suggestibility: An openness and responsiveness to new ideas or information. (p. 88)

Suggestibility tests: Brief hypnotic interactions in which specific responses are suggested in order to determine an individual's degree of responsiveness. (p. 130)

Symptom prescription: A therapeutic strategy of encouraging the client to deliberately continue the symptomatic patterns. Also known as "paradoxical intention," the apparent mechanism is establishing intentional control over a previously spontaneous pattern. (pp. 315–316)

Temporal disorientation: Using suggestions to confuse the individual's sense of time in order to facilitate regression or progression. (p. 262)

Trance: A state of focused attention characterized by dissociation and responsiveness to suggestion. (p. 41)

Trance logic: The lack of need for the hypnotized person to have objectivity in processing suggestions. (p. 139)

Trance phenomena: The subjective experiences of people that are best thought of as the building blocks of one's personal reality. Amplified in hypnosis, these experiences can be combined in new configurations for therapeutic purposes. (pp. 250–253)

Transderivational search: The process of attaching words (symbols) to experience in order to make meaning. (p. 58)

Truism: An obvious truth so self-evident as to be beyond refutation. (p. 172)

Ultradian cycle theory: Proposed by Ernest Rossi, the theory emphasizes a biological view of trance by relating it to the biological cycles of alternating attentiveness and relaxation that physiologically occur about every 90–120 minutes. (p. 65)

Bibliography

Allee, J. (Ed.) (1978). *Webster's Encyclopedia of Dictionaries: New American Edition.* Literary Press.

American Society of Clinical Hypnosis, Education and Research Foundation. (1973). *A Syllabus on Hypnosis and a Handbook of Therapeutic Suggestions.*

Anderson-Evangelista, A. (1980). *Hypnosis: A Journey into the Mind.* New York: Arco Publishing.

Aronson, E. (1984). *The Social Animal.* 4th Ed. San Francisco: W.H. Freeman and Co.

Bandler, R. & Grinder, J. (1975). *Patterns of the Hypnotic Techniques of Milton H. Erickson, M.D.* (Vol. I). Cupertino, Ca.: Meta Publications.

Bandler, R. & Grinder, J. (1979). *Frogs into Princes.* Moab, Ut.: Real People Press.

Barber, J. (1980). Hypnosis and the unhypnotizable. *American Journal of Clinical Hypnosis, 23,* 4–9.

Barber, J. & Gitelson, J. (1980). Cancer pain: Psychological management using hypnosis. *CA-A Cancer Journal for Clinicians,* published by the American Cancer Society, *30,* 130–135.

Barber, T. (1962). Hypnotic age regression: A critical review. *Psychosomatic Medicine, 24,* 286–299.

Barber, T. (1964). Hypnotizability, suggestibility, and personality: A critical review of research findings. *Psychological Reports, 14,* 299–320.

Barber, T. (1969). *Hypnosis: A Scientific Approach.* New York: Van Nostrand Reinhold.

Barker, P. (1985). *Using Metaphors in Psychotherapy.* New York: Brunner/Mazel.

Bateson, G. (1972). *Steps to an Ecology of Mind.* New York: Ballantine Books.

Buscaglia, L. (1982). *Living, Loving and Learning.* New York: Ballantine Books.

Cheek, D. & LeCron, L. (1968). *Clinical Hypnotherapy.* New York: Grune and Stratton.

Erickson, M. (May, 1948). Hypnotic psychotherapy. *The Medical Clinics of North America,* pp. 571–583.

Erickson, M. (1952). Deep hypnosis and its induction. In L.M. LeCron (Ed.), *Experimental Hypnosis,* (pp. 70–114). New York: Macmillan.

Erickson, M. (1954). Pseudo-orientation in time as a hypnotherapeutic procedure. *International Journal of Clinical and Experimental Hypnosis, 2,* 261–283.

Erickson, M. (1958). Naturalistic techniques of hypnosis. *American Journal of Clinical Hypnosis, 1,* 3–8.

Erickson, M. (1964a). A hypnotic technique for resistant patients. *American Journal of Clinical Hypnosis, 1,* 8–82.

Erickson, M. (1964b). The confusion technique in hypnosis. *American Journal of Clinical Hypnosis, 6,* 183–207.

Erickson, M. (1965). The use of symptoms as an integral part of therapy. *American Journal of Clinical Hypnosis, 8,* 57–65.

Erickson, M. & Rossi, E. (1974). Varieties of hypnotic amnesia. *American Journal of Clinical Hypnosis, 16,* 225–239.

Erickson, M. & Rossi, E. (1979). *Hypnotherapy: An Exploratory Casebook.* New York: Irvington Publishers.

Erickson, M. & Rossi, E. (1981). *Experiencing Hypnosis: Therapeutic Approaches to Altered States.* New York: Irvington Publishers.

Erickson, M., Rossi, E., & Rossi, S. (1976). *Hypnotic Realities.* New York: Irvington Publishers.

Festinger, L. (1957). *A Theory of Cognitive Dissonance.* Stanford, Ca.: Stanford University Press.

Fromm, E. & Shor, R. (Eds.) (1972). *Hypnosis: Research Developments and Perspectives.* Chicago: Aldine Atherton.

Gilligan, S. (1982). Ericksonian approaches to clinical hypnosis. In J. Zeig (Ed.), *Ericksonian Approaches to Hypnosis and Psychotherapy.* New York: Brunner/Mazel.

Gilligan, S. (1985). Generative autonomy: Principles for an Ericksonian hypnotherapy. In J. Zeig (Ed). *Ericksonian Psychotherapy, Volume I: Structures.* New York: Brunner/Mazel.

Gilligan, S. (1987). *Therapeutic Trances: The Cooperation Principle in Ericksonian Hypnotherapy.* New York: Brunner/Mazel.

Gordon, D. (1980). *Therapeutic Metaphors.* Cupertino, Ca.: Meta Publications.

Gordon, D. & Meyers-Anderson, M. (1981). *Phoenix: Therapeutic Patterns of Milton H. Erickson.* Cupertino, Ca.: Meta Publications.

Grinder, J. & Bandler, R. (1981). *Trance-Formations: Neuro-Linguistic Programming and the Structure of Hypnosis.* Moab, Utah: Real People Press.

Grinder, J. & Bandler, R. (1982). *Reframing: Neuro-Linguistic Programming and the Transformation of Meaning.* Moab, Utah: Real People Press.

Grinder, J., Delozier, J., & Bandler, R. (1977). *Patterns of the Hypnotic Techniques of Milton H. Erickson, M.D.* (Vol. II). Cupertino, Ca.: Meta Publications.

Haley, J. (1963). *Strategies of Psychotherapy.* New York: Grune and Stratton.

Haley, J. (Ed.) (1967). *Advanced Techniques of Hypnosis and Therapy: Selected Papers of Milton H. Erickson, M.D.* New York: Grune and Stratton.

Haley, J. (1973). *Uncommon Therapy: The Psychiatric Techniques of Milton H. Erickson, M.D.* New York: Norton.

Haley, J. (1984). *Ordeal Therapy.* San Francisco: Jossey-Bass.

Hammond, D. (1984). Myths about Erickson and Ericksonian hypnosis. *American Journal of Clinical Hypnosis, 26,* 236–245.

Hilgard, E. (1965). *Hypnotic Susceptibility.* New York: Harcourt, Brace, and World.

Hilgard, E. (1973). Dissociation revisited. In M. Henle, J. Jaynes, and J. Sullivan (Eds.) *Historical Conceptions of Psychology.* New York: Springer.

Hilgard, E. (1977). *Divided Consciousness: Multiple Controls in Human Thought and Action.* New York: John Wiley and Sons.

Hilgard, E. & Hilgard, J. (1975). *Hypnosis in the Relief of Pain.* Los Altos, Ca.: Kaufmann.

Kroger, W. (1977). *Clinical and Experimental Hypnosis in Medicine, Dentistry, and Psychology,* 2d ed. Philadelphia: Lippincott.

Lankton, S. (1980). *Practical Magic.* Cupertino, Ca.: Meta Publications.

Lankton, S. & Lankton, C. (1983). *The Answer Within: A Clinical Framework of Ericksonian Hypnotherapy.* New York: Brunner/Mazel.

Lankton, S. & Lankton, C. (1986). *Enchantment and Intervention in Family Therapy.* New York: Brunner/Mazel.

Lazarus, A. (1971). *Behavior Therapy and Beyond.* New York: McGraw-Hill.

Madanes, C. (1984). *Behind the One-Way Mirror.* San Francisco: Jossey-Bass.

Massey, M. (1979). *The People Puzzle: Understanding Yourself and Others.* Reston, Va.: Reston Publishing.

McConnell, J. (1983). *Understanding Human Behavior.* 4th Ed. New York: Holt Rinehart and Winston.

Milgram, S. (1974). *Obedience to Authority.* New York: Harper & Row.

Mills, J. & Crowley, R. (1986). *Therapeutic Metaphors for Children and the Child Within.* New York: Brunner/Mazel.

O'Hanlon, W. (1987). *Taproots.* New York: Norton.

Orne, M. (1959). The nature of hypnosis: Artifact and essence. *Journal of Abnormal and Social Psychology, 58,* 277–299.

Orne, M. (1966a). Hypnosis, motivation, and compliance. *American Journal of Psychiatry, 122,* 721–726.

Orne, M. (1966b). On the mechanisms of posthypnotic amnesia. *International Journal of Clinical Hypnosis, 14,* 121–134.

Perls, F. (1970). *Gestalt Therapy: Verbatim.* New York: Bantam Books.

Reiser, M. (1980). *Handbook of Investigative Hypnosis.* Los Angeles: LEHI Publishing Co.

Rosen, S. (Ed.) (1982). *My Voice Will Go With You: The Teaching Tales of Milton H. Erickson.* New York: Norton.

Rosenhan, D. (1973). On being sane in insane places. *Science, 179,* 250–258.

Rossi, E. (1973). Psychological shocks and creative moments in psychotherapy. *American Journal of Clinical Hypnosis 16,* 9–22.

Rossi, E. (Ed.). (1980). *The Collected Papers of Milton H. Erickson on Hypnosis* (4 vols.). New York: Irvington Publishers.

Rossi, E. (1982). Hypnosis and ultradian cycles: A new state(s) theory of hypnosis? *American Journal of Clinical Hypnosis, 1,* 21–32.

Rossi, E. (1986). *The Psychobiology of Mind-Body Healing.* New York: Norton.

Rossi, E, & Cheek, D. (1988). *Mind-Body Therapy: Methods of Ideodynamic Healing in Hypnosis.* New York: Norton.

Rossi, E. & Ryan, M. (Eds.). (1985). *Life Reframing in Hypnosis: The Seminars, Workshops, and Lectures of Milton H. Erickson* (Vol. II). New York: Irvington.

Rossi, E., Ryan, M. & Sharp, F (Eds.). (1983). *Healing in Hypnosis: The Seminars, Workshops, and Lectures of Milton H. Erickson* (Vol. I). New York: Irvington.

Ruesch, J. & Bateson, G. (1968). *Communication: The Social Matrix of Psychiatry.* New York: Norton.

Ruesch, J. (1973). *Therapeutic Communication.* New York: Norton.

Samko, M. (1986). Rigidity and pattern interruption: Central issues underlying Milton Erickson's approach to psychotherapy. In M. Yapko (Ed.), *Hypnotic and Strategic Interventions: Principles and Practice,* (pp. 47–55). New York: Irvington.

Sarbin, T. (1950). Contributions to role-taking theory: I. Hypnotic behavior. *Psychological Review, 57,* 255–270.

Sarbin, T. & Coe. W. (1972). *Hypnosis: A social psychological analysis of influence communication.* New York: Holt Rinehart and Winston.

Satir, V. (1967). *Conjoint Family Therapy.* Palo Alto, Ca.: Science and Behavior Books.

Satir, V. (1972). *Peoplemaking.* Palo Alto, Ca.: Science and Behavior Books.

Schachter, S. & Singer, J. (1962). Cognitive, social and physiological determinants of emotional state. *Physiological Review, 69,* 379–389.

Seligman, M. (1975). *Helplessness: On Depression, Development, and Health.* San Francisco: Freeman.

Seligman, M. (1988). Boomer blues. *Psychology Today, 22,* 50–55.

Shor, R. (1959). Hypnosis and the concept of the generalized reality-orientation. *American Journal of Psychotherapy, 13,* 582–602.

Shor, R. & Orne, E. (1962). *The Harvard Group Scale of Hypnotic Susceptibility, Form A.* Palo Alto, Ca.: Consulting Psychologists Press.

Simon, N. (1976a). *Advanced Hypnotic Techniques for Professionals.* An unpublished hypnosis training manual.

Simon, N. (1976b). *Diagnosis and Brief Hypnotherapeutic Techniques.* An unpublished hypnosis training manual.

Simonton, O. (1975). Belief systems and management of the emotional aspects of malignancy. *Journal of Transpersonal Psychology, 7,* 24–47.

Simonton, O., Mathews-Simonton, S. & Creighton, J. (1978). *Getting Well Again.* Los Angeles: Tarcher.

Spiegel, D. (1986). Dissociating damage. *American Journal of Clinical Hypnosis, 29,* 123–131.

Spiegel, H. (1972). An eye-roll test for hypnotizability. *American Journal of Clinical Hypnosis, 15,* 25–28.

Spiegel, H. (1974). The Grade Five Syndrome: The highly hypnotizable person. *International Journal of Clinical and Experimental Hypnosis, 22,* 303–319.

Spiegel, H. & Spiegel, D. (1978). *Trance and Treatment: Clinical Uses of Hypnosis.* New York: Basic Books.

Sternbach, R. (Ed.). (1978). *The Psychology of Pain.* (p. 237). New York: Raven Press.

Tart, C. (Ed.). (1969). *Altered States of Consciousness: A Book of Readings.* New York: John Wiley and Sons.

Watzlawick, P. (1976). *How Real is Real?* New York: Basic Books.

Watzlawick, P. (1978). *The Language of Change.* New York: Basic Books.

Watzlawick, P. (1982). Erickson's contribution to the interactional view of psychotherapy. In J. Zeig (Ed.), *Ericksonian Approaches to Hypnosis and Psychotherapy.* (pp. 147–154). New York: Brunner/Mazel.

Watzlawick, P. (1983). *The Situation Is Hopeless, But Not Serious.* New York: Norton.

Watzlawick, P. (1985). Hypnotherapy without trance. In J. Zeig (Ed.), *Ericksonian Psychotherapy, Volume I: Structures.* (pp. 5–14). New York: Brunner/Mazel.

Watzlawick, P., Bavelas, J., & Jackson, D. (1967). *Pragmatics of Human Communication.* New York: Norton.

Watzlawick, P., Weakland, J., & Fisch, R. (1974). *Change.* New York: Norton.

Weitzenhoffer, A. (1953); (Paperbound edition, 1963). *Hypnotism: An Objective Study in Suggestibility.* New York: Wiley.

Weitzenhoffer, A. (1957). *General Techniques of Hypnotism.* New York: Grune and Stratton.

Weitzenhoffer, A. (1960). Unconscious or co-conscious? Reflections upon certain recent trends in medical hypnosis. *American Journal of Clinical Hypnosis, 2,* 177–196.

Weitzenhoffer, A. (1974). When is an "instruction" an "instruction?" *International Journal of Clinical and Experimental Hypnosis, 22,* 258–269.

Weitzenhoffer, A. & Hilgard, E. (1959). *Stanford Hypnotic Susceptibility Scale, Forms A and B.* Palo Alto, Ca.: Consulting Psychologists Press.

Weitzenhoffer, A. & Hilgard, E. (1963). *Stanford Profile Scales of Hypnotic Susceptibility, Forms I and II.* Palo Alto, Ca.: Consulting Psychologists Press.

Weitzenhoffer, A. & Weitzenhoffer, G. (1958). Personality and hypnotic susceptibility. *American Journal of Clinical Hypnosis, 1,* 79–82.

Yapko, M. (1981). The effect of matching primary representational predicates on hypnotic relaxation. *American Journal of Clinical Hypnosis, 23,* 169–175.

Yapko, M. (1983). A comparative analysis of direct and indirect hypnotic communication styles. *American Journal of Clinical Hypnosis, 25,* 270–276.

Yapko, M. (1984). The implications of the Ericksonian and Neuro-Linguistic Programming approaches for responsibility of therapeutic outcomes. *American Journal of Clinical Hypnosis, 27,* 137–143.

Yapko, M. (1985a). The Erickson hook: Values in Ericksonian approaches. In J. Zeig (Ed.), *Ericksonian Psychotherapy, Volume I: Structures.* (pp. 266–281). New York: Brunner/Mazel.

Yapko, M. (1985b). Therapeutic strategies for the treatment of depression. In S. Lankton (Ed.), *Elements and Dimensions of an Ericksonian Approach. Ericksonian Monographs, 1,* 89–110. New York: Brunner/Mazel.

Yapko, M. (1986). Ericksonian hypnosis. In B. Zilbergeld, G. Edelstein, & D. Araoz (Eds.), *Hypnosis: Questions and Answers.* (pp. 223–231). New York: Norton.

Yapko, M. (1988a). *When Living Hurts: Directives for Treating Depression.* New York: Brunner/Mazel.

Yapko, M. (1988b). Individuation: Alone together. In J. Zeig & S. Lankton (Eds.), *Developing Ericksonian Therapy: State of the Art.* (pp. 237–254). New York: Brunner/Mazel.

Yapko, M. (1988c). Confusion methodologies in the management of pain. *Hypnos: Swedish Journal of Hypnosis in Psychotherapy and Psychosomatic Medicine, 15,* 163–173.

Yapko, M. (Ed.) (1989). *Brief Therapy Approaches to Treating Anxiety and Depression.* New York: Brunner/Mazel.

Zeig, J. (1974). Hypnotherapy techniques with psychotic inpatients. *American Journal of Clinical Hypnosis, 17,* 59–69.

Zeig, J. (Ed.) (1980a). *A Teaching Seminar with Milton H. Erickson.* New York: Brunner/Mazel.

Zeig, J. (1980b). Symptom prescription and Ericksonian principles of hypnosis and psychotherapy. *American Journal of Clinical Hypnosis, 23,* 16–22.

Zeig, J. (1980c). Symptom prescription techniques: Clinical applications using elements of communication. *American Journal of Clinical Hypnosis, 23,* 23–32.

Zeig, J. (Ed.) (1982). *Ericksonian Approaches to Hypnosis and Psychotherapy.* New York: Brunner/Mazel.

Zeig, J. (Ed.). (1985a). *Ericksonian Psychotherapy* (2 Vols.). New York: Brunner/Mazel.

Zeig, J. (1985b). The clinical use of amnesia: Ericksonian methods. In J. Zeig (Ed.), *Ericksonian Psychotherapy, Volume I: Structures.* (pp. 317–337). New York: Brunner/Mazel.

Zeig, J. (1985c). *Experiencing Erickson: An Introduction to the Man and His Work.* New York: Brunner/Mazel.

Zeig, J. (Ed.). (1987). *The Evolution of Psychotherapy.* New York: Brunner/Mazel.

Zeig, J. & Lankton, S. (1988). *Developing Ericksonian Therapy: State of the Art.* New York: Brunner/Mazel.

Name Index

443

Subject Index